HUMAN
JUDGMENT
AND
SOCIAL
INTERACTION

HUMAN JUDGMENT AND SOCIAL INTERACTION

Edited by
Leon Rappoport
Kansas State University

David A. Summers
University of Kansas

HOLT, RINEHART AND WINSTON, INC.
New York   Chicago   San Francisco   Atlanta
Dallas   Montreal   Toronto   London   Sydney

Copyright © 1973 by Holt, Rinehart and Winston, Inc.
All rights reserved
Library of Congress Catalog Card Number: 72–84872
ISBN: 0–03–085870–4
Printed in the United States of America
3 4 5 6   038   9 8 7 6 5 4 3 2 1

Preface

If it is hard to second guess the confusions of the past—historians never seem to agree about anything—it is even harder to guess how future generations will see present day confusions. In our own immediate context of social science research and education, the confusion is very great these days, and there is a fair chance that some future essayist will describe it as follows:

> It was a time when social science stood at bay, brought up short, as it seemed to many professionals, unfairly, by the demands of a new generation seeking relevance (whatever-the-hell *that* was). Colleges were closing or cutting back. If you were a recently minted unblack, unbrown, unfemale Ph.D. without good connections, it was difficult to find the teaching or research work you thought you deserved. Consequently, none of the intellectuals could understand exactly why increasing numbers of students were turning up in psychology courses, or what it was they thought they would find there.

This brings us to the contents of this book: At a time like this, what possible use can there be for an original collection of papers describing basic research on human judgment and social interaction? Furthermore, how can anyone reasonably venture to talk the esoterica of such work in print when most potential readers seem committed to either more mystical or more traditional bodies of esoterica? In this connection, let it be acknowledged that our ten-year-olds (we have two between us) already know their astrological signs and how to consult daily newspaper horoscope columns. What can probability theory, regression statistics, or lens model parameters offer people like them in a few more years?

No easy answers. But to those who cry for relevance it may be suggested that in addition to hasty leaps forward guided by good intentions and whatever existing knowledge seems appropriate, the cause of relevance may also be served by a few careful steps sideways designed to provide newer, better knowledge. In keeping with the adage that nothing is so practical as a good theory, we are happy to note that some of the work introduced in this book has already been adapted for use in social action programs.

On the other hand, to those who would ignore both practical action and basic research in favor of a more mystical, intuitive vision, it may be suggested that there is no fundamental antithesis between scientific and metaphysical concerns. In fact, one may have no choice but to serve different masters in this respect, because some of the material to be presented here indicates that analytical and intuitive thinking are closely joined together.

Finally, to those turning up unbidden and unexpected as students in advanced undergraduate and graduate classes, it may be suggested that this book offers a great deal. We know from our own recent experience that students concerned with such diverse topics as perception, group social processes, child rearing practices, business decision-making, and international conflict, can all appreciate the importance of work on human judgment. Among other reasons, this is why so many different scholars with such different backgrounds are represented here as contributors.

Apart from diversity, however, the book also offers students a rare unitary view of what is involved in an extended program of basic research. Presented within a coherent framework, the contributions include philosophical perspectives, theoretical formulations, reviews of past work, reports of current experiments, interpretations of findings, and discussions of long-range implications. True, it is a body of work still in progress. But any student or teacher ready to be challenged by material requiring breadth, depth, and more than a simple puzzle-solving view of science will not be disappointed.

And then there are those horoscope-reading children of ours who, together with all the others, are probably going to have to face things more seriously as life on Earth proceeds into another century. Speaking for all the contributors to this book, we are immodest enough to think that it may contain some of the ideas they will need in order to survive their future.

L. R.
D. A. S.

Acknowledgments

The contributors to this volume deserve very special thanks for working hard to produce new material at a time when it was not clear whether a book of this type could be properly organized and put into print. We are grateful to Sylvia Link for typing all of the papers with unfailing care and good humor. Karene Will, long a mainstay at the Institute of Behavioral Science in Boulder, Colorado, gave us her customarily superb help arranging computer runs and making figures. In Manhattan, Kansas, along with much other work, Carolyn Tessendorf managed to keep correspondence and manuscripts perfectly organized as they flowed across three continents for almost three years.

Above all, we have had one silent, senior partner always present when we needed him. As our teacher, colleague, and friend, Kenneth R. Hammond has given us more than we can ever acknowledge in words. He has been the primary source of energy and inspiration behind this book.

Contents

HUMAN
JUDGMENT
AND
SOCIAL
INTERACTION

Origins, Aims, and Scope:
A General Introduction

This book presents a very diverse, but systematically related, set of papers concerning recent research on human judgment processes. For several reasons, which will gradually be made clear, we believe all the selections fit together to provide the rudiments of a new general theoretical framework for research on human judgment. But the major reason why the work of so many scholars, working on so many different substantive problems, in so many different places can be brought together here, lies in the *raison d'être* for the book itself. And this reason for being involves the scientific and intellectual legacy of one man: Egon Brunswik.

When Egon Brunswik died in 1955, some of his colleagues took it upon themselves to see his last book, *Perception and the Representative Design of Experiments* (1956), through publication. They also wrote a dedication:

> He was a true pioneer who was constantly striving to break out of the confines of orthodoxy and to develop a new methodology which would increase the scope and validity of psychological research .... Brunswik's creative genius will have an ever-increasing impact on the development of psychology.

The work in this book is at least a partial confirmation of the prediction made by Brunswik's colleagues. We say this for two reasons. First, the research reported and reviewed in this volume makes it clear that Brunswik's ideas are meaningful to scholars throughout most of the world wherever there is active research on human judgment.

Second, and perhaps more important, Brunswik's ideas have been extended from perceptual processes (his own primary research area) to problems that he could not possibly have anticipated—surely an outstanding criterion for "creative genius." The papers in this volume show that Brunswik's work is seminal to problems of human judgment and social interaction in the broadest sense—ranging over such areas as clinical judgment, individual learning, disordered thought, interpersonal conflict, and group processes. That his thinking can be applied to such a diversity of problems by such a diversity of scholars attests to the "ever-increasing impact" foreseen by his colleagues over 15 years ago.

But despite, or perhaps because of, the breadth and depth of his ideas, Brunswik's impact has not been made easily. Moreover, he is difficult to read. One could possibly grow rich making book and giving odds that any student or professional looking through his writings for the first time will be repelled. It is an uncomfortable fact that one of his sentences from the 1956 book was printed in the *New Yorker* under some such heading as "Our Wayward Authors." In short, for the casual reader to return to Brunswik's original writing as a means of grasping the underlying unity of "Brunswikian" research efforts is often a frustrating task.

We have begun with discussion of Brunswik, not only to acknowledge the main theoretical source of the work in this book, but also to indicate an important part of our attitude toward the book. It has not been put together lightly, at the inspiration of a publisher seeking to capitalize on a fashionable line of research—ours is not fashionable. Nor are we eager to publish to avoid perishing—our academic security rests on other ground. Instead, speaking for all those involved, it must be said explicitly that we are putting the work in this form so that we and others can properly *get at it.* The issue here is ultimately one of professional and scientific need.

The book was first conceived at a conference organized by Kenneth Hammond at the University of Colorado, in March, 1968. Approximately 20 of us spent three days discussing our programs of research on human judgment. Three remarkable things happened at the conference. First, we discovered that although our individual efforts ranged over a great spectrum, defined at one end by individual judgment in the absence of feedback information, and at the other by judgment in large groups with variable feedback, we could nevertheless communicate and mutually stimulate one another. We encountered that wonderful sense of confirmation that only comes to a basic researcher when he discovers that others are working on relevant phenomena that he himself cannot reach. In fact, each of us recognized that our own particular work could fit as a component into a whole.

The second remarkable thing was that all of us could agree in our vision of what that hypothetical "whole" should look like. This is sketched in the next section. Suffice it to say here that we could see a general theoretical-methodological framework that could properly hold our individual efforts, and was also very exciting as a dynamic heuristic, an organizing force drawing us together toward a larger enterprise than we had anticipated.

The third thing to emerge at the conference was a strong sense of congruity in professional philosophy, insofar as this is encompassed by fundamental assumptions concerning the human organism. There was a time—as little as ten to twelve years ago—when Brunswik's contention that man must be understood as functioning in an uncertain, probabilistic environment, and that he, therefore, must frequently operate as an "intuitive statistician," was viewed as an eccentric, if not downright crackpot, idea. But the world turns, and today ideas of probabilism and uncertainty, or entropy if you wish, are accepted as major concepts in most of psychology. If human cognitive processes are functional with respect to uncertainty, then Brunswik's effort to scrutinize behavior by means of theory he called "probabilistic functionalism" must be acknowledged as at least connotatively correct.

This does not mean that everyone at the conference and every contributor to this book wishes to label himself as an explicit follower of Brunswik. It does mean, however, that whatever philosophical label they choose to wear, and whatever cognitive freedom of maneuver they wish to retain, their basic assumptions about the organism coincide significantly with Brunswik's. The reader will therefore find himself here in a company of social scientists who to some significant degree share a subject matter, a methodology, a theoretical framework, and a philosophy. The aim of the book is to lay it all on the line.

Planning for the structure, contents, and organization of the book was also begun at the conference. In this connection, two important decisions were made. A primary consideration was the quality of material to be included. The most convenient strategy for a work like this is to reprint material that has already been published elsewhere. This strategy, however, was felt to be inappropriate; nothing grows stale more quickly than old empirical studies, and, besides, there was a need for a comprehensive work showing the unitary viewpoints underlying our diverse individual efforts. As a result, it was decided to make a serious effort to produce and bring together papers that had never before been published. On the whole, things turned out well: All but one of the articles included here were written specifically for this volume.

Our final problem was the choice of editors. A number of tactical considerations entered at this point. Some could not take it on simply because they were fully occupied. Others, by virtue of long-term commitments in substantive problem areas, would have found it inconvenient to work over the full spectrum of material planned for this book. And so, for a variety of reasons, it fell upon two of us to act as trustees for all the others.

The Organizational Framework

Judgment as Purposive Thought

All of the material in this book can be understood as an elaborate effort to define and understand the workings of human judgment, to expose it *in vitro,* empirically, as an anatomist exposes the structure and function of a particular organ. Therefore, rather than beginning with a formal theoretical discussion, we will list four relatively informal basic assumptions underlying the work to be presented, and then proceed toward the work itself.

1. Along with the major writers on cognitive development, we see think-
    ing as an adaptive process, a "tool" gradually shaped out of experience
    with the physical and social environment.
2. Judgment is a uniquely important functional aspect of thinking that allows
    persons to cope with, or adapt to, uncertainty. It provides the psycholog-
    ical means of going beyond perceptual and cognitive "givens," while main-
    taining organization and continuity in behavior.
3. Because of its central role of mediating between intentions or purposes
    of the person and uncertainties in his environment, judgment can only
    be understood by scrutinizing person-environment interactions.
4. Because judgment is here conceived of as centering upon *relationships*
    between proximal "givens" and distal "unknowns," the person-environ-
    ment interaction can best be understood as an interaction between cog-
    nitive and environmental *systems*.

All of the ideas outlined above will eventually be developed in detail.
However, since the final point provides an immediate basis for the organization of material in this book, it requires immediate elaboration.

A *cognitive system* is any minimally organized set of relationships
between an individual's judgments and the information ("cues") on which
the judgments are based. In connection with judgment phenomena, cognitive systems can be thought of as *policies*. That is, to the extent that
an individual finds meaning in a body of uncertain information, he does
so through application of an implicit or explicit policy concerning (1) the
causal relationships indicated by the information, and (2) the relation
of his outstanding goals or purposes to that information. Policy can include anything from the use of certain criteria by a graduate student selection committee, to a political leader's reliance upon reconnaissance
photographs (rather than statements by Soviet leaders) when making a
judgment about the presence of "offensive" missiles in Cuba. Technically,
a policy may be seen as a set of rules for utilizing available evidence in
order to reach a decision in an uncertain situation.

The *environmental* system is the situation itself. Just as a cognitive
system is definable according to the relationships between information
and judgments, an environmental system is definable according to the
relationships among environmental events—including the information
upon which judgments may be based. For the hypothetical admissions
committee mentioned above, the environmental system consists of relationships among various characteristics of the applicants, as well as the
relationship between each characteristic and actual graduate school (or
professional) success. The same is true for the political leader example.
The environmental system involved relationships among the various kinds
of information available during the Cuban missile crisis, as well as relations
between this information and the "larger events" that could only be inferred—for example, the presence or absence of offensive missiles in Cuba.

Briefly, it is suggested that judgment must be understood as the interaction between cognitive and environmental systems, each having its own depth, texture, and organization. Techniques for studying judgment from this standpoint will become clear in later chapters. A more direct problem is posed by the many different cognitive-environmental interactions that are possible. Where is one to start? And how is one to gain a theoretical perspective broad enough to embrace judgment as a basic process, apart from the substantive content of different problematic situations? The following framework offers a preliminary taxonomy for human judgment.

Four different types or "cases" of cognitive-environmental relationships define the range of judgmental phenomena examined in this book. These cases form an exhaustive general systems-theory hierarchy that cuts across traditional psychological problem areas.

1. *The single-system case.* This case includes all instances in which persons must make judgments on the basis of uncertain information, under conditions in which the environmental system is largely unknown, or even unknowable. Characteristic of this case is the fact that learning is either very slow, or nonexistent, because feedback is either absent, confounded, or irrelevant. In his *Memoirs* (1967), George Kennan suggests that foreign policy judgments are often of this type; that is, decisions are made on the basis of ambiguous information, and by the time they are put into effect it may be impossible to get reliable outcome information, or conditions may have changed so drastically that outcomes cannot be related to decisions. Military strategy judgments also have this character. Battle plans may succeed or fail for reasons that have nothing to do with the conditions that existed when they were formulated. And, closer to home, psychiatric practice provides further examples. Given ambiguous symptomatic information, the diagnostician must categorize patients and recommend treatment. He may then never see the outcome or he may receive outcome information that can be attributed to many factors other than those leading to the diagnosis.

The single-system case must therefore be understood as largely focused on the cognitive system of the judge, because the environmental or task system remains obscure. This case is of great theoretical and practical interest for a number of reasons. It covers, for example, many real-life situations where behavior ultimately appears to have been very stupid, because "experienced" decision makers have made serious mistakes.[1] And it raises intriguing questions for research: What kind of policies are shaped by conditions prevailing in the single-system case? What unique

[1] Vietnam is an obvious example. But what really makes this example of great theoretical interest is the effort that was made to *create* unambiguous outcome information. Body counts, target destruction data, and other reports were organized and funneled back to decision makers who treated them as reliable outcome evidence when in fact they were not.

properties must characterize these policies? And how can such policies be changed?

2. *The two-system case.* Here the properties of the environmental system *can* be ascertained, thus making it possible for decision makers to obtain reliable feedback about the consequences of their judgments. The ideal illustration for this case is the traditional scientific experiment. The scientist's hypothesis is his initial judgment; his experiment is designed to provide precise outcome information on the basis of which he may wish to revise his initial judgment. In more conventional, everyday affairs, the two-system case is illustrated by such diverse activities as weather forecasting and horse-race handicapping. All odds-makers are judges of the two-system variety.

This case requires equal emphasis on the cognitive system and the environmental system for two reasons: (1) because an understanding of the environmental system frequently facilitates an understanding of the judge's policy, and (2) because information about the environment enables the judge to adapt his cognitive system to that environment. Therefore, the important research issues concern evolution and change in policies occurring in relation to the characteristics of both the cognitive and environmental systems.

3. *The three-system case.* Now we move into the traditional territory of social psychology: How is judgment to be understood when, as commonly happens, *two* persons cooperate and consult in order to make decisions in uncertain situations? Abstractly, the three-system case concerns two different cognitive systems, each seeking to adapt to the same environmental system.

Typical examples include all varieties of partnerships that require mutual or shared decision making in the face of uncertainty: husbands and wives, business associates, and so on. And while the research questions here include those mentioned previously, they also extend to such interpersonal matters as conflict, compromise, and learning from and about the other person.

4. *The n-system case.* This case serves as an open-ended theoretical repository for decision making by three or more persons in an uncertain situation. The environmental system is engaged by n cognitive systems that also engage one another. If this is clearly the most complex of cases, it is, for at least two reasons, also probably the most important.

First, group decision making is an increasingly ubiquitous human occupation. It can be argued that, in the long run, man's survival as a species will grow more dependent on group decisions. The increasing amount of knowledge needed to make intelligent decisions about our resources demands this, advances in communication technology make such decision making more feasible, and rising population density makes it more probable.

Any attempt to understand the workings of *n* cognitive systems facing the same ambiguous environmental system will obviously involve a multitude of important issues. Furthermore, as one of the papers in this book makes clear, traditional efforts to study group decision making appear grossly inadequate because they include little or no representation of environmental systems, and only superficial representation of cognitive systems.

Methodology

In addition to their organization in the four-system framework, the studies to be presented here also share a common methodology. Cognitive and environmental systems that range over the four cases outlined above and that may pertain to a wide variety of subject matters, may all be represented through elaborations of Brunswik's original lens model for perception. Figure 1 shows the four specific cases diagrammed according to the lens model scheme.

The shared methodology illustrated in Figure 1 is important because it provides an operational continuity fitted to the whole spectrum of judgment described in the general framework. It allows us to see, for example, that environmental systems essentially consist of a distal object, event, or variable, that is, a *criterion* that is presented to cognitive systems as

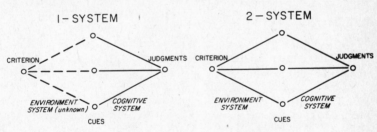

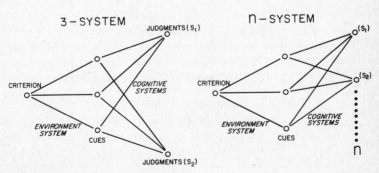

Figure 1. The four-systems framework

an array of cues. The criterion usually generates *multiple* cue information, and we denote this condition by consistently showing three cues. However, depending upon the particular problem, the number of cues can be either larger or smaller. The lines running from the cues to the criterion denote the relationship of each cue to the criterion. These relationships will, of course, also vary with the substantive judgment problem. We agree with Brunswik, however, that virtually all environmental systems to which man tries to adapt are uncertain, rather than fully determined. Thus, with the possible exception of contrived laboratory experiments, man rarely encounters situations in which cues are *perfectly* related to a distal event.

Similarly, the cognitive systems depicted by the lens scheme essentially consist of a set of relationships between judgments *about* the distal variable (or criterion) and the multiple, probabilistic cues upon which these judgments are based. The lines connecting the cues to the judgment denote the relationship between each cue and the individual's judgments. Again, these relationships will vary with the substantive judgment problem, and will often vary from person to person even in the same judgment situation. (As will be made clear in several of the articles, the latter is a frequent source of interpersonal conflict.)

It should be clear enough how each of the lens models can serve as a methodological and conceptual skeleton for each of the four different, but related, cases of judgment. But the most important value of the lens scheme is that it provides a common set of measures with direct operational meaning and relatively direct theoretical meaning, *which can be employed across the whole four-case spectrum of judgment.* This is something that can be appreciated better at the end of the book than at the beginning. For the moment, however, we might mention four specific advantages of the lens model methodology.

1. Any environmental system may be described by assessing cue-criterion relationships (environmental or ecological "cue validities") and overall uncertainty (variance in the criterion not accounted for by all the cues).
2. Any cognitive system can be described by determining the manner in which each cue is used by the individual ("functional cue validities") as well as by the uncertainty in the individual's policy (variance in the policy not accounted for by all the cues).
3. The general efficiency or utility of any policy can be described by establishing the accuracy of the judgments it produces. The efficiency (or inefficiency) of that policy can be explicated by comparing functional cue validities with environmental cue validities.
4. Each of the technical points mentioned above, as well as others to be mentioned elsewhere, allows specific empirical studies to be linked together. And because the technical language of our methodology extends across all cases of judgment, it is possible to express regularities extending across the whole spectrum in a form that is both testable and theoretically mean-

ingful. More concretely, this means that an hypothesis about judgment obtained in a three-system study, for example, might be tested in a two-system study, and vice versa.

Some Larger Implications

Taken together, all the material we have so far discussed should indicate that the main thrust of this book is toward a purposive, functionalist psychology of thinking. The purposive quality of human thought is nowhere more evident than in instances of judgment. And because the work to be presented shows judgment as an *adaptive* process—whether it occurs in clinical diagnosis or in political decision making by a group—it is ultimately tied to one of the key scientific principles underlying understanding of all biosocial systems.

Another point to note is that the work in this book has both a reductionist and expansionist character. This may seem contradictory, but since judgment is here examined in simple and complex forms, the work transcends conventional research strategies as well as conventional problem areas.

Readers should finally be warned that whereas all of the work follows traditional research *practices*—experimental procedures and analytical techniques are all in keeping with standard journal publication criteria—the enterprise as a whole is quite novel. Insofar as what is presented here is theory, it is open-ended, multifaceted theory. Thus, what may be learned about the judgment process *qua* process in studies of clinical inference and interpersonal conflict, may also yield substantive knowledge important to those specific areas. The word "may" is used advisedly: We do not lay claim to a general theory of judgment in this book. Instead, we offer summaries and demonstrations within an open, general framework that promises to move us toward general theory.

The Contributions

As indicated earlier, all of the contributed papers can be understood in relation to one another by placing them within the system scheme described above. The papers are arranged in such a way as to present increasing systems complexity as the reader moves through the book. Moreover, for reasons of conceptual and editorial clarity, the book is divided into two parts. Part I concerns individual judgment in the single- and two-system cases; Part II concerns judgment in the context of social interaction, the three- and *n*-system cases.

Although the systems scheme holds everything together, providing a larger unity that makes this book more than a simple collection or anthology, readers will quickly discover that each contribution can stand on its own without editorial commentaries. But while this means that one may easily and properly dip into the book, either at random or according to some personal design, it also means that a short, final briefing about the salient features of our conceptual terrain ought to be useful at this point.

Part I begins with a review by Slovic and Lichtenstein that gives an exhaustive survey of current research relevant to both the single- and two-system case. This reading also contains some valuable comparative discussions, most notably an evaluation of how the lens model approach to judgment relates to the Bayesian work on decision making.

Two more articles in Part I explore problem areas only briefly touched upon by Slovic and Lichtenstein. Wiggins provides a discussion of current multivariate approaches to capturing judgment policy in the single-system case, and Bjorkman offers a detailed analysis of the two-system case when cue information is in a nonmetric (nominal) form. Finally, the fourth selection by Gillis and Davis indicates how the lens model approach can be employed to investigate disordered thinking.

Part II is equally straightforward in substance, but more complex in organization, because when judgment is examined in connection with social interaction, as it must be if we are to gain understanding relevant to many real-life situations, a number of important problems reveal themselves.

In a newly revised version of a prize-winning article, Hammond begins Part II by describing a laboratory research paradigm for investigating the three-system phenomenon we call "cognitive conflict"—disagreement among persons trying to reach consensus in the face of uncertainty. Specific aspects of this phenomenon are then followed up in a series of brief independent reports.

Helenius presents evidence showing that laboratory-induced cognitive conflicts are not essentially different from those occurring as a result of natural social experience.

Bonaiuto reviews material and provides new data indicating how different types of feedback information influence both learning and conflict.

Miller, Gungor, and Kuhlman investigate the role of language, suggesting among other things that disagreements about the denotative meanings of cue material are easier to resolve than disagreements over connotative meanings.

The three-system case also generates the phenomenon we call "interpersonal learning"—persons working together may acquire task-relevant knowledge *from* one another and/or learn *about* one another. These two kinds of interpersonal learning are discussed in detail and demonstrated in studies reported, respectively, by Earle and Miller.

Finally, the *n*-system case involving three or more persons is presented in three papers. Reports by Kessel and by Moscovici, Lage, and Naffrechoux indicate that the traditional problem of group pressure may be investigated from a new perspective and with interesting new results when the lens model approach is employed. Cvetkovich reviews the general implications of this approach for small group research and describes findings obtained with five-person judgment groups.

The book ends with a long article by Hammond and Brehmer which is partly a summary of what has been learned about judgment, partly a description of a new computer-based technique ("cognograph") for enhancing judgment capacities, and, most importantly, a challenge to move ahead to further research and practical applications.

The potential benefits of applying cognograph in practical situations can in many ways stagger the imagination. But it should be emphasized most emphatically that although the technique has remarkable facilitating effects upon judgment and related phenomena, the effects are *not* accomplished by programming persons to think according to predetermined patterns. The computer is used to give persons information about how they themselves are thinking. To put it simply and candidly, this is a type of process information that has never before been available in the history of mankind. Just as technical developments in the field of electrophysiology now permit men to gain process information (biofeedback) about the workings of the central nervous system, the development of cognograph technology provides a similar caliber of information about higher mental processes associated with judgment. It remains to be seen how far this system may be applied in practical decision-making situations, but readers will see that progress already made in the laboratory is quite impressive.

PART I
The Single- and Two-System Cases for Individual Judgment

Introduction
to Reading 1

Although the primary aim of this volume is to illustrate how a conceptual and methodological framework derived from Brunswik's ideas can be applied to a broad range of judgment problems, it is important to recognize at the outset that other approaches are available to the investigator. Unfortunately, to make a choice among the available approaches is not an easy matter—not only are there great differences in terminology, but the methods used and the questions asked by proponents of the various approaches are frequently so different that it is often unclear that all are concerned with "judgment." A comparison of two or more different approaches to judgment research can be, quite simply, a bewildering affair promoting confusion rather than clarity.

The following reading by Slovic and Lichtenstein is particularly valuable because it avoids such pitfalls. These authors provide an exceptionally clear description of Brunswik's Lens Model, and show how it can be related to other important research models. In addition, they review the empirical literature associated with different approaches, and point out some of the practical implications of judgment research that have emerged in the form of "decision aids."

It is also noteworthy that this reading has had an interesting history of its own. After first being discussed as a possibility for this book during the 1968 conference in Boulder, a preliminary draft was circulated among authorities in the field during 1970. Their reactions were so favorable that early publication was arranged in the *Journal of Organizational Behavior and Human Performance* (1971, *6*, 649–744). It is reprinted here with the permission of Academic Press, Inc.

1 Comparison of Bayesian and Regression Approaches to the Study of Information Processing in Judgment[1]

PAUL SLOVIC
SARAH LICHTENSTEIN[2]
Oregon Research Institute

Our concern in this paper is with human judgment and decision making and, in particular, with the processing of information that precedes and determines these activities. The distinction between judgments and decisions is a tenuous one and will not be maintained here; we shall use these terms interchangeably.

Regardless of terminology, one thing is certain. Judgment is a fundamental cognitive activity that vitally affects the well being—or more accurately, the survival—of us all. Decisions are frighteningly more important and more difficult than ever before. Ancient man's most important decisions concerned his personal survival, and only a limited number of alternatives were available to him. Technological innovation has placed modern man in a situation where his decisions now control the fate of large population masses, sometimes the whole earth, and his sights are now set on outer space. Even the personal decisions that direct an individual's daily life have become increasingly complicated. To cite but one example, consider the bewildering array of career choices that confront today's bright youth. And consider the extreme commitment of time, effort, and money necessary to obtain the specialized training most of

[1] Sponsorship for this work comes from the Personnel and Training Research Programs, Psychological Sciences Division, Office of Naval Research, under Contract No. N00014-68-C-0431, Contract Authority Ident. No. NR 153-311, and from Grants MH-15414 and MH-12972 from the United States Public Health Service.

[2] We are indebted to many individuals for their comments on an early draft of this paper. In particular, we would like to thank Norman Anderson, Mats Bjorkman, Berndt Brehmer, Robyn Dawes, Lewis Goldberg, Kenneth Hammond, Leon Rappoport, David Summers, and Amos Tversky for their careful and critical reading of the manuscript. Thanks are also due William Chaplin for his help in conceptualizing the relationships among the various paradigms.

these opportunities require. The result is a high gain–high risk decision, much more difficult and complex than that faced by his parents.

The difficulties attendant to decision making are usually blamed on the inadequacy of the available information, and, therefore, our technological expertise has been mobilized to remedy this problem. Devices proliferate to supply the professional decision maker with an abundance of data. The physician, for example, has access to sophisticated electronic sensors, and satellites now relay masses of strategic data for military intelligence. However, the problem of interpreting and integrating this information has received surprisingly little attention. At this point, the decision maker is typically left to his own devices. More likely than not he will proceed, as will the physician, businessman, or military commander, in much the same manner that has been relied upon since antiquity, and when you ask him what distinguishes a good judge from a poor one he will reply, "It's a kind of locked in concentration, an intuition, a feel, nothing that can be schooled [Smith, 1968, p. 20]."

However, things have begun to change. Specialists from many disciplines have started to focus on the integration process itself. Their efforts center around two broad questions—"What is the decision maker doing with the information available to him?" and "What should he be doing with it?" The first is a psychological problem—that of understanding how man uses information. The second problem is a more practical one and involves the attempt to make decision making more effective and efficient.

The Focus of This Paper

Information processing occurs at several levels. Our concern here is not with events at the neural level but rather with cognitive operations performed on such grosser phenomena as symbols, signs, and facts. We shall focus on the processes and strategies that humans employ in order to integrate these discrete items of information into a decision. These are the deliberative processes commonly referred to by the terms "integrating," "weighing," "balancing," "trading off," or "combining" information.

Prior to 1960 there was relatively little research on information processing at this molar, judgmental level. However, the intellectual groundwork had already been laid by studies such as Brunswik's pioneering investigations of inference in uncertain environments (Brunswik, 1956; Hammond, 1955); the work on "probability learning" (Estes, 1959); investigations of gambling decisions, utility, and subjective probability (Edwards, 1954); Miller's (1956) elaboration of the limitations on the number of conceptual items that can be processed at one time; the concept formation studies by Bruner, Goodnow, and Austin (1956); and the research on computer simulation of thought by Newell, Shaw, and Simon (1958).

Since 1960, this early work has been supplemented by several hundred studies within the rather narrowly defined topic of information utilization in judgment and decision making. The yearly volume of studies has been increasing exponentially, stimulated by a growing awareness of the significance of the problems and the aid of the ubiquitous computer. The importance of the latter cannot be overestimated. When Smedslund (1955) published the first multiple-cue probability learning study, he bemoaned having to compute 3200 correlations on a desk calculator. It's not surprising that the next study of its kind was not forthcoming for five more years.

Much of the recent work has been accomplished within two basic schools of research. We have chosen to call these the "regression" and the "Bayesian" approaches. Each has its characteristic tasks and characteristic information that must be processed to accomplish these tasks. For the most part, researchers have tended to work strictly within a single approach and there has been minimal communication between the resultant subgroups of workers.

Our objective in this reading is to present a review and comparative analysis of these two approaches. Within each, we shall examine (1) the models that have been developed for describing and prescribing the use of information in decision making; (2) the major experimental paradigms, including the types of judgment, prediction, and decision tasks and the kinds of information that have been available to the decision maker in these tasks; (3) the key independent variables that have been manipulated in experimental studies; and (4) the major empirical results and conclusions.

In comparing these approaches, we seek the answers to two basic questions. First, do the specific models and methods characteristic of different paradigms direct the researcher's attention to certain problems and cause him to neglect others that may be equally important? Second, can a researcher studying a particular substantive problem, such as the use people make of inconsistent or conflicting information, increase his understanding by employing diverse models and experimental methods?

Areas Omitted

Space limitations have forced us to omit several other paradigms that have made significant contributions to the study of human judgment. One of these is the process-tracing approach described by Hayes (1968) and exemplified by the work of Kleinmuntz (1968) and Clarkson (1962). Researchers following this approach attempt to build sequential, branching models of the decision maker based upon his verbalizations as he works through actual decision problems. Yet another important approach to the study of judgment uses multidimensional scaling procedures to infer the cognitive structure of the judge. For coverage of this work the reader is referred to the reading by Nancy Wiggins in this book. There have been several attempts to apply information theory to the study of human judgment. One of the most notable recent efforts along these lines is the work of Bieri, Atkins, Briar, Leaman, Miller, and Tripodi (1966), which examines the transmission of information in social judgment along the lines of Miller's (1956) well-known paradigm. Another area we shall omit here is that of probability learning. A recent and thorough review emphasizing the information processing implications of this work is presented by Jones (in press). Lastly, we have not attempted to review signal detection theory, an approach that has produced a geat deal of research concerning the integration of sensory information into decisions. The reader is referred to books by Swets (1964) and Green and Swets (1966) for detailed coverage of this area.

The Regression Approach

The regression approach is so named because of its characteristic use of multiple regression and its close relative, analysis of variance (ANOVA), to study the use of information by a judge. Within this broad approach we shall distinguish two different paradigms which we have labeled the "correlational" paradigm and the "ANOVA" paradigm.

The Correlational Paradigm

In the correlational paradigm, a judge's integration of information is described by means of correlational statistics. The basic approach requires the judge to make quantitative evaluations of a number of stimuli, each of which is defined by one or more quantified cue dimensions or characteristics. For example, a judge might be asked to predict the grade point average for each of a group of college students on the basis of high school grades and aptitude test scores. Sarbin and Bailey (1966) elaborate the aims of the correlational analyst in a study such as this:

> He correlates the information cues available to the inferring person with the judgments or inferences. . . . What usually results is that the coefficients of correlation between cues and judgment make public the subtle, and often unreportable, inferential activities of the inferring person. That is, the coefficients reveal the relative degrees that the judgments depend on the various sources of information available to the judge [pp. 193–194].

The development of the correlational paradigm has followed two streams. One stream has focused on the judge; its goal is to describe the judge's idiosyncratic method of combining and weighting information by developing mathematical equations representative of his combinatorial processes (Hoffman, 1960).

The other stream developed out of the work of Egon Brunswik, whose philosophy of "probabilistic functionalism" led him to study the organism's successes and failures in an uncertain world. Brunswik's main emphasis was not on the organism itself, but on the adaptive interrelationship between the organism and its environment. Thus, in addition to studying the degree to which a judge used cues, he analyzed the manner in which the judge learned the characteristics of his environment. He developed the "lens model" to represent the probabilistic interrelations between organismic and environmental components of the judgment situation (Brunswik, 1952, 1956).

Because of his concern about the environmental determinants of judgment, Brunswik was also the foremost advocate of what he called "representative design." The essense of this principle is that the organism should be studied in realistic settings, in experiments that are representative of its usual ecology. The lens model provides a means for appropriately specifying the structure of the situational variables in such an experiment.

The lens model. The lens model has proved to be an extremely valuable framework for conceptualizing the judgment process. Hammond (1955) described the relevance of the model for the study of clinical judgment, and recent work by Hursch, Hammond, and Hursch (1964), Tucker (1964), and Dudycha and Naylor (1966b) has detailed some important relationships among its components in terms of multiple regression statistics. A diagrammatic outline of a recent version of the lens model (based on Dudycha & Naylor) is shown in Figure 1.1. The variables X_1, X_2, . . . X_k are cues or information sources that define each stimulus object. For example, if the stimuli being evaluated are students whose grade point averages are to be predicted, the X_i can represent high school rank, aptitude scores, etc. The cue dimensions must be quantifiable, if only to the extent of a 0–1 (e.g., high vs. low or yes vs. no) coding. Each cue dimension has a specific degree of relevance to the true state of the world. This true state, also called the criterion value, is designated Y_e (e.g., the student's actual grade point average). The relevance of the ith information source in the environment is indicated by the correlation, $r_{i,e}$, across stimuli, between cue X_i and Y_e. This value, $r_{i,e}$, is called the *ecological validity* of the ith cue. The intercorrelations among cues, again across stimuli, are given by the $r_{i,j}$ values. On the subject's side, his response or judgment is Y_s (the judged grade point average), and the correlation of his judgments with the ith cue is $r_{i,s}$ also known as his *utilization coefficient* for the ith cue.

Both the criterion and the judgment can be predicted from linear combinations of the cues as indicated by the following regression equations:

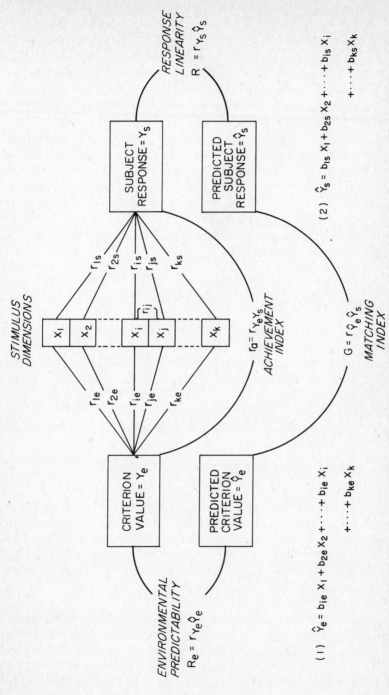

Figure 1.1 Diagram of lens model showing the relationship among the cues, criteria, and subjects' responses (Based on Dudycha & Naylor, 1966b. Reprinted by permission of Academic Press, Inc., and the authors.)

$$\hat{Y}_e = \sum_{i=1}^{k} b_{i,e} \, X_i \qquad\qquad (1.1)$$

$$\hat{Y}_s = \sum_{i=1}^{k} b_{i,s} \, X_i \qquad\qquad (1.2)$$

Equation 1.1 represents the prediction strategy that is optimal in the sense of minimizing the sum of squared deviations between $\hat{Y}_e$ and Y_e. The multiple correlation coefficient, $R_e = r_{Y_e \hat{Y}_e}$, indicates the degree to which the weighted combination of cues serves to predict the state of Y_e.

Equation 1.2 provides one possible model of the subject's decision-making strategy or *policy*. The multiple correlation coefficient, $R_s = r_{Y_s \hat{Y}_s}$, indicates how well his judgments can be predicted by a linear combination of cue-values. It is also known as the subject's *response linearity*. The values of $b_{i,e}$ and $b_{i,s}$ provide measures of importance of each cue in the environment and for the judge.

The two most important summary measures of the judge's performance are:

$r_a = r_{Y_e Y_s}$, the achievement index, and
$G = r_{\hat{Y}_e \hat{Y}_s}$, the matching index.

All of the above equations apply to linearly predictable relations and dependencies. The model has been further expanded by Hursch et al. to express nonlinear cue-utilization by the introduction of the C coefficient. C is the correlation between the residual that cannot be linearly predicted in the criterion and the residual that cannot be linearly predicted in the judgment. If either of these residuals is random, C will be zero.

Tucker (1964) has shown that the indices of the lens model are related in a general equation for achievement:

$$r_a = R_e R_s G + C \left[(1 - R_e^2)(1 - R_s^2) \right]^{1/2} \qquad\qquad (1.3)$$

Equation 1.3 plays an extremely important role in many empirical studies and has come to be called the *lens model equation*. It demonstrates that achievement is a function of the statistical properties of the environment *(R_e)*, as well as the statistical properties of the subject's response system *(R_s)*, the extent to which the linear weightings of the two systems match one another *(G)*, and the extent to which nonlinear variance of one system is correlated with nonlinear variance of the other *(C)*. As Hammond (1966) has noted, the lens model permits an analysis of the relative contributions of environmental factors to a judge's achievement and thus serves as a valuable adjunct to research in the Brunswikian tradition.

Mathematical models of the judge. As we have seen, the lens model was developed to study the effects of the decision maker's environment on his performance. Because of this environmental emphasis, the focal components of the model are r_a, the achievement index, and the factors such as R_s, G, and C that determine achievement. Workers following the other stream of correlational research have had a different emphasis. They have been more interested in the judge's weighting process—his policy. In contrast with the Brunswikian tradition, they have placed less importance upon modeling the environment and, instead, have stressed the need to control the environmental situation. They tend to make the stimulus dimensions explicit and to vary their levels systematically, even though some degree of realism may be lost in the process.

A wide variety of mathematical models have been developed to capture judgmental policies. The first and most prominent of these is the *linear model* (Hoffman, 1960) which is exemplified by Equation 1.2 of the lens model. Alternatively, when the judge is classifying stimuli into one of two categories, the *linear discriminant function,* rather than the multiple regression equation, can be used to analyze the way that cues are weighted (Rodwan & Hake, 1964). In either form, the model captures the notion that the judge's predictions are a linear combination of each of the available cues. When judgment is represented by the linear model, the $b_{i,s}$ values of Equation 1.2 and the utilization coefficients, $r_{i,s}$, are used to represent the relative importance given each cue. Hoffman (1960) proposed an alternative index, "relative weight," designed for this purpose. Relative weights are computed as follows:

$$RW_{i,s} = \frac{B_{i,s} r_{i,s}}{R_{s.}^2} \; .$$

Since the sum of relative weights is 1.0, Hoffman's index describes the relative contribution of each of the predictors as a proportion of the predictable linear variance.

However, as Darlington (1968) has recently emphasized, all indices of relative weight become suspect when the factors are intercorrelated. This problem has led many judgment researchers to work with sets of stimuli in which the cues are made orthogonal to one another. One device used to insure orthogonality has been to construct stimuli by producing factorial combinations of the cues. Of course, this practice is anathema to Brunswikians, since it is the antithesis of representative design. Brunswik observed (1955; pp. 204–205) that factorial designs may produce certain combinations of values that are inherently incompatible or otherwise unrealistic and disruptive of the very process they were meant to disclose. This criticism cannot be taken lightly and some evidence does exist that judgment processes differ as a function of cue interrelationships (Dudycha & Naylor, 1966a; Slovic, 1966). But to the researcher who is primarily interested in relative weights, rather than achievement, orthogonal designs often seem preferable to designs in which the cues are correlated in a representative fashion. Attempts are usually made, however, to mitigate potential disruptive effects by telling the judge that he will be dealing with a selected, rather than a random, sample of cases and by eliminating combinations of factors that are obviously unreal (See, e.g., Hoffman, Slovic, & Rorer, 1968).

As we shall see, the linear model does a remarkably good job of predicting human judgments. However, judges' verbal introspections indicate that they believe they use cues in a variety of nonlinear ways, and researchers have attempted to capture these with more complex equations. One type of nonlinearity occurs when an individual cue relates to the judgments in a *curvilinear* manner. For example, the following quotation from a leading authority on the stock market suggests a curvilinear relation between the volume of trading on a stock and its future prospects:

> If you are driving a car you can get to your destination more quickly at 50 mph than at 10 mph. But you may wreck the car at 100 mph. In a similar way, increasing volume on an advance up to a point is bullish and decreasing volume on a rally is bearish, but in both cases only up to a point [Loeb, 1965, p. 287].

Such functions can be modeled by including exponential terms (i.e., X_i^2, X_i^3, etc.) as predictors in the judge's policy equation.

A second type of nonlinearity occurs when cues are combined in a *configural* manner. Configurality means that the judge's interpretation or weighting of an item of information varies according to the nature of other available information. An example of configural reasoning involving price changes, volume of trading, and market cycle was given by the same stock market expert:

> Outstanding strength or weakness can have precisely opposite meanings at different times in the market cycle. For example, consistent strength and volume in a particular issue, occurring after a long general decline, will usually turn out to be an extremely bullish indication . . . . On the other hand, after an extensive advance which finally spreads to issues neglected all through the bull market, belated individual strength and activity not only are likely to be shortlived but may actually suggest the end of the general recovery . . . [p. 65].

When decision makers state that their judgments are associated with complex, sequential, and interrelated rules, it is likely that they are referring to some sort of configural process. It is important, therefore, that techniques used to describe judgment be sensitive to configurality. The C coefficient, described earlier, is unsatisfactory from a descriptive standpoint because of its lack of specificity.

The ANOVA Paradigm

One way of making the linear model sensitive to configural effects has been to incorporate cross-product terms into the policy equation of the judge. Thus, if the meaning of factor X_1 varies as a function of the level of factor X_2, the term $b_{12}X_1X_2$ can be added to the equation. When models become this complex, however, the proliferation of highly inter-correlated terms in the equations becomes so great that estimation of the weighting coefficients is unreliable unless vast numbers of cases are available (Hoffman, 1968). For this reason, investigators such as Hoffman, Slovic, and Rorer (1968), Rorer, Hoffman, Dickman, and Slovic (1967), and Slovic (1969) have turned to the use of analysis of variance (ANOVA) to describe complex judgmental processes.

The structural model underlying ANOVA is quite similar to that of multiple regression, both being alternative formulations of a general linear model (Cohen, 1968). Although the factors that describe the cases can be either continuous or categorical, each must be partitioned into a relatively few discrete levels. In addition, the factors are typically made orthogonal to one another, although this is not a necessity. In return for these restrictions, the ANOVA technique provides a statistically efficient mechanism for detecting curvilinear and configural use of information.

When judgments are analyzed in terms of an ANOVA model, a significant main effect for cue X_1 implies that the judges' responses varied systematically with X_1 as the levels of the other cues were held constant. If sufficient levels of the factor were included in the design, and if these levels can be assigned interval scale values, the main effect may be divided into effects due to linear, quadratic, cubic, and so on, trends. Similarly, a significant interaction between cues X_1 and X_2 implies that the judge was responding to particular patterns of those cues; that is, the effect of variation of cue X_1 upon judgment differed as a function of the corresponding level taken by cue X_2.

The ANOVA model thus has potential for describing the linear, curvilinear, and configural aspects of the judgmental process. Within the framework of the model, it is possible to calculate an index of the importance of individual or patterned use of a cue, relative to the importance of other cues. One such index is based upon the degree to which the mean judgment shifts as the levels of a factor are varied (See Slovic, 1969). Another is simply a transformation of these mean effects into an estimate of the proportion of the total variation in a person's judgments that can be predicted from knowledge of the particular levels of a given cue or pattern of cues (See Hays, 1963, p. 324, or Hoffman et al., 1968). The latter index includes linear and nonlinear variance and, therefore, it is analogous to, but more general than, Hoffman's index of relative weight.

In an ANOVA design, the usual way to produce orthogonal stimulus dimensions is to construct all possible combinations of the cue levels in a completely crossed factorial arrangment. Such an arrangement becomes unmanageable when the number of cues is large, or when it is desirable to include many levels of each cue. However, if one is willing to assume that some of the higher-order interactions are negligible, then it is possible to employ a fractional replication design and evaluate the importance of the main effects and lower-order interactions with a considerably reduced number of stimuli (Anderson, 1964; Cochran & Cox, 1957; Shanteau, 1970; Slovic, 1969).

Integration theory. Integration theory can be considered one extension of the regression approaches described above. As such, it has formed the basis of an intensive program of research in the areas of clinical and psychophysical judgment, personality impression formation, and decision making. The essential ideas stem from the work of Norman Anderson, and are summarized in Anderson (1968b, 1969, 1970, 1971, in press).

Integration theory is concerned simultaneously with two problems. The first is scaling the stimulus items and determining the weighting parameters. This component of the theory is called "valuation." The second concern, called "integration," tests theories about the specific composition rules used by the subjects. Particular attention has been given to tasks in which a simple algebraic model, involving adding, averaging, subtracting, or multiplying the informational inputs, serves as the substantive theory of judgment that is being tested.

Technically, integration theory relies upon factorial designs, due to the fact that the substantive theories studied thus far have almost always been reducible to an ANOVA model. Therefore, ANOVA has been the principal analytical tool, serving to represent the theoretical postulates and providing a goodness-of-fit test of the models. An invalid response scale could cause a valid model to fail the test of fit. Therefore, an important feature of Anderson's approach is the use of monotone rescaling procedures for the response variable. If the model is correct, it serves as a frame on which to rescale the response. Failure to obtain an adequate fit after rescaling argues against the model, and success argues for it. Once the model and response scale are established, the subjective values of the information items can be derived. Anderson has used the term "functional measurement" to describe this interplay between theory and scaling.

According to integration theory, each piece of information is represented by two properties: a subjective scale value, s, and a weight, w. The weight represents the salience or importance of the information. The basic theoretical model is:

$$R = C + \sum_{k=0}^{n} w_k s_k \tag{1.4}$$

where R is the subject's response or judgment. The first term in the sum, $w_0 s_0$, represents the weight and scale value of the initial opinion prior to receiving any information. This basic model has been expanded in a variety of ways to encompass different substantive theories. The following description will focus on an additive model as applied to a two-way factorial design. Here, the subject is shown a stimulus containing two descriptive items—one from the row dimension and one from the column dimension. His response is considered to be the resultant of the two items and his initial opinion:

$$R_{ij} = w_0 s_0 + w_R s_{Ri} + w_C s_{Cj} \tag{1.5}$$

where w_R and w_C are the weights associated with the row and column dimensions, s_{Ri} is the scale value of the information item in Row i of Dimension R, and s_{Cj} is the scale value of the item in Column j Dimension C.

An example of the kind of task to which Equation 1.5 is applicable is the study by Sidowski and Anderson (1967) in which subjects judged the attractiveness of working at a certain occupation (Doctor, Lawyer, Accountant, or Teacher) in a certain city (City A, B, C, or D). Each cell of the design corresponds to a pair of items (a city–occupation combination) that the judge is to integrate. Another example is an impression formation task similar to that used by Lampel and Anderson (1968), in which each cell is a person described by an adjective and a photograph. The adjective represents the row source and the photograph represents the column source. The salience of each of the two sources, represented by w_R and w_C in Equation 1.5, is assumed to be constant. The values of the adjectives and photographs are captured by s_{Ri} and s_{Cj}.

The important properties of this model are that the weights are constant across levels of each dimension and that the model permits the scaling of subjective values for each item. Thus, Equation 1.5 is similar to the linear model of Equation 1.2 except that subjective scale values, rather than the physical or objective values, are employed in the linear equation. It is not assumed that the objective values of the stimulus dimensions are linearly related to the responses. If, for example, the judgment task involved the rating of occupations, and salary was one of the factors, the actual salary levels would enter into the linear model of Equation 1.2 as predictors of the judgments. But it is quite likely that the judge perceives salary in a nonlinear fashion. The subjective difference between $20,000 and $25,000 is probably less than the difference between $5,000 and $10,000. Integration theory attempts to discover these subjective scale values and to determine rules of composition based on *these* values, whereas the regression and ANOVA approaches described earlier attempt to discover the combination rule based on the objective dimensions.

Equation 1.5 implies that the row by column interaction should be zero in principle and nonsignificant in practice. Therefore, ANOVA serves to test the model's goodness of fit. If the model passes this test, it may be used to estimate the subjective values s_{Ri} and s_{Cj}. When Equation 1.5 is averaged over columns, the mean response for Row i is:

$$R_{i.} = w_R s_{Ri} + \text{constant} \tag{1.6}$$

where the dot subscript on R denotes the average over the column index. The constant expression represents the influence of the columns and is the same for all rows. Equation 1.6 says that these row means form a linear function of the subjective values of the row stimuli. Thus, the row means constitute an interval scale of the row stimuli. Similarly, the column means constitute an interval scale of the column stimuli.

The above results hold for an additive model. Similar analyses for subtractive and multiplicative models may be found in Shanteau and Anderson (1969) and Anderson and Shanteau (1970). Anderson (1971, in press) summarized these results and presented averaging versions of these models in which the weights are constrained to sum to unity. In some of these models, w_k can be scaled but not s_k, or vice versa. In others, both parameters can be scaled.

Anderson (1969) noted that caution is required in interpreting the meaning of significant interactions when these occur. Interactions may result from cognitive configurality that is theoretically meaningful or from defects in the response scale, such as floor and ceiling effects. In some cases, a monotonic rescaling of the judgments can be used to eliminate the interaction (See, e.g., Bogartz & Wackwitz, 1970). Whether or not to rescale the judgments is a delicate matter—one that depends upon the researcher's degree of confidence in the theoretical model that is being tested and his confidence in the validity of the scale on which the judgments are measured. For example, Lampel and Anderson (1968) found a significant interaction between visual and verbal information in an impression formation task. This interaction could have been eliminated by monotonic rescaling of the responses. However, as Anderson (1970) observed, they did not remove the interaction because previous experimentation had given them confidence in the response scale. Thus the interaction was retained and given a psychological interpretation.

Anderson and colleagues have also applied integration theory to study the effects of serial position in information integration. In these studies the stimuli were presented successively and the serial positions corresponded to factors in the design. The weights indicated by the main effects thus produced a serial-position curve that was used to assess whether information was given more salience earlier (primacy) or later (recency) in the sequence (Anderson, 1965b, 1968a; Shanteau, 1970). Anderson (1965b) noted that when information is presented serially, the weighted average model can be reformulated in a manner that makes it particularly valuable for studying the step-by-step buildup of a judgment in response to each item. This form, called the proportional change model, asserts that the judgment, R_k, produced after receipt of the kth item of information, is given by:

$$R_k = R_{k-1} + w_k(s_k - R_{k-1}) \tag{1.7}$$

where R_{k-1} is the judgment prior, and R_k is the judgment posterior, to presentation of the kth item. The scale value of the kth item is denoted by s_k, and w_k is a change parameter that measures the influence of the kth item.

Conjoint measurement. The theory of conjoint measurement (Krantz & Tversky, 1970; Luce & Tukey, 1964; Tversky, 1967b) is analogous in many respects to integration theory. Both are concerned with discovering the psychological laws that govern the composition of several attributes (for our purposes, several items of information). However, integration theory deals with *quantitative* laws, whereas conjoint measurement is concerned with *qualitative* laws.

When the stimuli and the judgments can be measured independently on interval scales, the rule of combination can be tested directly. However, when the assumption of interval-scale measurement is of dubious validity, conjoint measurement is valuable, since it uses only *ordinal* properties of the judgments to test the proposed combination rule.

Krantz and Tversky delineated the testable ordinal relationships among judgments that can be used to diagnose which, if any, of several polynomial composition rules is appropriate. For example, one class of testable properties, called independence conditions, serves a valuable diagnostic function. The essence of ordinal independence is that the ordering of the judgments within any row of the factorial matrix is constant across rows.

Krantz and Tversky argued that the ordinal approach to the study of composition rules, exemplified by conjoint measurement, should be regarded as complementary to numerical approaches such as the lens model or integration theory. From a practical standpoint, they noted that direct tests of ordinal properties are generally more powerful in their ability to discriminate alternative composition rules than are overall tests of goodness of fit. From a theoretical standpoint, they contended that qualitative properties may sometimes lead to a more fundamental understanding of psychological principles than do numerical analyses.

Conjoint measurement has been applied in only a few judgment studies thus far (See, e.g., Coombs & Huang, 1970; Tversky, 1967a, 1967c; Tversky & Krantz, 1969; Wallsten, 1970) but the explication of its analysis techniques by Krantz and Tversky should stimulate greater use of this approach in the future.

The Bayesian Approach

Brunswik proposed the use of correlations to assess relationships in a probabilistic environment. He could have used conditional probabilities instead; had he done so, he undoubtedly would have built his lens model around Bayes' theorem, an elementary fact about probabilities described in 1763 by the Reverend Thomas Bayes. The modern impetus for what we are calling the Bayesian paradigm can be traced to the work of von Neumann and Morgenstern (1947) who revived interest in maximization of expected utility as a core principle of rational decision making, and to L. J. Savage, whose book *The Foundations of Statistics* fused the concepts of utility and personal probability into an axiomatized theory of decision in the face of uncertainty, "a highly idealized theory of the behavior of a 'rational' person with respect to decisions [Savage, 1954, p. 7]." The Bayesian approach was communicated to businessmen by Schlaifer (1959) and to medical diagnosticians by Ledley and Lusted (1959). Psychologists were introduced to Bayesian notions by Ward Edwards (Edwards, 1962; Edwards, Lindman, & Savage, 1963) and much of the empirical work to be discussed was stimulated directly by the ideas in the latter two papers.

The Bayesian approach is thoroughly embedded within the framework of decision theory. Its basic tenets are that opinions should be expressed in terms of subjective or personal probabilities, and that the optimal revision of such opinions, in the light of relevant new information, should be accomplished via Bayes' theorem. Edwards (1966) noted that, although revision of opinion can be studied as a separate phenomenon, it is most interesting and important when it leads to decision making and action. Because of this concern with decision making, the output of a Bayesian anlaysis is not a single prediction but rather a distribution of probabilities over a set of hypothesized states of the world. These probabilities can then be used, in combination with information about payoffs associated with various decision possibilities and states of the world, to implement any of a number of decision rules, including the maximization of expected value or expected utility.

Bayes' theorem is thus a normative model. It specifies certain internally consistent relationships among probabilistic opinions and serves to prescribe, in this sense, how men should think. Much of the psychological research has used Bayes' theorem as a standard against which to compare actual behavior and to search for systematic deviations from optimality.

The Bayesian model. Given several mutually exclusive and exhaustive hypotheses, H_i, and a datum,[3] D, Bayes' theorem states:

$$P(H_i/D) = \frac{P(D/H_i)P(H_i)}{\Sigma P(D/H_i)P(H_i)} \tag{1.8}$$

In Equation 1.8, $P(H_i/D)$ is the posterior probability that H_i is true, taking into account the new datum, D, as well as all previous data. $P(D/H_i)$ is the conditional probability that the datum D would be observed if hypothesis H_i were true. For a set of mutually exclusive and exhaustive hypotheses H_i, the values of $P(D/H_i)$ represent the impact of the datum D on each of the hypotheses. The value $P(H_i)$ is the prior probability of hypothesis H_i. It, too, is a conditional probability, representing the probability of H_i conditional on all information available prior to the receipt of D. The denominator serves as a normalizing constant. Although Equation 1.8 is appropriate for discrete hypotheses, it can be rewritten, using integrals, to handle a continuous set of hypotheses and continuously varying data.

It is often convenient to form the ratio of Equation 1.8 taken with respect to two hypotheses, H_i and H_j:

$$\frac{P(H_i/D)}{P(H_j/D)} = \frac{P(D/H_i)}{P(D/H_j)} \cdot \frac{P(H_i)}{P(H_j)}$$

For this ratio form, new symbols are introduced:

$$\Omega_1 = LR \cdot \Omega_o$$

where Ω_1 represents the *posterior odds*, *LR* is called the *likelihood ratio*, and Ω_o stands for the *prior odds*.

Bayes' theorem can be used sequentially to measure the impact of several data. The posterior probability computed for the first datum is used as the prior probability when processing the impact of the second datum, and so on. The order in which data are processed makes no difference to their impact on posterior opinion. The final posterior odds, given n items of data, are

[3] Within the regression and ANOVA paradigms, a datum refers to a response made by a judge; for Bayesians, however, a datum is an item of information presented to the judge.

$$\Omega_n = \prod_{k=1}^{n} LR_k \cdot \Omega_o \tag{1.9}$$

Equation 1.9 shows that data affect the final odds multiplicatively. If the $\log_{10}$ of this equation were taken, the log likelihood ratios would combine additively with the log prior odds. The degree to which the prior odds change, upon receipt of a new datum, is dependent upon the likelihood ratio for that datum. Thus the likelihood ratio is an index of data diagnosticity or importance analogous to the weights employed in regression models.

The use of Bayes' theorem assumes that data are conditionally independent, that is,

$$P(D_j/H_i) = P(D_j/H_i, D_k)$$

If this assumption is not met, then the combination rule has to be expanded. For two data, the expanded version is:

$$P(H_i/D_1, D_2) \propto P(D_2/H_i, D_1) P(D_1/H_i) P(H_i) \tag{1.10}$$

As more data are received, the equation requires further expansion and becomes difficult to implement.

The meaning of the conditional independence assumption might be clarified by an example. Height and hair length are negatively correlated, and thus nonindependent, in the adult U.S. population (even these days), but within subgroups of males and females, height and hair length are, we might suppose, quite unrelated. Thus if the hypothesis of interest is the identification of a person as male or female, height and hair length data are *conditionally* independent, and the use of Bayes' theorem to combine these cues is appropriate. In contrast, height and weight are related both across sexes and within sexes, and are thus both unconditionally and conditionally nonindependent. These cues could not be combined via Bayes' theorem without altering it as shown in Equation 1.10. One way of thinking about the difference between these two examples is that in the first case the correlation between the cues is mediated by the hypothesis: The person is tall and has short hair *because* he is male. In the case of conditional nonindependence, however, the correlation between the cues is mediated by something other than the hypothesis: The taller person tends to weigh more because of the structural properties of human bodies.

Experimental paradigms. A hypothetical experiment, similar to one actually performed by Phillips and Edwards (1966), will illustrate a common use of the Bayesian paradigm. The subject is presented with the following situation: Two bookbags are filled with poker chips. One bookbag has 70 red chips and 30 blue chips, while the other bag holds 30 red chips and 70 blue chips. The subject does not know which bag is which. The experimenter flips a coin to choose one of the bags and then begins to draw chips from the chosen bag. After drawing a chip he shows it to the subject and then replaces it in the bag, stirring vigorously before drawing the next chip. The subject is asked to estimate the probability that the predominantly red bag is the one being sampled. At the start, before the first chip is drawn, the subject is required to give a probability estimate of .5, indicating that each bag is equally likely to have been chosen. Then, after each chip is drawn, the subject reflects the revision of his opinion by changing his probability estimate. The subject sees 10 successive chips drawn; the basic data for analysis are the 10 posterior probability estimates the subject made after each chip.

The optimal responses are computed from Bayes' theorem. The data (poker chips) are conditionally independent because each sampled chip is replaced before the next is drawn. The prior odds are 1 (the bookbags were equally likely to be chosen), and the likelihood ratios associated with red and blue chips are a function of the 70/30 proportions in each bag:

$$LR_{\text{Red Chip}} = \frac{P\,(\text{Red Chip}/H_{70\ \text{Red}})}{P\,(\text{Red Chip}/H_{70\%\ \text{Blue}})} = \frac{.7}{.3}$$

$$LR_{\text{Blue Chip}} = \frac{P\,(\text{Blue Chip}/H_{70\%\ \text{Red}})}{P\,(\text{Blue Chip}/H_{70\%\ \text{Blue}})} = \frac{.3}{.7}$$

The posterior odds of the predominently red bag having been chosen, given a sample of, say, 6 red chips and 4 blue chips, are calculated from Equation 1.9:

$$\Omega_{10} = \left(\frac{7}{3}\right)^6 \cdot \left(\frac{3}{7}\right)^4 \cdot 1 \simeq 5.44$$

The odds are greater than 5 to 1 that the predominantly red bag is the bag being sampled. This corresponds to a posterior probability for that bag of approximately .845.

The primary data analysis compares subjects' probability revision upon receipt of each chip with those of Bayes' theorem. To supplement direct comparisons of Bayesian probabilities and subjective estimates, Peterson, Schneider, and Miller (1965) introduced a measure of the degree to which performance is optimal, called the accuracy ratio:

$$AR = \frac{SLLR}{BLLR}$$

where *SLLR* is the log likelihood ratio inferred from the subjects' probability estimates (using Equation 1.9) and *BLLR* is the optimal (Bayesian) log likelihood ratio. The conversion to log likelihood ratios is made because the optimal responses then become linear with the amount of evidence favoring one hypothesis over the other. The accuracy ratio can be computed for each datum, or it can serve as a summary measure across many responses made to a variety of data. In the latter case, it is the slope of the regression line relating *SLLR*s to *BLLR*s, and is thus similar to a beta weight in the correlational model.

The task just described illustrates the use of a binomial data generating model. The Bayesian paradigm, however, is capable of dealing with a great variety of different types of data—discrete or continuous, from the same or different sources, and so on. For example, some Bayesian experiments have employed multinomial distributions to generate samples of data. Table 1.1 provides a hypothetical illustration. In this example three hypotheses concerning a college student's grade point average (GPA) are related to three data sources (e.g., verbal ability, achievement motivation, and credit hours attempted). Each data source is comprised of several subclasses of information (e.g., below average or above average achievement motivation). The entries in the cells of the resulting evidence-

Table 1.1   Some Multinomial Data Generating Hypotheses

| | Hypotheses about a Student's GPA | | |
| | H_1 | H_2 | H_3 |
	Lower 33%	*Middle 33%*	*Upper 33%*
D_1: Verbal ability			
1. Below average	.55	.30	.15
2. Average	.30	.40	.35
3. Above average	.15	.30	.50
D_2: Achievement motivation			
1. At or below average	.75	.50	.50
2. Above average	.25	.50	.50
D_3: Credit hours attempted			
1. Below 12	.15	.25	.20
2. 12–15	.25	.30	.20
3. 16–18	.30	.30	.30
4. Above 18	.30	.15	.30

hypothesis matrix are conditional probabilities of the form $P(D_{jk}/H_i)$, that is, the probability that the kth subclass of data class j would occur, given H_i.

If the data subclasses are mutually exclusive and exhaustive, as is the case here, the conditional probabilities within any data source and any one hypothesis must sum to 1.00 (e.g., a student must be either above, at, or below average on achievement motivation). Across hypotheses, the conditional probabilities need not sum to any constant (e.g., relatively few college students, regardless of GPA, take less than 12 credit hours of course work).

The critical measure of relatedness between a cue and a hypothesis is represented here by three conditional probabilities, $P(D_{jk}/H_1)$, $P(D_{jk}/H_2)$, and $P(D_{jk}/H_3)$, rather than by a single correlation. The diagnosticity of a particular datum, D_{jk}, rests on the ratios of the conditional probabilities across hypotheses. Thus below average verbal ability (D_{11}) is highly diagnostic, whereas 16–18 credit hours attempted (D_{33}) gives no information at all concerning GPA.

A typical experiment, based on a multinomial task, proceeds as follows: The subject would be asked to assume some prior probability distribution across the hypothesis set (e.g., that each of the three GPA categories was equally likely). He then would receive a set of data, describing a student (e.g., verbal ability average, motivation above average, 16 credit hours). Following this he must revise his prior opinion about the likelihood that the various hypotheses had generated the evidence. To do this he needs some indication of the importance of each item of evidence. Either the $P(D_{jk}/H_i)$ values can be presented to him in the form of a table or he can be given feedback that will enable him to estimate these values on the basis of the relative frequency of occurrence of each item. The subject's estimates can be in the form of posterior probabilities or some analog such as posterior odds. These estimates are then compared with the optimal responses prescribed by Bayes' theorem.

Some Bayesian experiments require the subjects to estimate both $P(D/H)$ and $P(H/D)$. The goal of such a study is to see if the estimates are consistent; that is, to explore whether the $P(H/D)$ estimates can be predicted by aggregating the $P(D/H)$ estimates according to the optimal composition rule, Bayes' theorem.

Information seeking experiments. The decision maker often has the option of deferring his decision while he gathers relevant information, usually at some additional cost. The information presumably will increase his certainty about the true state of the world and increase his chances of making a good decision. In seeking additional information, the decision maker must weight the relative advantage of the new information against its cost. When the probabilistic characteristics of the task are well defined, an optimal strategy can be specified that will, in conjunction with the reward for making a correct decision, the penalty for being wrong, and the cost of the information, determine a stopping point that is optimal in the sense of maximizing expected value (Edwards, 1965; Raiffa & Schlaifer, 1961; Wald, 1947). This task is a natural extension of the probabilistic inference tasks described above, since it requires the decision maker to link payoff considerations with his inferences in order to arrive at a decision. A large number of studies have investigated man's ability to make such decisions. For example, one commonly studied task uses the bookbag and the poker chip problem described earlier. As before, a sequence of chips is sampled, with replacement, from a bag with proportion of red chips equal to P_1 or P_2. Instead of estimating the posterior probabilities for each bag, the subject must decide from which bag the sample is coming. In some cases, he must decide, prior to seeing the first chip, how many chips he wishes to see (fixed stopping). In other cases, he samples one chip at a time and can stop at any point and announce his decision (optional stopping). Space limitations prohibit further analysis of this body of research here. The interested reader is referred to papers by Fried and Peterson (1969), Pitz (1969b, 1969c), Rapoport (1969), and Wallsten (1968) for examples of this research.

Comparisons of the Bayesian and Regression Approaches

Having completed our overview of the basic elements of the regression and Bayesian approaches, it is appropriate to consider briefly some of the similarities and differences between them. At first glance, it would seem that the dissimilarities predominate. This impression is fostered, primarily, by the grossly different terminology used within each approach. However, closer examination reveals many points of isomorphism. In particular, each paradigm is based on a theoretical model of the composition rules whereby informational input is integrated into a judgmental response. The schematic diagram in Figure 1.2 depicts some general relationships between input, process, and response, and will serve as the organizational framework for the present discussion.

Input

The information that serves as input to the decision maker varies somewhat both within and between each approach. The correlational paradigm typically involves dimensions of quantitative information. Data presented

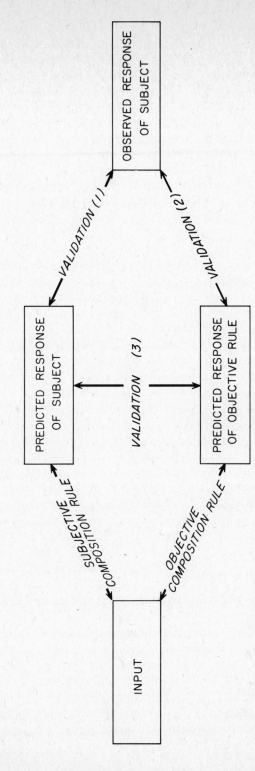

Figure 1.2. General schema for comparing research paradigms

within the ANOVA and Bayesian studies, by contrast, are often discrete, categorical, or qualitative items, although these approaches can also process dimensional data. As to the relationships among data sources, ANOVA techniques require factorially combined information elements, and workers within the descriptive stream of correlational research also prefer orthogonal structure. Lens model research often uses items that are correlated in a fashion representative of the real world. Bayes' theorem, in its analytically convenient forms (Equations 1.8 and 1.9), requires conditionally independent data. A rough translation of this requirement in correlational terms would be that the residual correlations between cues, with the criterion dimension partialed out, must be zero.

The Subject's Response

The response required of the subject also differs across paradigms. The correlational and ANOVA approaches usually deal with a single-valued prediction (point estimate) about some conceptually continuous hypothesis. Bayesians would say that there is a probability distribution over this continuous distribution and that the subject's single judgment must represent the output of some covert decision process in which some implicit decision rule is applied (e.g., the response may be interpreted as specifying the criterion value having the largest probability of occurrence), based on some implicit payoff matrix. Some Bayesian studies also require subjects to make predictions, usually concerning discrete hypotheses. When they do, the payoffs accompanying correct and incorrect predictions are usually made explicit to the decision maker. Most often, however, subjects in Bayesian studies estimate the posterior or conditional probability distribution (or some function thereof, such as odds) across various hypotheses. Although Bayes' theorem can, in principle, be applied to continuous hypotheses, the emphasis on probability distributions rather than point estimates makes such a task experimentally awkward (See, however, Peterson & Phillips, 1966).

Subjective Composition Rules

From the standpoint of psychological theory, the rule by which the subject combines or integrates the input information is the most important element being investigated. Each paradigm is based upon a theoretical model of this composition process. Furthermore, these various algebraic models are closely related. The simple additive model plays a key role in both correlational and ANOVA studies and more complex polynomial rules can also be studied within these paradigms. Bayes' theorem is multiplicative in form, much like the multiplicative models within integration theory and conjoint measurement. In addition, the proportional change model of integration theory (Equation 1.7) and the Bayesian model both conceptualize the step-by-step buildup of judgment in terms of a weighted combination of the present datum and prior opinion.

Each of these composition models contains descriptive parameters that assess the subjective impact or importance of information. Correlational studies rely on global measures that reflect importance across an entire dimension or data source, such as correlations $(r_{i,s})$, regression weights $(b_{i,s})$, or relative weights $(RW_{i,s})$. In contrast, Bayesians are usually interested in the subjective impact of each individual datum, as measured by its subjective likelihood ratio. In the Bayesian approach, the source of dimensionality of the datum is irrelevant. Integration theory makes a conceptual distinction between two kinds of impact that are confounded in the above measures: w_k reflects the importance of one dimension or source of data relative to other sources, and s_k measures the subjective value of a single datum relative to other data from the same source.

The Bayesian paradigm looks at fixed hypotheses and examines the manner in which the subjective probabilities of these hypotheses are revised in the light of new information. For this reason it has sometimes been called a "dynamic" paradigm. In contrast, most of the correlational research deals with "static" aspects of information processing: When a subjective weight is inferred from a subject's responses over 50 trials, it is assumed that the subject's view of the world remains unchanged over this period. However, the static versus dynamic distinction is not inherent in the models. A good example of this point is found within integration theory, where the weighted average model takes both a static form (Equation 1.4) and a dynamic form—the proportional change model of Equation 1.7. In like manner, a regression equation could process information sequentially, and the item-by-item revisions of the judgments could be compared to optimal revisions specified by the equation although such a study has not been reported.

Objective Composition Rules

Objective composition rules can be thought of as representing the environmental aspect of the judgment situation, and they encompass the same sorts of models as are applied to the subjects' judgments. In some cases, logical considerations suggest a normative rule (such as Bayes' theorem). In other situations, the rule is determined primarily on empirical grounds (e.g., the use of multiple regression in the lens model to predict some criterion variable).

Both the lens model and the Bayesian approach share a deep concern about the relationship between the decision maker and his environment. Both models compare what the decision maker does with what he should be doing. The optimality of multiple regression rests on the acceptance of a built-in payoff function: the least squares criterion of goodness of fit. The posterior probabilities of the Bayesian model, however, can be combined with *any* payoff function to determine the best action. In certain circumstances, Bayesian and multiple regression models lead to identical solutions, as in the case of determining an optimal decision boundary between two hypotheses on the basis of normally distributed and standardized data (Koford & Groner, 1966).

Testing the Composition Rules

Validation of composition rules can take a number of different forms. Most important are comparisons between predicted responses (or other critical properties of subjective and objective rules) and the observed responses of the judge. These have been designated as validation types Number 1 and Number 2 in Figure 1.2. The predictions of a particular subjective rule can also be compared with those of a particular objective rule. We have designated this as validation type Number 3. An example of this type of validation is the *G* index in the lens model.

With regard to validation types Number 1 and Number 2, researchers differ in their attitudes towards testing the models. Workers within correlational and Bayesian settings have typically been satisfied that high correlations between their model's predictions and the subject's responses provide adequate evidence for the validity of the model. For example, Beach (1966) observed correlations in the .90s between subjects' *P(H/D)* estimates and Bayesian values that were calculated using subjects' earlier *P(D/H)* estimates. He concluded that:

> . . . *S*s possess a rule for revising subjective probabilities that they apply to whatever subjective probabilities they have at the moment . . . .
> As has been amply demonstrated, the *S*s' revision rule is essentially Bayes' theorem. That is to say, *S*s' revisions can be predicted with a good deal of precision using Bayes' theorem as the model [p. 36].

However, Anderson, working within the framework of integration theory, has chided researchers for neglecting to test goodness of fit:

> Tests of quantitative predictions clearly require evaluation of the discrepancies from prediction. Much of the earlier work . . . is unsatisfactory in this regard since it is based on regression statistics and goes no further than reporting correlations between predicted and observed [1969, p. 64].

Anderson goes on to note that high correlations may occur despite a seriously incorrect model. As evidence he cites a study by Sidowski and Anderson (1967), which found a correlation of .986 between the data and a simple additive model, despite the fact that the ANOVA showed a statistically significant and substantively interpretable interaction. Finally, as we noted earlier, conjoint measurement provides qualitative, localized tests that may be quite powerful for discriminating among alternative composition models.

The paramorphic representation problem. Hoffman (1960, 1968) raised an issue particularly germane to the discrimination of alternative subjective composition functions. He observed that: (1) two or more models of judgment may be algebraically equivalent yet suggestive of radically different underlying processes; and (2) two or more models may be algebraically different yet equally predictive, given fallible data. Drawing an analogy to problems of classification in minerology, Hoffman introduced the term "paramorphic representation" to remind psychologists that "the mathematical description of judgment is inevitably incomplete . . . , and it is not known how completely or how accurately the underlying process has been represented [1960, p. 125]." Although Hoffman raised the paramorphic issue in connection with models based upon correlational techniques, all of the models we have discussed face the same problem when they are used descriptively.

Empirical Research

As the preceding discussion indicated, judgment researchers are studying similar phenomena but with somewhat different methods. In the remainder of this chapter we shall survey the empirical research spawned by the theory and methodology described above. Table 1.2 outlines the organization of our coverage. We have partitioned regression studies according to whether they were conducted within the correlational or ANOVA paradigms. We have further categorized the work according to five broad problem areas relating to the use of information by the decision maker.

The first category is devoted to a focal topic of research within each paradigm. For the correlational paradigm, this focal topic is the specification of the policy equation for the judge, including the closely related problem of whether to include nonlinear terms in the policy equation.[4] A focal topic of ANOVA research is the distinction between two variants of the linear model, the summation model, and the averaging model, in impression formation. In Bayesian research, the focal topic is a particular form of suboptimal performance called conservatism. These topics are

---

[4] This is not the only focal topic of correlational research. For workers in the Brunswik-Hammond tradition, the judge's learning or adaptation in an uncertain environment is a focal topic.

Table 1.2. Overview of Topics in Bayesian and Regression Studies of Judgment

	Regression Studies		Bayesian Studies
	Correlational Paradigm	*ANOVA Paradigm*	*Probability Estimation Paradigm*
Typical Dependent Variables	$R_s, r_{i,s}, b_{i,s}, r_a, G, C$	weights (w_k) and subjective scale values (s_k) significance tests for the models	estimates of $P(H/D)$, $P(D/H)$, or ratios thereof deviations from Bayes' theorem
Categories of Research			
I. The focal topic	modeling a judge's policy	models of impression formation	conservatism
II. Task determinants of information use	cue consistency cue variability cue format number of cues response mode	set size extremity of meaning redundancy interitem consistency contextual effects sequential effects	response mode payoffs data diagnosticity prior probabilities sequential effects
III. Learning to use information	single-cue functional learning positive versus negative cues multiple-cue learning type of feedback interpersonal learning use of nonmetric cues	little or no research	effects of payoffs percent and type of feedback
IV. Alternative subjective composition strategies	strategies in correlational research	little or no research	strategies for estimating $P(H/D)$
V. Aiding the decision maker	bootstrapping	little or no research	probabilistic information processing systems

not closely interrelated. They are emphasized here simply because they have received a great deal of attention in the three areas of research.

The second category is devoted to the task determinants of information use. While many of these task variables are similar across differing paradigms, the dependent variables of such studies are less comparable, because they are so often closely related to the focal topics of the paradigms. For example, consider the number of items of information as a task variable. In the correlational paradigm, Einhorn (1971) has shown a decrease in R_s, subjects' linear consistency, as the number of cues increased. Anderson (1965a) used varying set sizes in an ANOVA paradigm to test predictions of an averaging model. In a Bayesian setting, Peterson, DuCharme, and Edwards (1968) have shown that larger sample sizes yield greater conservatism. Because task variables such as these are so closely linked to the focal topic in each area, we will report each group of studies directly after the relevant focal topic. We will restrict our coverage to what are primarily performance studies—that is, studies in which the judge either has learned the relevant characteristics about the information he is to use prior to entering the experiment, or, alternatively, is given this information at the start. In other words, this particular research is concerned with evaluating how the judge uses the information he has and not with how he learns to use this information.

Additional research categories are devoted to learning to use information, subjective composition strategies other than those investigated as part of the focal topics, and techniques for helping the decision maker integrate information.

Focal Topic of Correlational Research: Modeling a Judge's Policy

The Linear Model

In a large number of studies, researchers have attempted to represent the judge's idiosyncratic weighting policy by means of the linear model (Equation 1.2). Examination of more than 30 of these studies illustrates the tremendous diversity of judgmental tasks to which the model has been applied. The tasks include judgments about personality characteristics (Hammond, Hursch, & Todd, 1964; Knox & Hoffman, 1962); performance in college (Dawes, 1970; Einhorn, 1971; Newton, 1965; Sarbin, 1942) or on the job (Madden, 1963; Naylor & Wherry, 1965); attractiveness of common stocks (Slovic, 1969) and other types of gambles (Slovic & Lichtenstein, 1968); physical and mental pathology (Goldberg, 1970; Hoffman, Slovic, & Rorer, 1968; Oskamp, 1962; Wiggins & Hoffman, 1968); and legal matters (Kort, 1968; Ulmer, 1969).[5] In some cases, the stimuli were artificial and the judges were unfamiliar with the task. Typical of these are a study by Knox and Hoffman (1962) in which college students were asked to judge the intelligence of other students on the basis of grade point average, aptitude test scores, credit hours attempted, and so on; and a study by Summers (1968) in which students were asked to rate the potential for achieving minority group equality as a function of legislated opportunities and educational opportunities. At the other extreme are studies of judgments made in complex but familiar situations by skilled decision makers who had other cues available besides those included in the prediction equation. For example, Kort (1968) modeled judicial decisions in workmen's compensation cases using various facts from the cases as cues. Brown (1970) modeled caseworkers' suicide probability estimates for persons phoning a metropolitan suicide prevention center; the cues were variables such as sex, age, suicide plan, etc., obtained from the telephone interview. And Dawes (1970) used a linear model to predict the ratings given applicants for graduate school by members of the admissions committee.

In all of these situations the linear model has done a fairly good job of predicting the judgments, as indicated by R_s values in the .80s and .90s for the artificial tasks and the .70s for the more complex real-world situations. Although most of these models were not cross-validated, the few studies that have applied the linear model derived from one sample of judgments to predict a second sample have found remarkably little shrinkage (Einhorn, 1971; Slovic & Lichtenstein, 1968; Summers & Stewart, 1968; and Wiggins & Hoffman, 1968).

Capturing a Judge's Policy

The various cues that define a stimulus are certainly not equally important and judges do not weight them equally. One of the purposes of using a linear model to represent the judgmental process is to make the judge's weighting policy explicit. Large individual differences among weighting policies have been found in almost every study that reports individual equations. For example, Rorer, Hoffman, Dickman, and Slovic (1967) examined the policies whereby hospital personnel granted weekend passes to patients at a mental hospital. For five of the six cues there was at least one judge for whom that cue was the most important item and at least

---

[5] Drs. Arthur Elstein and Lee Shulman have recently brought to our attention a study by Henry A. Wallace (who was later to become Secretary of Agriculture and Vice President) that used linear equations to model corn judges, and, in anticipation of the lens model, compared the judges' models with a model of the environment. Published in 1923, this study predates all other known work of this kind by several decades. Wallace, H. A., What is in the corn judge's mind? *Journal of the American Society of Agronomy,* 1923, *15,* pp. 300–304.

one judge for whom it was nonsignificant. A striking example of individual differences in a task demanding a high level of expertise comes from a study of nine radiologists by Hoffman, Slovic, and Rorer (1968). The stimuli were hypothetical ulcers, described by the presence or absence of seven roentgenological signs. Each ulcer was rated according to its likelihood of being malignant. There was considerable disagreement among radiologists' judgments as indicated by a median interjudge correlation, across stimuli, of only .38. A factor analysis of these correlations disclosed four different types of judges, each of which was associated with a particular kind of policy equation.

Even when expert judges don't disagree with one another, an attempt to model them can be enlightening. For example, seven of the nine radiologists studied by Hoffman et al. viewed small ulcer craters as more likely to be malignant than large craters. Yet a follow-up study by Slovic, Rorer, and Hoffman (1971) described statistical evidence obtained by other researchers indicating just the opposite—that large craters are more likely than small ones to be malignant.

The ability of regression equations to describe individual differences in judgment policies has led to the development of a number of techniques for grouping or clustering judges in terms of the homogeneity of their equations (Christal, 1963; Dudycha, 1970; Maguire & Glass, 1968; Naylor & Wherry, 1965; Wherry & Naylor, 1966; Williams, Harlow, Lindem, & Gab, 1970). Although a few of these studies have compared the methods, their relative utility remains to be demonstrated.

In summary, it is apparent that the linear model is a powerful device for predicting quantitative judgments made on the basis of specific cues. It is capable of highlighting individual differences and misuse of information as well as making explicit the causes of underlying disagreements among judges in both simple and complex tasks.

Nonlinear Cue-Utilization

Despite the strong predictive ability of the linear model, a lively interest has been maintained in what Goldberg (1968) has referred to as "the search for configural judges." The impetus for this search comes from Meehl's (1954) classic inquiry into the relative validity of clinical versus actuarial prediction. Meehl proposed that one possible advantage of the clinical approach might arise from the clinician's ability to make use of configural relationships between predictors and a criterion.

A clue to one outcome of the search was provided by Yntema and Torgerson (1961) who hypothesized that, whenever predictor variables are monotonically related to a criterion variable, a simple linear combination of main effects will do a remarkably accurate job of predicting, even if interactions are known to exist. Yntema and Torgerson demonstrated their contention by presenting an example in which they showed that 94 percent of the variance of a truly configural function could be predicted from an additive combination of main effects.

Early work by Hoffman, some reported in Hoffman (1960) and some unpublished, indicated that configural terms based on the judge's verbalizations added little or no increment of predictable response variance to that contributed by the linear model. The R_s values were approximately as great as the retest reliabilities would permit, thus casting additional doubt about the existence of meaningful nonlinearities. Hursch, Hammond, and Hursch (1964); Hammond, Hursch, and Todd (1964); and Newton (1965) reported unsuccessful attempts to find evidence of nonlinearity using the C coefficient. However, these findings do not preclude the possibility of configural judgment processes, since either a lack of nonlinearity in the environment or a difference between the nonlinearity in the environment and in the judgmental systems is sufficient to produce low C values.

In light of the simple but compelling arithmetic underlying Yntema and Torgerson's "main effect hypothesis" the results of this early research should not have been too surprising. Yet the search continued, buoyed by (1) the repeated assertions of judges to the effect that their processes really were complex and configural, (2) the possibility that previous experimenters had not yet studied the right kinds of tasks—tasks that were "truly configural," and (3) the possibility that the experimental designs and statistical procedures used in previous studies were not optimally suited for uncovering the existing configural effects.

For example, Wiggins and Hoffman (1968) used a more sophisticated approach in their study of the diagnosis of neuroticism versus psychoticism from the MMPI. Their data, 861 MMPI profiles, were selected because MMPI lore considered it to be highly configural with respect to this type of diagnosis. In addition to criterion diagnoses, the judgments of 29 clinical psychologists were available for each profile. Besides using the linear model, Wiggins and Hoffman employed a "quadratic model," which included the 11 MMPI scale scores (X_i) as in the linear model along with all 11 squared values of these scales (X_i^2) and the 55 cross-product terms (X_iX_j). The third model tested was a "sign model" that included 70 diagnostic signs from the MMPI literature, many of which were nonlinear. The coefficients for each model and each judge were derived using a stepwise regression procedure. Cross validation of the models in a new sample indicated that 13 subjects were best described by the sign model, three by the quadratic model, and 12 by the linear model. But even for the most nonlinear judge the superiority of his best model over the linear model was slight (.04 increase in R_s).

Studies in which judges predicted the effects of various foreign policies (Summers & Stewart, 1968), rated the attractiveness of gambles (Slovic & Lichtenstein, 1968), evaluated the quality of patient care in hospital wards (Huber, Sahney, & Ford, 1969), and made decisions about workmen's compensation cases in a court of law (Kort, 1968) also found only minimal improvements in predictability as a consequence of including curvilinear and configural terms.

In an attempt to demonstrate the existence of configural effects, a number of investigators dropped the regression approach in favor of ANOVA designs applied to systematically constructed stimuli in tasks ranging from medical diagnosis to stock market forecasting (Hoffman, Slovic, & Rorer, 1968; Rorer, Hoffman, Dickman, & Slovic, 1967; Slovic, 1969). These studies did succeed in uncovering numerous instances of interaction among cues but the increment in predictive power contributed by these configural effects was again found to be small.

This line of research, employing both correlational and ANOVA techniques, can be summarized simply and conclusively. The hypothesis of Yntema and Torgerson has clearly been substantiated. The linear model accounts for all but a small fraction of predictable variance in judgments across a remarkably diverse spectrum of tasks.

However, the ANOVA research and other recent studies aimed at assessing the predictive power of nonlinear effects have exposed a different view of the problem, one that accepts the limited predictive benefits of nonlinear models but, simultaneously, asserts the definite, indeed widespread, existence of nonlinear judgment processes, and emphasizes their substantive meaning. To illustrate the complexity inherent in judgments that are quite predictable with a linear model, consider the data from the study of ulcer diagnosis conducted by Hoffman et al. An ANOVA technique showed that each of the nine radiologists who served as subjects exhibited at least two statistically significant interactions. One showed 13. Across radiologists there were 24 significant two-way, 17 three-way, and 14 four-way interactions. A subset of only 17 cue-configurations, out of a possible 57, accounted for 43 of the 57 significant interactions. Thus numerous instances of configurality were evidenced and a subset of specific interactions occurred repeatedly across radiologists. Hoffman et al. did not attempt to probe into the content of the interactions they observed but Slovic (1969), in his study of stockbrokers, and Kort (1968), in his study of workmen's compensation decisions, did and both uncovered information about the rationale behind their judges' nonlinear use of the cues.

Anderson had also paid careful attention to interactions obtained in his ANOVA studies of impression formation and has found several of substantive interest. For example, Anderson and Jacobson (1965) asked subjects to judge the likableness of persons described by sets of three adjectives. They found an interaction which implied that the weight given a particular adjective was less for sets where that adjective was inconsistent with the implications of the other adjectives than for sets in which it was consistent. Sidowski and Anderson (1967) asked subjects to judge the attractiveness of working at a certain job in a certain city. While the judgments of each city–job combination were found to be a weighted sum of the values for the two components, the attractiveness of being a teacher was more dependent upon the attractiveness of the city than were the other occupations—perhaps because teachers are in more direct contact with the cities' socioeconomic milieu. Other interesting examples of interactive cue-utilization have been found by Lampel and Anderson (1968) and Gollob (1968).

Hoffman (1968) has observed that an undirected search for configural relations within a finite set of data is fraught with statistical difficulties. Green (1968) concurred and criticized standard regression and ANOVA techniques for being essentially fishing expeditions. A better strategy, he suggested, is to form some specific hypothesis about configurality and seek support for it. In this vein, Slovic (1966) hypothesized and found differences in subjects' strategies for combining information as a function of whether cues were in conflict. When the implications of important cues were congruent, subjects seemed to use both. When they were inconsistent, subjects focused on one of the cues or turned to other cues for resolution of the conflict. This study, and related experiments reported in Hoffman (1968) and in Anderson and Jacobson (1965), indicate that the linear model may need to be amended to include a term sensitive to the level of incompatibility among important cues.

Tversky (1969) and Einhorn (1971) also hypothesized, and found, specific nonlinear uses of information. Tversky's subjects sometimes chose among a pair of two-dimensional gambles by a lexicographic procedure in which they selected the gamble with the greater probability of winning, provided that the difference between gambles on this dimension exceeded some small value ϵ. If the probability difference was less than or equal to ϵ, these subjects selected the gamble with the higher payoff. In contrast to the linear model, this sort of strategy is noncompensatory, inasmuch as no amount of superiority with regard to payoff can overcome a deficiency greater than ϵ on the probability dimension.

Einhorn developed mathematical functions that could be incorporated into a prediction equation to approximate conjunctive and disjunctive judgmental processes as postulated by Coombs (1964) and Dawes (1964). Dawes described the evaluation of a potential inductee by a draft board physician as one example of a conjunctive process. The physician requires that the inductee meet an entire set of minimal criteria in order to be judged physically fit. A disjunctive evaluation, on the other hand, depends solely on the attribute with highest value. For example, a scout for a professional football team may evaluate a player purely in terms of his best specialty, be it passing, running, or kicking. Neither the conjunctive nor the disjunctive model balances one attribute against another as does the linear model. Einhorn pitted his conjunctive and disjunctive models against the linear model in two tasks—one where faculty members ranked applicants for graduate school, the other where students ranked jobs according to their preferences. He found that many subjects were fit better by the conjunctive model than by the linear model, particularly in the job preference task. Einhorn concluded by criticizing the notion that cognitive complexity and mathematical complexity go hand in hand. He argued that nonlinear, noncompensatory strategies may be more simple, cognitively, than the linear model, despite their greater mathematical complexity.

At this point, it seems appropriate to conclude that notions about nonlinear processes are likely to play an increasing role in our understanding of judgment despite their limited ability to outpredict linear models.

Subjective Policies and Self-Insight

Thus far we have been discussing weighting policies that have been assessed by fitting a regression model to the judge's responses. We think of these as "computed" or "objective" policies. Judges in a number of studies were asked to describe the relative weights they had used in the task. The correspondence between these "subjective weights" and the computed weights serves as an indicant of the judge's insight into his own policy. Martin (1957) and Hoffman (1960) proposed a technique that has been used to examine these "after the fact" opinions—that of asking the judge to distribute 100 points according to the relative importance of each attribute. Martin found that the linear model based on subjective weights produced a mean R_s of .77 in predicting evaluations of a student's sociability. A linear model computed in the usual way, but not cross validated, did better, producing a mean R_s of .89. Hoepfl and Huber (1970), Hoffman (1960), Oskamp (1962), Pollack (1964), Slovic (1969), and Slovic, Fleissner, and Bauman (in press) all found serious discrepancies between subjective and computed relative weights for their judges.

One type of error in self-insight has emerged in all of these studies. Judges strongly overestimate the importance they place on minor cues (i.e., their subjective weights greatly exceed the computed weights for these cues) and they underestimate their reliance on a few major variables. Subjects apparently are quite unaware of the extent to which their judgments can be predicted by only a few cues. Across a number of studies, varying in the number of cues that were available, three cues usually sufficed to account for more than 80 percent of the predictable variance in the judge's responses. The most important cue usually accounted for more than 40 percent of this variance.

Shepard (1964) presented an interesting explanation of the subjective underweighting of important cues and overweighting of minor cues. He hypothesized:

> Possibly our feeling that we can take into account a host of different factors comes about because, although we remember that at some time or other we have attended to each of the different factors, we fail to notice that it is seldom more than one or two that we consider at any one time [p. 266].

Slovic, Fleissner, and Bauman (in press), studying the policies of stockbrokers, examined the relationship between number of years as a broker and accuracy of self-insight. The latter was measured by correlating a broker's subjective weights with his computed weights across eight cue factors. Across 13 brokers, the Spearman rank correlation between the insight index and experience was —.43. Why should greater experience lead to less valid self-insight? Perhaps the recent training of the young brokers necessitated an explicit awareness of the mechanics of the skill that they were attempting to learn. Skills generally demand a great deal of conscious attention as they are being acquired. With increasing experience, behaviors become more automatic and require much less attention. Because of this they may also be harder to describe. It may be that the most experienced judges produce verbal rationales for their evaluations that are less trustworthy than those of their inexperienced colleagues. This hypothesis is an intriguing one and needs to be investigated with more precision than was done in this study. In fact, all of the studies described in this section need to be replicated using a variety of psychophysical methods to assess subjective weights. Some methods that could be used in such studies are suggested by Eckenrode (1965), Klahr (1969), Yntema and Klem (1964), and Yntema and Torgerson (1961).

Task Determinants in Correlational Research

Cue Interrelationships

Several studies have examined the role of intercorrelational structure and conflict among cues in determining the weighting of those cues. Slovic (1966; see also Hoffman, 1968) found that, when important cues agreed in their implications, subjects typically used both and weighted them equally. When they disagreed, subjects focused on one of the cues or turned to other cues for resolution of the conflict. Also, in situations of higher cue conflict, linear consistency (R_s) was much lower. These effects were found both when cue conflict and cue intercorrelations varied together and when conflict was varied while keeping the cues orthogonal (uncorrelated). Dudycha and Naylor (1966a) have also studied the effect of varying the intercorrelations among cues upon policy equations. They found that profiles of cue-utilization correlations $(r_{i,s})$ showed more variance and R_s decreased as the correlation between cues decreased. However, the regression weights ($b_{i,s}$ values) remained relatively stable across sets varying in cue correlation and, therefore, much of the decrease in R_s may have been a statistical artifact (See Schenck & Naylor, 1968).

Cue-Variability and Cue-Utilization

Uhl and Hoffman (1958) hypothesized that an increase in the variability of a salient cue, across a set of stimuli, would lead to greater weighting of this cue by a judge. This increased weight would persist, they proposed, even among subsets of stimuli for which this cue was not unusually variable. Underlying this hypothesis was the assumption that the judge is motivated to make differential predictions and that cues that increase his ability to differentiate will reinforce his use of those attributes. The variability of a salient cue is one such feature that correlates with differentiability. Presumably judges will focus their attention on the more highly variable cues, other things being equal.

Uhl and Hoffman tested this hypothesis in a task where subjects judged IQ on the basis of profiles made up of nine cues. Each subject judged several sets of profiles on different days. The variability of a particular cue was increased on one day by providing a greater number of extreme levels. On the following day, the cue was returned to normal and its relative weight was compared with the weight it received prior to the manipulation of variability. The hypothesized effect was found in seven out of ten subjects when a strong cue was manipulated. Increasing the variability of a minor cue had no effect upon its subsequent use. The authors concluded that the judge may alter his system of judgment because of the characteristics of samples he sees.

Morrison and Slovic (1962) independently tested a version of the variability hypothesis in a different type of setting. Each of their stimuli consisted of a circle (Dimension 1) paired with a square (Dimension 2). Subjects had to rank order a set of these stimuli on the basis of their total area (circle and square combined). The results indicated that if the variability of circle area was greater than the variability of square area in the set of stimuli, then circle area would be assigned much heavier weight in the judgment. If the variability of square area was higher in the set, then square area became the dominant dimension.

Cue Format

Knox and Hoffman (1962) examined the effect of profile format on judgments of a person's intelligence and sociability. Each subject based his judgments on profiles of cues. In one condition, the cues were presented as T-scores with a mean of 50 and standard deviation of 10. A second condition presented the information in percentile scores. The percentile profiles showed considerably more scatter and had more extreme values than did the T-scores, which tended to appear rather "squashed." Judgments were made on a stanine scale with a normal distribution suggested but not forced. Judgments made to percentile scores were found to be much more variable. It appeared that judges were responding not only to the underlying meaning of the scores but to the graphical position of the points on the profile in an absolute sense. Subjects were reluctant to make ratings on the judgment scale that were more extreme than the stimulus scores. Being statistically naive, they were unable to guage the true extremeness of certain T-scores. Judgments made to percentile scores were also more reliable and produced higher values of R_s when linear models were fitted to them. Regression weights did not differ significantly between formats.

Number of Cues

There has been surprisingly little correlational research on the effects of varying the number of cues. A pilot study by Hoffman and Blanchard (1961) obtained some interesting results but was limited by a small number of subjects. Hoffman and Blanchard had subjects predict a person's weight on the basis of either 2, 5, or 7 physical characteristics. Increased numbers of cues led to lower R_s values, decreased accuracy, lower test-retest reliability, and lower response variance. This latter finding may be the cause of some of the other results and may itself be due to an increased number of conflicts among cues in the larger data sets.

Hayes (1964) and Einhorn (in press) also found that linear consistency decreased as the number of cues increased. Einhorn interpreted this decrease in R_s as indicating that his subjects were using more complex models in the high information conditions—models whose variance was not predictable from the linear and nonlinear models he tested. However, the reliability of his subjects' judgments was not assessed and it is possible that greater information merely produced more unreliable rather than more complex judgments. Hayes found that increased numbers of cues also led to a reduction in decision quality when subjects were working under a time limit.

Oskamp (1965) had 32 judges, including eight experienced clinical psychologists, read background information about a case. The information was divided into four sections. After reading each section of the case the judge answered 25 questions about the attitudes and behaviors of the subject and gave a confidence rating with each answer. The correct answers were known to the investigator. Oskamp found that, as the amount of information about the case increased, accuracy remained at about the same level while confidence increased dramatically and became entirely out of proportion to actual correctness.

In summary, there is a small amount of evidence that increasing the amount of information available to the decision maker increases his confidence without increasing the quality of his decisions and makes his decisions more difficult to predict.

Cue-Response Compatibility

Fitts and Deininger (1954) introduced the concept of stimulus-response compatibility to explain the results of several studies of paired-associates learning and reaction time. Compatibility was defined as a function of the similarity between the spatial position of the stimulus in a circular array and the position of the correct response in the same sort of array. High compatibility produced the quickest learning and fastest reaction time. In an experiment concerned with risk-taking judgments, Slovic and Lichtenstein (1968) observed a related type of compatibility effect that influenced cue-utilization. They found that when subjects rated the attractiveness of a gamble, probability of winning was the most important factor in their policy equations. In a second condition, subjects were required to indicate the attractiveness of a gamble by an alternative method, namely, equating the gamble with an amount of money such that they would be indifferent between playing the gamble and receiving the stated amount. Here it was found that attractiveness was determined more by a gamble's outcomes than by its probabilities. The outcomes, being expressed in units of dollars, were readily commensurable with the units of the responses—also dollars. On the other hand, the probability cues had to be transformed by the subject into values commensurable with dollars before they could be integrated with these other cues. It seems plausible that the cognitive effort involved in making this sort of transformation greatly detracted from the influence of the probability cues in the second task.

This finding suggests the general hypothesis that greater compatibility between a cue and the required response should enhance the importance of that cue in determining the response. Presumably, the more complex the transformation needed to make a cue commensurable with other important cues and with the response, the less that cue will be used.

Focal Topic of the ANOVA Paradigm: Models of Impression Formation

There is a substantial body of literature concerned with the problem of understanding how component items of information are integrated into impressions of people. Much of this research can be traced to the work of Asch (1946) who asked subjects to evaluate a person described by various trait adjectives. In one of Asch's studies, the adjective "warm" was added to the set of traits. Another group saw the trait "cold." All other adjectives were identical. The subjects wrote a brief description of the person and completed an adjective checklist. Asch found that substitution of the word "warm" for "cold" produced a decided change in the overall characterization of the person being evaluated. He interpreted this as being due to a shift in meaning of the traits associated with the key adjectives "warm" and "cold." This view has much in common with the notions of configurality and interaction we have been discussing.

More recent endeavors have centered around the search for quantitative models of the integration process. That is, they attempt to develop a mathematical function of the scale values of the individual items to predict the overall impression. Although Asch explicitly denied that an impression could be derived from a simple additive combination of stimulus items, the additive model and its variations have received the most attention (Rosenberg, 1968). Most of these studies have used rigorous experimental control, factorial designs, and statistical techniques such as ANOVA as the basis for their analyses.

One of the first studies to test the additive model was carried out by Anderson (1962). His subjects rated a number of hypothetical persons, each described by three adjectives, on a 20-point scale of likableness. Within each set there was one item each of high, medium, and low scale value as determined in a separate normative study. An additive model gave an excellent fit to the data.

The additive model serves as a more general case for two derivative models—one based on the principle of summation of information, the other an averaging formulation. In the summation model, the values of the stimulus items are added to arrive at an impression. The averaging model asserts that an impression is the mean, rather than the sum, of the separate item values. The adding versus averaging question has fundamental importance in integration theory. It governs the theoretical interpretation of the results and it affects the scaling of the stimuli (Anderson, 1971, in press).

The study by Anderson (1962) did not attempt to distinguish between the averaging and summation formulations. To do so requires careful attention to subtle facets of stimulus construction and experimental design. Recent research has taken on this challenge, varying task and design characteristics in an attempt to determine the validity of these and other competing models. The following section will review briefly the types of situational manipulations that have been brought to bear on this problem.

Task Determinants of Information Use in Impression Formation

Set Size

The number of items of information in a set is one factor that has been varied in attempts to distinguish summation and averaging models. Fishbein and Hunter (1964) provided four groups of subjects with different amounts of positively evaluated information about a fictitious person. The information was presented sequentially in such a way that the total summation of effect increased as a function of the number of items while the mean decreased, that is, the more highly evaluated items came first. The subjects used a series of bipolar adjective scales to evaluate the stimulus persons. The judgments became more favorable as the amount of information increased, presumably supporting the summation model. The Fishbein and Hunter study has been criticized by Rosenberg (1968) who argued that presenting the most favorable adjective first permitted possible sequential effects to influence the results. Also, the intended decrease in mean evaluation of the individual adjectives as a function of set size was not statistically significant. As Anderson (1971, in press) observed, increased extremity of judgment with sequential presentation of essentially equal adjectives can be accounted for by a version of the averaging model.

Anderson (1965a) also used set size to contrast the two models. He had subjects rate the likableness of persons described by either two or four traits. He found that sets consisting of two moderately valued traits and two extremely valued traits produced a less extreme judgment than sets consisting of the two extreme traits alone. This result was taken as support for the averaging model and was later replicated by Hendrick (1968). Another result of Anderson's study, that sets of four extreme adjectives were rated more extreme than sets with two extreme adjectives, confirmed earlier findings by Anderson (1959), Podell (1962), and Stewart (1965) to the effect that increased set size produces more extreme ratings. While this result seems to support a summation model, Anderson showed how it could be accommodated using an averaging model that incorporates an initial impression with non-zero weight and scale value s_0. Anderson (1967b) provided further support for this model.

Extremity of Information

The adjectives in Anderson's (1965a) study were presumed to be of equal weight. Thus the averaging model predicted that the judgment of a stimulus set containing four items having extreme scale values averaged with the judgment of a set containing four items of moderate value would equal the judgment of a set containing two extreme and two moderate items. Anderson found that this prediction did not hold for negatively evaluated items. The discrepancy suggested that the extreme negative items carried more weight than did moderately negative information.

Studies by Himmelfarb (1970), Kerrick (1958), Manis, Gleason, and Dawes (1966), Oden and Anderson (1971), Osgood and Tannenbaum (1955), Podell and Podell (1963), Weiss (1963), and Willis (1960) also found indications that the weight of an information item is associated with the extremity of its scale value. Manis et al. found that two positive or two negative items of information of different value would lead to a judgment less extreme than the most extreme item but more extreme than that predicted by a simple averaging of the items. At the same time these judgments were not extreme enough to be produced by the summation model. To account for these results, the authors suggested a version of the averaging model that weights items in proportion to their extremity. Himmelfarb found support for an averaging model in which neutral information received less weight than more polarized information. Oden and Anderson found that the importance of a stimulus dimension depended on its value but the direction of dependence varied across different types of judgment tasks.

Redundancy

Both summation and averaging models assume that the values of the stimulus items are independent of the other items in the set. This assumption has been the focus of concern for a number of studies. Dustin and Baldwin (1966), for example, had subjects evaluate persons described by single adjectives, A and B, and by the combined pair AB. Ratings of AB pairs tended to be more extreme than the mean of the individual items: this tendency was dependent upon the degree of redundancy or implication between A and B as measured by their intercorrelation in a normative sample. Schmidt (1969) did a similar study but varied the relatedness of the items differently. He combined trait sentences (Mr. A is kind) with instance sentences (Mr. A is kind to B). The two sentences just given are obviously highly redundant. By changing the trait adjectives this redundancy can be greatly reduced. Schmidt found that judgments based on less redundant sets were consistently more extreme than those based on more redundant information. Wyer reported similar findings in studies where redundancy was measured by the conditional probability of A given B (Wyer, 1968) and by the degree to which the joint probability of occurrence (P_{AB}) exceeded the product of the two unconditional probabilities (P_A and P_B) (Wyer, 1970). It seems apparent that models in this area will need further revision to handle the effects of redundancy.

Interitem Consistency

The data just described indicate that highly redundant information has less impact. But information with too great a "surprise value" shares a similar fate. Anderson and Jacobson (1965) found that an item whose scale value is highly inconsistent with its accompanying items (as in the trait "gloomy" in the set "honest-considerate-gloomy") was likely to be discounted—that is, given less weight. The discounting was slight when subjects were told that all three traits were accurate and equally important, but increased when subjects were cautioned that one of the items might be less valid than the others. Anderson and Jacobson argued that the averaging model might have to include differential weights to accommodate the reduced impact of inconsistent information.

Wyer (1970) defined inconsistency among two adjectives as the degree to which their joint probability (P_{AB}) was less than the product of their unconditional probabilities (P_A and P_B). Note that this places high inconsistency at the negative end of a continuum defined by $P_{AB}-P_AP_B$, with maximum redundancy at the positive end. After constructing stimuli according to this definition, Wyer found that inconsistency produced a discounting of the less polarized of a pair of adjectives, leading to a more extreme evaluation. However, when inconsistency became too great, both adjectives appeared to be discounted, producing a less extreme evaluation.

Himmelfarb and Senn (1969) studied the effects of stimulus inconsistency in experiments concerned with judgments of a person's social class. The stimulus persons were described by dimensional attributes—occupation, income, and education. Surprisingly, discounting of inconsistent information was not found. The authors speculated that their failure to find discounting might have been due to the lack of directly contradictory information or to the possibility that social class stimuli, being objective aspects of an individual, might be less easily discounted than personality traits.

Other Contextual Effects

Anderson and Lampel (1965) and Anderson (1966) had subjects form an impression based on three adjectives and then rate one of the component traits alone. Both studies produced context effects, judgments of the single trait being displaced towards the values of the other traits. A natural interpretation of this effect is that the value or meaning of the test word has changed as a function of the impression formation process, much as Asch originally suggested. Wyer and Watson (1969) argued in favor of this change of meaning interpretation over several competing hypotheses but their data are equivocal. Anderson and Lampel (1965) hypothesized that positive context effects are due to a generalized halo effect rather than a change of meaning. According to this theory, once a component has been integrated into the whole, it no longer has a distinct individual meaning. The subject then rates the individual component according to a weighted average of its context-free meaning and the overall impression. Anderson (1971) describes two experiments supporting this position.

Primacy and Recency Effects

Several dozen studies of impression formation have attempted to determine whether information presented early in a sequence is more or less influential than information presented later, other things being equal. Greater influence of early information is called primacy. Its opposite effect is called recency.

These studies can be categorized according to whether the subject's task was to average verbal items of information such as adjectives, or quantitative and perceptual items such as numbers, weights, lines, and loudness of sounds. A typical experimental design in such studies goes as follows: First the items are scaled individually with respect to the criterion. These items are then sorted into homogeneous subsets having high *(H)* or low *(L)* scale values. Then blocks of *H* and *L* items are presented in varying order. For example, primacy would lead the final judgment for an *HHLL* sequence to be higher than that for a *LLHH* sequence, whereas recency would produce the opposite effect.

The results of these investigations indicate that order effects are highly pervasive phenomena, appearing in studies that employ quite diverse stimuli and response modes. However, whether primacy or recency effects occur is dependent upon task characteristics. When adjectives are used as stimuli and the subject responds only at the end of the information sequence, primacy is usually found (Anderson, 1965b; Anderson & Barrios, 1961; Anderson & Norman, 1964; Asch, 1946; Luchins, 1957). Primacy effects in these studies have been attributed to decreased attention being given the later adjectives and to discounting of the inconsistent information provided by the later adjectives (Anderson, 1968a). When attentional demands were changed by having subjects recall the adjectives after making their rating, pronounce each adjective, or make a rating after each new item was presented, recency predominated (Anderson, 1959, 1968a; Anderson & Hubert, 1963; Hendrick & Costantini, 1970a; Levin & Schmidt, 1969; Luchins, 1958; Rhine, 1968; Rosenkrantz & Crockett, 1965; Stewart, 1965). When numbers, weights, lines, or sounds are used as stimuli, the information items are homogeneous and not likely to create feelings of incongruity. In these studies recency is observed, regardless of whether the judgments are made during the sequence or only at the end (Anderson, 1964, 1967a; Anderson & Jacobson, 1968; Hendrick & Costantini, 1970b; Parducci,

Thaler, & Anderson, 1968; Weiss & Anderson, 1969). Although many hypotheses have been proposed to account for these effects, their causes remain to be determined precisely.

Focal Topic of Bayesian Research: Conservatism

The most common Bayesian study deals with probability estimation, often in some variant of the bookbag and poker chip experiment described earlier. The primary finding has been labeled *conservatism:* Upon receipt of new information, subjects revise their posterior probability estimates in the same direction as the optimal model, but the revision is typically *too small;* subjects act as if the data are less diagnostic than they truly are. Subjects in some studies (Peterson, Schneider, & Miller, 1965; Phillips & Edwards, 1966) have been found to require from two to nine data observations to revise their opinions as much as Bayes' theorem would prescribe for one observation.

Much of the Bayesian research has been motivated by a desire to discover the determinants of conservatism in order that its effects might be minimized in practical diagnostic settings. A spirited debate has been raging among Bayesians about which part of the judgment process leads subjects astray. The principal competing explanations as to the "locus of conservatism" are the misperception, misaggregation, and artifact hypotheses (Edwards, 1968).

Misperception

In order to perform optimally, subjects must have some understanding of the data generator—the model, device, equations, or other assumptions used by the experimenter to generate the stimuli shown to the subject. If the subject misunderstands the data generator, he may misperceive the conditional probability of the data given the hypothesis, $P(D/H)$; this misperception is hypothesized by some to be the source of conservatism. For example, Lichtenstein and Feeney (1968) showed that subjects performed very poorly when dealing with a circular normal data generator despite 150 training trials with feedback. But subjects' data and comments suggested an entirely different (and incorrect) model regarding the meaning of each datum, and reanalyses of their responses showed them to be quite consistent with this simpler yet incorrect view of the data generator. Does such a simple and popular data generator as the binomial distribution also lead to misperceptions about the meaning of data? Vlek and Bientema (1967) and Vlek and van der Heijden (1967) showed that it does. Vlek and Bientema presented subjects with samples (e.g., five black and four white) drawn from an urn whose constituent proportions were known to the subject, and asked them how often such a sample might be expected to occur in 100,000 samples of the same size. Vlek and van der Heijden asked for the probability that such a sample would occur in 100 trials. Both studies showed that subjects had poor understanding of the likelihood of data.

If such misperceptions are the cause of conservatism, then one would expect estimates of posterior probabilities to be consistent with, and predictable from, estimates about the data generator, that is, estimates of $P(D/H)$. Peterson, DuCharme, and Edwards (1968) had subjects in a binomial task estimate $P(H/D)$, then $P(D/H)$. Then they were instructed in $P(D/H)$ by being shown several theoretical sampling distributions which they discussed with the experimenter. For example, they observed how the distribution became more peaked as the number of draws and the dominant proportion increased. Finally they were again asked to estimate $P(H/D)$. Peterson et al. found that subjects' conservative $P(H/D)$ estimates could be explained by the deviations of their $P(D/H)$ estimates from the optimal values. They also found that instruction about the sampling distributions reduced conservatism in the final stage, but the reduction was small in relation to the amount of conservatism.

Subjects in the study by Peterson et al. did not have the theoretical sampling distribution available at the time they made post-instruction $P(H/D)$ estimates. Pitz and Downing (1967) gave subjects similar instruction and, in addition, allowed them to refer to histogram displays of the theoretical sampling distributions as they made predictions about which of two populations was generating the data. However, their predictions were not improved by this instruction. Wheeler and Beach (1968) trained subjects by having them observe samples of eight draws, make a bet on which of two populations generated the data, and then observe the correct answer. Prior to training the subjects' sampling distributions were too flat, their betting responses were conservative, and these two errors were consistent with one another. After training, the subjects' sampling distributions were more veridical, their betting responses were less conservative, and again the two sets of responses were consistent.

A particular kind of misperception error relates to the impact of rare events. Vlek (1965) suggested that unlikely events, when they occur, are seen as uninformative. He argued for the compelling nature of this error by giving an exaggerated example:

The posterior probability that a sample of 2004 chips, 1004 of which are red, is taken from bag A ($P_r = .70$), and not from B ($P_r = .30$), is equal to .967. But who will accept hypothesis A as a possible generator of these data, and, if forced to do so, who dares to base an important decision on such a small difference in the—seemingly biased—sample [p. 15]?

The answer to his question is, of course, that Bayes' theorem dares. In the optimal model, it matters not at all that a datum may be highly unlikely under both hypotheses. The only determinant of its impact is the relative possibility of its occurrence—the likelihood ratio. The violation of this likelihood principle has been demonstrated by Vlek (1965) and Vlek and van der Heijden (1967), who showed a systematic increase in conservatism as a function of the rarity of the data, and this violation can serve as an explanation for Lichtenstein and Feeney's (1968) results. Beach (1968) directly tested Vlek's hypothesis. Beach constructed decks of cards, each with a letter, from *A* to *F,* written on it in green or red ink. The task of the subjects was to estimate the posterior probability that the letters sampled were drawn from the green deck rather than the red deck, given complete information about the frequency of each letter in each deck. Two groups of subjects used different decks of cards; the likelihood ratios were the same between groups, but the relative frequencies of the letters differed between groups. This permitted a test of whether the impact of rare events was misperceived, with likelihood ratio held constant. The results verified Vlek's hypothesis; subjects were more conservative when responding to less likely events.

Misaggregation

Another explanation of conservatism is that subjects have great difficulty in aggregating or putting together various pieces of information to produce a single response. Proponents of this view draw support from several sources (Edwards, 1968). First, they point out that in the studies just reported as supporting the misperception hypothesis, subjects were shown samples of several data at once. When shown a sample of, say, six red and three blue chips, and asked to state the probability that such a sample might occur, the subject must, in a sense, aggregate the separate impact of each chip, even though the sample is presented simultaneously. Viewed in this light, both estimation of $P(H/D)$ and of $P(D/H)$ in studies like Wheeler and Beach (1968) are aggregation tasks; thus the consistency between the two tasks does not provide a discrimination between the misperception and misaggregation hypotheses. Beach (1968), testing the rare event hypothesis, did present subjects with only one datum at a time, but he presented three data per sequence. Gettys and Manley (1968) reported two experiments in which five levels of frequency of data and five levels of likelihood ratios were factorially combined in 100 binomial problems. For each problem the subject was shown the contents of two urns and the result of a single sampling of one datum. In this situation, with no aggregation required, the rare event effect was not found. The subjects were sensitive to changes in likelihood ratio but not to differing event frequencies. The authors argued that the rare event effect found in other studies is attributable to aggregation difficulties.

A related source of support for the misaggregation hypothesis comes from the finding that subjects perform best on the first trial of a sequence. DuCharme and Peterson (1968) reported this finding based on a task using normal data generators. The subjects were shown samples of heights and asked the posterior odds that the population being sampled was of men or women. They were virtually optimal for single-datum sequences and for the first trial of four-data sequences, but conservative on subsequent trials. Similar results were obtained by Peterson and Swensson (1968).

It might be noted that Peterson and Miller (1965) found conservatism with just one datum per problem, but this presents no special problem for the misaggregation hypothesis, since in that study the one datum had to be aggregated with a varying value for the prior probability of the hypothesis. Peterson and Phillips (1966) also found first-trial conservatism. However, they, like Peterson and Miller, used a probability response mode. This mode, as will be discussed later, is highly susceptible to a nonoptimal but simple strategy that produces artifactual results. DuCharme and Peterson (1968) and Peterson and Swensson (1968) avoided this criticism by asking for responses in terms of posterior odds rather than probabilities, and found first-trial optimality.

Both the misperception and misaggregation hypotheses received support in a study by Phillips (1966; also reported in Edwards et al., 1968). His subjects misperceived the impact of each datum, and, in addition, were not consistent with that misperception in a subsequent aggregation task.

Additional evidence for the misaggregation hypothesis was given by Hammond, Kelly, Schneider, and Vancini (1967) who found that the log likelihood ratios inferred from subjects' $P(D/H)$ estimates did not match the log likelihood ratios inferred from these subjects' $P(H/D)$ estimates. Similar results were recently obtained by Grinnell, Keeley, and Doherty (1970).

Finally, man's difficulties in aggregating data have been demonstrated in a series of man–machine systems studies. A system where men estimate $P(D/H)$ separately for each datum and the machine combines these into posterior probabilities via Bayes' theorem has consistently been found superior to a system where the man, himself, must aggregate the data into a $P(H/D)$ estimate (Edwards, Phillips, Hays, & Goodman, 1968; Kaplan & Newman, 1966; Schum, Southard, & Wombolt, 1969).

Artifact

The third explanation of conservatism, that conservatism is artifactual, was originally suggested by Peterson (See Edwards, 1968), and has been recently supported and renamed *response bias* by DuCharme (1970). Du-

Charme hypothesized that subjects are capable—and optimal—when dealing with responses in the odds range from 1:10 to 10:1, but are conservative when forced, either by the accumulation of many data or by the occurrence of one enormously diagnostic datum, to go outside that range. He pointed out that such a response bias would explain many of the conservatism effects reported in the literature, including increased conservatism attributed to increasing diagnosticity and the superiority of first-trial performance. DuCharme tested his hypothesis directly in a task where subjects had to determine whether observed samples of heights came from a male or female population. His subjects gave sequential posterior odds estimates to sequences varying in length from one to seven data. The results supported the response bias hypothesis. First-trial estimates and later-trial estimates in the same probability range were similarly optimal. Second- and third-trial estimates were more conservative following a highly diagnostic first datum ($LR = 99$) than were estimates of those same data following an undiagnostic first trial ($LR = 1.3$). Optimality of response was exhibited within a central range of posterior odds, while conservatism occurred outside this range.

Task Determinants in Bayesian Research

The Effects of Response Mode

Direct estimation methods. Direct estimation of posterior probabilities has several drawbacks. First, the amount of change in $P(H/D)$ induced by a single datum decreases as the probabilities prior to the receipt of that datum become more extreme. Subjects may have difficulty coping with this nonlinear relationship between stimulus and response. In addition, there is a potential problem with floor and ceiling effects because of the boundedness of the probability scale at zero and one. The subject may be reluctant to give an extreme response early in the sequence, for fear of "using up" the scale before the last data arrive. If subjects estimate odds or log odds (odds spaced logarithmically on a scale), the above difficulties are avoided. Phillips and Edwards (1966) compared these various response modes in a binomial task and found, as expected, that "odds" and "log odds" responses showed less conservatism than did estimates of probabilities.

Indirect methods. Instead of asking the subject for probabilities, indirect methods infer his probabilities from some other response. Sanders (reported in Edwards, 1966) used bookbag and poker chip situations to compare a direct response, verbal odds, with two different indirect responses, choice among bets and bidding for bets. He found substantial agreement, as measured by similarity of Accuracy Ratios, between the direct, verbal estimates of odds and the estimates inferred from choices among bets. The bidding mode produced considerably more optimal behavior than the other two modes.

Beach and Phillips (1967) compared direct probability estimates with probabilities inferred from choices among bets, and found high correlations between the two responses. Strong agreement between probability estimates and probabilities inferred from bids has also been found in two studies by Beach and Wise (1969a, 1969b). However, Beach and Olson (1967) have shown that probabilities inferred from choices among bets were highly susceptible to the gambler's fallacy (e.g., subjects overestimated the probability of a red after four greens were sampled, and underestimated it after four reds occurred), while direct estimates of probabilities were much more optimal. Geller and Pitz (1968) have explored the use of decision speed, measured without the subject's knowledge, as an indirect measure of probability in a bookbag and poker chip task. A high correlation was found between the speed of decision and the Bayesian probability that the decision was correct. In addition, relative changes in decision speed approximated optimal changes in probability more closely than did changes in subjects' confidence estimates.

Effects of intermittent responding. Perhaps the very act of making repeated responses, once after each datum is presented, affects the final response of the subject. This hypothesis was tested by Beach and Wise (1969b), who compared verbal estimates of posterior probabilities made only at the end of a sequence of three data with estimates made after each datum. They found satisfactory correspondence between the two estimate methods. Pitz (1969a), however, did find differences attributable to repeated responses. When subjects responded after each new datum and their previous responses were displayed, confidence increased with increased sample size, holding diagnosticity constant. However, when the responses made after each datum were not continuously displayed, or when the subject made confidence responses only at the end of the sequence, such nonoptimal tendencies were not observed. Halpern and Ulehla (1970), using a signal detection task, also found differences between repeated responses and a single, final response.

Nominal versus probability responses. Is there any difference between a nominal response (yes–no; predominantly red–predominantly blue) and a probability response which is later converted to a nominal response by the experimenter? Swets and Birdsall (1967), using an auditory detection task, found that the probability response data provided a better fit to the signal detection model than the nominal response data. Similar results were found by Ulehla, Canges, and Wackwitz (1967). However, Halpern and Ulehla (1970) found exactly the opposite results in a visual discrimination task.

Using a Bayesian task with three hypotheses, Martin and Gettys (1969) found better performance using a nominal response than using a probability response. Attaching probabilities to *two* less likely hypotheses as well as to the favored hypothesis was apparently difficult enough to degrade subjects' performance.

The Effects of Payoffs

The use of payoffs in probability estimation tasks may have a motivational effect, persuading the subjects to try harder, and an instructional effect, helping subjects to understand what the experimenter wants from them (Winkler & Murphy, 1968). These effects were explored by Phillips and Edwards (1966), who used three different payoff schemes and a control group in a bookbag and poker chip task. The subjects estimated the posterior probability of each bag for 20 sequences of 20 draws each. The control group received no payoff but were told which hypothesis was correct after each sequence. The three payoff groups were paid $v(p)$ points, later converted to money, where p was the subject's estimate for the correct hypothesis, and $v(p)$ was calculated as follows:

$$\text{Quadratic:} \quad v(p) = 10,000 - 10,000 (1 - p)^2$$
$$\text{Logarithmic:} \quad v(p) = 10,000 + 5,000 \log_{10} p$$
$$\text{Linear:} \quad v(p) = 10,000 p$$

The quadratic and log payoffs share the characteristic that the only way the subject can maximize his expected winnings is by reporting his true subjective probability (Toda, 1963). For the linear payoff, the subject should always estimate 1.0 for the more likely hypothesis. The results indicated that payoffs help to decrease conservatism, but do not eliminate it. The instructional value of payoffs was reflected in more learning by the payoff groups than the control groups, and by the lower between-subject variance for the payoff groups.

These findings were amplified in a study by Schum, Goldstein, Howell, and Southard (1967) using a complex multinomial task with six hypotheses and 4, 8, or 12 data, of varying diagnosticity, in each of 324 sequences. A log payoff group was found to be conservative. A linear payoff group was not conservative, but their responses were highly variable: Their posterior odds were as likely to be 50 times too great or too small as they were to be accurate. When the responses were simply scored as "correct," meaning that the true hypothesis received the largest estimated posterior probability, or "incorrect," differences among the payoff groups were eliminated.

Pitz and Downing (1967) manipulated payoffs in a binary prediction task to test subjects' sensitivity to changes in strategy required by the optimal model. Subjects were asked to guess which of two specially constructed dice was being rolled, after five data were presented. Five different payoff matrices were used. The first matrix was symmetric, in that rewards and penalties were the same for both dice. The other matrices were biased. In order to maximize their expected winnings, subjects should alter their strategies when payoff matrices are biased. For example, they should guess the less likely die when the reward for being correct is great and the cost for being wrong is small. The subjects were highly optimal when using the symmetric matrix. With the biased payoff matrices, they altered their predictions as a function of varying payoffs, but they did not change nearly enough; they were unwilling to make responses that had a smaller probability of being correct, even though, because of the biased payoffs, these responses would have increased their expected gains. Pitz and Downing suggested that subjects have a high utility for making a correct guess. A similar suggestion was made by Ulehla (1966), who found essentially the same result in a study of perceptual discrimination of lines tilted left or right. With a symmetric payoff scheme, subjects closely fit the signal detection model, but biased payoffs led to insufficient change in strategy.

The Effects of Diagnosticity

One of the simplest ways of varying the diagnosticity of the data in a probability estimation task is to change the data generator. In a bookbag and poker chip experiment, the diagnostic impact of a sample of one red chip is greater when the bag being sampled contains 80 red and 20 green versus 20 red and 80 green than when the possible contents of the bag are more similar, say, 60 red and 40 green versus 40 red and 60 green. In several experiments (Peterson, DuCharme, & Edwards, 1968; Peterson & Miller, 1965; Phillips & Edwards, 1966; Pitz, Downing, & Reinhold, 1967; and Vlek, 1965) diagnosticity was manipulated in this way and all showed greater conservatism with more diagnostic data. Very low levels of diagnosticity sometimes produce the opposite of conservatism: Subjects' responses are more extreme than Bayes' theorem specifies (Peterson & Miller, 1965).

When the data generator is a complex multinomial system, different samples can differ greatly in total diagnosticity, that is, in the certainty with which the sample points to one of several hypotheses. Studies by Martin and Gettys (1969), Phillips, Hays, and Edwards (1966), and Schum, Southard, and Wombolt (1969) all showed that samples of higher overall diagnosticity lead to greater conservatism. Martin and Gettys found that their least diagnostic samples produced the same extremeness of response (opposite of conservatism) as found by Peterson and Miller (1965) in a binomial task.

Another way of varying diagnosticity is to vary sample size. In general, the larger the sample, the more diagnostic it is. Vlek (1965), Pitz, Downing, and Reinhold (1967), and Peterson, DuCharme, and Edwards (1968), using binomial tasks, and Schum (1966b; also Schum, Southard, & Wombolt, 1969), using a multinomial task, have shown that larger sample sizes yield greater conservatism. Diagnosticity can be held constant across different sample sizes, however. In any symmetric binomial task, diagnosticity is solely a function of the difference between the number of occurrences of one type and of the other type. Thus the occurrence of 4 reds and 2 blues in a sample of 6 chips has the same diagnosticity as the occurrence of 12 reds and 10 blues in a sample of 22 chips. Studies by Vlek (1965) and Pitz (1967) showed that when this difference was held constant, the larger sample sizes yielded lower posterior estimates, hence greater conservatism. However, when Schum, Southard, and Wombolt (1969) held diagnosticity constant in a multinomial task, variations in sample length had no effect upon the size of subjects' final posterior probability estimates. The method used for holding sample diagnosticity constant as sample size increases differed in the binomial and multinomial task. In the binomial task, diagnosticity is held constant by holding constant the differences between red and blue chips as the sample size increases. But in the multinomial task used by Schum et al., the total diagnosticity of a large sample was equated with that of a small sample by using data in the large sample each of which was, on the average, less diagnostic than the average datum used in the small sample. Since data of low diagnosticity have been shown to produce less conservatism, this may account for the discrepancy between Schum's findings of no sample size effect and the finding of large effects by Vlek (1965) and Pitz (1967).

Sample size and diagnosticity can also be varied by holding the total number of data constant and varying the number of data presented to the subject at any one time. Peterson, Schneider, and Miller (1965) presented subjects with 48 trials of one datum each, with 12 trials of 4 data each, with 4 trials of 12 data each, and with a single trial containing 48 data. Conservatism was large when subjects responded after each single datum, but was even larger when the number of data (and hence the average diagnosticity) per trial increased. Vlek (1965) also found poorer performance with larger blocks of data presented simultaneously.

All these studies tell the same story: Increased diagnosticity, no matter how produced, increases conservatism. The sole exception to this statement is reported by Schum and Martin (1968), who used a multinomial task — six hypotheses and six data per sample. They used two different data-generating models, Model A and Model B. Diagnosticity was varied both within and between the two models. The results for Model A were typical of diagnosticity studies—subjects were sensitive to changes in diagnosticity within the model, but as diagnosticity increased, subjects became increasingly conservative. The results from Model B represented a unique finding—as diagnosticity increased in Model B samples, the responses deviated further from Bayes' theorem, but in a nonconservative direction (i.e., they became increasingly more extreme). This finding is unexplained by Schum and Martin. One possible explanation is that subjects completely disregarded the difference between Model A and Model B, responding solely to the number of items favoring the most likely hypothesis. The subsequent comparison of such responses with the optimal responses derived from the two different models would make similar responses look conservative in one case and extreme in the other case.

The Effects of Manipulating Prior Probabilities

A decision maker's beliefs about the state of the world before he receives relevant information are expressed in the prior probabilities he attaches to the hypotheses. Prior probabilities may be manipulated in a bookbag and poker chip experiment, for example, by showing the subject not two, but ten bookbags, n of which are predominantly red and $(10 - n)$, predominantly blue. When the experimenter chooses one bag at random, the subject has reason to believe, before the first chip is drawn, that the prior probability of the bag being predominantly red in $n/10$. Variation of n thus constitutes variation of prior probabilities.

When subjects' responses are analyzed in terms of inferred likelihood ratios or Accuracy Ratios, such measures should not change when prior probabilities are varied. Phillips and Edwards (1966) and Schum (1966b) reported such invariance. However, Peterson and Miller (1965) did find a systematic relationship between prior probability and Accuracy Ratio in a binomial task. Across nine levels of prior probability, from .1 to .9, subjects' Accuracy Ratios increased (the subjects became less conservative) as the priors became more extreme (departed from .5). This finding, however, may be an artifactual result of the response mode—probabilities expressed with a sliding pointer on an equal-interval scale. If subjects simply moved the slider a constant amount, up for a black datum, down for a white datum, regardless of its initial setting, the reported relationship between the Accuracy Ratio and prior probabilities would occur.

The one general characteristic of the Bayesian research summarized so far is that subjects are never as sensitive to the experimental conditions as they ought to be. This statement characterizes conservatism itself, as well as the effects of payoffs and diagnosticity. Partial sensitivity to variations in prior probabilities has been found using signal detection models by Ulehla (1966) and Galanter and Holman (1967). Wendt (1969) found partial sensitivity to prior odds. He asked his subjects to bid for each datum; this bid was interpreted as the value of the datum for the subject. Wendt found that the bids were closer to optimal when the prior odds were 1:1 than when the prior odds were extreme.

The Effects of Sequence Length

Several studies have found that subjects are more hesitant to commit themselves fully to a probability revision when they know that there will be opportunity for additional revision on later trials than when they know any revision taking place must be made immediately. Vlek (1965) compared $P(H/D)$ estimates made after the ninth trial in a 19-trial sequence with estimates made after the simultaneous presentation of nine data items (no more were to be presented). The probability estimates were less extreme in the former condition where subjects knew they had ten additional opportunities for revisions. This effect might be attributed to the difference between simultaneous versus serial presentation in the above study. However, Pitz, Downing, and Reinhold (1967) used serial presentation with responding after each item and found the average revision of $P(H/D)$ to be greater for shorter sequences than for longer ones. Similarly, Shanteau (1970) found that shorter sequences produced more extreme $P(H/D)$ responses at any serial position, holding the evidence constant. Although none of the above studies put any pressure on subjects to make their intermediate responses maximally accurate, Roby (1967) used a payoff system to motivate subjects to be accurate at every response point and he, too, found that they tended to delay for several trials before modifying their estimates. These results should be viewed with caution, however, because each of these studies employed a response mode highly susceptible to ceiling effects. Replication of these findings using odds or log odds response modes is needed to discover if subjects are affected by sequence length even when they feel comfortable that they cannot "use up" the response scale.

Primacy and Recency Effects

Studies investigating sequential use of probabilistic information have generally required subjects to make judgments after each new datum was presented. Three of these studies have reported primacy effects (Dale, 1968; Peterson & DuCharme, 1967; Roby, 1967) and two have obtained recency (Pitz & Reinhold, 1968; Shanteau, 1970). Both primacy and recency violate the Bayesian model. The occurrence of primacy here contrasts with the recency effects generally found when subjects make intermittent judgments upon receipt of verbal or perceptual information. One possible explanation for this is that studies showing primacy effects each presented subjects with a long sequence of items of information that first pointed strongly to one hypothesis and then suddenly changed in character so that the less favored hypothesis became at least as probable as the first. The resulting inconsistency of the latter data is extremely implausible in a stationary environment, and it is not surprising that subjects tended to discount those data. Neither of the two studies obtaining recency effects used such inconsistent sequences of data.

An Inertia Effect in Bayesian Research

Anderson (1959) invoked the concept of inertia in discussing the "basal component" of an opinion—that part that becomes increasingly resistant to change as information accumulates. More recently Pitz and his associates have conducted a series of studies demonstrating the existence of inertia in opinions that are formed and revised on the basis of probabilistic evidence. Pitz, Downing, and Reinhold (1967) found that subjects revised their $P(H/D)$ estimates much less following evidence contradictory to their currently favored hypotheses than they did after confirming evidence. Revision should have been equal in either direction. Especially interesting was the finding that probability estimates sometimes moved towards greater certainty after a single disconfirming datum was observed. This phenomenon, labeled an "inertia effect," was also found by Geller and Pitz (1968).

Geller and Pitz investigated two possible explanations of the inertia effect. The first was that inertia stems from strong commitment to a hypothesis whereby subjects become unwilling to change their stated level of confidence even though their opinions might change. This hypothesis was suggested by findings in studies by Gibson and Nichol (1964), Brody (1965), and Pruitt (1961). Pruitt found that subjects required more information to change their minds about a previous decision than to arrive at that decision in the first place. Brody found that initial commitment to an incorrect decision slowed down the rate of increase in confidence for the correct choice. Geller and Pitz obtained data indicating that subjects' speed of decision decreased markedly following disconfirming evidence even though the stated confidence in that decision had not decreased. They argued that this supported the commitment hypothesis and also concluded that stated confidence may not indicate subjects' true opinions. A second hypothesis tested by Geller and Pitz was that subjects may expect an occasional disconfirming event to occur when information is probabilistic. For example, if the task is to determine whether the samples of marbles are coming from an urn that is 60 percent red and 40 percent blue or vice versa and the first nine draws produce six red and three blue marbles, the drawing of a blue on the next trial may not be upsetting to subjects who believe the urn to contain 40 percent blue marbles. When subjects were asked to predict the next event in the sample, Geller and Pitz found that the inertia effect was greater following predicted disconfirming events than nonpredicted disconfirming events, and this was taken as support for the second hypothesis.

Further evidence for the commitment hypothesis comes from a study by Pitz (1967). His subjects stated their confidence in their opinions only after an entire sample was presented. When confidence was plotted as a function of increasing sample size, with Bayesian probabilities held constant, mean confidence judgments decreased, rather than increased, as would be predicted from the inertia effect. This lack of inertia was attributed to the fact that there was no prior judgment to which subjects would have been committed. A later study (Pitz, 1969a) found that when subjects were not allowed to keep track of their trial-by-trial responses, inertia was eliminated.

Pitz (1966) had subjects make sequential judgments of the proportion of particular events in a sample. When subjects' previous judgments were displayed to them or could be recalled, their estimates showed a delay in revision towards .5 that seems analogous to the inertia effect found in studies of confidence or subjective probability. Here, too, a group whose previous judgments were not displayed showed no such effect.

Learning To Use Information

There has been considerable investigation into the learning of information processing and judgmental skills. Our focus here will be on studies in which the subject has to learn to use information to make a prediction or judgment. We shall neglect a rather sizable literature that explores whether subjects can learn to detect correlational or probabilistic contingencies among events when not required to use this knowledge in decisions.

Regression Studies of Learning

Researchers working within the regression framework, and in particular with the lens model, have been quite interested in learning. In fact, learning could be categorized, along with the problem of modeling, as a focal topic within the correlational paradigm. One way to partition the studies that have been conducted is according to whether subjects had available only one cue or multiple cues in the learning task.

Single-cue learning. Research with single cues has focused upon what Carroll (1963) has called "functional learning." Carroll attempted to discover whether subjects could learn the functional relationships between a scaled cue or stimulus variable, X, and a scaled criterion, Y. The environment was deterministic; that is, there was a perfect 1 to 1 correspondence between all values of X and Y. Across tasks, Carroll varied the mathematical complexity of the functions as determined by the number of parameters needed to describe them. He found that subjects' responses seemed to follow continuous subjective functions even when the stimuli and criterion feedback were randomly ordered. Not surprisingly, simple functions were learned more accurately. Later work by Björkman (1965) and Naylor and Clark (1968) centered around the relative ease of learning positive versus negative linear functions both in deterministic and probabilistic settings. The results of these studies indicated that positive relationships between cue and criterion are learned much more readily than negative ones.

Björkman (1968) defined "correlation learning" as functional learning where error ($R_e < 1.00$) was involved. He observed that correlational learning requires a subject to learn both the function relating stimulus and response, and the probability distributions around this function. In one experiment he found that the variance of a subject's responses about his own regression curve decreased as a consequence of training. A second experiment varied the extent to which there was a definite function to learn. Conditions with less pronounced cue-criterion trends resulted in larger ratios of subjects' response variance to criterion variance. From these results, Björkman concluded that correlational tasks are learned through a two-stage process involving both functional learning and probability learning, with the former occurring temporally prior to the latter.

Conservatism in single-cue learning. Do subjects in single-cue learning experiments exhibit conservatism such as occurs in Bayesian studies of performance? The results of several studies have been brought to bear upon this question but they must be viewed cautiously because of the problems in assessing conservatism in correlational tasks. For example, Naylor and Clark (1968) measured conservatism by dividing the stimulus distribution into thirds and computing the variance of each subject's responses within each third of the range. These variances were compared with the variances of the criterion values computed over the same sub-ranges. The assumptions underlying this measure are (1) that the criterion distribution reflects the true probabilities of the various hypothesis states within each sub-range of cue-values, and (2) that a subject's distribution of point responses represents an adequate picture of his perceived subjective probabilities for each of these hypothesis states. Given these assumptions, Naylor and Clark's subjects were conservative, inasmuch as the average dispersion of their judgments was found to exceed the dispersion of the criterion values in the upper and lower thirds of the cue distribution.

Naylor and Clark also proposed that the standard error of estimate $(\sqrt{1 - R_s^2})$ could be taken as an index of conservatism. Conservatism was presumed to increase this index, leading subjects to scatter their responses rather than consistently predicting the same criterion value, given a particular cue-value. By this measure, Naylor and Clark's subjects, as well as subjects in studies by Björkman (1965), Gray (1968), Gray, Barnes, and Wilkinson (1965), were not conservative. In these studies, R_s typically exceeded R_e and the discrepancy $(R_s - R_e)$ was inversely related to R_e. Thus the two measures proposed by Naylor and Clark lead to opposite conclusions about conservatism.

Brehmer and Lindberg (1970) have criticized the above conclusions, arguing that conservatism really means that subjects do not changs their inferences as much as they should when the cue-values change. They argued that the indices used by Naylor and Clark confound two sources of variance—the consistency of the subjects and their conservatism or extremeness. Therefore, Brehmer and Lindberg proposed that conservatism be assessed by the relationship between b_e and b_s, the slopes of the regression lines relating the criterion values and judgments to the cue dimension.[6]

The experiments by Gray (1968), Gray et al. (1965) and Naylor and Clark (1968) found that b_s exceeded b_e for low values of R_e (and b_e) but not for high values. Since R_e and b_e were confounded in these studies, Brehmer and Lindberg decided to vary R_e, holding b_e constant. Lower values of R_e simply had greater deviation about a regression line that was the same for each condition. They found that subjects' judgments were consistently more extreme than the criterion values; that is, b_s was greater than b_e. This was especially true when R_e was low. This result, along with similar findings by Gray and Naylor and Clark, was interpreted as indicating that subjects are not conservative in this type of task.

Multiple-cue learning. Multiple-cue research is assumed to have relevance for a variety of "real-world" situations in which an individual must integrate information from several sources. Most of the studies rely upon the lens model for conceptual and analytical guidance. Independent variables are the number of cues, their $r_{i,e}$ values and the multiple correlation, R_e, the forms of the functional relationships between cues and criterion, and the intercorrelation between cues. Typically, the subject is presented with a set of cues, he makes a quantitative judgment on the basis of these cues, and then receives the criterion value as feedback. Among the major results are (1) subjects can learn to use linear cues appro-

[6] In single-cue studies, $r_{i,e}$ is equivalent to R_e; similarly, $r_{i,s}$ equals R_s, while $b_{i,e}$ and $b_{i,s}$ equal b_e and b_s, respectively.

priately (Lee & Tucker, 1962; Smedslund, 1955; Summers, 1962; and Uhl, 1963); (2) learning of nonlinear functions occurs but is slower and less effective than learning of linear relationships (Brehmer, 1969a; Hammond & Summers, 1965; Sheets & Miller, in press; Summers, 1967; and Summers, Summers, & Karkau, 1969) and is especially difficult if subjects are not properly forewarned that the relations may be nonlinear (Earle, 1970; Hammond & Summers, 1965; and Summers & Hammond, 1966); (3) subjects can learn to detect changes in relative cue-weights over time although they do so slowly (Peterson, Hammond, & Summers, 1965a; Summers, 1969); (4) it is easier for subjects to learn which cue to use than to discover which functional rule relates a known valid cue to the criterion; learning both of these simultaneously is especially difficult (Summers, 1967, 1969); (5) in a two-cue task, pairing a cue of low or medium validity with one of high validity is detrimental to performance (a distraction effect), while pairing a cue of low validity with another of medium or low validity is facilitative (Dudycha & Naylor, 1966b); and (6) subjects can learn to use valid cues even when they are not perceived with perfect reliability (Brehmer, 1970).

Cue intercorrelations (redundancies) have been varied in several learning studies (Armelius & Lenntoft, 1970; Miller & Sarafino, in press; Naylor & Schenck, 1968). The major result is that subjects' beta-weights match the cue-criterion correlations rather than the cue-criterion beta-weights. Thus subjects fail to take appropriate account of redundancies.

Conservatism has not been an explicit concern in many multiple-cue learning studies. However, Peterson, Hammond, and Summers (1965b) found that subjects failed to weight the most valid of three cues heavily enough and slightly overweighted the cue with lowest validity. Peterson et al. noted the similarity of these results to those of Bayesian performance tasks in which conservatism and data diagnosticity are positively related.

A few studies have investigated the effects of different modes of feedback upon correlational learning. When subjects are given the correct answer on every trial ("outcome feedback"), learning is relatively slow. Lens model feedback, indicating how a subject's cue-utilization coefficients compare with the ecological validities, is far more effective (Hammond & Boyle, 1970; Newton, 1965; Todd & Hammond, 1965). Magnusson and Nystedt (1969) found that providing subjects with the ecological validities was more effective than providing feedback about their cue-utilization coefficients.

The lens model paradigm has also been extended to the problem of analyzing interpersonal learning and conflict between pairs of individuals (e.g.. Hammond, 1965; Hammond & Brehmer, this volume; Hammond, Todd, Wilkins, & Mitchell, 1966; Hammond, Wilkins, & Todd, 1966; Rappoport, 1965). A typical experiment trains pairs of subjects to use one of two cues in either linear or nonlinear fashion. Each subject learns to use a different cue, perhaps in different ways as well. After training, subjects are brought together to learn to predict a new criterion, using the same cues. Typically both cues must be used in this second task, and the subjects' training leads them initially to disagree with one another and with the outcome feedback they receive from the task. Lens model analysis of each subject's individual judgments and the pair's joint judgments provides a great deal of information about the mechanisms whereby subjects learn from the task and from one another. A study by Brehmer (1969b) found that the differences between subjects' weighting policies are rapidly reduced in the joint task but this reduction is accompanied by increased inconsistency such that overt discrepancies are not very much diminished by the end of the conflict period. Because of such findings, Hammond and Boyle (1970) and Hammond and Brehmer (Reading 14, this volume) argued that it is necessary to invent methods to display to the subjects the real sources of their disagreement and both of these studies describe a computer system that does this. Another interesting result from this area is that persons initially trained to have nonlinear policies are more likely to change than are persons with more linear policies (Brehmer, 1969b; Earle, 1970).

Bayesian Studies of Learning

Bayesian researchers have been notably uninterested in the topic of learning. Many Bayesian studies have used situations like bookbags and poker chips, with which the experimenters assume the subject is already familiar. Others (e.g., Lichtenstein & Feeney, 1968) have given initial training trials, with feedback; however, this training data is usually not analyzed. The epitome of indifference to learning is illustrated in a study by Peterson (1968). Although his subjects responded to more than 8000 four-data sequences, Peterson did not mention whether feedback was given (presumably it was not), and all analyses were based on all the data, without any attention paid to changes over time. Peterson, like most other Bayesian researchers, was interested in how subjects *behave*— not how they learn. Nonetheless, a few Bayesian studies do consider learning and thus merit attention.

The effects of feedback. Edwards, Phillips, Hays, and Goodman (1968) reported a study which compared two groups of subjects who gave likelihood ratio responses; these responses were then cumulated, that is, converted into posterior odds estimates, by the experimenters, using Bayes' theorem. One group received feedback of these cumulated posterior odds after each estimate; the other group received no feedback. This type of feedback was found to degrade the cumulated posterior odds—making them more conservative—although changes over time were not reported.

Martin and Gettys (1969) gave subjects either nominal feedback (e.g., H_1 generated the data) or probabilistic feedback (e.g., the posterior probabilities that each hypothesis generated the data are .769 for H_1, .108 for H_2, and .123 for H_3) in a multinomial task. These authors found that probabilistic feedback produced more optimal responses than nominal feedback, but they found no evidence that learning had occurred, either across four blocks of 50 trials, within the first 50 trials, or in a 20-trial replication. However, learning may have occurred in the 5 preexperimental practice trials.

The effects of payoff. Phillips and Edwards (1966) presented 20 sequences of binomial data to three groups, each with different payoff schemes, and to one group which received no payoff. They found that the no-payoff group showed a small amount of learning (decreasing discrepancy from optimal responses); all payoff groups showed more learning, with no evidence of asymptote by the end of the experiment. Performance showed greater improvement in the latter half of these 20-item sequences than in the first half, suggesting that the subjects learned to use large probabilities as the evidence for one hypothesis mounted.

Learning specific aspects of a probabilistic setting. Schum (1966a) showed that subjects can learn and utilize existing conditional nonindependence in multinomial data. The subjects were warned which data sources might be nonindependent, but they were not told the form of the relationship, nor which of the hypotheses mediated the relationship. They were taught to tabulate the frequencies with which the data occurred in such a way that the nonindependence could be seen. Thus the outstanding achievement of the subjects was not that they could learn what interdependencies existed, but that they could utilize this information appropriately in their posterior probability estimates—their responses more closely matched a model utilizing the nonindependence than a model in which independence was falsely assumed.

Two additional learning studies were oriented to the misperception explanation of conservatism. In order to strengthen the point that subjects' conservatism resulted from their misunderstanding of the kinds of samples to expect from a given population, Peterson, DuCharme, and Edwards (1968) found that subjects were less conservative after they had been shown 100 illustrative samples of data from a binomial population. Wheeler and Beach (1968) not only showed their subjects 200 binomial samples, but they asked the subjects to make a bet on which population generated the data, for each sample. Outcome feedback was given immediately after each bet. The effects of such training were seen in increased accuracy of subjects' estimated sampling distributions and decreased conservatism.

Descriptive Strategies: A Search
for Alternative Subjective Composition Rules

Thus far we have tied our presentation of theoretical notions and empirical results rather closely to the Bayesian and regression paradigms. In doing so, we have accepted the validity of their models rather uncritically as descriptive indicators of cognitive processes. However, despite the fairly adequate global fit provided by these models, close examination of judgmental data often reveals discrepancies that may carry important theoretical implications. In this section we shall discuss some of the alternative subjective composition strategies suggested by these discrepancies.

Strategies in Correlational Research

Starting-point and adjustment strategies. The present authors have recently conducted several experiments that seem to provide insight into the cognitive operations performed by decision makers as they attempt to integrate information into an evaluative judgment. In a study by Slovic and Lichtenstein (1968), the stimuli were gambles, described by four risk dimensions— probability of winning (P_W), amount to win ($\$_W$), probability of losing (P_L), and amount to lose ($\$_L$). One group of subjects was asked to indicate their strength of preference for playing each bet on a bipolar rating scale. Subjects in a second group indicated their opinion about a gamble's attractiveness by equating it with an amount of money such that they would be indifferent between playing the gamble or receiving the stated amount. This type of response is referred to as a "bid." The primary data analysis consisted of correlating each subject's responses with each of the risk dimensions across a set of gambles. These correlations indicated that the subjects did not weight the risk dimensions in the same manner when bidding as when rating a gamble in monetary units. Ratings correlated most highly with P_W, while bids were influenced most by $\$_W$ and $\$_L$.

Both bids and ratings presumably reflect the same underlying characteristic of a bet—namely, its worth or attractiveness. Why should subjects employ probabilities and payoffs differently when making these related responses? The introspections of one individual in the bidding group are especially helpful in providing insight into the type of cognitive process that could lead bidding responses to be overwhelmingly determined by just one payoff factor. This subject said,

> If the odds were . . . heavier in favor of winning . . . rather than losing . . . , I would pay about ¾ of the amount I would expect to win. If the reverse were true, I would ask the experimenter to pay me about . . . ½ of the amount I could lose.

Note this subject's initial dependence on probabilities followed by a complete disregard for any factor other than the winning payoff for attractive bets or the losing payoff for unattractive bets. After deciding he liked a bet, he used the amount to win, the upper limit of the amount he could bid, as a starting point for his response. He then reduced this amount by a fixed proportion in an attempt to integrate the other dimensions into the response. Likewise, for unattractive bets, he used the amount to lose as a starting point and adjusted it proportionally in an attempt to use the information given by the other risk dimensions. Such adjustments, neglecting to consider the exact levels of the other dimensions, would make the final response correlate primarily with the starting point—one of the payoffs in this case.

It is interesting to note that this starting-point and adjustment process is quite similar to the fixed-percent markup rule that businessmen often use when setting prices (Katona, 1951). This type of process can be viewed as a cognitive shortcut employed to reduce the strain of mentally weighting and averaging several dimensions at once.

The observation of simple starting-point and adjustment procedures in bidding and pricing judgments has led the first author to examine the strategies by which subjects average two numerical cues into an evaluative judgment. Preliminary analysis of the data indicates that, even in this relatively simple task, subjects tend to use a single cue as a starting point for their judgment. Next, they adjust this starting judgment rather imprecisely in an attempt to take the other cue into account. These data suggest that the subjects, although college students of above average intelligence, resorted to simple strategies in order to combine the two cue-values. They were not skilled arithmeticians, able to apply regression equations or produce weighted averages without computational aids.

Strategies in multiple-cue learning. Close examination of multiple-cue learning studies provides further evidence for the occurrence of simple strategies. For example, Azuma and Cronbach (1966) studied the manner in which subjects learned to predict a criterion value on the basis of several cues. When subjects' responses were correlated with the cue-values over blocks of trials, the results indicated an orderly progression towards proper weighting of the cues. However, when successful learners were asked to give introspective accounts of the process by which they made their judgments, these reports bore little resemblance to the weighting function employed by the experimenters. Instead they typically described a sequence of rather straightforward mechanical operations. Azuma and Cronbach observed that, although the experimenter regards the universe of stimuli as an undifferentiated whole, their subjects isolated sub-universes and employed different rules within each of these. The imposition, by the experimenter, of a correlational composition model may obscure the more local rules used by the subjects.

Strategies for Estimating P(H/D)

Students of the theory of probability have been continually amazed at its subtlety and the extent to which results derived from it conflict with their intuitive expectations. Nevertheless, a recent review by Peterson and Beach (1967) concerning man's capabilities as an "intuitive statistician" came to an optimistic conclusion. Peterson and Beach asserted that:

> Experiments that have compared human inferences with those of statistical man show that the normative model provides a good first approximation for a psychological theory of inference. Inferences made by subjects are influenced by appropriate variables and in appropriate directions [Pp. 42–43].

Even the specter of conservatism has failed to dampen the optimism of many Bayesian researchers who have attributed conservatism to erroneous subjective probabilities rather than an inadequate (i.e., non-Bayesian) processing of this information.

Our own examination of the experimental literature suggests that the Peterson and Beach view of man's capabilities as an intuitive statistician is too generous. Instead, the intuitive statistician appears to be quite confused by the conceptual demands of probabilistic inference tasks. He seems capable of little more than revising his response in the right direction upon receipt of a new item of information (and the inertia effect is evidence that he is not always successful in doing even this). After that, the success he obtains may be purely a matter of coincidence—a fortuitous interaction between the optimal strategy and whatever simple rule he arrives at in his groping attempts to ease cognitive strain and to pull a number "out of the air."

Constant Δp strategy. There are several simple strategies that seem to highlight subjects' difficulties in conceptualizing the requirements of probabilistic inference tasks and, at the same time, explain many of the ethereal phenomena that comprise the "conservatism" effect. The first such strategy is to revise one's $P(H/D)$ response by a constant, $\Delta p,$ regardless of the prior probability of the hypothesis or the diagnosticity of the data. The strongest evidence for this strategy comes from Pitz, Downing, and Reinhold (1967). Subjects saw sequences of either 5, 10, or 20 data items and made a probability revision after each datum. Three different levels of data diagnosticity were employed, using a binomial task. The results indicated the usual inverse relationship between diagnosticity and conservatism, with some subjects overreacting to data of low validity. Longer sequences produced greater conservatism. Pitz et al. noted that events that confirmed the favored hypothesis resulted in approximately equal changes in subjective probability, regardless of a subject's prior probability. There was little difference between changes for sequences of lengths 5 and 10, but the average change for sequences of length 20 was considerably lower, as if subjects were holding back in anticipation of a greater amount of future information. The experimenters also reported the average change was not a function of the nature of the two hypotheses but, instead, was approximately the same across the three levels of diagnosticity. They concluded with the observation:

> The fact that changes in subjective probability were a constant function of prior probabilities, were independent of the nature of the hypotheses, yet were not independent of the length of the sequence of data, implies that a subject's performance in a probability revision task is nonoptimal in a more fundamental way than is implied by discussions of conservatism. Performance is determined in large part by task characteristics which are irrelevant to the normative model. . . . It may not be unreasonable to assume that . . . the probability estimation task is too unfamiliar and complex to be meaningful [p. 392].

This same sort of insensitivity to gross variations in diagnosticity is evident in studies by Martin (1969), Peterson and Miller (1965), Peterson, Schneider, and Miller (1965), and Schum and Martin (1968) and serves to explain many of their results.

Similarity strategies. The second type of strategy for making probability estimates appears in several studies. The subjects base their responses on the similarity of the sample data with whatever representative feature of the hypothesis seems most salient. This strategy was observed by Dale (1968) in a pseudomilitary task. The values of $P(D_j/H_i)$ were displayed as histograms—one for each of the four hypotheses. Data categories were represented on the X-axis of these histograms and probabilities on the Y-axis. As the subjects received the data reports, they often physically arranged these reports to form a frequency histogram which they then compared with the four conditional probability displays. The relative magnitudes of their responses appeared to be based upon the similarity between the pattern formed by the data and the pattern formed by each of the conditional distributions. Dale noted that the subjects were at a loss to know what magnitude of probability to assign a given level of similarity. One subject, when he had assessed the probability of the correct hypothesis at .38 (the Bayesian probability was .98) remarked: "Getting mighty high!"

Lichtenstein and Feeney (1968) also observed a kind of similarity strategy. Their subjects were shown the locations of bomb blasts and had to estimate the probability that the intended target was City *A* or City *B*. The subjects were told that the errors were unbiased, in that a bomb was just as likely to miss its target in any direction. They were also told that a bomb was more likely to fall near its target than far from it. The subjects' responses were clearly discrepant from the optimal responses derived from the circular normal data generator. Several subjects reported that they compared the distances of the bomb site from the two cities and based their estimates on this comparison, that is, on the similarity between the location of the datum and the locations of the cities. A model assuming that probability estimates were simply a function of the ratio of the two distances did a much better job of predicting the responses of most subjects than did the "correct" circular normal model.

Use of sample proportions. The results of several independent studies using binomial tasks suggest that the subjects were matching their responses to the sample proportions. For example, Beach, Wise, and Barclay (1970), using a task with a simultaneous sample of items, found a remarkably close relationship between the sample proportion and the mean posterior probability estimates. Several of their subjects remarked that sample proportions were very compelling because they were available (and somehow relevant) numbers in a difficult and foreign task. Studies by Kriz (1967) and Shanteau (1970) also revealed evidence that sample proportions are the primary determinant of estimates. Such behavior does not take into account the likelihood of the data, as specified by the population proportions. Subjects thus would not change their responses across tasks that varied in population proportion (diagnosticity). This lack of sensitivity has been reported by Beach, Wise, and Barclay (1970) and by Vlek (1965), who suggested that ". . . subjects do not look further than the sample presented to them [p. 22]."

For the usual levels of diagnosticity found in binomial tasks, a strategy of using the sample proportion to estimate $P(H/D)$ will produce very conservative performance. Beach et al. (1970) concluded that this strategy is a spurious one that invalidates the bookbag and poker-chip task as an indicant of subjective probability revision. It seems to us that this may be too harsh a judgment in light of the ubiquity of simple strategies for inference across a variety of laboratory and real-life judgment situations.

Aiding the Decision Maker

Experimental work such as we have just described documents man's difficulties in processing multidimensional and probabilistic information. Unfortunately, there is abundant evidence indicating that these difficulties persist when the subject leaves the artificial confines of the laboratory and resumes the task of using familiar sources of information to make decisions that are important to himself and to others. Examples of overly simplistic use of information have been found in business decision making (Katona, 1951), military decision making (Wohlstetter, 1962), governmental policy (Lindblom, 1964), design of scientific experiments (Tversky & Kahneman, in press), and management of our natural resources (Kates, 1962; Russell, 1969; White, 1966). Agnew and Pyke (1969, p. 39) note that a decision maker left to his own devices ". . . uses, out of desperation, or habit, or boredom, or exhaustion, whatever decision aids he can—anything that prepackages information." Among the vast assortment of decision aids described by Agnew and Pyke are rumors, cultural biases and self-evident truths, common sense, appeals to authority, and appeals to experts who, themselves, are all too fallible.

The need for effective decision aids has not gone unnoticed, however. This is an age of technological advancement that creates more difficult and more important decision problems as it provides man with ever more power to manipulate his environment. It is not surprising, therefore, that this same technological bent has been focused upon the decision-making process itself. One interesting new development is the cognograph, a computer system that provides lens model feedback to the judge (Hammond & Boyle, 1971; Hammond, 1971).

The aim of this section is to describe two other recent and distinctive contributions to the regression and Bayesian approaches to the improvement of decision making.

Probabilistic Information Processing Systems

A great deal of Bayesian research has centered about the use of probability assessments in applied diagnostic systems. Edwards (1962) introduced the notion of a probabilistic information processing (PIP) system because of his concern about the optimal use of information in military and business settings. He distinguished two types of probabilistic outputs for such a system. The first was diagnosis (what is the probability that this activity indicates an enemy attack?), and the second was parameter estimation (how rapidly is that convoy moving and in what direction?). Edwards proposed the following design for a PIP system: Let men estimate $P(D/H)$, the probability that a particular datum would be observed given a specified hypothesis, and let machines integrate these $P(D/H)$ estimates across data and across hypotheses by means of Bayes' theorem. After all the relevant data have been processed, the resulting output is a posterior probability, $P(H/D)$, for each hypothesis. Edwards originally designed the PIP system with the intention of using Bayes' theorem as a labor-saving device. However, when research subsequently indicated that difficulties in aggregating data led subjects' unaided posterior probability estimates to be markedly conservative, the need to develop an antidote for conservatism added considerable impetus to the development of such systems.

Edwards and Phillips (1964) promoted the PIP system as a promising alternative to traditional command and control systems. They hypothesized that this system would produce faster and more accurate diagnoses for several reasons. First, Bayes' theorem is an optimal procedure for extracting all the certainty available in data. It automatically screens information for relevance, filters noise, and weights each item appropriately. In addition, PIP systems promise to permit men and machines to complement one another, using the talents of each to best advantage.

Sometimes $P(D/H)$ values are readily calculable from historical information or from some explicit model of the data-generating device. However, in many cases, no such probabilities exist. For example, what is the probability that Russia would have launched 25 reconnaissance satellites in the last three days if she planned a missile attack on the United States? As Edwards and Phillips observed, only human judgment can evaluate this type of information; PIP systems attempt to obtain and use such judgments systematically.

The basic idea of a PIP system suggested a number of questions for research. Edwards and Phillips discussed the need to verify the basic premise that men can be taught to be good estimators for probabilities. One question concerned the most effective method for making such estimates. For example, should men estimate $P(D/H)$ values directly or estimate other quantities from which $P(D/H)$ can be inferred? Subsequent research indicated that it is easier to estimate likelihood ratios than to estimate $P(D/H)$ values themselves, because the latter are influenced by many irrelevant factors such as the level of detail with which the datum is specified (Edwards, Lindman, & Phillips, 1965).

Perhaps the most important research need was to evaluate the effectiveness of PIP systems in realistically complex environments. A number of such studies have been completed in recent years. One of the most extensive studies was by Edwards, Phillips, Hays, and Goodman (1968). They constructed an artificial future world (complete with "history" up to 1975). The subjects related sequences of data to six hypotheses concerning war within the next 30 days, for example, H_1 was "Russia and China are about to attack North America," while H_6 was "Peace will continue to prevail." Four groups of subjects received intensive training in the characteristics of the "world," and then each group was trained in a particular response task. The *PIP group's* responses were likelihood ratios. To each datum five ratios were given, comparing in turn the likelihood of the datum given each of the war hypotheses against the likelihood of the datum given the peace hypothesis. The responses were registered on log-odds scales. The *POP group* responded with posterior odds, estimated upon receipt of each new datum. Again, each of the war hypotheses was compared in turn to the peace hypothesis. The *PEP group* responded by naming, for each war hypothesis, the fair price for an insurance policy that would pay 100 points in the event of that particular war, and nothing in the event of peace. The *PUP group* gave probability estimates comparable to the PEP group's price estimates. Thus, of the four groups, only the PIP group, who gave likelihood ratios, were relieved of the task of cumulating evidence across the data in each sequence. In this group, the aggregation was done by machine to compute posterior odds.

No optimal model could be devised for this simulation. The "true" hypothesis for any sequence of data was not known. Results showed that the PIP group arrived at larger final odds than other groups. When the PIP system showed final odds of 99:1, other groups showed final odds from 2:1 to 12:1. Because of this greater efficiency, the authors concluded that PIP was superior to the other systems.

The problem of finding a task complex enough to warrant the comparison of $P(D/H)$ responses (PIP) with $P(H/D)$ responses (POP), while still providing an optimal model against which to evaluate both methods, was tackled by Phillips (1966; also reported in Edwards, 1966). The data were thirty bigrams, combinations of two letters such as "th" or "ed." The hypotheses were that the bigrams were drawn either from the first two letters of words, or from the last two letters of words. The bigram "ed" might thus be viewed as beginning a word (like *ed*itor) or ending a word (like look*ed*). Phillips' subjects were six university newspaper editorial writers; data came from their own editorials. Frequency counts using the subjects' editorials (not shown to them) provided the veridical probabilities against which their responses could be compared. For the PIP task, all subjects estimated the likelihood ratio $(P(D/H_1) / P(D/H_2))$ for each bigram. Then, for the POP task, they were asked to imagine that the bigrams had been placed in two bookbags according to their frequencies of use, that is, if "my" had occurred 20 times at the beginning of words and 40 times at the end of words, the 20 "my" bigrams were placed in bag B, and 40 in bag E. One bag was chosen by the flip of a coin, and 10 bigrams were successively sampled. The subjects gave posterior odds estimates after each draw. Following this POP task, they repeated the PIP task. Results showed that in the PIP task subjects were modestly successful at estimating the relative frequencies of their own use of bigrams, but five of the six subjects were conservative. In the POP task they were much more conservative; they treated all but two of the bigrams as if they provided little or no diagnostic information.

Kaplan and Newman (1966) reported the results of three experiments designed to evaluate PIP in a military setting. In two of these studies the PIP technique showed a definite superiority over a POP condition. This superiority was particularly evident early in the data sequence. The authors speculated that the relatively poor performance of the PIP system in the other experiment may have been due to the fact that subjects there were provided with the output of Bayes' theorem after each datum was presented, making it difficult to evaluate each item of information on its own merit. Edwards, Phillips, Hays, and Goodman (1968) and Schum, Southard, and Wombolt (1969) also found a detrimental effect from showing $P(D/H)$ estimators the current state of the system.

A major effort to evaluate the idea of a PIP system within the context of threat evaluation has been carried out at Ohio State University under the direction of David Schum and his colleagues. The results are described in Briggs and Schum (1965), Howell (1967), Schum (1967, 1968, 1969), Schum, Goldstein, and Southard (1966), and Schum, Southard, and Wombolt (1969). The Ohio State research employed a situation in which the experimenters specified an arbitrarily constructed $P(D/H)$ matrix that governed the sampling of data. Subjects had to learn the import of various data items by accumulating relative frequencies linking data and hypotheses. The subjects were intensively trained in making probabilistic judgments and were quite familiar with the characteristics of the information with which they were dealing. Howell (1967) has summarized the first six years of research at Ohio State, concluding that automation of the aggregation process (i.e., PIP) can be expected to improve the quality of decisions in a wide variety of diagnostic conditions. He also observed that the superiority of a PIP system is most pronounced under degraded, stressful, or otherwise difficult task conditions.

In contrived or simulated diagnostic situations, the PIP system seems to be a promising device for improving estimates of posterior probabilities. Future work will undoubtedly see the extension of the system to nonmilitary settings along with greater attention to the practical details of implementing such systems in applied contexts. PIP systems have already been proposed for medicine (Gustafson, 1969; Gustafson, Edwards, Phillips, & Slack, 1969; Lusted, 1968) and probation decision making (McEachern & Newman, 1969), and applications to weather forecasting, law, and business seem imminent.

As promising as the PIP idea seems to be, however, a number of serious problems have yet to be faced. Some problems of particular importance noted by Schum, Southard, and Wombolt (1969) include hypothesis definition, source unreliability (uncertainty about which datum is being observed), nonstationarities of the environment, and nonindependence of data. Schum (1969) observed that in systems where data accumulate rapidly, experts who assess $P(D/H)$ may have to aggregate their judgments over a series of data (i.e., judge $P(D_1, D_2, D_3, \ldots D_n/H_i)$. When data items are nonindependent, these conditional probabilities can become quite complex. Three experiments reported by Schum, Southard, and Wombolt (1969) found that highly trained subjects could adequately aggregate diagnostic import across small samples of conditionally non-independent data. However, the subjects were given access to the relative frequencies of the lower-order conditional probabilities and, as the experimenters noted, the results gave little indication about "how one uses his educated intuition in assigning import to evidence in the absence of a relative frequency 'crutch' [p. 44]."

Tversky and Kahneman have recently scrutinized subjects' "educated intuitions" about probabilities in a series of experiments (Kahneman & Tversky, 1970; Tversky & Kahneman, 1970, in press) and their results imply that man may be as poor at estimating $P(D/H)$ values as he is at estimating posterior probabilities. One of their hypotheses is that the number of instances of an event that are readily retrieved from memory or the ease with which they come to mind are major clues used for estimating the probability of that event. The "availability" of instances is affected by many subtle factors such as recency, salience, and imaginability, all of which may be unrelated to the correct probability. Tversky and Kahneman point out the implications of these biases for PIP systems and they suggest that informing the decision maker of his susceptibility to these influences might be valuable, although by doing so one risks imparting new biases.

Bootstrapping

Can a system be designed to aid the decision maker that is based on his own judgments of complex stimuli? One possibility is based on the finding that regression models, such as the linear model, can do a remarkably good job of simulating such judgments. An intriguing hypothesis about cooperative interaction between man and machine is that these simulated judgments may be better, in the sense of predicting some criterion or implementing the judge's personal values, than were the actual judgments themselves. Dawes (1970) has termed this phenomenon "bootstrapping."

The rationale behind the bootstrapping hypothesis is quite simple. Although the human judge possesses his full share of human learning and hypothesis generating skills, he lacks the reliability of a machine. As Goldberg (1970) noted:

> He 'has his days': Boredom, fatigue, illness, situational and interpersonal distractions all plague him, with the result that his repeated judgments of the exact same stimulus configuration are not identical. He is subject to all these human frailties which lower the reliability of his judgments below unity. And, if the judge's reliability is less than unity, there must be error in his judgments—error which can serve no other purpose than to attenuate his accuracy. If we

could . . . [eliminate] the random error in his judgments, we should thereby increase the validity of the resulting predictions [p. 423].

Of course, the bootstrapping procedure, by foregoing the usual process of criterion validation, is vulnerable to any misconceptions or biases that the judge may have. Implicit in the use of bootstrapping is the assumption that these biases will be less detrimental to performance than the inconsistency of unaided human judgment.

Bootstrapping seems to have been explored independently by at least four groups of investigators. Yntema and Torgerson (1961) reported a study that suggested its feasibility. Their subjects were taught, via outcome feedback, to predict a criterion that was nonlinearly related to the cues. After 12 days of practice, their average correlation with the criterion was found to be .84. Then a linear regression model was computed for each subject on the basis of his responses during the final practice day. When these models were used to predict the criterion, the average correlation rose to .89. Thus consistent application of the linear model improved the predictions, even though the subjects had presumably been taking account of nonlinearities in making their own judgments. Yntema and Torgerson saw in these results the possibility that "artificial, precomputed judgments may in some cases be better than those the man could make himself if he dealt with each situation as it arose [p. 24]." More recently, Dudycha and Naylor (1966b) have reached a similar conclusion on the basis of their observation that subjects in a multiple-cue learning task were employing the cues with appropriate relative weights but were being inaccurate due to the inconsistency of their judgments. They concluded that although humans may be used to generate strategies, they should then be removed from the system and replaced by their strategies.

Bowman (1963) outlined a bootstrapping approach within the context of managerial decision making that has stimulated considerable empirical research (See Gordon, 1966; Hurst & McNamara, 1967; Jones, 1967; Kunreuther, 1969). Kunreuther, for example, developed a linear model of production scheduling decisions in an electronics firm. Coefficients were estimated to represent the relative importance of sales and inventory variables across a set of decisions made by the production manager. Under certain conditions, substitution of the model for the manager was seen to produce decisions superior to those the manager made on his own.

At about the time that Bowman was proposing his version of bootstrapping, Ward and Davis (1963) were advocating the same kind of approach to man–computer cooperation. Although they presented no data, Ward and Davis outlined several applications of the method in tasks such as estimating the time it would take to retrain 500 people, who now hold 500 existing jobs, to 500 new, possibly different jobs. Here a model would be built to capture an expert judge's policy on the basis of a relatively small number of cases. The model could then be substituted for the expert on the remaining cases. Ward and Davis also outlined an application of boot-strapping for the purpose of assigning personnel to jobs so as to maximize the payoff of the assignments.

Goldberg (1970) evaluated the merits of bootstrapping in a task where 29 clinical psychologists had to predict the psychiatric diagnoses of 861 patients on the basis of their MMPI profiles. A linear model was built to capture the weighting policy of each clinician. When models of each clinician were constructed on the basis of all 861 cases, 86 percent of these models were more accurate predictors of the actual criterion diagnoses than the clinicians from whom the models were derived. There was no instance of a man being greatly superior to his model. When a model was constructed on only one-seventh of the cases and used to predict the remaining cases, it was still superior to its human counterpart 79 percent of the time. While the average incremental validity of model over man was not large, the consistent superiority of the model suggested considerable promise for the bootstrapping approach.

Another demonstration of bootstrapping comes from a study of a graduate student admissions committee by Dawes (1971). Dawes built a regression equation to model the average judgment of the four-man committee. The predictors in the equation were overall undergraduate grade point average, quality of the undergraduate school, and a score from the Graduate Record Examination. To evaluate the validity of the model and the possibility of bootstrapping, Dawes used it to predict the average committee rating for his sample of 384 applicants. The R_s value for predicting the new committee ratings was .78. Most important, how-ever, was the finding that it was possible to find a cutting point on the distribution of predicted scores such that no one who scored below it was invited by the admissions committee. Fifty-five percent of the applicants scored below this point, and thus could have been eliminated by a pre-liminary screening without doing any injustice to the committee's actual judgments. Furthermore, the weights used to predict the committee's behavior were better than the committee itself in predicting later faculty ratings of the selected students. In an interesting cost-benefit analysis, Dawes estimated that the use of such a linear model to screen applicants to the nation's graduate schools could result in an annual savings of about $18 million worth of professional time.

A recent paper by Dawes and Diller (1970) derives a formula based on observable properties of judgments that indicates when bootstrapping with linear models may be expected to occur. In addition, a procedure is presented for amalgamating the judge's predictions with the predictions of his linear model in such a way that the amalgamation is superior to both the judge and model.

Concluding Remarks

Some Generalizations about the State of Our Knowledge

What have we learned about human judgment as a result of the efforts detailed on the preceding pages? Several generalizations seem appropriate. First, it is evident that the judge responds in a highly predictable way to the information available to him. Furthermore, much of what we call "intuition" can be explicated in a precise and quantitative manner. When this is done, the judge's insight into his own cognitive processes is often found to be inaccurate.

Second, we find that judges have a very difficult time weighting and combining information—be it probabilistic or deterministic in nature. To reduce cognitive strain, they resort to simplified decision strategies, many of which lead them to ignore or misuse relevant information.

The order in which information is received affects its use and integration but the specific form of sequential effects that occur is dependent upon particular circumstances of the decision task. Similarly, the manner in which information is displayed and the nature of the required response greatly influence the use of that information. In other words, the structure of the judgment situation is an important determinant of information use.

Finally, despite the great deal of research already completed, it is obvious that we know very little about many aspects of information use in judgment. Few variables have been explored in much depth—even such fundamental ones as the number of cues, cue-redundancy, or the effects of various kinds of stress. And the enormous task of integrating this area with the mainstream of cognitive psychology—work on concept formation, problem solving, memory, learning, attention, and so on—remains to be undertaken.

Does the Paradigm Dictate the Research?

One of the objectives of this chapter was to determine whether the specific models and methods characteristic of each research paradigm tend to focus the researcher's attention on certain problem areas while causing him to neglect others. Such focusing has obviously occurred. For example, the Bayesians have been least concerned with developing descriptive models of subjective composition rules, concentrating instead on comparing subjects' performance with that of an optimal model, Bayes' theorem. They have paid little attention to the learning of optimality, however. Researchers within the correlational paradigm have spent a great deal of effort using correlational methods to describe a judge's idiosyncratic weighting process, and researchers using ANOVA designs to study impression formation have concentrated on distinguishing various additive and averaging models and delineating sequential effects at the group level.

These different emphases are further illustrated by the fact that experimental manipulations that are similar from one paradigm to the other have been undertaken for quite different purposes. For example, the Bayesians have studied sequence length to gauge its effects on conservatism; set size was studied in impression formation in order to distinguish additive and averaging models; and the number of cues was varied by correlational researchers to study the effects upon consistency and complexity of subjects' strategies.

Can these differences in focus be attributed to the influence of the model used? Is a researcher inevitably steered in a particular direction by his chosen model? To some small extent, this is certainly true. A correlationalist will find it difficult to use, as his cues, intelligence reports such as: "General Tsing was seen last Monday lunching with Ambassador Hsieh." Instead, he will feel more comfortable with cues such as MMPI scores, or Grade Point Averages. Similarly, a Bayesian is most comfortable working with a small number of hypotheses, while the correlationalist can work conveniently with many, provided they are unidimensionally scaled.

In general, however, we believe that the major differences in research emphasis cannot be traced to differences among the models. On the one hand, we see neglected problems for which a model is well suited. For example, the Bayesians neglect learning although they have a numerical response, which can easily be compared to a numerical optimal response, for every trial; they need not partition the data into blocks (as correlationalists must in order to compute a beta weight). On the other hand, we see persistent, even stubborn, pursuit of topics for which the model is awkward. Correlationalists have devoted much effort to the search for configural cue-utilization, yet the linear model is extraordinarily powerful in suppressing such relationships, and interactions in ANOVA must be viewed with suspicion because the technique lacks invariance properties under believable data transformations.

Several research paradigms have been wound up around common points of interest and are chugging rapidly down diverging roads. Since any study almost always raises additional questions for investigation, there has been no dearth of interesting problems to fuel these research vehicles. Unfortunately, these vehicles lack side windows, and few investigators are looking far enough to the left or right. Of several hundred studies, only a handful indicate any awareness of the existence of comparable research under another paradigm. The fact remains, however, that all these investigators are interested in the same general problem—that of understanding how humans integrate fallible information to produce a judgment or decision. Single-minded dedication to one paradigm is disturbing since it suggests a lack of concern with basic, substantive issues. As Platt (1964) put the matter:

> To paraphrase an old saying, Beware of the man of one method or one instrument, either experimental or theoretical. He tends to become method oriented rather than problem oriented. The method oriented man is shackled; the problem oriented man is at least reaching freely toward what is most important [p. 351].

Applied versus Theoretical Objectives

If one is problem oriented, the distinction between applied and theoretical objectives becomes relevant to the selection of an experimental design. Methods suited for one of these general aims may be inadequate for the other. Thus correlational research, with its emphasis on predictability, may be quite useful for certain applied work but less adequate for theoretical endeavors which require sharper hypotheses and tests of fit. Similarly, in an applied man-machine system, the response scale is often valid by definition. But when the research emphasis shifts from practical problems and normative models to theoretical issues, the choice of a response scale may become critical. A clear awareness of these distinctions would seem to be important for both theoretical and applied research.

Towards an Integration of Research Efforts

We suggest that researchers should employ a multiparadigm approach, searching for the most appropriate tasks and models to attack the substantive problems of interest to them. We will try to show, for several such problems, how such a broader perspective might be advantageous.

Sequential effects. The potential value of a diverse approach is illustrated by research on primacy and recency effects. Hendrick and Costantini (1970a) found no effect of varying information inconsistency in an impression formation task, where adjectives served as cues. They argued that attention decrement, not inconsistency, accounts for the primacy commonly found in studies of impression formation. Yet a number of Bayesian studies did obtain primacy when early and late data were, to varying degrees, inconsistent (Dale, 1968; Peterson & DuCharme, 1967; Roby, 1967) and recency when later data were not inconsistent (Pitz & Reinhold, 1968; Shanteau, 1970). The discrepancy between the Hendrick and Costantini data and the Bayesian results would seem to be worth investigating.

The study by Shanteau (1970) provides a nice example of the utility of applying methods and tasks from different paradigms when studying sequential effects. Shanteau used an ANOVA design with a Bayesian task. He presented subjects with sequences of data constructed according to factorial combinations of binary events. Their task was to estimate $P(H/D)$ after each datum was received. Sequential effects appear as main effects of serial position in such a design. Two experiments clearly showed that recency was operating throughout all stages of sequences as long as 15 items.

The inertia effect in Bayesian research can be viewed as a type of primacy effect. The fact that inertia is so dependent upon the degree to which subjects' previous judgments are displayed or otherwise highlighted suggests that this same factor might also be operating in studies of primacy and recency. It is perhaps relevant that most of the studies of impression formation that employed intermittent responding and obtained recency effects used spoken ratings, slash marks, or required subjects to fill out detailed questionnaires. None of these formats gives particular salience to previous judgments. The one study that exhibited primacy effects (Anderson, 1959) employed a more standard written response, although subjects did have to turn the page for each new item of information. In addition, in each of the Bayesian studies that obtained primacy (Dale, 1968; Peterson & DuCharme, 1967; Roby, 1967), subjects were asked to make estimates on some mechanical device that preserved the previous response and required it to be physically manipulated when changes were made. While all this is obviously "post hoc" analysis, future research on primacy and recency effects should take a close look at the manner in which the previous response in the sequence is made and stored.

Novelty. How do subjects handle data that are rare or novel? Wyer (1970) examined the effects of novelty, defined in terms of the unconditional probability of an adjective, upon impression formation. Novel adjectives were seen to carry greater weight, making impressions more polarized. This increased weight attached to rare data appears to be in contradiction with findings from Bayesian research on rare events (Beach, 1968; Vlek, 1965; Vlek & van der Heijden, 1967). These studies have presented evidence that rare events are viewed as uninformative, that is, they are not given enough weight in the decision process.

Learning. Hammond and his colleagues (e.g., Hammond & Brehmer, Reading 14, this volume; Todd & Hammond, 1965) have long contended that specific feedback derived from the lens model (i.e., feedback about the weight the subject gives to each cue, and the weight the environment gives to each cue) is more effective than nonspecific feedback (i.e., the "correct" answer). How does this result relate to the finding by Martin and Gettys (1969) that probabilistic feedback is better than nominal feedback, or to the evidence from Wheeler and Beach (1968) and Peterson, Du-

Charme, and Edwards (1968) that subjects give more optimal $P(H/D)$ estimates after they have received training in $P(D/H)?$ If specific feedback enhances performance, why then did Pitz and Downing (1967) find that subjects' binary predictions were not improved by detailed information about the sampling distributions?

Diagnosticity and conservatism. Both the Bayesian and the correlational models have well-defined measures of the diagnosticity of data— $P(D/H)$ and $b_{i,e}$, respectively. A unified approach to this topic seems natural. In the past, correlationalists have done little exploration in performance (nonlearning) studies where diagnosticity was varied. Bayesian research on this topic has been extensive and has demonstrated the difficulties subjects have in integrating probabilistic information. The different data and response formats possible within the correlational paradigm would seem to provide an excellent opportunity to investigate the generality of these difficulties. Subjects could be taught how to use various linear and curvilinear cues individually and could then be asked to integrate them into their judgments.

From a theoretical standpoint the question of conservatism rests upon the validity of the response scale. We have already seen that different response modes produce different degrees of conservatism, but these responses have been selected on the basis of practical, not theoretical considerations. Response rescaling and model testing, as practiced within integration theory and conjoint measurement, could be quite useful in evaluating conservatism.

Self insight. The analysis of the judge's insight into his own subjective composition function is a fascinating and important area that has been investigated only within the correlational paradigm. And in these studies, only one rather arbitrary technique has been used to scale the judge's perceptions of a cue's importance—the "distribute-100-points" technique. Besides the obvious step of employing new scaling techniques in correlational studies, it would seem valuable to test the accuracy of self-insight in a variety of tasks, using Bayesian and ANOVA models as well.

Decision aids. The idea of bootstrapping, which was developed in the context of regression equations, has some interesting relationships with the PIP system designed by Bayesians to improve human judgment. Both view human judgments as essential and attempt to blend them optimally (See Pankoff & Roberts, 1968, for an elaboration of this point). However, advocates of the PIP system assume that the aggregation process is faulty and attempt to circumvent this by having subjects estimate $P(D/H)$ values and letting a machine combine them. They decompose the judgment task into a number of presumably simpler estimation tasks. Bootstrapping assumes that subjects can aggregate information appropriately except for unreliability that must be filtered out. The success of bootstrapping and PIP systems suggests that the assumptions of both have some validity— judges are biased *and* unreliable in their weighting of information. Perhaps a system can be designed to minimize both these sources of error or, at least, to differentiate situations where PIP might excel bootstrapping or vice versa.

New Directions

Although a diverse program, integrating Bayesian and regression paradigms, might be quite valuable in increasing our understanding of information processing, some new approaches might be even more illuminating. Our own inclination is to move towards more molecular analyses of the heuristic strategies that subjects employ when they integrate information— along the lines we discussed earlier in this reading. At this level, the evidence to date seems to indicate that subjects are processing information in ways fundamentally different from Bayesian and regression models. Thus, if we are to pursue this line of research we will have to develop new models and different methods of experimentation. Use of eye movements, introspection, and tasks where subjects have to search for or request information as they need it may help provide insights into molecular strategies. The search for new models should bring judgment research into closer contact with the more traditional areas of psychology. For example, Bruner, Goodman, and Austin's (1956) work on the role of cognitive strain in determining concept formation strategies, and Simon's analyses of cognitive limitations and their influence on problem solving (Simon, 1956, 1969) seem likely to have much relevance for our understanding of composition strategies in judgment.

REFERENCES

Agnew, N. M., & Pyke, S. W. *The science game: An introduction to research in the behavioral sciences.* Englewood Cliffs, N.J.: Prentice-Hall, 1969.

Anderson, N. H. Test of a model for opinion change. *Journal of Abnormal and Social Psychology,* 1959, *59,* 371–381.

Anderson, N. H. Application of an additive model to impression formation. *Science,* 1962, *138,* 817–818.

Anderson, N. H. Test of a model for number-averaging behavior. *Psychonomic Science,* 1964, *1,* 191–192.

Anderson, N. H. Averaging versus adding as a stimulus-combination rule in impression formation. *Journal of Experimental Psychology,* 1965, *70,* 394–400. (a)

Anderson, N. H. Primacy effects in personality impression formation using a generalized order effect paradigm. *Journal of Personality and Social Psychology,* 1965, *2,* 1–9. (b)

Anderson, N. H. Component ratings in impression formation. *Psychonomic Science,* 1966, *6,* 279–280.

Anderson, N. H. Application of a weighted average model to a psychophysical averaging task. *Psychonomic Science,* 1967, *8,* 227–228. (a)

Anderson, N. H. Averaging model analysis of set-size effect in impression formation. *Journal of Experimental Psychology,* 1967, *75,* 158–165. (b)

Anderson, N. H. Application of a linear-serial model to a personality-impression task using serial presentation. *Journal of Personality and Social Psychology,* 1968, *10,* 354–362. (a)

Anderson, N. H. A simple model for information integration. In R. P. Abelson, E. Aronson, W. J. McGuire, T. M. Newcomb, M. J. Rosenberg, & P. H. Tannenbaum (Eds.), *Theories of cognitive consistency: A sourcebook.* Skokie, Ill.: Rand McNally, 1968. (b)

Anderson, N. H. Comment on "An analysis-of-variance model for the assessment of configural cue utilization in clinical judgment." *Psychological Bulletin,* 1969, *72,* 63–65.

Anderson, N. H. Functional measurement and psychophysical judgment. *Psychological Review,* 1970, *77,* 153–170.

Anderson, N. H. Two more tests against change of meaning in adjective combinations. *Journal of Verbal Learning and Verbal Behavior,* 1971, *10,* 75–85.

Anderson, N. H. Integration theory and attitude change. *Psychological Review,* in press.

Anderson, N. H., & Barrios, A. A. Primacy effects in personality impression formation. *Journal of Abnormal and Social Psychology,* 1961, *63,* 346–350.

Anderson, N. H., & Hubert, S. Effects of concomitant verbal recall on order effects in personality impression formation. *Journal of Verbal Learning and Verbal Behavior,* 1963, *2,* 379–391.

Anderson, N. H., & Jacobson, A. Effect of stimulus inconsistency and discounting instructions in personality impression formation. *Journal of Personality and Social Psychology,* 1965, *2,* 531–539.

Anderson, N. H., & Jacobson, A. Further data on a weighted average model for judgment in a lifted weight task. *Perception and Psychophysics,* 1968, *4,* 81–84.

Anderson, N. H., & Lampel, A. K. Effect of context on ratings of personality traits. *Psychonomic Science,* 1965, *3,* 433–434.

Anderson, N. H., & Norman, A. Order effects in impression formation in four classes of stimuli. *Journal of Abnormal and Social Psychology,* 1964, *69,* 467–471.

Anderson, N. H., & Shanteau, J. C. Information integration in risky decision making. *Journal of Experimental Psychology,* 1970, *84,* 441–451.

Armelius, B., & Lenntoft, K. Effect of cue intercorrelation in a multiple cue probability learning task with different cue validities. Umeå Psychological Report No. 20, Department of Psychology, University of Umeå, 1970.

Asch, S. E. Forming impressions of personality. *Journal of Abnormal and Social Psychology,* 1946, *41,* 258–290.

Azuma, H., & Cronbach, L. J. Cue-response correlations in the attainment of a scalar concept. *The American Journal of Psychology,* 1966, *79,* 38–49.

Beach, L. R. Accuracy and consistency in the revision of subjective probabilities. *IEEE Transactions on Human Factors in Electronics,* 1966, *7,* 29–37.

Beach, L. R. Probability magnitudes and conservative revision of subjective probabilities. *Journal of Experimental Psychology*, 1968, *77*, 57–63.

Beach, L. R., & Olson, J. B. Data sequences and subjective sampling distributions. *Psychonomic Science*, 1967, *9*, 309–310.

Beach, L. R., & Phillips, L. D. Subjective probabilities inferred from estimates and bets. *Journal of Experimental Psychology*, 1967, *75*, 354–359.

Beach, L. R., & Wise, J. A. Subjective probability and decision strategy. *Journal of Experimental Psychology*, 1969, *79*, 133–138. (a)

Beach, L. R., & Wise, J. A. Subjective probability revision and subsequent decisions. *Journal of Experimental Psychology*, 1969, *81*, 561–565. (b)

Beach, L. R., Wise, J. A., & Barclay, S. Sample proportion and subjective probability revisions. *Organizational Behavior and Human Performance*, 1970, *5*, 183–190.

Bieri, J., Atkins, A. L., Briar, S., Leaman, R. L., Miller, H., & Tripodi, T. *Clinical and social judgment: The discrimination of behavioral information.* New York: Wiley, 1966.

Björkman, M. Learning of linear functions: Comparison between a positive and a negative slope. Report No. 183 from the Psychological Laboratories of the University of Stockholm, 1965.

Björkman, M. The effect of training and number of stimuli on the response variance in correlation learning. Umeå Psychological Report No. 2, Department of Psychology, University of Umea, 1968.

Bogartz, R. S., & Wackwitz, J. H. Transforming response measures to remove interactions or other sources of variance. *Psychonomic Science*, 1970, *19*, 87–89.

Bowman, E. H. Consistency and optimality in managerial decision making. *Management Science*, 1963, *9*, 310–321.

Brehmer, B. Cognitive dependence on additive and configural cue-criterion relations. *The American Journal of Psychology*, 1969, *82*, 490–503. (a)

Brehmer, B. The roles of policy differences and inconsistency in policy conflict. Umeå Psychological Report No. 18, Department of Psychology, University of Umeå, 1969. (b) Also published as Program on Cognitive Processes Report No. 118, Institute of Behavioral Science, University of Colorado, 1969.

Brehmer, B. Inference behavior in a situation where the cues are not reliably perceived. *Organizational Behavior and Human Performance*, 1970, *5*, 330–347.

Brehmer, B., & Lindberg, L. A. The relation between cue dependency and cue validity in single-cue probability learning with scaled cue and criterion variables. *Organizational Behavior and Human Performance*, 1970, *5*, 542–554.

Briggs, G. E., & Schum, D. A. Automated Bayesian hypothesis-selection in a simulated threat-diagnosis system. In J. Spiegel & D. E. Walker (Eds.), *Information systems sciences: Proceedings of the second congress.* Washington, D.C.: Spartan Books, 1965.

Brody, N. The effect of commitment to correct and incorrect decisions on confidence in a sequential decision-task. *American Journal of Psychology*, 1965, *78*, 251–256.

Brown, T. R. The judgment of suicide lethality: A comparison of judgmental models obtained under contrived versus natural conditions. Unpublished doctoral dissertation, University of Oregon, 1970.

Bruner, J. S., Goodnow, J. J., & Austin, G. A. *A study of thinking*. New York: Wiley, 1956.

Brunswik, E. *The conceptual framework of psychology*. Chicago: University of Chicago Press, 1952.

Brunswik, E. Representative design and probabilistic theory in a functional psychology. *Psychological Review*, 1955, *62*, 193–217.

Brunswik, E. *Perception and the representative design of experiments*. Berkeley: University of California Press, 1956.

Carroll, J. D. Functional learning: The learning of continuous functional mappings relating stimulus and response continua. Research Bulletin (RB-63-26), Princeton, N.J.: Educational Testing Service, 1963.

Christal, R. E. JAN: A technique for analyzing group judgment. Technical Documentary Report PRL-TDR-63-3, Personnel Research Laboratory, Aerospace Medical Division, Air Force Systems Command, Lackland AFB, Texas, 1963.

Clarkson, G. P. E. *Portfolio selection: A simulation of trust investment*. Englewood Cliffs, N.J.: Prentice-Hall, 1962.

Cochran, W. G., & Cox, G. M. *Experimental designs*. (2nd ed.) New York: Wiley, 1957.

Cohen, J. Multiple regression as a general data-analytic system. *Psychological Bulletin*, 1968, *70*, 426–443.

Coombs, C. H. *A theory of data*. New York: Wiley, 1964.

Coombs, C. H., & Huang, L. C. Polynomial psychophysics of risk. *Journal of Mathematical Psychology*, 1970, *7*, 317–338.

Dale, H. C. A. Weighing evidence: An attempt to assess the efficiency of the human operator. *Ergonomics*, 1968, *11*, 215–230.

Darlington, R. B. Multiple regression in psychological research and practice. *Psychological Bulletin*, 1968, *69*, 161–182.

Dawes, R. M. Social selection based on multidimensional criteria. *Journal of Abnormal and Social Psychology*, 1964, *68*, 104–109.

Dawes, R. M. Graduate admissions: A case study, *American Psychologist*, 1971, *26*, 180–188.

Dawes, R. M., & Diller, R. D. The prediction of bootstrapping and a method of amalgamation. *Oregon Research Institute Research Bulletin*, 1970, *10* (6).

DuCharme, W. M. A response bias explanation of conservative human inference. *Journal of Experimental Psychology*, 1970, *85*, 66–74.

DuCharme, W. M., & Peterson, C. R. Intuitive inference about normally distributed populations. *Journal of Experimental Psychology*, 1968, *78*, 269–275.

Dudycha, A. L. A Monte Carlo evaluation of JAN: A technique for capturing and clustering rater's policies. *Organizational Behavior and Human Performance*, 1970, *5*, 501–516.

Dudycha, A. L., & Naylor, J. C. The effect of variations in the cue R matrix upon the obtained policy equation of judges. *Educational and Psychological Measurement*, 1966, *26*, 583–603. (a)

Dudycha, A. L., & Naylor, J. C. Characteristics of the human inference process in complex choice behavior situations. *Organizational Behavior and Human Performance*, 1966, *1*, 110–128. (b)

Dustin, D. S., & Baldwin, P. M. Redundancy in impression formation. *Journal of Personality and Social Psychology,* 1966, *3,* 500–506.

Earle, T. C. Task learning, interpersonal learning, and cognitive complexity. *Oregon Research Institute Research Bulletin,* 1970, *10*(2).

Eckenrode, R. T. Weighting multiple criteria. *Management Science,* 1965, *12,* 180–192.

Edwards, W. The theory of decision making. *Psychological Bulletin,* 1954, *51,* 380–418.

Edwards, W. Dynamic decision theory and probabilistic information processing. *Human Factors,* 1962, *4,* 59–73.

Edwards, W. Optimal strategies for seeking information: Models for statistics, choice reaction times, and human information processing. *Journal of Mathematical Psychology,* 1965, *2,* 312–329.

Edwards, W. Nonconservative probabilistic information processing systems. Report from Decision Sciences Laboratory, Electronic Systems Division, Air Force Systems Command, USAF, ESD-TR-66-404, 1966.

Edwards, W. Conservatism in human information processing. In B. Kleinmuntz (Ed.), *Formal representation of human judgment.* New York: Wiley, 1968.

Edwards, W., Lindman, H., & Phillips, L. D. Emerging technologies for making decisions. *New directions in psychology II.* New York: Holt, Rinehart and Winston, 1965.

Edwards, W., Lindman, H., & Savage, L. J. Bayesian statistical inference for psychological research. *Psychological Review,* 1963, *70,* 193–242.

Edwards, W., & Phillips, L. D. Man as transducer for probabilities in Bayesian command and control systems. In G. L. Bryan & M. W. Shelley (Eds.), *Human judgments and optimality.* New York: Wiley, 1964.

Edwards, W., Phillips, L. D., Hays, W. L., & Goodman, B. C. Probabilistic information processing systems: Design and evaluation. *IEEE Transactions on Systems Science and Cybernetics,* 1968, SSC-*4,* 248–265.

Einhorn, H. J. The use of nonlinear, noncompensatory models in decision making. *Psychological Bulletin,* 1970, *73,* 221–230.

Einhorn, H. J. Use of nonlinear, noncompensatory models as a function of task and amount of information. *Organizational Behavior and Human Performance,* 1971, *6,* 1–27.

Estes, W. K. The statistical approach to learning theory. In S. Koch (Ed.), *Psychology: A study of a science.* Vol. *2.* New York: McGraw-Hill, 1959.

Fishbein, M., & Hunter, R. Summation versus balance in attitude organization and change. *Journal of Abnormal and Social Psychology,* 1964, *69,* 505–510.

Fitts, P. M., & Deininger, R. L. S-R compatibility: Correspondence among paired elements within stimulus and response codes. *Journal of Experimental Psychology,* 1954, *48,* 483–492.

Fried, L. S., & Peterson, C. R. Information seeking: Optional vs. fixed stopping. *Journal of Experimental Psychology,* 1969, *80,* 525–529.

Galanter, E., & Holman, G. L. Some invariances of the iso-sensitivity function and their implications for the utility function of money. *Journal of Experimental Psychology,* 1967, *73,* 333–339.

Geller, E. S., & Pitz, G. F. Confidence and decision speed in the revision of opinion. *Organizational Behavior and Human Performance,* 1968, *3,* 190–201.

Gettys, C. F., & Manley, C. W. The probability of an event and estimates of posterior probability based upon its occurrence. *Psychonomic Science,* 1968, *11,* 47–48.

Gibson, R. S., & Nichol, E. H. The modifiability of decisions made in a changing environment. Report from Decision Sciences Laboratory, Electronic Systems Division, Air Force Systems Command, USAF, ESD-TR-64-657, 1964.

Goldberg, L. R. Simple models or simple processes? Some research on clinical judgments. *American Psychologist,* 1968, *23,* 483–496.

Goldberg, L. R. Man versus model of man: A rationale, plus some evidence, for a method of improving on clinical inferences. *Psychological Bulletin,* 1970, *73,* 422–432.

Gollob, H. F. Impression formation and word combination in sentences. *Journal of Personality and Social Psychology,* 1968, *10,* 341–353.

Gordon, J. R. M. A multi-model analysis of an aggregate scheduling decision. Unpublished doctoral dissertation, Sloan School of Management, Massachusetts Institute of Technology, Cambridge, 1966.

Gray, C. W. Predicting with intuitive correlations. *Psychonomic Science,* 1968, *11,* 41–43.

Gray, C. W., Barnes, C. B., & Wilkinson, E. F. The process of prediction as a function of the correlation between two scaled variables. *Psychonomic Science,* 1965, *3,* 231–232.

Green, B. F., Jr. Descriptions and explanations: A comment on papers by Hoffman and Edwards. In B. Kleinmuntz (Ed.), *Formal representation of human judgment.* New York: Wiley, 1968.

Green, D. M., & Swets, J. A. *Signal detection theory and psychophysics.* New York: Wiley, 1966.

Grinnell, M., Keeley, S., & Doherty, M. E. Bayesian predictions of faculty judgments of graduate school success. Paper presented at the meeting of the Midwestern Psychological Association, Cincinnati, 1970.

Gustafson, D. H. Evaluation of probabilistic information processing in medical decision making. *Organizational Behavior and Human Performance,* 1969, *4,* 20–34.

Gustafson, D. H., Edwards, W., Phillips, L. D., & Slack, W. V. Subjective probabilities in medical diagnosis. *IEEE Transactions on Man-Machine Systems,* 1969, MMS-*10*(3), 61–65.

Halpern, J., & Ulehla, Z. J. The effect of multiple responses and certainty estimates on the integration of visual information. *Perception and Psychophysics,* 1970, *7,* 129–132.

Hammond, K. R. Probabilistic functioning and the clinical method. *Psychological Review,* 1955, *62,* 255–262.

Hammond, K. R. New directions in research on conflict resolution. *Journal of Social Issues,* 1965, *21,* 44–66.

Hammond, K. R. Probabilistic functionalism: Egon Brunswik's integration of the history, theory, and method of psychology. In K. R. Hammond (Ed.), *The Psychology of Egon Brunswik.* New York: Holt, Rinehart and Winston, 1966.

Hammond, K. R. Computer graphics as an aid to learning. *Science,* 1971, *172,* 903–908.

Hammond, K. R., & Boyle, P. J. R. Quasi-rationality, quarrels, and new conceptions of feedback. *Bulletin of the British Psychological Society,* 1971, *24,* in press. (Paper read as invited address at annual meeting of the British Psychological Society, 1970.)

Hammond, K. R., Hursch, C. J., & Todd, F. J. Analyzing the components of clinical inference. *Psychological Review,* 1964, *71,* 438–456.

Hammond, K. R., Kelly, K. J., Schneider, R. J., & Vancini, M. Clinical inference in nursing: Revising judgment. *Nursing Research,* 1967, *16,* 36–45.

Hammond, K. R., & Summers, D. A. Cognitive dependence on linear and non-linear cues. *Psychological Review,* 1965, *72,* 215–234.

Hammond, K. R., Todd, F. J., Wilkins, M. M., & Mitchell, T. O. Cognitive conflict between persons: Application of the "Lens Model" paradigm. *Journal of Experimental Social Psychology,* 1966, *2,* 343–360.

Hammond, K. R., Wilkins, M. M., & Todd, F. J. A research paradigm for the study of interpersonal learning. *Psychological Bulletin,* 1966, *65,* 221–232.

Hayes, J. R. Human data processing limits in decision making. In E. Bennett (Ed.), *Information system science and engineering. Proceedings of the First Congress on the Information Systems Sciences.* New York: McGraw-Hill, 1964.

Hayes, J. R. Strategies in judgmental research. In B. Kleinmuntz (Ed.), *Formal representation of human judgment.* New York: Wiley, 1968.

Hays, W. L. *Statistics for psychologists.* New York: Holt, Rinehart & Winston, 1963.

Hendrick, C. Averaging vs. summation in impression formation. *Perceptual and Motor Skills,* 1968, *27,* 1295–1302.

Hendrick, C., & Costantini, A. F. Effects of varying trait inconsistency and response requirements on the primacy effect in impression formation. *Journal of Personality and Social Psychology,* 1970, *15,* 158–164. (a)

Hendrick, C., & Costantini, A. F. Number averaging behavior: A primacy effect. *Psychonomic Science,* 1970, *19,* 121–122. (b)

Himmelfarb, S. The impact of neutral information about a person. Unpublished manuscript, University of California at La Jolla, 1970.

Himmelfarb, S., & Senn, D. J. Forming impressions of social class: Two tests of an averaging model. *Journal of Personality and Social Psychology,* 1969, *12,* 38–51.

Hoepfl, R. T., & Huber, G. P. A study of self-explicated utility models. *Behavioral Science,* 1970, *15,* 408–414.

Hoffman, P. J. The paramorphic representation of clinical judgment. *Psychological Bulletin,* 1960, *47,* 116–131.

Hoffman, P. J. Cue-consistency and configurality in human judgment. In B. Kleinmuntz (Ed.), *Formal representation of human judgment.* New York: Wiley, 1968.

Hoffman, P. J., & Blanchard, W. A. A study of the effects of varying amounts of predictor information on judgment. *Oregon Research Institute Research Bulletin,* 1961.

Hoffman, P. J., Slovic, P., & Rorer, L. G. An analysis-of-variance model for the assessment of configural cue utilization in clinical judgment. *Psychological Bulletin,* 1968, *69,* 338–349.

Howell, W. C. Some principles for the design of decision systems: A review of six years of research on a command-control system simulation. Aerospace Medical Research Laboratories, Aerospace Medical Division, Air Force Systems Command, Wright-Patterson Air Force Base, Ohio. AMRL-TR-67-136, 1967.

Huber, G. P., Sahney, V. K., & Ford, D. L. A study of subjective evaluation models. *Behavioral Science,* 1969, *14,* 483–489.

Hursch, C., Hammond, K. R., & Hursch, J. L. Some methodological considerations in multiple cue probability studies. *Psychological Review,* 1964, *71,* 42–60.

Hurst, E. G., Jr., & McNamara, A. B. Heuristic scheduling in a woolen mill. *Management Science,* 1967, *14,* B-182-B-203.

Jones, C. Parametric production planning. *Management Science,* 1967, *13,* 843–866.

Jones, M. R. From probability learning to sequential processing: A critical review. *Psychological Bulletin,* in press.

Kahneman, D., & Tversky, A. Subjective probability: A judgment of representativeness. *Oregon Research Institute Research Bulletin,* 1970, *10*(5).

Kaplan, R. J., & Newman, J. R. Studies in probabilistic information processing. *IEEE Transactions on Human Factors in Electronics,* 1966, *7,* 49–63.

Kates, R. W. Hazard and choice perception in flood plain management. Department of Geography Research Paper No. 78, University of Chicago, 1962.

Katona, G. *Psychological Analysis of Economic Behavior.* New York: McGraw-Hill, 1951.

Kerrick, J. S. The effect of relevant and non-relevant sources on attitude change. *Journal of Social Psychology,* 1958, *47,* 15–20.

Klahr, D. Decision making in a complex environment: The use of similarity judgments to predict preferences. *Management Science,* 1969, *15,* 595–618.

Kleinmuntz, B. The processing of clinical information by man and machine. In B. Kleinmuntz (Ed.), *Formal representation of human judgment.* New York: Wiley, 1968.

Knox, R. E., & Hoffman, P. J. Effects of variation of profile format on intelligence and sociability judgments. *Journal of Applied Psychology,* 1962, *46,* 14–20.

Koford, J. S., & Groner, G. F. The use of an adaptive threshold element to design a linear optimal pattern classifier. *IEEE Transactions on Information Theory,* 1966, IT-*12,* 42–50.

Kort, F. A nonlinear model for the analysis of judicial decisions. *The American Political Science Review,* 1968, *62,* 546–555.

Krantz, D. H., & Tversky, A. Conjoint measurement analysis of composition rules in psychology. Report No. 70-10, Ann Arbor, Mich.: Michigan Mathematical Psychology Program, 1970.

Kriz, J. Der likelihood-quotient zur erfassung des subjektiven signifikanzniveaus. Forschungsbericht No. 9, Institute for Advanced Studies, Vienna, 1967.

Kunreuther, H. Extensions of Bowman's theory on managerial decision-making. *Management Science,* 1969, *15,* 415–439.

Lampel, A. K., & Anderson, N. H. Combining visual and verbal information in an impression-formation task. *Journal of Personality and Social Psychology,* 1968, *9,* 1–6.

Ledley, R. S., & Lusted, L. B. Reasoning foundations of medical diagnosis. *Science,* 1959, *130,* 9–21.

Lee, J. C., & Tucker, R. B. An investigation of clinical judgment: A study in method. *Journal of Abnormal and Social Psychology,* 1962, *64,* 272–280.

Levin, I. P., & Schmidt, C. F. Sequential effects in impression formation with binary intermittent responding. *Journal of Experimental Psychology,* 1969, *79,* 283–287.

Lichtenstein, S., & Feeney, G. J. The importance of the data-generating model in probability estimation. *Organizational Behavior and Human Performance,* 1968, *3,* 62–67.

Lindblom, C. E. The science of "muddling through." In W. J. Gore & J. W. Dyson (Eds.), *The making of decisions.* London: Collier-Macmillan, 1964.

Loeb, G. *The battle for investment survival.* New York: Simon and Schuster, 1965.

Luce, R. D., & Tukey, J. Simultaneous conjoint measurement: A new type of fundamental measurement. *Journal of Mathematical Psychology,* 1964, *1,* 1–27.

Luchins, A. S. Experimental attempts to minimize the impact of first impressions. In C. I. Hovland (Ed.), *The order of presentation in persuasion.* New Haven: Yale University Press, 1957.

Luchins, A. S. Definitiveness of impression and primacy-recency in communications. *The Journal of Social Psychology,* 1958, *48,* 275–290.

Lusted, L. B. *Introduction to medical decision making.* Springfield, Ill.: Charles C Thomas, 1968.

Madden, J. M. An application to job evaluation of a policy-capturing model for analyzing individual and group judgment. 6570th Personnel Research Laboratory, Aerospace Medical Division, Air Force Systems Command, PRL-TDR-63-15, May, 1963.

Magnusson, D., & Nystedt, L. Cue relevance and feedback in a clinical prediction task. Report No. 272 from the Psychological Laboratories, University of Stockholm, 1969.

Maguire, T. O., & Glass, G. V. Component profile analysis (COPAN)—An alternative to PROF. *Educational and Psychological Measurement,* 1968, *28,* 1021–1033.

Manis, M., Gleason, T. C., & Dawes, R. M. The evaluation of complex social stimuli. *Journal of Personality and Social Psychology,* 1966, *4,* 404–419.

Martin, D. W. Data conflict in a multinomial decision task. *Journal of Experimental Psychology,* 1969, *82,* 4–8.

Martin, D. W., & Gettys, C. F. Feedback and response mode in performing a Bayesian decision task. *Journal of Applied Psychology,* 1969, *53,* 413–418.

Martin, H. T., Jr. The nature of clinical judgment. Unpublished doctoral dissertation, Washington State College, 1957.

McEachern, A. W., & Newman, J. R. A system for computer-aided probation decision-making. *Journal of Research on Crime and Delinquency,* 1969, *6,* 184–198.

Meehl, P. E. *Clinical versus statistical prediction.* Minneapolis: University of Minnesota Press, 1954.

Miller, G. A. The magical number seven, plus or minus two: Some limits on our capacity for processing information. *Psychological Review,* 1956, *63,* 81–97.

Miller, M. J., & Sarafino, E. The effects of intercorrelated cues on multiple probability learning. *Organizational Behavior and Human Performance,* in press.

Morrison, H. W., & Slovic, P. Effects of context on relative judgments of area. Paper presented at the meeting of the Eastern Psychological Association, Atlantic City, 1962. (Also in IBM Research Note NC-104, Watson Research Center, 1962.)

Naylor, J. C., & Clark, R. D. Intuitive inference strategies in interval learning tasks as a function of validity magnitude and sign. *Organizational Behavior and Human Performance,* 1968, *3,* 378–399.

Naylor, J. C., & Schenck, E. A. The influence of cue redundancy upon the human inference process for tasks of varying degrees of predictability. *Organizational Behavior and Human Performance,* 1968, *3,* 47–61.

Naylor, J. C., & Wherry, R. J., Sr. The use of simulated stimuli and the "JAN" Technique to capture and cluster the policies of raters. *Educational and Psychological Measurement,* 1965, *25,* 969–986.

Newell, A., Shaw, J. C., & Simon, H. A. Elements of a theory of human problem solving. *Psychological Review,* 1958, *65,* 151–166.

Newton, J. R. Judgment and feedback in a quasi-clinical situation. *Journal of Personality and Social Psychology,* 1965, *1,* 336–342.

Oden, G. C., & Anderson, N. H. Differential weighting in integration theory. *Journal of Experimental Psychology,* 1971, *89,* 152–161.

Osgood, C. E., & Tannenbaum, P. H. The principle of congruity in the prediction of attitude change. *Psychological Review,* 1955, *62,* 42–55.

Oskamp, S. How clinicians make decisions from the MMPI: An empirical study. Paper presented at the American Psychological Association, St. Louis, 1962.

Oskamp, S. Overconfidence in case study judgments. *Journal of Consulting Psychology,* 1965, *29,* 261–265.

Pankoff, L. D., & Roberts, H. V. Bayesian synthesis of clinical and statistical prediction. *Psychological Bulletin,* 1968, *70,* 762–773.

Parducci, A., Thaler, H., & Anderson, N. H. Stimulus averaging and the context for judgment. *Perception and Psychophysics,* 1968, *3,* 145–150.

Peterson, C. R. Aggregating information about signals and noise. *Proceedings, 76th Annual Convention, APA,* 1968, 123–124.

Peterson, C. R., & Beach, L. R. Man as an intuitive statistician. *Psychological Bulletin,* 1967, *68,* 29–46.

Peterson, C. R., & DuCharme, W. M. A primacy effect in subjective probability revision. *Journal of Experimental Psychology,* 1967, *73,* 61–65.

Peterson, C. R., DuCharme, W. M., & Edwards, W. Sampling distributions and probability revisions. *Journal of Experimental Psychology,* 1968, *76,* 236–243.

Peterson, C. R., Hammond, K. R., & Summers, D. A. Multiple probability learning with shifting cue weights. *American Journal of Psychology,* 1965, *78,* 660–663. (a)

Peterson, C. R., Hammond, K. R., & Summers, D. A. Optimal responding in multiple-cue probability learning. *Journal of Experimental Psychology,* 1965, *70,* 270–276. (b)

Peterson, C. R., & Miller, A. J. Sensitivity of subjective probability revision. *Journal of Experimental Psychology,* 1965, *70,* 117–121.

Peterson, C. R., & Phillips, L. D. Revision of continuous subjective probability distributions. *IEEE Transactions on Human Factors in Electronics,* 1966, *7,* 19–22.

Peterson, C. R., Schneider, R. J., & Miller, A. J. Sample size and the revision of subjective probabilities. *Journal of Experimental Psychology,* 1965, *69,* 522–527.

Peterson, C. R., & Swensson, R. G. Intuitive statistical inferences about diffuse hypotheses. *Organizational Behavior and Human Performance,* 1968, *3,* 1–11.

Phillips, L. D. Some components of probabilistic inference. Technical Report No. 1, Human Performance Center, University of Michigan, 1966.

Phillips, L. D., & Edwards, W. Conservatism in a simple probability inference task. *Journal of Experimental Psychology,* 1966, *72,* 346–357.

Phillips, L. D., Hays, W. L., & Edwards, W. Conservatism in complex probabilistic inference. *IEEE Transactions on Human Factors in Electronics,* 1966, *7,* 7–18.

Pitz, G. F. The sequential judgment of proportion. *Psychonomic Science,* 1966, *4,* 397–398.

Pitz, G. F. Sample size, likelihood, and confidence in a decision. *Psychonomic Science,* 1967, *8,* 257–258.

Pitz, G. F. An inertia effect (resistance to change) in the revision of opinion. *Canadian Journal of Psychology,* 1969, *23,* 24–33. (a)

Pitz, G. F. The influence of prior probabilities on information seeking and decision making. *Organizational Behavior and Human Performance,* 1969, *4,* 213–226. (b)

Pitz, G. F. Use of response times to evaluate strategies of information seeking. *Journal of Experimental Psychology,* 1969, *80,* 553–557. (c)

Pitz, G. F., & Downing, L. Optimal behavior in a decision-making task as a function of instructions and payoffs. *Journal of Experimental Psychology,* 1967, *73,* 549–555.

Pitz, G. F., Downing, L., & Reinhold, H. Sequential effects in the revision of subjective probabilities. *Canadian Journal of Psychology,* 1967, *21,* 381–393.

Pitz, G. F., & Reinhold, H. Payoff effects in sequential decision-making. *Journal of Experimental Psychology,* 1968, *77,* 249–257.

Platt, J. R. Strong inference. *Science,* 1964, *146,* 347–353.

Podell, J. E. The impression as a quantitative concept. *American Psychologist,* 1962, *17,* 308. (Abstract)

Podell, H. A., & Podell, J. E. Quantitative connotation of a concept. *Journal of Abnormal and Social Psychology,* 1963, *67,* 509–513.

Pollack, I. Action selection and the Yntema-Torgerson worth function. In E. Bennett (Ed.), *Information system science and engineering: Proceedings of the First Congress on the Information Systems Sciences.* New York: McGraw-Hill, 1964.

Pruitt, D. G. Informational requirements in making decisions. *American Journal of Psychology,* 1961, *74,* 433–439.

Raiffa, H., & Schlaifer, R. *Applied statistical decision theory.* Boston: Harvard University, Graduate School of Business Administration, Division of Research, 1961.

Rapoport, A. Effects of observation cost on sequential search behavior. *Perception & Psychophysics,* 1969, *6,* 234–240.

Rappoport, L. Interpersonal conflict in cooperative and uncertain situations. *Journal of Experimental Social Psychology,* 1965, *1,* 323–333.

Rhine, R. J. Test of models and impression formation. Paper presented at the meeting of the Western Psychological Association, San Diego, March, 1968.

Roby, T. B. Belief states and sequential evidence. *Journal of Experimental Psychology,* 1967, *75,* 236–245.

Rodwan, A. S., & Hake, H. W. The discriminant-function as a model for perception. *American Journal of Psychology,* 1964, *26,* 380–392.

Rorer, L. G., Hoffman, P. J. Dickman, H. D., & Slovic, P. Configural judgments revealed. *Proceedings of the 75th Annual Convention of the American Psychological Association,* 1967, *2,* 195–196.

Rosenberg, S. Mathematical models of social behavior. In G. Lindzey & E. Aronson (Eds.), *The Handbook of Social Psychology*, 1968, *1*, 186–203.

Rosenkrantz, P. S., & Crockett, W. H. Some factors influencing the assimilation of disparate information in impression formation. *Journal of Personality and Social Psychology*, 1965, *2*, 397–402.

Russell, C. S. Losses from natural hazards. Working Paper No. 10, Natural Hazard Research Program, Department of Geography, University of Toronto, 1969.

Sarbin, T. R. A contribution to the study of actuarial and individual methods of prediction. *American Journal of Sociology*, 1942, *48*, 593–602.

Sarbin, T. R., & Bailey, D. E. The immediacy postulate in the light of modern cognitive psychology. In K. R. Hammond (Ed.), *The psychology of Egon Brunswik*. New York: Holt, Rinehart & Winston, 1966.

Savage, L. J. *The foundations of statistics*. New York: Wiley, 1954.

Schenck, E. A., & Naylor, J. C. A cautionary note concerning the use of regression analysis for capturing the strategies of people. *Educational and Psychological Measurement*, 1968, *28*, 3–7.

Schlaifer, R. *Probability and statistics for business decisions*. New York: McGraw-Hill, 1959.

Schmidt, C. F. Personality impression formation as a function of relatedness of information and length of set. *Journal of Personality and Social Psychology*, 1969, *12*, 6–11.

Schum, D. A. Inferences on the basis of conditionally nonindependent data. *Journal of Experimental Psychology*, 1966, *72*, 401–409. (a)

Schum, D. A. Prior uncertainty and amount of diagnostic evidence as variables in a probabilistic inference task. *Organizational Behavior and Human Performance*, 1966, *1*, 31–54. (b)

Schum, D. A. Concerning the evaluation and aggregation of probabilistic evidence by man-machine systems. In D. E. Walker (Ed.), *Information System Science and Technology*. Washington, D.C.: Thompson Book, 1967.

Schum, D. A. Behavioral decision theory and man-machine systems. Report No. 46-4, Interdisciplinary Program in Applied Mathematics and Systems Theory. Houston: Rice University, 1968.

Schum, D. A. Concerning the simulation of diagnostic systems which process complex probabilistic evidence sets. Technical Report 69-10, Aerospace Medical Research Laboratory, Wright-Patterson Air Force Base, Ohio, April 1969.

Schum, D. A., Goldstein, I. L., Howell, W. C., & Southard, J. F. Subjective probability revisions under several cost-payoff arrangements. *Organizational Behavior and Human Performance*, 1967, *2*, 84–104.

Schum, D. A., Goldstein, I. L., & Southard, J. F. Research on a simulated Bayesian information-processing system. *IEEE Transactions on Human Factors in Electronics*, 1966, *7*, 37–48.

Schum, D. A., & Martin, D. W. Human processing of inconclusive evidence from multinomial probability distributions. *Organizational Behavior and Human Performance*, 1968, *3*, 353–365.

Schum, D. A., Southard, J. F., & Wombolt, L. F. Aided human processing of inconclusive evidence in diagnostic systems: A summary of experimental evaluations. AMRL-Technical Report 69-11. Aerospace Medical Research Laboratory, Wright-Patterson Air Force Base, Ohio, May 1969.

Shanteau, J. C. An additive decision-making model for sequential estimation and inference judgments. *Journal of Experimental Psychology,* 1970, *85,* 181–191.

Shanteau, J. C., & Anderson, N. H. Test of a conflict model for preference judgment. *Journal of Mathematical Psychology,* 1969, *6,* 312–325.

Sheets, C., & Miller, M. J. The effect of cue-criterion function form on multiple cue probability learning. *American Journal of Psychology,* in press.

Shepard, R. N. On subjectively optimum selection among multiattribute alternatives. In M. W. Shelly, II, & G. L. Bryan (Eds.), *Human judgments and optimality.* New York: Wiley, 1964.

Sidowski, J. B., & Anderson, N. H. Judgments of city-occupation combinations. *Psychonomic Science,* 1967, *7,* 279–280.

Simon, H. A. Rational choice and the structure of the environment. *Psychological Review,* 1956, *63,* 129–138.

Simon, H. A. *The sciences of the artificial.* Cambridge, Mass.: MIT Press, 1969.

Slovic, P. Cue consistency and cue utilization in judgment. *American Journal of Psychology,* 1966, *79,* 427–434.

Slovic, P. Analyzing the expert judge: A descriptive study of a stockbroker's decision processes. *Journal of Applied Psychology,* 1969, *53,* 255–263.

Slovic, P., Fleissner, D., & Bauman, W. S. Quantitative analysis of investment decisions. *Journal of Business,* in press.

Slovic, P., & Lichtenstein, S. C. The relative importance of probabilities and payoffs in risk taking. *Journal of Experimental Psychology Monograph Supplement,* 1968, *78,* (3, pt. 2).

Slovic, P., Rorer, L. G., & Hoffman, P. J. Analyzing the use of diagnostic signs. *Investigative Radiology,* 1971, *6,* 18–27.

Smedslund, J. *Multiple-probability learning.* Oslo: Akademisk Forlag, 1955.

Smith, A. *The money game.* New York: Random House, 1968.

Stewart, R. H. Effect of continuous responding on the order effect in personality impression formation. *Journal of Personality and Social Psychology,* 1965, *1,* 161–165.

Summers, D. A. Rule versus cue learning in multiple probability tasks. *Proceedings of the 75th Annual Convention of the American Psychological Association,* 1967, *2,* 43–44.

Summers, D. A. Conflict, compromise, and belief change in a decision-making task. *Journal of Conflict Resolution,* 1968, *12,* 215–221.

Summers, D. A. Adaptation to change in multiple probability tasks. *American Journal of Psychology,* 1969, *82,* 235–240.

Summers, D. A., & Hammond, K. R. Inference behavior in multiple-cue tasks involving both linear and nonlinear relations. *Journal of Experimental Psychology,* 1966, *71,* 751–757.

Summers, D. A., & Stewart, T. R. Regression models of foreign policy judgments. *Proceedings of the 76th Annual Convention of the American Psychological Association,* 1968, *3,* 195–196.

Summers, S. A. The learning of responses to multiple weighted cues. *Journal of Experimental Psychology,* 1962, *64,* 29–34.

Summers, S. A., Summers, R. C., & Karkau, V. T. Judgments based on different functional relationships between interacting cues and a criterion. *American Journal of Psychology,* 1969, *82,* 203–211.

Swets, J. A. (Ed.) *Signal detection and recognition by human observers: Contemporary readings.* New York: Wiley, 1964.

Swets, J. A., & Birdsall, T. G. Deferred decision in human signal detection: A preliminary experiment. *Perception and Psychophysics,* 1967, *2,* 15–28.

Toda, M. Measurement of subjective probability distribution. Report No. 3, Pennsylvania State College, Institute of Research, Division of Mathematical Psychology, 1963.

Todd, F. J., & Hammond, K. R. Differential feedback in two multiple-cue probability learning tasks. *Behavioral Science,* 1965, *10,* 429–435.

Tucker, L. R. A suggested alternative formulation in the development by Hursch, Hammond, & Hursch, and by Hammond, Hursch, & Todd. *Psychological Review,* 1964, *71,* 528–530.

Tversky, A. Additivity, utility, and subjective probability. *Journal of Mathematical Psychology,* 1967, *4,* 175–202. (a)

Tversky, A. A general theory of polynomial conjoint measurement. *Journal of Mathematical Psychology,* 1967, *4,* 1–20. (b)

Tversky, A. Utility theory and additivity analysis of risky choices. *Journal of Experimental Psychology,* 1967, *75,* 27–36. (c)

Tversky, A. Intransitivity of preferences. *Psychological Review,* 1969, *76,* 31–48.

Tversky, A., & Kahneman, D. The judgment of probability by retrieval and construction of instances. *Oregon Research Institute Research Bulletin,* 1970, *11* (2).

Tversky, A., & Kahneman, D. The belief in the law of small numbers. *Psychological Bulletin,* in press.

Tversky, A., & Krantz, D. H. Similarity of schematic faces. A test of interdimensional additivity. *Perception & Psychophysics,* 1969, *5,* 124–128.

Uhl, C. Learning of interval concepts. I. Effects of differences in stimulus weights. *Journal of Experimental Psychology,* 1963, *66,* 264–273.

Uhl, C. N., & Hoffman, P. J. Contagion effects and the stability of judgment. Paper read at Western Psychological Association, Monterey, California, 1958.

Ulehla, Z. J. Optimality of perceptual decision criteria. *Journal of Experimental Psychology,* 1966, *71,* 564–569.

Ulehla, Z. J., Canges, L., & Wackwitz, F. Integration of conceptual information. *Psychonomic Science,* 1967, *8,* 223–224.

Ulmer, S. S. The discriminant function and a theoretical context for its use in estimating the votes of judges. In J. B. Grossman & J. Tanenhaus (Eds.), *Frontiers of judicial research.* New York: Wiley, 1969.

Vlek, C. A. J. The use of probabilistic information in decision making. Psychological Institute Report No. 009-65, University of Leiden, The Netherlands, 1965.

Vlek, C. A. J., & Bientema, K. A. Subjective likelihoods in posterior probability estimation. Psychological Institute Report No. E 014-67, University of Leiden, The Netherlands, 1967.

Vlek, C. A. J., & van der Heijden, L. H. C. Subjective likelihood functions and variations in the accuracy of probabilistic information processing. Psychological Institute Report No. E 017-67, University of Leiden, The Netherlands, 1967.

von Neumann, J., & Morgenstern, O. *Theory of games and economic behavior.* (3rd ed.) Princeton: Princeton University Press, 1953.

Wald, A. *Sequential analysis.* New York: Wiley, 1947.

Wallsten, T. S. Failure of predictions from subjectively expected utility theory in a Bayesian decision task. *Organizational Behavior and Human Performance,* 1968, *3,* 239–252.

Wallsten, T. S. The likelihood-ratio principle and conjoint measurement. Paper read at the tenth annual meeting of the Psychonomic Society, San Antonio, November 1970.

Ward, J. H., Jr., & Davis, K. Teaching a digital computer to assist in making decisions. 6570th Personnel Research Laboratory, Aerospace Medical Division, Air Force Systems Command, PRL-TDR-63-16, June 1963.

Weiss, W. Scale judgments of triplets of opinion statements. *Journal of Abnormal and Social Psychology,* 1963, *66,* 471–479.

Weiss, D. J., & Anderson, N. H. Subjective averaging of length with serial presentation. *Journal of Experimental Psychology,* 1969, *82,* 52–63.

Wendt, D. Value of information for decisions. *Journal of Mathematical Psychology,* 1969, *6,* 430–443.

Wheeler, G., & Beach, L. R. Subjective sampling distributions and conservatism. *Organizational Behavior and Human Performance,* 1968, *3,* 36–46.

Wherry, R. J., Sr., & Naylor, J. C. Comparison of two approaches—JAN and PROF —for capturing rater strategies. *Educational and Psychological Measurement,* 1966, *26,* 267–286.

White, G. F. Optimal flood damage management: Retrospect and Prospect. In A. V. Kneese & S. C. Smith (Eds.), *Water research.* Baltimore: Johns Hopkins Press, 1966.

Wiggins, N., & Hoffman, P. J. Three models of clinical judgment. *Journal of Abnormal Psychology,* 1968, *73,* 70–77.

Williams, J. D., Harlow, S. D., Lindem, A., & Gab, D. A judgment analysis program for clustering similar judgmental systems. *Educational and Psychological Measurement,* 1970, *30,* 171–173.

Willis, R. H. Stimulus pooling and social perception. *Journal of Abnormal and Social Psychology,* 1960, *60,* 365–373.

Winkler, R. L., & Murphy, A. H. "Good" probability assessors. *Journal of Applied Meteorology,* 1968, *7,* 751–758.

Wohlstetter, R. *Pearl Harbor: Warning and decision.* Stanford, Calif.: Stanford University Press, 1962.

Wyer, R. S., Jr. The effects of information redundancy on evaluations of social stimuli. *Psychonomic Science,* 1968, *13,* 245–246.

Wyer, R. S., Jr. Information redundancy, inconsistency, and novelty and their role in impression formation. *Journal of Experimental Social Psychology,* 1970, *6,* 111–127.

Wyer, R. S., Jr., & Watson, S. F. Context effects in impression formation. *Journal of Personality and Social Psychology,* 1969, *12,* 22–33.

Yntema, D. B., & Klem, L. Telling a computer how to evaluate alternatives as one would evaluate them himself. In E. Bennett (Ed.), *Information system science and engineering: Proceedings of the First Congress on the Information System Sciences.* New York: McGraw-Hill, 1964.

Yntema, D. B., & Torgerson, W. S. Man-computer cooperation in decisions requiring common sense. *IRE Transactions of the Professional Group on Human Factors in Electronics,* 1961, HFE *2*(1), 20–26.

Introduction
to Reading 2

It is all too often made painfully clear to each of us that our judgments in a particular situation differ substantially from those of another person; what is not so clear is why these judgments differ, or how different they may be in comparison with judgments made by a third person. These problems are reflected in the research questions examined by Wiggins; that is, how can individual differences in judgment be most accurately characterized, and how can clusters of individuals having similar judgment policies be identified and described? When judgments concern multidimensional objects or events, the identification and description of individual differences is a very complex (and frequently discouraging) matter.

Fortunately, the "general individual difference model" described by Wiggins is an appropriate tool for work in this problem area. Her reading presents the statistical techniques (multimodal factor analysis and multidimensional scaling) underlying the model and illustrates how it can facilitate judgment research. Wiggins also notes the importance of *other* individual differences associated with judgmental differences and shows how these may be incorporated in the general model.

2 Individual Differences in Human Judgments: A Multivariate Approach[1]

NANCY WIGGINS[2]

University of Illinois

A research strategy that emphasizes individual differences in cognitive and perceptual judgments is at variance with more classical research approaches. In the tradition of experimental psychology, the judgments obtained are summarized by averaging across all experimental subjects. Should individual differences among judges emerge, these differences would be treated as error and an "average judge" would be considered the most meaningful summary of all the judges. That approach has the advantage of ensuring generalizability to other judges, similar to the ones being studied, at the expense of ignoring individual differences. It is assumed that the mean judgment is representative of all the judges in the sample, or alternatively, that the judges are replications of one another within error of measurement.

By contrast, in the spirit of correlational psychology with its emphasis on individual differences, the mean judgment is not assumed to be representative of all the judges in the sample. Rather, each judge is treated separately; his data are enumerated and compared with the results of each of the other judges. For example, Hoffman (1960) compared the judgmental models of two judges asked to predict the intelligence of persons represented by a series of nine-cue profiles. Hoffman derived a linear model for each judge by obtaining the cue weights from the multiple regression of the nine input cues with the judge's predictions. The resultant regression weights indicated the relative emphasis each judge placed on the various cues. When judges are treated individually in this manner, generalizability becomes restricted. One would be willing to generalize the results, or model, for a single judge *only* to that same judge for future

[1] The research of the author for this reading was supported by NIMH Grant No. MH-13892 and the reading was supported in part by Grant No. MH-12972 to Oregon Research Institute.
[2] The author is extremely indebted to Jerry S. Wiggins for his painstaking editorial assistance, and to Sarah Lichtenstein, Paul Slovic, and Lewis R. Goldberg for their critical editorial comments.

occurrences of a similar task. Further, when the number of judges becomes large, comparison among judges may become unwieldy.

Despite these problems, the main rationale for an individual difference analysis is that judgments obtained on the basis of a group average will often distort the judgmental strategies of many individual subjects. In the extreme of this situation, there may not exist any real subjects to whom a group average result applies (Tucker & Messick, 1963). On the other hand, individual differences would be unimportant provided the judgmental responses of the majority of judges were quite similar to the average judgment. Such judgmental complexity can be characterized as arising from two distinct sources: individuals and stimuli. The complexity of individuals, or individual differences, will be defined in terms of the number of dimensions necessary to reproduce the covariation among individuals. Similarly, the complexity of stimuli will be defined in terms of the number of psychophysical dimensions necessary to account for the perceived stimulus interrelationships.

The complexity of individuals and stimuli will be discussed in the context of cue-utilization; the particular judgmental paradigm considered is embedded in Hammond, Hursch, and Todd's (1964) conceptualization of Brunswik's Lens Model. That model is based primarily on three elements and their interrelationships: judge, cues, and criterion. In particular, a number of judges are asked to make a judgment for each of a series of profiles (representing patients, applicants, etc.), where each profile consists of a set of previously quantified cues. As a mirror to the real world, the model assumes that the relationships existing among cues, criterion, and judge are probabilistic.

The cue-weighting scheme of each judge is "captured" (Naylor & Wherry, 1965), or "represented" (Hoffman, 1960) by treating the judgments as the dependent variable and the cue-values as the independent variables in a multiple regression equation. The regression equation relating cues and judgments can be thought of as the linear "model" of man (Goldberg, 1970). The corresponding multiple correlation indicates the *linear predictability of man*. Similarly, the multiple regression equation relating cues to an external criterion is termed the "actuarial" formula. The ecological validity of the cues is indicated by their regression weights in that formula, and the corresponding multiple correlation between cues and criterion represents the *linear predictability of the criterion*. The correlation between the judgments and the external criterion represents the *accuracy of the judge*. Within this context, the purpose of this chapter is fourfold: (1) to discuss several multivariate approaches to individual differences in cue-utilization; (2) to examine the relevance of stimulus multidimensionality to studies of cognitive judgment; (3) to outline a general model for the simultaneous study of individual differences and stimulus complexity; and (4) to provide empirical examples that illustrate the usefulness of a multivariate approach for the study of individual differences.

Multivariate Approaches to Individual Differences

Historically, factor analysis has been associated primarily with the detection and isolation of different human abilities in the area of intelligence testing. The basic data matrix on which a factor analysis is performed ordinarily consists of a set of Pearson product-moment correlations among a set of variables, or tests. The resulting factor matrix can be conceptualized as representing the correlations between the tests, or manifest variables, and the underlying factors, or latent variables. Tests that are themselves highly intercorrelated should mark (i.e., correlate with) the same factor or factors. Factor analysis is one convenient method for summarizing the interrelationships among a large number of tests, since, ideally, the number of factors should be considerably less than the number of tests. As an alternative to factor analysis for parsimoniously describing the intercorrelations among a set of variables, cluster analysis is a method whereby tests are discretely grouped, or clustered, in terms of their intercorrelations. Tests are usually clustered in such a way that tests within a cluster correlate more highly with one another than do tests between clusters. The interested reader is referred to Harman (1967) for a sophisticated treatment of factor analysis and to Tryon (1966) for the principles underlying cluster analytic techniques.

Each of the multivariate individual difference models to be discussed in this chapter employs a variant of either a factor analytic or a cluster analytic technique. However, instead of factoring tests or variables that have been correlated across subjects, the individual difference models factor, or cluster, *persons* whose judgment responses are similar (i.e., highly intercorrelated). This section briefly reviews some of the individual difference models employing factor analysis, and describes the various interpretations placed on the resulting subject factors. Particular attention will be paid to Tucker's (Tucker & Messick, 1963; Tucker, 1966a) approach to individual differences due to the popularity in the literature this approach has enjoyed.

Tucker's model. A unique approach to the problem of systematically isolating individual differences in human judgment without a concomitant loss of generalizability is provided by the multivariate models of Tucker and his associates (Tucker, 1960, 1964, 1966a, 1966b, 1966c, 1968, 1972; Tucker & Messick, 1963). By specifying a procedure that allows for the emergence of *types* of judges, this approach provides considerably more parsimony than is the case when each judge is treated individually. The results (judgmental models for different types of judges) can be generalized to similar samples of judges. It would not be expected that an "identical twin" of any single judge would emerge in a new sample of judges but only that the model describing similar types of judges would be generalizable. Specifically, Tucker's models involve, first, a factor analysis of judges. Although a standard factor analysis is ordinarily performed on a matrix of intercorrelations, Tucker's models involve factoring the sums of squares and cross-products among subjects. A Pearson correlation is simply the mean of a sum of cross-products among standard scores; for the Tucker model neither the means nor variances are removed from the raw scores. Thus, an element in the intersubject cross-product matrix is simply the sum of cross products between the *raw scores* of two subjects. The complete intersubject cross-product matrix is factored and the resultant subject factors are then positioned in such a way as to represent meaningful "idealized" or conceptual individuals (Cliff, 1968b), where an idealized individual is represented by a vector (factor) in the subjects' factor space. The judgment models, or regression of judgments on cues, are obtained for the idealized individuals rather than for each judge individually. This conceptualization of judgment types expands Brunswik's Lens Model to include types of judges, rather than a single judge. The same relationships between cues, criterion, and judgments would hold except in this case the judgments of an idealized individual would be treated as the basic data, instead of the judgments of a single judge or the average judge.

It should be noted that when a factor analytic model for subjects is applied and there emerges only one subject factor, it would be difficult to argue the case for individual differences. A single subject factor would indicate that the average judgment is a reasonable approximation to the judgments of any of the individual judges. On the other hand, should the number of subject factors approximate the number of subjects in the sample, it would be difficult to argue for "types" of judges. In that case, the parsimony usually inherent in a factor analytic model would be missing. Empirically, factorial studies of individual differences in human judgment generally indicate more than one subject factor, with the number of meaningful factors being considerably less than the number of subjects in the sample (e.g., Messick & Kogan, 1966; Walters & Jackson, 1966; Wiggins, 1966; Wiggins & Fishbein, 1969; Wiggins, Hoffman, & Taber, 1969).

JAN and its extensions. Although a number of studies based on Tucker's conceptualization of individual differences have appeared in the psychophysical and social perception literature (e.g., Cliff, 1968a; Helm & Tucker, 1962; Jackson & Messick, 1963), comparatively few studies of this sort have been carried out *explicitly* in the context of cue-utilization within the framework of Brunswik's Lens Model. The *JAN* technique

(Christal, 1963; Naylor & Wherry, 1965) and its extensions, *PROF* (Wherry & Naylor, 1966) and *COPAN* (Maguire & Glass, 1968), attempt to isolate types of judges in terms of the weights applied to different cues. Similar in conception to Tucker's models, *PROF* and *COPAN* involve an obverse factor analysis among subjects, *not* with respect to the original judgments but rather in terms of the correlations between each of the cues and the subjects' judgments. The basic data matrix of intersubject correlations, or cross-products, is factored. Judges are thus typed or classified into groups on the basis of their similarity of cue-weighting or rating policy. Although these techniques tend to isolate individual judgmental differences only with respect to cue-weights, data from the *JAN* technique (Naylor & Wherry, 1965) nevertheless suggested considerable variability among individual judges. From an initial sample of 50 subjects judging "Air Force worth" based on 23 traits, *JAN* indicated 25 judge types who differed from one another in their rating policies.

The above types of multivariate models can be said to represent a compromise between a strictly nomothetic (group) and a purely idiographic (individual) analysis of judgmental responses. The advantages of such approaches are: (1) the detection of individual differences in judgmental styles, (2) the parsimonious description of such individual differences, and (3) the possibility of generalizing differences in judgmental styles to other samples of judges and stimuli.

Stimulus Multidimensionality

Although the majority of studies of cue-utilization have employed a unidimensional rating scale for the response class, several writers have emphasized the fruitfulness of studying the judgment process in terms of the judge's perception of the *dimensionality* of the stimuli (Jackson, 1969; Tucker & Messick, 1963; Wiggins & Hoffman, 1968a). Jackson (1969) presents a strong case for multidimensional scaling techniques in the area of social perception:

> These simple [unidimensional] methods of an earlier age are unequal to the task of representing complex areas such as the perception of personality, because they impose unrealistic simplicity upon a complex domain. Furthermore, whereas traditional unidimensional scaling methods require the investigator to be in a position to specify and communicate the relevant dimensions to his judges, modern multivariate methods of scaling do not [p. 228].

Most studies of cue-utilization assume that both the experimenter and the subject know and agree upon the relevant stimulus dimensions.

Although this assumption *may* hold for physical stimuli, for most types of social stimuli the underlying dimensions are unknown. Multidimensional scaling models that utilize a response class, such as similarity or difference, allow, but do not force, the perceived relevant stimulus dimensions to emerge, constrained only by the set of stimuli sampled. Although much recent work has been concerned with the development of mathematical models for multidimensional scaling (Coombs, 1958; Guttman, 1967; Hays & Bennett, 1961; Kruskal, 1964; Messick & Abelson, 1956; Shepard, 1962a, 1962b; Torgerson, 1952, 1958), few explicit applications of these types of models are found in the cue-utilization literature. The rationale for a multidimensional approach to judgmental stimuli (e.g., profiles) stems from research in three major areas: (1) studies of the effect of stimulus dimensionality on information transmission, (2) studies of the effect of cue-inconsistency on rater policy, and (3) investigations of the predictability of unidimensional responses from the perceived multidimensional stimulus configurations.

Stimulus dimensionality and information transmission. In the area of clinical judgment, a number of studies have been concerned with the effect of the stimulus dimensionality on such judgmental variables as amount of information transmitted. Miller & Bieri (1963) gave experienced clinicians one of three sets of information regarding a group of clients: their case histories, current behavior, and interview excerpts. Each case was judged on rating scales for object-relations, defenses, and clinical diagnosis. The different types of input information were then combined to yield what the authors interpreted as more "multidimensional" stimuli (Tripodi & Bieri, 1964). It was found that the resulting increase in stimulus complexity did not lead to an increase in the judge's channel capacity for processing information, that is, in his ability to discriminate stimuli on the criterion dimension. These results contrast with those generally found with physical stimuli (Engen & Pfaffmann, 1960; Eriksen & Hake, 1955; Klemmer & Frick, 1953; Pollack, 1953). In fact, under certain circumstances, information transmission decreased with an increase in stimulus complexity (Bieri et al., 1966).

Since in these studies each of the judgmental responses was obtained on a unidimensional response scale it was not possible to assess the judge's *perceived* stimulus dimensionality. Although it may be the case that simply adding more pieces of clinical information leads to increased stimulus dimensionality, this assumption should be investigated by multidimensional psychophysical methods. Unlike the scaling of physical stimuli for which the dimensionality can be "built in," the dimensionality of social and clinical stimuli can only be determined by multidimensional scaling methods (Jackson, 1969).

Cue-discrepancy and cue-weighting. A useful application of multi-dimensional scaling methods in the study of cue-utilization is found in studies of judgmental strategy as a function of cue-discrepancy. These investigations raise the question of whether judgmental strategies will be different when cues are discrepant as compared to situations in which cues are not discrepant. Such studies generally treat two numerical cues as discrepant if they differ by some absolute amount (e.g., Slovic, 1966). An interesting case of cue-discrepancy occurs when the discrepancy generates a certain amount of conflict for the subject. Such would be the case only if the subject presumed the two cues to be related positively and perceived differences between them as discrepant. It is here suggested that multidimensional scaling methods be employed initially to determine the perceived relationships between cues before the cue values are experimentally manipulated. How a judge reacts to inconsistent or discrepant cue information would be expected to be a function of how he initially perceived the cue interrelationships. In this context, the multidimensional scaling methods can be thought of as an indirect technique for determining the subjective cue interrelationships for a given set of profiles.

Prediction of unidimensional from multidimensional judgments.
Perhaps the most compelling empirical evidence for the importance of perceived stimulus dimensionality comes from the pioneering work of Cliff and his associates (Cliff, 1965, 1966; Cliff, Pennell, & Young, 1966; Cliff & Young, 1968). Cliff has argued that unidimensional judgments for a given set of stimuli are mediated by the judge's subjective multidimensional configuration of these stimuli. Thus, various unidimensional judgments derive directly from the judge's internalized configuration or multidimensional "map" of the stimuli. Psychometrically, this means that a significant multiple correlation would obtain between the stimulus dimensions uncovered from the multidimensional scaling (independent variables) and the scale values of the stimuli on a unidimensional scale (dependent variable). This notion has received empirical support from a series of studies conducted by Cliff and his colleagues. In a study of facial expressions it was possible to locate a vector of *unidimensional* judgments of emotional intensity in the multidimensional space generated by similarity judgments among facial expressions (Cliff & Young, 1968). Cliff (1968a) also found that subjects' unidimensional responses to trait adjectives under both "self-description" and "fake good" instructions were mediated by the multidimensional space generated from similarity judgments between pairs of adjectives. Two studies (Cliff & Young, 1968; Rigney & DeBow, 1967) found that unidimensional judgments of "air raid threat" based on such cues as range, course, etc., were predictable from (i.e., correlated with) the first dimension uncovered from a multidimensional scaling analysis of the same air raids. On the basis of these studies,

Cliff and Young (1968) have argued that one can interpret judgments in terms of a "subjective organization of the objective stimuli which can itself be recovered by means of multidimensional scaling (p. 282)."

Studies of political judgment (e.g., Warr, Schroder, & Blackman, 1969) have indicated a close relationship between the evaluation of political figures (unidimensional judgment) and the perceived dimensionality among political figures (multidimensional judgment). This relationship was, in turn, mediated by the subjects' political party affiliation. Thus, the correlation between the first dimension from the multidimensional task and the evaluative factor scores for the stimuli was .55 for the left wing group whereas it was .89 for the right wing group. Shikiar (1970) found that 80 percent of the variance of preference for political figures was predictable on the basis of the multidimensional configuration of these political figures. This type of preference-similarity relationship also was supported in a study of the judgments of college admissions officers based on hypothetical profiles of admission candidates (Klahr, 1969). In an unpublished study of cue-utilization, the present author found a relationship between unidimensional judgments of intelligence for nine-cue profiles and the corresponding multidimensional judgments of a selected set of these profiles.

Taken together the above studies suggest the provocative possibility of predicting unidimensional judgments on the basis of the judge's perceived dimensionality of the stimulus pool. As Cliff and Young (1968) note, ". . . the various decisions, evaluations, and judgments which an individual makes concerning the members of a collection of stimuli are all relatable to an organization or underlying structure for the collection [p. 270]." This is not to say that one type of judgment is more basic than the other nor that any type of unidimensional judgment is predictable from a multidimensional stimulus configuration. Indeed, in Shikiar's study of political figures, although unidimensional evaluative ratings of political figures were predictable from the perceived similarity among political figures, this was *not* the case for unidimensional potency and activity ratings. One would expect certain "relevant" unidimensional judgments to be related to the perceived multidimensional stimulus space although the precise nature of "relevance" cannot yet be specified.

Although most studies of cue-utilization have tended to employ only unidimensional rating procedures, Cliff's theory, if viable, suggests that the dynamics of judgment tend to be a function of the subject's internalized stimulus map or implicit theory of the stimuli. Further, it is presumed that the judges' internal configurations, or implicit theories of cue-interrelationships, would also be subject to systematic individual differences (Wiggins & Hoffman, 1968a). This notion, along with the earlier points made with reference to individual differences, argues for the simultaneous study of both stimulus and subject dimensionality in judgmental studies.

The General Individual Differences Model

The remainder of this chapter is directed primarily to the application of Tucker's multivariate models (Tucker, 1964, 1966a, 1972; Tucker & Messick, 1963) in the area of cue-utilization. Such models allow for the uncovering of multiple orderings with respect to both stimuli and judges. Thus, individual differences can be studied in terms of Tucker's "idealized individual" notion while allowing for the possibility of more than one stimulus dimension for a given idealized judge.

A unidimensional judgment will be defined as one for which a response dimension attribute is presented to the subject (e.g., judgment of amount of extraversion). A multidimensional judgment is one in which, usually, no attribute is supplied to the subject; the response class must involve a similarity or difference measure that can be mapped into Euclidian distance. (Non-Euclidian distance models are beyond the scope of this chapter.) However, a task for which a similarity judgment is made with respect to an attribute will also be termed multidimensional; for example, subjects might be asked to judge the similarity between profiles with respect to extraversion. Such a task should uncover the relevant dimensions of extraversion. Because a similarity judgment was made the task is considered multidimensional. It is noted that the attributes defining the dimensions presumed to underly the stimuli are not specified to the subject but are allowed to emerge. The reader is referred to Torgerson (1958) and Green and Carmone (1970) for a comprehensive treatment of multidimensional scaling.

The individual difference models presented here assume: (1) For unidimensional judgments, subjects will differ in the unidimensional scale values assigned to the stimuli. Thus, different orderings of the stimuli will hold for different types of judges. In studies of cue-utilization this is tantamount to saying that differential cue-weightings should hold for different judge types. (2) For a multidimensional task, individuals will differ in both the number and kinds of perceived stimulus dimensions. Tucker's general model of individual differences will be reviewed briefly for both unidimensional and multidimensional judgments. A recent individual differences model for multidimensional scaling (Carroll & Chang, 1970) will be discussed. Then illustrative research examples will be presented under the following headings: (1) unidimensional judgments, (2) multidimensional judgments, and (3) multimode data matrices.

Case I. Unidimensional Judgments

The basic experimental paradigm for this case is as follows: a number *(n)* of judges *(j)* make a series of responses (e.g., diagnostic judgments) on a unidimensional scale for a set of N profiles. Each profile consists of a quantified set of k cues. Thus, the basic data matrix, $_nX_N$, is a subject by profile matrix whose elements are the responses given to each profile by each judge.

The analysis begins by obtaining sums of squares and cross-products among subjects. Thus one calculates $_nX_{NN}X'_n$. Although an individual difference analysis can be performed on intersubject correlation matrices or on intersubject matrices consisting of various interaction terms (e.g., Gollob, 1968), the present discussion will be based on the use of inter-subject sums of squares and cross-products, as originally proposed and later defended by Tucker (1968). It is assumed that the original response scale is similar for all subjects and has a meaningful zero point, comparable across subjects. An example of such a response scale would be a rating of intelligence on a seven-place scale ranging from extremely unintelligent (-3) through neutral (0) to extremely intelligent ($+3$). The zero point is employed to rate profiles that are judged as neither intelligent nor unintelligent.

The second step of the analysis involves a principal axis factor analysis (Harman, 1967) of the sums of squares and cross-products among subjects. That is, factors are extracted from the basic data matrix post-multiplied by its transpose with sums of squares among subjects in the diagonals. The number of "meaningful" factors is chosen on the basis of some criteria for factor "significance" (Harman, 1967; Horn, 1965; Linn, 1968; Tucker, 1966b). The resultant subject factor matrix, $_nF_r$, yields the projections of the n judges on the r significant unrotated subject factors.

In order to obtain the corresponding projections of the profiles (stimuli) on the subject factors, the subject factor matrix is premultiplied by the transpose of the basic data matrix and postmultiplied by the inverse of the diagonalized eigenvalue matrix. That is

$$_NY_r = {_NX'_n} {_nF_r} {_r(\Gamma)_r}^{-1}$$

where $Y =$ stimulus projections on the r subject factors
   $X' =$ transpose of the raw data matrix
   $F =$ subject projections on the r subject factors
   $\Gamma =$ eigenvalues corresponding to the first r subject factors.

If the subject factor matrix is rotated via a transformation matrix, T, then the matrix of stimulus projections on the subject factors is similarly rotated by T^{-1}. Thus, if $FT = F^*$, then $YT^{-1} = Y^*$. It is important to bear in mind the distinction between these two rotated factor matrices. The rotated *subject* factors of the F^* matrix are termed "idealized" or conceptual individuals. The Y^* matrix represents the projections of the *stimuli* on the rotated subject factors, which are termed "idealized" ratings.

These ratings are proportional to those that would be given by a real individual in the same position in the factor space as the idealized individual.

Properties of idealized individuals. An idealized individual is best conceptualized as a *meaningfully* rotated subject factor (Cliff, 1968b). The positioning of subject factors is directly analogous to factor rotation in an ordinary factor analysis. An idealized individual would represent judges only to the extent that the subject factors were marked by, or graphically passed through, or near, real subjects. To the extent that simple structure (Thurstone, 1940) was exhibited by the data, an idealized individual could be conceptualized as a continuous representation of a subgroup of response-homogeneous judges.

Of course it would be possible to position a subject factor in such a manner that it was not located near any of the real subjects; as such, the factor would represent a hypothetical, or imaginary, subject. Although it also would be possible to locate all subject factors such that each one was marked only by a single judge, such a procedure would be no more parsimonious than idiographic treatment. Compared to a single judge, however, a subject factor that was marked primarily by a single judge would have some additional reliability in that all of the judges in the sample would have projections, albeit small, on that subject factor.

Although the original Tucker-Messick model specified a particular factor-analytic approach for isolating idealized individuals, any number of cluster-analytic methods could be applied to detect "types" of judges. Provided the number of subject factors (or clusters) was greater than one, the basic unit for further analysis would be the judgments given either by an idealized individual or by a discrete cluster of judges. If an idealized individual is conceptualized as a subject factor, the idealized ratings, or judgments given by an idealized individual, represent the basic unit of analysis. When types of judges have been isolated by discrete cluster-analytic solutions, the mean judgment of each of the subgroups of judges would represent the basic responses. If only one subject or cluster emerged, the average judgment, as representative of the individuals in the sample, would constitute the basic data for analysis.

Properties of idealized ratings. For each idealized individual (i.e., subject factor), there is a corresponding set of idealized ratings. These idealized ratings are simply the projections of the stimuli on the subject factors obtained by matrix multiplication, as already described. The projections of the stimuli (profiles) on a given subject factor represent unidimensional ratings of the profiles that are proportional to those ratings given by a judge (or judges) in the same spatial location as the subject factor. It is noted that the projections of the stimuli on the first, *unrotated* subject factor have been shown to be highly correlated with the group average judgments of the stimuli (Tucker & Messick, 1963). Should it be the case that only one subject factor emerged as significant, the mean judgments for the group of judges can be taken as representative of all the judges in the sample; or *alternatively,* the projections of the stimuli on the first unrotated subject factor can be interpreted as proportional to "average" ratings.

When the number of subject factors is greater than one, there is a set of idealized ratings that corresponds to each idealized individual. Within the context of Brunswik's Lens Model, these idealized ratings are treated in *exactly* the same manner as a set of real ratings by a given judge. For example, the linear model of an idealized individual is obtained by regressing the idealized ratings onto the cue values of a set of profiles. In the present context, instead of modeling each of the judges in the sample individually, the regression model is applied to the "judgments" of each of the idealized individuals. To the extent that the cue-values represent a completely crossed factorial design, it is also possible to treat the idealized ratings in the analysis-of-variance design suggested by Hoffman, Slovic, and Rorer (1968) and Anderson (1969). If a significant interaction emerges between cues (factors in the analysis of variance), one could argue for configurality in cue usage for a given idealized individual. Thus, it is possible to capture the judgment policies of idealized individuals in terms of their weighting schemes for the cues. It is also possible to detect and isolate possible configurality of cue-usage (Hoffman, 1968). The important point to note is that whatever model of cue-utilization is applied to a set of judgments given by a single judge, that model can equally well be applied to the idealized individuals' judgments. In this manner individual differences can be isolated while preserving both parsimony and generalizability.

Case II. Multidimensional Judgments

The basic concept of multidimensional scaling is that of psychological distance or similarity between stimuli. For example, in studies of cue-utilization the subject might be presented with all possible pairs of profiles and asked to judge the distance, or the similarity, between each pair of profiles. The pair-comparison format is but one of a number of experimental techniques for obtaining estimates of interstimulus distances (Torgerson, 1958). The basic assumption is that the more dissimilar a pair of profiles is judged to be, the more distant it is, and, conversely, the more similar, the less distant. The basic multidimensional scaling model involves the conversion of these judged differences or similarities to actual Euclidean distances, if possible. An attempt is then made to determine the smallest number of *dimensions* necessary to reproduce the Euclidean distances.

In practice, the general multidimensional scaling model is applied to empirical estimates of psychological distances between all pairs of stimuli. These distances are first assembled into an interstimulus relative distance matrix. An additive constant is then applied to each of these relative distances to convert them to absolute distances (i.e., distances having an absolute origin). The characteristic roots and vectors are obtained from the scalar products of these distances (with origin located at the centroid) and the number of "large" roots are interpreted as corresponding to the minimum number of dimensions necessary to reproduce the original Euclidean interstimulus distances. The final matrix consists of the projections of each of the stimuli on the "significant" dimensions. Recently, several multidimensional scaling models have been developed (Guttman, 1967; Kruskal, 1964; Shepard, 1962a) that make fewer assumptions about the metric involved in the original judgments. However, all of these models initially require some similarity or distance estimate among stimuli. Although distance estimates can be obtained directly from experimental subects, the distances may be obtained by nonreactive procedures as well. One such ingenious distance measure was employed in the multidimensional scaling of psychological journals (Coombs, 1964, pp. 463–480; Jakobovits & Osgood, 1967; Xhignesse & Osgood, 1967). The assumption made was that the more references one journal had to another, the *closer* the two journals. Here, number of references was interpreted as relative distance.

An example using physical stimuli with known dimensionality such as colors easily distinguishes a unidimensional scaling task from a multidimensional one. When subjects are asked to judge a single color dimension, such as hue or brightness, the task is a unidimensional one. It is noted that in these unidimensional judgment tasks the experimenter supplies the attribute (e.g., hue). However, when subjects are asked to judge the similarity, or difference between pairs of color chips, the task becomes a multidimensional one. When Munsell color chips are selected to vary, physically, with respect to both hue and brightness, two psychological dimensions, hue and brightness, are reproduced independently of the experimental method for obtaining the distance estimates (Messick, 1956; Shepard, 1958; Torgerson, 1952). In obtaining the interstimulus distances, the experimenter usually does not supply an attribute or construct, but merely obtains from the subject some type of distance estimate between pairs of stimuli. The dimensions that emerge from the multidimensional scaling of these relative distances indicate the important attributes, or dimensions, on which the judged distances were based. As Jackson (1969) has argued, although the multidimensional scaling of physical stimuli can help validate the scaling models, the results of these studies add little to our knowledge of physical stimuli, the dimensionality of which is well known. However, ". . . when we move into the domain of personality and social processes, we leave the sanctuary of well-chartered waters. Here there are few criteria for evaluating the goodness of fit of our results against an external standard. But it is precisely when we know little about the nature of the important underlying dimensions that it is hazardous to attempt to specify these to subjects [p. 231]."

The majority of multidimensional scaling studies employing non-physical stimuli have generally scaled for the average subject. Thus, a scaling procedure such as the method of equal intervals or the method of successive intervals (Torgerson, 1958) is applied to the average judgments, and an "average" interstimulus relative distance matrix is obtained. The application of standard multidimensional scaling techniques to this inter-stimulus distance matrix yields a final factor matrix consisting of the projections of the stimuli on the significant factors. The important dimensions underlying the stimuli are thus uncovered for the "average" judge or subject.

Multidimensional scaling methods may easily be extended to incorporate the notion of individual differences as originally outlined by Tucker and Messick (1963). The Tucker and Messick model is applied to inter-stimulus distance estimates that have been obtained from each subject by some experimental method. The basic data matrix, then, consists of all possible *pairs* of stimuli $[N(N-1)/2]$ by subjects, the elements of the matrix representing psychological distances. As outlined previously, sums of squares and cross-products among subjects are factored and the factors corresponding to the "large" eigenvalues are retained and rotated to represent meaningful idealized individuals. Next, the projections of the *pairs* of stimuli on the subject factors are calculated. These interstimulus pair projections are interpreted as proportional to distance judgments corresponding to each of the idealized individuals. As before, two basic matrices are considered: (1) the projections of the *subjects* on the rotated subject factors, called idealized individuals, and (2) the projections of the *stimulus-pairs* on the rotated subject factors, called idealized distance ratings. The methods for obtaining these two matrices were outlined under the section on unidimensional judgments. The only difference here is that for the multidimensional case, the stimulus projections consist of each pair of stimuli. These projections are interpreted as proportional *distance* estimates.

For each idealized individual (subject factor), there is a corresponding set of interstimulus factor projections, or proportional distances. This vector of $[N(N-1)/2]$ interstimulus factor projections is assembled into an $N \times N$ interstimulus "distance" matrix and standard multidimensional procedures are applied to the matrix. The projections of the N stimuli are obtained on the "significant" dimensions for each idealized individual. These dimensions may, of course, be rotated if desired. The Tucker-Messick model thus allows for the possibility of systematic individual differences in the perception of both the number and type of stimulus dimensions. For example, in a multidimensional scaling study of color chips, Helm and Tucker (1962) used a Tucker-Messick analysis and isolated idealized individuals who differed in their color perceptions, both from one another and from the average judge. These idealized individuals were further distinguished from one another on the basis of color blindness versus normal color vision.

In studies of cue-utilization, the stimuli would consist of N profiles, each of which contained k cues. A variety of experimental procedures exist for obtaining psychological distance estimates among the profiles; perhaps the simplest procedure is to ask subjects directly to rate the difference (or similarity) between the pairs of persons or objects represented by the profiles. "No difference" or "exactly alike" would represent the zero point. Although, ideally, all possible pairs of stimuli would be judged, an incomplete pair-comparison design may be utilized when subject time is limited (Bock & Jones, 1968).

The final results of the Tucker-Messick analysis yield the projections of the N stimuli on the "significant" dimensions for each idealized individual. In order to interpret these final factor matrices, it is necessary to determine the common elements underlying those profiles that mark the same factor. A factor is named on the basis of those stimuli (profiles) that have high projections on it. Since each stimulus itself consists of more than one cue, it is sometimes difficult for the investigator to determine the similar properties of profiles marking a given factor.

One possible means of factor identification involves correlating the factor projections of the profiles with each of the cue-values to determine those cues which vary as a function of the profile projections. A sophisticated version of this method of factor naming might involve canonical correlations between the factors (independent variables) and the cue-values (dependent variables) obtained across all profiles. If the number of profiles is not large enough to permit canonical correlations, multiple correlations might be obtained between the cue-values (independent variables) and each of the factors (dependent variables). When the multiple correlations are significant, the corresponding regression weights indicate those cues perceived as important for the profiles defining a given factor. To the extent that subjects might be judging distance among profiles in terms of complex relationships among cues, it would be possible to correlate cue-combinations (e.g., the difference or product between two cues) with the stimulus factor.

A recent model for individual differences in multidimensional scaling (Carroll & Chang, 1970) assumes that individuals differentially weight the several dimensions of a *common* psychological space. This model uncovers the psychological dimensions underlying the stimuli; it is assumed that these perceived dimensions are the *same* for each individual but that individual differences may occur in the weighting (importance) of each of the stimulus dimensions. Since these weights may vary between zero and one it is possible that an individual may not weight one or more dimensions. This model differs primarily from that of Tucker in that: (1) the perceived stimulus dimensions are assumed to be common to all individuals, and (2) each individual receives a set of weights indicating the relative importance he places on the various dimensions. It is noted that unless there is a means for clustering individuals with respect to their dimensional weightings, subjects must still be treated idiographically. Applying this model to the perception of fellow psychological laboratory workers, Jones and Young (1970) found that: (1) three dimensions (status, professional interests, and political persuasion) described the stimulus person configurations; (2) these three dimensions were differentially weighted by faculty versus students; and (3) these differential weighting schemes predicted independently measured behavioral indexes of sociometric choice. It should be noted that Tucker's most recent multidimensional scaling model (1970) isolates individual differences for the weighting of the perceived stimulus dimensions as well as for the correlations between these stimulus dimensions. Under certain restrictive assumptions this model subsumes the Carroll-Chang model. Although the Carroll-Chang model appears extremely promising for the study of individual differences, it applies primarily to multidimensional judgments.

As described above, the Tucker-Messick procedure is equally applicable to either a unidimensional judgment situation or a multidimensional one. In both cases the assumption of individual differences is tested and the resultant differences in judgmental styles can be specified. Although a number of studies attest to the usefulness of Tucker's models of individual differences (Helm & Tucker, 1962; Messick & Kogan, 1966; Posavac, 1971; Walters & Jackson, 1966; Wiggins, 1966; Wiggins & Fishbein, 1969), few studies have been conducted explicitly in the context of cue-utilization. The following sections describe some empirical research employing multivariate models for the detection and isolation of individual differences in cue-utilization. It is hoped that the usefulness of the approach will be revealed in the description of these empirical applications.

Empirical Studies of Individual Differences in Cue-utilization

Unidimensional Judgments

Perhaps the most widely cited data for studies of cue-utilization in clinical judgment are those initially collected by Meehl (1959) and subsequently analyzed in a number of studies (Goldberg, 1965, 1968, 1969, 1970; Wiggins & Hoffman, 1968b). These data involve the diagnosis of psychosis versus neurosis by 29 clinicians for 861 MMPI profiles gathered from seven hospitals and clinics around the country. The MMPI profiles consisted of the eight clinical scales (excluding Mf) and the three validity scales. Thirteen of the subjects were Ph.D. clinical psychologists (staff) and the remaining 16 subjects were predoctoral trainees at the University of Minnesota. These 29 judges were given seven samples of MMPI profiles, one sample at a time, and were asked to sort each group of profiles on an 11-step forced-normal distribution ranging from most (likely) neurotic to most (likely) psychotic. The only information given the clinicians was that the samples represented males under psychiatric care who were diagnosed as psychotic or neurotic. In terms of the actual hospital diagnosis, the percentage of psychotics in each sample ranged from 37 percent to 64 percent, with a median of 51 percent over all 861 profiles.

Although not explicitly using Tucker's individual differences model, one study utilized the Meehl data in an attempt to isolate individual differences in the judgments of the 29 clinicians. Horn and Stewart (1968) factor analyzed the judgments of the 29 clinical judges, plus the actual criterion diagnosis, across the 861 MMPI profiles. Three subject factors were retained and a varimax rotation of these factors indicated that the first factor was correlated with the criterion, suggesting a "validity" component of judgment. No interpretations of the remaining two factors were made. Except for the variable "amount of clinical training" (which was unrelated to any of the subject factors) Horn and Stewart had no additional variables that would serve to identify their subject factors. The varimax rotation performed on the subject factors in no way guaranteed that the factors represented meaningful idealized individuals; that is, passed through or near any of the 29 clinical judges.

In light of the above considerations, the present author (Wiggins, 1971) reanalyzed the original data following the Tucker-Messick rationale. It was hypothesized, on the basis of the Horn and Stewart analysis, that individual differences in judgmental viewpoints would emerge. It was further predicted that such differences would be manifested in significant judgmental correlates of the idealized subject types, provided these idealized individuals represented real judges in the subjects' factor space. Psychometrically, these hypotheses can be restated: (1) more than one subject factor would be necessary to account for the sums of squares and cross-products among clinicians; (2) these factors could be rotated in such a way as to represent meaningful idealized individuals (i.e., subgroups of response-homogeneous judges or a single real judge); and (3) these idealized individuals should differ on available judgmental and personological measures. It was further expected that if different idealized individuals emerged they would exhibit different judgmental models in the sense of differential cue-utilization.

From the extensive research on these data, a variety of judgmental variables were available. These variables, taken primarily from Goldberg (1970), were obtained separately for each of the 29 clinical judges and were based on analyses using the total group of 861 MMPI profiles. Goldberg (1970) described these variables as follows:

1. *Validity coefficient of the judge.* The correlation between the judge's predictions and the actual criterion values.
2. *Linear predictability of the judge.* The multiple correlation between the 11 MMPI scale scores and the judge's predictions.
3. *Reliability of the judge.* The correlation between a judge's responses to 100 pairs of empirically matched profiles.
4. *Validity of the judge's linear model.* The correlation between the predicted judgments, based on the judge's linear regression model, and the actual criterion values.
5. *Linear component of judgmental accuracy.* The correlation between the predicted values from the judge's linear regression model and the predicted values for the linear model relating MMPI scale scores to the criterion. This variable is perfectly correlated with the validity of the judge's model (4) and provides an alternative interpretation of that measure.
6. *Nonlinear component of judgmental accuracy.* The correlation between residual values of the criterion and the residuals of the judge's predictions after the linear components are removed.
7. *Incremental validity of model over judge.* The arithmetic difference between the validity of the judge's model and the actual validity of the judge (4 − 1).
8. *Relationship to composite judge.* The correlation between the clinician's judgments and those of the "composite" judge (the average of all of the 29 judgments for each profile).

In addition, the categorical variables of sex and staff versus trainee were employed. All of these variables were utilized in the analysis in an attempt to relate individual differences in clinical judgments derived from the Tucker-Messick procedure to independently measured judgmental and personological subject variables.

The method of analysis involved, first, a principal components analysis of sums of squares and cross-products among the 29 judges across the 861 MMPI profiles. Three factors were retained as meaningful by an examination of the successive distribution of eigenvalues, as well as by Tucker's (1966b) mean square ratio test for factor significance. Each of the three unrotated subject factors was correlated with all of the judgmental variables. The first factor was significantly correlated with linear predictability, reliability, and the correlation of the judge with the composite judge. Sex, amount of training, and the nonlinear component of accuracy were not related to any of the subject factors.

A graphic plot of the second and third unrotated principal components revealed that Component II, a bipolar factor, discriminated the most valid judges from the least valid judges, and that Component III was marked by a single, idiosyncratic judge. Consequently, the three principal components were rotated in such a way that one factor passed through the most valid judge, one factor passed through the least valid judge, and one factor passed through the idiosyncratic judge. The projections of all of the remaining judges on these three rotated factors were obtained. The factor rotation was performed in such a way that each of the three marker judges had a loading of unity on their corresponding rotated factor and zero loadings on the other two factors. Each of these rotated factors provided a representation of a meaningful "idealized individual"; that is, the factors were relatively unipolar with respect to all of the judges, and they were marked by three real judges (Wiggins, 1971).

The correlations of the three idealized individuals (rotated subject factors) and each of the judgmental variables were obtained. The first idealized individual was represented by valid judges, that is, the correlation between the subjects' factor loadings and their validity coefficients was .93. The linear models for these judges were more valid than the judges themselves. The second idealized individual was not valid ($r = -.58$), but tended to be linearly predictable. Further, this idealized individual was negatively related to the validity of the judges' models; that is, the judges' models tended to fare worse than the judges themselves. The third idealized individual was negatively related to reliability. This type of individual tended to have an invalid model and was negatively correlated with the composite judge. Of interest was the fact that the "valid" idealized individual tended to have a judgment model that fared better in predicting the criterion than the valid judges themselves, while the "invalid" idealized individual represented judges whose models fared even worse than their own invalid judgments.

In order to discriminate among these three idealized individuals in terms of their judgment models, the linear regression models relating input cues to judgments were obtained for the three judges marking the three idealized individuals. These judgment models were compared to the optimal weights derived from regressing the actual criterion onto the cues (Goldberg, 1965). Marker Judge I, defining the first, valid, idealized individual, correctly weighted four out of the five most valid scales. In addition, he tended to overweight slightly two less valid scales. Marker Judge II, the least valid judge, correctly weighted two clinical scales but tended to underweight three valid scales while overweighting four less valid scales. The third marker judge, an invalid and unreliable judge, correctly weighted one valid scale but positively weighted a negatively valid scale.

In identifying the linear models for these idealized individuals, only the models of the three marker judges were obtained. Thus, no attempt was made to determine the "idealized" ratings corresponding to the idealized individuals, thereby limiting the generalizability of the study. However, Posavac (1969) has indicated the similarity of results between "marker" judges and the corresponding idealized individual. It was predicted, on the basis of these preliminary results, that at least three major judgmental viewpoints should distinguish different viewpoints of clinical judgments of the MMPI. Further, these viewpoints should be related to the judge's validity, predictability, and reliability and to the validity of the judge's model.

In order to test this individual differences hypothesis in another judgmental task, Kohen (1971) asked 98 psychology graduate students to predict first year grade point averages for 110 graduate student profiles, 20 of which were repeated. These profiles represented real graduate students in psychology at the University of Illinois. The profiles consisted of the following ten cues: (1) Graduate Record Examination (GRE)—Verbal, (2) GRE—Quantitative, (3) GRE—Advanced test, (4) undergraduate grade point average (GPA), (5) "selectivity" of undergraduate school (Astin, 1956), (6) mean peer rating received as a first year student (Wiggins, Blackburn, & Hackman, 1969) on need achievement, (7) mean peer rating on extraversion, (8) mean peer rating on anxiety, (9) self-rating on conscientiousness, and (10) sex of student. Each of these cues was carefully explained to the subjects and appropriate anchor points were given. The subjects' task was to choose a number from 3.00 (C) to 5.00 (A), in steps of .2, which best indicated each student's first year grade point average.

For each subject, the judgmental variables were: (1) validity of judge, (2) linear predictability of judge, (3) validity of judge's model, and (4) incremental validity of judge's model over judge. The reliabilities for each judge were obtained by a test-retest correlation between the 20 repeated profiles. In addition to these judgmental variables, a variety of biographical, personological, intellectual, and attitudinal variables were available describing each judge. It was predicted that individual differences in this judgment task would be reflected in differential correlations with both the judgmental and the background variables.

The basic data matrix consisted of the 110 grade-point-average judgments by the 98 judges. Since the judgment scale did not have an absolute origin, the grand mean was subtracted from each of the individual's judgments. Sums of squares and cross-products among subjects' deviation scores were factored and five subject factors were retained as significant. The subjects' projections on each of the five unrotated factors were correlated with the judgmental variables as well as with all of the additional background variables. Finally, the projections of all of the profiles were obtained for each subject factor (idealized ratings), and the multiple regressions of the idealized ratings on the ten cues were calculated to yield the linear judgment model corresponding to each of the subject factors.

Before describing the five subject types, it is of interest to consider the actual validities of the cues as well as the validities of the judges. The regression of the actual first year grade point averages onto the ten cues yielded a multiple correlation of .69 ($p < .001$). The highest regression weights were obtained for GRE—advanced, undergraduate grade point average, selectivity, and peer rating of need achievement. These validities are in accord with other studies of grade-point-average predictions in graduate school (Wiggins, Blackburn, & Hackman, 1969). The present group of judges was fairly accurate in the predictions of first year grade point average—the mean validity coefficient for the 98 judges was .33, the median was .34 and the range was .07 to .48. Of interest is the fact that the most accurate model of a judge had a validity of .64, only .05 correlation points lower than the best actuarial prediction! The differences in judgmental accuracies were reflected more parsimoniously by the isolation of the five subject factors.

The first unrotated subject factor was significantly correlated with the judge's validity, linear predictability, and the accuracy of the judge's model. It was not related to reliability nor to the incremental validity of the model over the man. Thus, for these data, the first unrotated subject factor represented valid judges whose models performed about as well as they did. The judgment model (regressing the idealized ratings onto the ten cues) corresponding to the first subject factor indicated a heavy reliance on aptitude and achievement variables (e.g., GRE—verbal, quantitative, advanced, GPA) in forecasting grade point average. Judges marking the first unrotated factor tended to weight the more valid cues, although they underweighted the valid personological variable of need achievement.

The second subject factor was represented by judges who tended to be only slightly invalid ($r = -.23$), who were not linearly predictable, and whose models fared considerably worse than their own judgments. Their judgment models indicated only a weighting for undergraduate grade point average and virtually no weighting for any of the other cues.

The third subject factor represented judges who were linearly predictable. The projections of the judges on that factor were not related to any of the other judgmental variables. The paramorphic model for these linearly predictable judges indicated that they weighted GRE—verbal most heavily, and also weighted GRE—quantitative, self-rating of conscientiousness, and sex.

The fourth subject factor represented judges whose model fared considerably worse than their own judgments, independently of the validity of their judgments. These judges placed a heavy negative weight on undergraduate grade point average and tended to underweight additional valid cues.

The fifth subject factor represented the unreliable judges whose models tended to outperform their own judgments in forecasting the criterion. The judgment model for these judges indicated that they weighted self-rating of conscientiousness most heavily and assigned negative weights to GRE—quantitative. The five types of judges were also differentially related to a variety of personological, biographical, and aptitude variables, lending additional support to the hypothesis of individual differences.

In comparing the study just described to the analysis of the MMPI data, it should be noted that the samples of subjects represented considerably different populations. Kohen's study utilized more subjects ($n = 98$) than did the MMPI study ($n = 29$) although far fewer profiles were judged. It is probable that the criterion of first year grade point average was more reliable than the criterion of hospital diagnosis of psychosis versus neurosis. Although the number of subject factors emerging in the Kohen study was greater than that from the MMPI study, this was probably due to the larger number of subjects and their presumably greater heterogeneity. However, the same judgmental variables emerged as significant correlates of the individuals in both studies although they emerged in a more complex manner in Kohen's study. The parsimony of the Tucker-Messick analysis in this study may be seen from the manner in which individual differences were described in terms of five subject types instead of the enumeration of judgmental models for 98 subjects. Since no attempt was made to rotate the subject factors in Kohen's study, the data are only suggestive. Future analyses planned for these data include the rotation of the subject factors in such a way as to maximize the correlations of the idealized individuals with the judgmental variables. Thus, an attempt will be made to find a location in the space of subjects that corresponds to the most valid judge, the most reliable judge, and so on.

The most compelling evidence for an individual differences approach to human judgment is found in a study by Wiggins, Hoffman, and Taber (1969). These authors hypothesized that "(1) judges will tend to differ in weights which they assign to different quantified input cues in judgments of the intelligence of others; (2) individual differences will emerge with respect to the manner in which judges combine input cues; that is, some judges will be more complex than others in that they combine cues configurally as opposed to linearly; and (3) these judgmental differences in weighting and combining cues should be predictable on the basis of outside personological characteristics of the judges, particularly their own intellectual and educational experiences [p. 54]." Using the Tucker-Messick approach, an obverse factor analysis of intelligence judgments by 145 subjects of 199 profiles with nine cues indicated eight distinct types of judges. Correlations of the subject factor projections with a variety of intellectual and personality variables indicated that types of judges who were themselves educated, bright, and verbal relied on a few relevant cues such as "high school rank" and "English effectiveness." Judges of lower intelligence either utilized many cues or utilized cues that were irrelevant to the concept of intelligence. Judges scoring high on authoritarianism scales, and who also did well only on performance ability tests, tended to view the intelligence of others as a function of the character traits of "responsibility" and "study habits." Finally judges with little education themselves perceived the cue, "status," as most central to their implicit theory of intelligence.

In obtaining the judgmental models for these intelligence judgments, all judges were discretely classified into one of the eight factorial groups on the basis of their factor loadings. A multiple regression equation was obtained between the cue-values and the mean judgments for each of the eight subgroups of judges. The resulting multiple correlations ranged from .80 to .99 with a median of .96; five of the groups of judges had multiple correlations above .95. Since the mean judgments for a subgroup of homogeneous judges removes unreliability, the linear predictability of the judgments is increased to such an extent that little variance remains. Rather than using subgroup means, Kohen obtained the idealized ratings corresponding to their idealized individuals. For the five idealized ratings, the multiple correlations between cue-values and idealized judgments were .81, .35, .42, .59, and .69. The magnitude of these multiple correlations are similar to those obtained from the judgments of a single judge (Wiggins & Hoffman, 1968b). One research question raised involves a comparison between idealized ratings and mean judgments of subgroups of judges in terms of their judgmental properties (e.g., linear predictability, accuracy of model, etc.). Psychometrically, this question involves a comparison of a factor analysis of subjects with a cluster analysis of subjects. The same data set would be used to contrast properties of idealized ratings with mean judgments of clusters of judges. Ideally, the discrete "clusters of subjects" would mark the corresponding idealized individuals, for purposes of comparison.

Although these three studies attest to the fruitfulness of a multivariate individual differences approach, a number of questions remain to be answered: (1) Would the same idealized individuals emerge for the same group of judges across different judgment tasks? This question relates to the issue of the transituational generality of idealized individuals. For example, since judgmental accuracy does not appear to be a general trait (e.g., Crow & Hammond, 1957), it is not expected that a judge who is accurate in one situation would be accurate in another. However, it is possible that idealized individuals who tend to be among the more valid judges would exhibit at least some transituational generality. (2) Does nonlinearity of cue-usage distinguish among idealized individuals for tasks that involve a nonlinear cue-criterion relationship? (3) What predictive properties do idealized ratings possess? Goldberg (1970) has shown that when a single judge possesses any validity at all, his linear model may exhibit even more validity. The question raised here involves comparisons for accuracy among: (1) the judgments of a single judge marking an idealized individual, (2) the predicted judgments generated by the model of that judge, (3) the idealized judgments corresponding to the idealized individual representing the judge, and (4) the predicted judgments generated by the model for the idealized judgments. These questions become extremely important for clinical judgment tasks for which criterion data are either absent or belated. Goldberg (1971) and Wiggins and Kohen (1971) have suggested that in the absence of criterion data and when clinicians' time is at a premium, it would be well to model either the judge with the highest correlations with the composite or the composite itself, thereby gaining some validity over the "typical" clinician's judgment. The present research suggests the possibility of using idealized ratings or the *models* of the idealized ratings in forecasting behavior. Such possibilities, however, will depend on the outcome of future studies employing idealized individuals and their ratings.

Multidimensional judgments. An example of the Tucker-Messick individual differences model applied to multidimensional studies of cue-utilization is found in a study by Wiggins and Hoffman (1968a). Thirty-one college students were asked to judge the distances among all possible pairs of 22 profiles containing eight cues. The cues were coded onto a ten-point scale and indicated: (1) father's education, (2) mother's education, (3) number of siblings, (4) high school grades, (5) aptitude test score, (6) English test score, (7) study habits rating, and (8) hours employed weekly. The 22 profiles were selected to insure maximal variability among the cue-values. In a design counterbalanced for order, the subjects made two sets of distance judgments. One set of instructions required them to judge simply the distance among the profiles; the second set of instructions asked them to judge the distance among the profiles with respect to intelligence. Thus for one set of instructions, no attribute was provided for the subjects, whereas the second set of instructions provided the attribute of intelligence as a basis for judgment.

The particular hypotheses put forth by the authors were: (1) the multivariate structure of profile judgments would differ as a function of the two instructional sets; (2) no single multivariate structure would be generalizable to all judges but rather judges would be idiosyncratic in their perceptual schemes for judging profiles; and (3) cue-consistency and individual differences between judges would interact; if cue-consistency (defined as a discrepancy between positively related cues) were an important determinant of profile judgments, it would be a function of individual differences.

A Tucker-Messick analysis was applied separately to the judged distances under the two instructional sets (an order effect was noted and the data were analyzed separately). Three idealized individuals emerged for both instructional sets and the multidimensional stimulus matrices were obtained for each of the six idealized individuals. In addition, the group average multidimensional space was obtained for each instructional set. As predicted, the number and the type of profile dimensions differed both within and across instructional sets. Not surprisingly, when subjects were provided with an explicit and relevant attribute, intelligence, the number of dimensions for the average perceptual space was less than when judges were not provided with this attribute. It is likely that when no attribute was provided, the dimensionality of the group space might have represented the multiplicity of attributes chosen by the subjects as important to profile similarity within the context of the particular cues involved.

In addition to group average differences across instructional sets, idealized individuals differed from one another and from their group average within an instructional set. For example, when instructed to judge similarity with respect to intelligence, judges tended to base their judgments primarily on achievement and aptitude cues. However, two idealized individuals within this instructional set were able to make more complex discriminations of intelligence involving more than one dimension. Of interest was the fact that these two idealized individuals based their profile judgments on the *discrepancy* (arithmetic difference between cues) between intellectual cues rather than on the single cues themselves. However, for the third idealized individual in the instructional set providing an attribute, the discrepancy among cues was not as important as their simple unweighted sum.

Although the small sample employed in this study limits the generality of the findings, the approach raises some provocative questions. If, as the data suggest, cue-inconsistency interacts with individual differences, it would be important to establish which sets of cues would be perceived as inconsistent by various idealized individuals. It might be the case that a pair of discrepant (i.e., large arithmetic difference) cues would not be perceived as such by a given group of judges, either because their difference was not noticeable or because the cues were not presumed to be related in the first place.

One interesting question raised by the Wiggins-Hoffman data is the possible relationship between the manner in which idealized individuals utilize cues in a unidimensional judgment task and the number and type of profile dimensions emerging in a multidimensional scaling task. If, as Cliff and Young (1968) suggest, the multidimensional scaling task yields the subject's underlying conceptual map of the profiles, then it should be possible to predict "relevant" unidimensional judgments on the basis of the underlying multidimensional framework.

Although little published data bear on the question of *cue-utilization* under multidimensional and unidimensional judgments (exceptions are Cliff & Young, 1968; Rigney & DeBow, 1967), data recently collected by the present author suggest that such a relationship exists. The subjects utilized by Wiggins, Hoffman, and Taber (1969) for determining cue-weightings for unidimensional judgments of intelligence were additionally instructed to make pair-comparison distance estimates between 28 profiles selected from the total set of 199. For each of the eight idealized individuals isolated in the unidimensional intelligence judgments (Wiggins, Hoffman, & Taber, 1969), the multidimensional space for the selected 28 profiles was determined. For each idealized individual, rank order correlations between the cue regression weights (all were positive) in the unidimensional task and the cue regression weights when each multidimensional factor was regressed onto the cues indicated a significant correlation with at least one multidimensional factor. This means that there was one multidimensional factor that was marked by just those cues used in a unidimensional task. At present, an attempt is being made to locate a vector corresponding to the unidimensional intelligence judgments in the multidimensional space. The possibility of locating such a vector for each idealized individual is suggested by the relationships between the cues emerging as important in the multidimensional task and those weighted in the unidimensional task. If it is possible to predict unidimensional judgments on the basis of multidimensional configurations, then the possibility is raised of studying the complexity of the judgment process in terms of multidimensional scaling.

Multimode data matrices. One of the most interesting applications of multivariate techniques in the judgment area can be found in those experimental situations that generate a data matrix of more than two modes. For example, if a number of judges were asked to forecast behavior from a series of profiles on a number of occasions, this experimental paradigm would generate a judge by profile by occasion matrix. It is certainly not uncommon to find three-mode data matrices in impression formation studies (e.g., Blackburn, 1970) where a group of raters are asked to judge a number of ratees on a variety of traits. Typical semantic differential studies (Heise, 1969; Osgood, Suci, & Tannenbaum, 1957) generate three-dimensional matrices consisting of raters (subjects) by concepts (e.g., nouns) by bipolar adjectival rating scales. Usually these types of data are analyzed by collapsing one of the three modes. However, when the subject mode is collapsed by obtaining mean judgments across all subjects, individual differences are not only obscured but the mean judgment may not, in fact, be representative of any of the individuals within the group (Snyder & Wiggins, 1970; Wiggins & Fishbein, 1969).

It is to these types of three-dimensional data matrices that Tucker's (1963a, 1963b, 1966b, 1966c, 1972) three-mode factor analytic model was addressed. Given a subject by profile by occasion data cube, the three-mode analysis generates the following types of matrices: (1) a factor matrix for each of the three modes—subjects, profiles, and occasions; and (2) a "core" matrix that yields the weights interrelating each of the factors from each of the three data modes. When properly scaled (Snyder & Wiggins, 1970) these core weights are proportional to the means of the variables marking each of the factors.

Mills and Tucker's (1966) application of the three-mode model to a clinical judgment situation will illustrate the usefulness of this approach. Five experienced clinical judges were asked to judge the "severity of pathology" (i.e., how schizophrenic was each response?) on a seven-place scale from WAIS vocabulary and comprehension items obtained from 23 patients. The patient sample included six normals, six psychoneurotics, six schizophrenics, and five brain-damaged patients. Thus, the basic data matrix consisted of five judges by 23 patients by 30 WAIS items (20 vocabulary and 10 comprehension). The elements of this matrix were the judge's seven-place ratings for severity of pathology.

A three-mode factor analysis of these data indicated one judge factor, two WAIS item factors, and two patient factors. The two WAIS item factors were labeled "vocabulary" and "comprehension," suggesting that the judges discriminated between these two types of items on which they based their diagnoses. The two patient factors were labeled: (1) organic impairment not present, and (2) absence of pathology (i.e., normal). The core matrix for these data indicated an interactional pattern between the two types of WAIS items and the two types of patients. In particular, organic impairment was related to vocabulary items; lack of pathology was related to comprehension items. One of the interesting, if not unusual, findings of this study was the fact that any analysis of individual differences in this task was *not* warranted based upon the large single first principal component emerging from the judge's data mode. This suggested that these five judges exhibited similar judgmental styles and, as such, their average judgment could be considered a reasonable representation of all these five judges.

A study in progress by Leonard Rorer and the present author provides an interesting, albeit complex, illustration of a three-mode analysis applied to a clinical judgment situation involving learning. As part of the study, 21 judges were asked to rate 769 MMPI profiles for psychoticism versus neuroticism on six separate occasions. The judges included three MMPI experts (Expert Group), nine graduate students in psychology (Middle Group), and nine subjects taken "off the street," who were completely unfamiliar with the MMPI (Naive Group). Each of the six occasions consisted of a week of training (outcome feedback provided) and a week of testing (no feedback). The MMPI profiles were selected from those originally used by Meehl (1959) and described earlier in this reading. Three hundred of these profiles were used during the training week and the remaining 469 were employed in the week of testing. All subjects made their judgments on a ten-point probability scale ranging from "0–9 percent chance of being psychotic" (i.e., 91–100 percent chance of neurosis) through 91–100 percent chance of being psychotic (i.e., 0–9 percent chance of neurosis). The naive group was not informed as to the construct being judged; they simply made their judgments on an "N versus P" probability scale. Nor were they informed as to the meaning of the names of the 11 MMPI scales on which they based their judgments.

These data were assembled into a three-mode matrix consisting of 21 judges by 6 occasions by 769 profiles. Preliminary analyses suggest at least 3 judge factors, 3 occasion factors, and 4 profile factors, and indicate that both the validity and reliability of the judges serve to identify the first two subject components. At the present time, an attempt is being made to rotate and interpret these factors. Since each of the 6 occasions involved training, it will also be possible to investigate individual differences in generalized learning curves, as specified by Tucker (1966a).

Concluding Remarks

Although the above studies are by no means exhaustive of the literature, each study illustrates an application of multivariate models to the study of cue-utilization. Among the assumptions underlying the application of such models are: (1) individual differences in judgments reflect the characteristic styles in which individuals perceive, construe, and organize their environment; (2) these individual differences are reflected in differences in the weighting and combining of cues in the judgment situation; (3) such judgmental differences are themselves mediated by and functionally related to a wide variety of intellective, personological, cognitive-stylistic and attitudinal characteristics of the judges; and (4) the dimensionality of the stimuli as well as of the individuals should be investigated simultaneously. One might wonder if the cues that define the perceived stimulus dimensions in a multidimensional task in any way relate to how a subject utilizes and weights those same cues in a unidimensional task.

It is hoped that future research in this area will be aimed at the investigation of the basic parameters of individual differences in human judgment: the reliability, internal consistency, and transituational generality of such individual differences. If it were the case that personological correlates of different judgmental styles exhibited some generality across situations, then the provocative possibility is raised of *a priori* identification of different types of judges; or alternatively, it would be possible to utilize judgments as indirect measures of personality (Kusyszyn & Jackson, 1968). Although the factor-analytic approach to individual differences described here is simply a descriptive (as opposed to inferential) model, should these factors exhibit reliability, consistency, and some transituational generality, the notion of an idealized individual would become a more viable scientific construct.

REFERENCES

Anderson, N. H. Comment on "An analysis-of-variance model for the assessment of configural cue utilization in clinical judgment." *Psychological Bulletin,* 1969, *72,* 63–65.

Astin, A. W. *Who goes where to college?* Chicago: Science Research, 1965.

Bieri, J., Atkins, A. L., Briar, S., Leaman, R., Miller, H., & Tripodi, T. *Clinical and social judgment: The discrimination of behavioral information.* New York: Wiley, 1966.

Blackburn, M. C. A multivariate study of some sources of person perception structure. Doctoral dissertation, Urbana, University of Illinois, 1970.

Bock, R. D., & Jones, L. V. *The measurement and prediction of judgment and choice.* San Francisco: Holden Day, 1968.

Carroll, J. D., & Chang, J. Analysis of individual differences in multidimensional scaling via an N-way generalization of "Eckhart-Young" decomposition. *Psychometrika,* 1970, *35,* 283–319.

Christal, R. E. JAN: A technique for analyzing group judgment. Technical Documentary Report PRL-TDR-63-3, Personnel Research Laboratory, Aerospace Medical Division, Air Force Systems Command, Lackland A.F.B., Texas, 1963.

Cliff, N. Multidimensional scaling and cognition: I. Relations among judgments obtained under varying conditions. University of Southern California: Unpublished technical report, Nonr 228 (32), November 1965.

Cliff, N. Multidimensional scaling and cognition: II. The relation of evaluation to multidimensional meaning spaces. University of Southern California: Unpublished technical report, Nonr 228 (32), August 1966.

Cliff, N. Adjective check list responses and individual differences in perceived meaning. *Educational and Psychological Measurement,* 1968, *28,* 1063–1077. (a)

Cliff, N. The "idealized individual" interpretation of individual differences in multidimensional scaling. *Psychometrika,* 1968, *33,* 225–232. (b)

Cliff, N., Pennell, R., & Young, F. Multidimensional scaling in the study of set. *American Psychologist,* 1966, *21,* 707. (Abstract)

Cliff, N., & Young, F. W. On the relation between unidimensional judgments and multidimensional scaling. *Organizational Behavior and Human Performance,* 1968, *3,* 269–285.

Coombs, C. H. An application of a nonmetric model for multidimensional analysis of similarities. *Psychological Reports,* 1958, *4,* 511–518.

Coombs, C. H. *A theory of data.* New York: Wiley, 1964.

Crow, W. J., & Hammond, K. R. The generality of accuracy and response sets in interpersonal perception. *Journal of Abnormal and Social Psychology,* 1957, *54,* 384–390.

Engen, T., & Pfaffmann, C. Absolute judgments of odor quality. *Journal of Experimental Psychology,* 1960, *59,* 214–219.

Ericksen, C. W., & Hake, H. W. Multidimensional stimulus differences and accuracy of discrimination. *Journal of Experimental Psychology,* 1955, *50,* 153–160.

Goldberg, L. R. Diagnosticians vs. diagnostic signs: The diagnosis of psychosis vs. neurosis from the MMPI. *Psychological Monographs,* 1965, *79* (9, Whole No. 602).

Goldberg, L. R. Simple models or simple processes? Some research on clinical judgments. *American Psychologist,* 1968, *23,* 483–496.

Goldberg, L. R. The search for configural relationships in personality assessment: The diagnosis of psychosis vs. neurosis from the MMPI. *Multivariate Behavioral Research,* 1969, *4,* 523–536.

Goldberg, L. R. Man versus model of man: A rationale, plus some evidence, for improving on clinical inference. *Psychological Bulletin,* 1970, *73,* 422–434.

Gollob, H. F. Confounding of sources of variation in factor-analytic techniques. *Psychological Bulletin,* 1968, *70,* 330–344.

Green, P. E., & Carmone, F. J. *Multidimensional scaling and related techniques in marketing analyses.* Boston: Allyn and Bacon, 1970.

Guttman, L. The development of nonmetric space analysis: A letter to Professor John Ross. *Multivariate Behavioral Research,* 1967, *2,* 71–82.

Hammond, K. R., Hursch, C. J., & Todd, F. J. Analyzing the components of clinical inference. *Psychological Review,* 1964, *71,* 438–456.

Harman, H. H. *Modern factor analysis.* (2nd ed.) Chicago: University of Chicago Press, 1967.

Hays, W. L., & Bennett, J. F. Multidimensional unfolding: Determining configuration from complete rank order preference data. *Psychometrika,* 1961, *26,* 221–238.

Heise, D. R. Some methodological issues in the semantic differential. *Psychological Bulletin,* 1969, *72,* 406–422.

Helm, C. E., & Tucker, L. R. Individual differences in the structure of color perception. *American Journal of Psychology,* 1962, *75,* 437–444.

Hoffman, P. J. The paramorphic representation of clinical judgment. *Psychological Bulletin,* 1960, *57,* 116–131.

Hoffman, P. J. Cue-consistency and configurality in human judgment. In B. Kleinmuntz (Ed.), *Formal representation of human judgment.* New York: Wiley, 1968. Pp. 53–90.

Hoffman, P. J., Slovic, P., & Rorer, L. G. An analysis-of-variance model for the assessment of configural cue utilization in clinical judgment. *Psychological Bulletin,* 1968, *69,* 338–349.

Horn, J. L. A rationale and technique for estimating the number of factors in factor analysis. *Psychometrika,* 1965, *30,* 179–185.

Horn, J. L., & Stewart, P. On the accuracy of clinical judgments. *British Journal of Social and Clinical Psychology,* 1968, *7,* 129–134.

Jackson, D. N. The multidimensional nature of human social perception. *Canadian Journal of Behavioral Science,* 1969, *1,* 227–262.

Jackson, D. N., & Messick, S. Individual differences in social perception. *British Journal of Clinical and Social Psychology*, 1963, *2*, 1–10.

Jakobovits, L. A., & Osgood, C. Connotations of twenty psychological journals to their professional readers. *American Psychologist*, 1967, *22*, 792–800.

Jones, L. E., & Young, F. W. The structure of a social environment: A longitudinal, individual difference scaling of an intact group. *Journal of Personality and Social Psychology*, 1972, in press.

Klahr, D. Decision making in a complex environment: The use of similarity judgments to predict preferences. *Management Science*, 1969, *15*, 595–618.

Klemmer, E. T., & Frick, F. C. Assimilation of information from dot and matrix patterns. *Journal of Experimental Psychology*, 1953, *45*, 15–19.

Kohen, E. S. An individual difference analysis of judgments of first year graduate success in psychology. Master's thesis, Urbana, University of Illinois, 1971.

Kruskal, J. B. Multidimensional scaling by optimizing goodness of fit to a nonmetric hypothesis. *Psychometrika*, 1964, *29*, 1–27.

Kusyszyn, I., & Jackson, D. N. A multimethod factor analytic appraisal of endorsement and judgment methods in personality assessment. *Educational and Psychological Measurement*, 1968, *28*, 1047–1061.

Linn, R. L. A Monte Carlo approach to the number of factors problem. *Psychometrika*, 1968, *33*, 37–72.

Maguire, T. O., & Glass, G. V. Component profile analysis (COPAN): An alternative to PROF. *Educational and Psychological Measurement*, 1968, *28*, 1021–1033.

Meehl, P. E. A comparison of clinicians with five statistical methods of identifying psychotic MMPI profiles. *Journal of Counseling Psychology*, 1959, *6*, 102–109.

Messick, S. An empirical evaluation of multidimensional successive intervals. *Psychometrika*, 1956, *21*, 367–376.

Messick, S., & Abelson, R. P. The additive constant problem in multidimensional scaling. *Psychometrika*, 1956, *21*, 1–15.

Messick, S., & Kogan, N. Personality consistencies in judgment: Dimensions of role construct. *Multivariate Behavioral Research*, 1966, *1*, 165–175.

Miller, H., & Bieri, J. An informational analysis of clinical judgment. *Journal of Abnormal and Social Psychology*, 1963, *67*, 317–325.

Mills, D. H., & Tucker, L. R. A three-mode factor analysis of clinical judgment of schizophrenicity. *Journal of Clinical Psychology*, 1966, *22*, 136–139.

Naylor, J. C., & Wherry, R. J., Sr. The use of simulated stimuli and the "JAN" technique to capture and cluster the policies of raters. *Educational and Psychological Measurement*, 1955, *25*, 969–986.

Osgood, C. E., Suci, G. J., & Tannenbaum, P. *The measurement of meaning*. Urbana: University of Illinois Press, 1957.

Pollack, I. The information of elementary auditory displays, II. *Journal of Acoustical Society of America*, 1953, *25*, 765–769.

Posavac, E. Dimensions of trait preferences and personality type. *Journal of Personality and Social Psychology*, 1971, *19*, 274–281.

Rigney, J. W., & DeBow, C. H. Multidimensional scaling analysis of decision strategies in threat evaluation. *Journal of Applied Psychology*, 1967, *51*, 305–310.

Shepard, R. N. Stimulus and response generalization: Tests of a model relating generalization to distance in psychological space. *Journal of Experimental Psychology*, 1958, *55*, 509–523.

Shepard, R. N. The analysis of proximities: Multidimensional scaling with an unknown distance function. I. *Psychometrika,* 1962, *27,* 125–140. (a)

Shepard, R. N. The analysis of proximities: Multidimensional scaling with an unknown distance function. II. *Psychometrika,* 1962, *27,* 219–246. (b)

Shikiar, R. The relationships among the multidimensional scaling of political judgments, preferences, and semantic differential judgments. Unpublished master's thesis, Urbana, University of Illinois, 1970.

Slovic, P. Cue consistency and cue utilization in judgment. *American Journal of Psychology,* 1966, *79,* 427–434.

Snyder, F. W., & Wiggins, N. Affective meaning systems: A multivariate approach. *Multivariate Behavioral Research,* 1970, 5, 453–468.

Thurstone, L. L. Experimental study of simple structure. *Psychometrika,* 1940, *5,* 153–168.

Torgerson, W. S. Multidimensional scaling: I. Theory and method. *Psychometrika,* 1952, *17,* 401–419.

Torgerson, W. S. *Theory and methods of scaling.* New York: Wiley, 1958.

Tripodi, T., & Bieri, J. Information transmission in clinical judgments as a function of stimulus dimensionality and cognitive complexity. *Journal of Personality,* 1964, *32,* 119–137.

Tryon, R. C. The BC TRY computer system of cluster and factor analysis. *Multivariate Behavioral Research,* 1966, *1,* 95–111.

Tucker, L. R. Intra-individual and inter-individual multidimensionality. In H. Gulliken & E. Messick (Eds.), *Psychological scaling: Theory and applications.* New York: Wiley, 1960. Pp. 155–167.

Tucker, L. R. The extension of factor analysis to three-dimensional matrices. In N. Fredericksen & A. Gulliksen (Eds.), *Contributions to mathematical psychology.* New York: Holt, Rinehart and Winston, 1963. (a)

Tucker, L. R. Implication of factor analysis of three-way matrices for measurement of change. In C. Harris (Ed.), *Problems in measuring change.* Madison: University of Wisconsin Press, 1963. (b)

Tucker, L. R. Systematic differences between individuals in perceptual judgments. In M. Shelly & G. L. Bryan (Eds.), *Human judgments and optimality.* New York: Wiley, 1964. Pp. 85–98.

Tucker, L. R. A. search for structure underlying individual differences in psychological phenomena. Conference on cluster analysis of multivariate data. Unpublished manuscript, 1966. (a)

Tucker, L. R. Learning theory and multivariate experiment: Illustration by determination of generalized learning curves. In R. B. Cattell (Ed.), *Handbook of multivariate experimental psychology.* Skokie, Ill.: Rand McNally, 1966. (b)

Tucker, L. R. Some mathematical notes on three-mode analysis. *Psychometrika,* 1966, *31,* 279–311. (c)

Tucker, L. R. Comments on "Confounding sources of variation in factor analytic techniques." *Psychological Bulletin,* 1968, *70,* 345–354.

Tucker, L. R. Relations between multidimensional scaling and three-mode factor analysis. *Psychometrika,* 1972, *37,* 3–27.

Tucker, L. R., & Messick, S. An individual differences model for multidimensional scaling. *Psychometrika,* 1963, *28,* 333–367.

Walters, H. A., & Jackson, D. N. Group and individual regularities in trait inference: A multidimensional scaling analysis. *Multivariate Behavioral Research,* 1966, *1,* 145–163.

Warr, P. B., Schroder, H. M., & Blackman, S. The structure of political judgment. *British Journal of Social and Clinical Psychology,* 1969, *8,* 32–43.

Wherry, R. J., Sr., & Naylor, J. C. Comparison of two approaches—JAN and PROF—for capturing rater strategies. *Educational and Psychological Measurement,* 1966, *26,* 267–286.

Wiggins, N. Individual viewpoints of social desirability. *Psychological Bulletin,* 1966, *66,* 68–73.

Wiggins, N. Individual differences in diagnostic judgments of psychosis and neurosis from the MMPI. *Educational and Psychological Measurement,* 1971, *31,* 199–214.

Wiggins, N., Blackburn, M., & Hackman, J. R. Prediction of first-year graduate success in psychology: Peer ratings. *The Journal of Educational Research,* 1969, *63,* 81–85.

Wiggins, N., & Fishbein, M. Dimensions of semantic space: A problem of individual differences. In J. R. Snider & C. E. Osgood (Eds.), *The semantic differential technique.* Chicago: Aldine, 1969. Pp. 138–193.

Wiggins, N., & Hoffman, P. J. Dimensions of profile judgments as a function of instructions, cue-consistency, and individual differences.*Multivariate Behavioral Research,* 1968, *3,* 3–20. (a)

Wiggins, N., & Hoffman, P. J. Three models of clinical judgment. *Journal of Abnormal Psychology,* 1968, *73,* 70–77. (b)

Wiggins, N., Hoffman, P. J., & Taber, T. Types of judges and cue-utilization in judgments of intelligence. *Journal of Personality and Social Psychology,* 1969, *12,* 52–59.

Wiggins, N., & Kohen, E. S. Man vs. model of man revisited: The forecasting of graduate school success. *Journal of Personality and Social Psychology,* 1971, *19,* 100–106.

Xhignesse, L. V., & Osgood, C. E. Bibliographic citation characteristics of the psychological journal network in 1950 and in 1960. *American Psychologist,* 1967, *22,* 778–791.

Introduction
to Reading 3

Björkman's application of lens model concepts to situations involving
binary or qualitative cues, and his description of an appropriate analytical
model are important contributions to the study of judgment. Equally
important, however, is his treatment of two critical issues in the areas
of judgment and learning—namely, cue congruency (or consistency) and
the role of outcome feedback. Problems relevant to cue congruency, in
which the information available to a judge is contradictory or inconsistent,
are quite common. How the judge responds to such situations is not only
theoretically important, but also of considerable practical significance.

The second issue, concerning the role of feedback, also raises
interesting theoretical and practical questions. For example, in what
respects are judgments likely to change when feedback about outcomes
is no longer available? Are there situations in which the removal of outcome
feedback may facilitate judgmental performance, rather than hinder it?
Björkman reviews experimental evidence relevant to these questions and
explains why the effects of nonfeedback will vary depending upon the
particular type of judgment task involved.

3 Inference Behavior in Nonmetric Ecologies

MATS BJÖRKMAN
University of Umea, Sweden

The quantitative formulations of the lens model, and the experiments designed in accordance with them, have one important characteristic in common— *they refer to a metric ecology.*

Now I think everyone can agree that nature is not always metric. In many situations we have to make inferences from qualitative cues; they don't appear as values that can be ordered along a continuum. Cues of this kind are, for example, colors, two- and three-dimensional shapes, certain features of people, and so on. Such nonmetric cues can be useful in a wide variety of inference situations; the red sign indicates that you should not cross, the shape of the moon tells you whether the illuminated area will increase or decrease, and the presence or absence of certain facial features may lead to inferences about the presence or absence of certain traits. These are but a few examples of situations that involve nonmetric (or "nominal") inferences made on the basis of nonmetric cues.

In short, our ecology often demands the use of nonmetric cues in order to adapt adequately to the environment. For this reason, how individuals learn to use nonmetric cues when making inferences assumes considerable importance. The purpose of this paper is to examine the nature of inference in nonmetric situations, and, in particular, to show how Brunswik's Lens Model can be brought to bear on this problem.

Some General Remarks about the Lens Model Approach to the Nonmetric Case

In experiments where the cues and the distal variable (criterion) are scaled variables, the subject is presented with a set of cue-values and asked to make an inference about the distal variable. The distal state of affairs presents itself as a lenslike scatter of cue-values (nature scatters its effects irregularly), each cue with a more or less uncertain relation to the distal variable. This idea was fundamental to Brunswik's theorizing and can be discerned in his early writing with Tolman (Tolman & Brunswik, 1935).

The lens analogy was considered so fundamental that it gave the name to the model. In the nonmetric case, however, *the lens characteristic* of the relation between cues and criterion disappears. For example, in the most widely used nonmetric situation with two cues and two events, often called discrimination learning, the distal state does not have the character of a focal point. This might at first seem to violate the idea of applying the lens model in nonmetric situations. Of primary importance, however, is not the lens characteristic itself but rather the conceptual framework associated with the lens model.

Another feature of the present approach should also be made clear at the beginning. The lens model grew from Brunswik's conceptualization of the real world, his probabilistic functionalism. Brunswik proposed that behavior is directed toward distal goals and that achievement of these goals is facilitated by learning the relations between these goals and their proximal effects. (These relations, Brunswik notes, are typically irregular and uncertain.) It follows then that inference becomes an important characteristic of adaptation to the environment. The purpose of the lens model is to reflect this and other characteristics of man's interaction with his environment. It is intended to be a model with high ecological relevance, but, as was argued in a recent paper (Björkman, 1969c), the lens model is not a *predictive* model; rather, it serves as a conceptual tool for a systematic *description* of inferential behavior and for generating new ideas and research, that are not directly derivable from a scrutiny of the model itself. With regard to the latter, studies of cognitive conflict (Hammond, 1965; Hammond, Bonaiuto, Faucheux, Moscovici, Fröhlich, Joyce, & Di Majo, 1968; Hammond & Brehmer, 1970) and the experiments on the effect of various forms of feedback (Brehmer & Lindberg, 1970a, 1970b; Todd & Hammond, 1965) may serve as examples.

Roughly speaking then, the lens model is a framework for studying "grand strategies" of inferential behavior in various contexts of high ecological relevance with a strong focus on achievement. In contrast, certain other models, for example, Estes (1959) stimulus sampling model, the component model for discrimination learning by Burke and Estes (1957), Atkinson's (1958) observing response model, and other models of statistical learning theory focus on what Brunswik would have called "process details." These models aim at precise predictions of relatively narrow aspects of predictive behavior, for example, characteristics of the response tendencies after they have stabilized at the asymptotic level, sequential effects, and so on. As noted earlier, the author's bias in the domain of human inference is admittedly Brunswikian, and he will thus be concerned with "grand strategies" rather than "process details." In this paper this bias will express itself as an attempt to apply concepts associated with the lens model as a frame of reference in nonmetric situations. Specifically, what do concepts like ecological validity, cue-utilization, response consistency, cue-redundancy, compromise, and vicarious functioning mean in the non-metric situation? Can these concepts contribute to our knowledge about inferential processes?If a generalization is possible, comparison between the metric and the nonmetric situations might become easier and might further our understanding of human inference in general.

This reading contains two main parts. The first part is methodological and presents certain lens model concepts defined in a way appropriate for the nonmetric situation. The second part illustrates the use of some of these concepts in experimental studies.

Defining Characteristics of a Nonmetric Inference Situation

In one of the introductory paragraphs a few examples of nonmetric situations were given. In laboratory work we try to mirror the formal characteristics of such real-life situations. When constructing inference tasks we are not interested primarily in whether cues and criteria are letters, various shapes, or colors, but in the formal relationships between cues and criterion and between the cues themselves. This is true also for the metric studies where cues and criteria most often have been numbers, lines varying in length, or graphs showing the magnitude of each cue and the criterion.

Most important of the formal characteristics is, of course, the *task uncertainty.* In the metric situations the relationships between cues and criterion are measured by correlation coefficients based on linear regression. Accordingly, the predictability of the ecological system is measured by multiple Rs. In the nonmetric case this methodology is not applicable since the variables are not scaled. Instead of correlation coefficients and multiple regression analysis, one has to introduce probabilities and conditional probabilities.

In order to illustrate a nonmetric experimental inference task, consider the following situation. In front of the subject there is a display with two windows, one for the cues and one for the criterion. The cue can be a spot of red, green, or blue color appearing in the window and the criterion may be either of two events, a square or a circle. After the color has been briefly exposed, the subject is asked to predict whether a circle or a square will then appear. After making his prediction, he receives feedback in the sense that he is shown which of the two forms appears in the window. On each trial a predictive response (circle or square) is obtained, and for blocks of trials the response frequency can be computed. This is a brief description of the kind of situation that will be our concern in this paper.

In the example just referred to, there are three cues, C_1, C_2, and C_3, and two criterion events, E_1 and E_2. The task is defined by the conditional probabilities of a certain shape following a certain color, $p(E_i/C_j)$. In the example there are six conditional probabilities and we can speak of a 3×2 nonmetric task; the first number (M) always refers to the cues and the second number (N) to the events. In general, the task is made up of M cues and N events and there is a total of $M \times N$ conditional probabilities.

Some definitions emerging from the lens model have been illustrated for the nonmetric case in Figure 3.1. To the left are the N events E_i $(i = 1 \ldots N)$. For each of them there is a conditional probability $p(E_i/C_j)$, indicating the relationship between the event and each of the M cues C_j $(j = 1 \ldots M)$. Thus, $p(E_i/C_j)$ defines the ecological validity of C_j with respect to event E_i, that is, how valid C_j is as a predictor of E_i.

To the right we have the responses, $R_k(k = 1 \ldots N)$, which are equal in number to the events. For each response there is a conditional probability $p(R_k/C_j)$, indicating its relationship to each of the cues. Thus, $p(R_k/C_j)$ represents cue-utilization; that is, how much response R_k depends on cue C_j.

The definition of achievement, however, is a little more complicated. Achievement in this case is the probability of a correct prediction. Now, this probability, in the following example denoted by A, can be decomposed into subprobabilities in two different ways. First, let A_{ii} represent the probability of the joint occurrence of R_i and E_i summated over all N instances. Since there are N responses and events, A is defined in the following way (Case I):

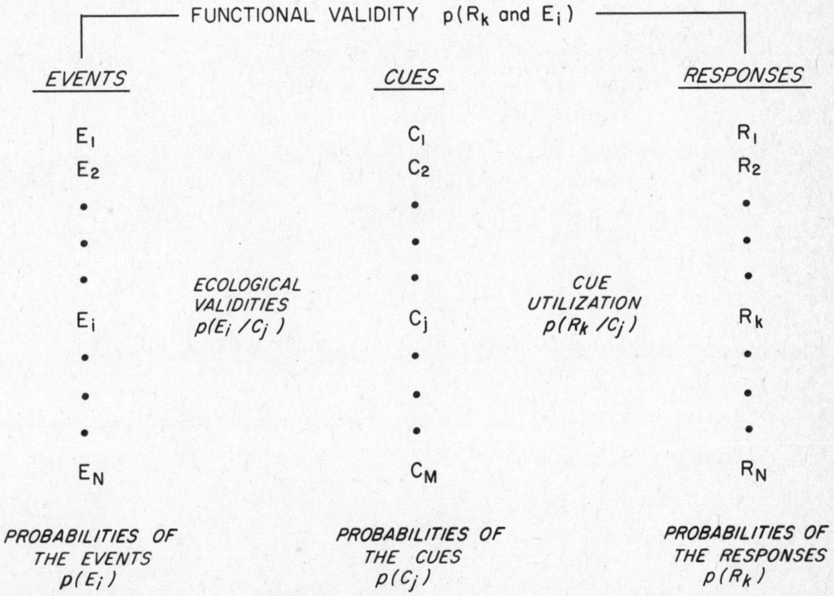

FUNCTIONAL VALIDITY $p(R_k$ and $E_i)$

EVENTS		CUES		RESPONSES
E_1		C_1		R_1
E_2		C_2		R_2
•		•		•
•		•		•
•	ECOLOGICAL VALIDITIES	•	CUE UTILIZATION	•
E_i	$p(E_i/C_j)$	C_j	$p(R_k/C_j)$	R_k
•		•		•
•		•		•
•		•		•
E_N		C_M		R_N
PROBABILITIES OF THE EVENTS $p(E_i)$		PROBABILITIES OF THE CUES $p(C_j)$		PROBABILITIES OF THE RESPONSES $p(R_k)$

Figure 3.1. Concepts of Brunswik's Lens Model applied to the case of an $M \times N$ nonmetric ecology

$$A = \sum_{i=1}^{N} A_{ii} \tag{3.1}$$

Second, let a_{jj} represent the probability of a correct prediction when cue C_j occurs. This means that all the responses $R_1, R_2, \ldots R_N$ contribute to a correct prediction as far as they occur jointly with the corresponding events $E_1, E_2, \ldots E_N$. In this case achievement is defined in the following way (Case II):

$$A = \sum_{j=1}^{M} c_j a_{jj} \tag{3.2}$$

where c_j is the probability of occurrence of cue s_j.

In the first case (Equation 3.1) achievement is decomposed into N parts each referring to the probability of the joint occurrence of R_i and E_i when $i = 1 \ldots N$. In the second case (Equation 3.2) the achievement is defined by M numbers each referring to the probability of a correct prediction for each cue $C_j(j = 1 \ldots M)$. Both ways of defining achievement have advantages depending on the purpose of the inquiry, as will be shown later in this paper.

Achievement as a Function of the Ecological System and the Response System

We first introduce some shortened notations together with the conditions for exhaustiveness and mutual exclusiveness.

$c_j = $ the probability of occurrence of cue C_j, $p(C_j)$
$e_i = $ the probability of occurrence of event E_i, $p(E_i)$
$r_k = $ the probability of occurrence of response R_k, $p(R_k)$
$v_{ij} = $ the conditional probability of E_i and C_j occurs, $p(E_i/C_j)$
$u_{jk} = $ the conditional probability of R_k when C_j occurs, $p(R_k/C_j)$
$V_{ij} = $ the probability of the joint occurrence of C_j and E_i

$$V_{ij} = p(C_j) \cdot p(E_i/C_j) = c_j v_{ij}$$

$A_{ik} = $ the probability of the joint occurrence of E_i and R_k

$$\sum_{j=1}^{M} c_j = 1 \qquad \sum_{i=1}^{N} e_i = 1 \qquad \sum_{k=1}^{N} r_k = 1$$

$$\sum_{i=1}^{N} v_{ij} = 1 \text{ for } j = 1 \ldots M \qquad \sum_{k=1}^{N} u_{jk} = 1 \text{ for } j = 1 \ldots M$$

$$\sum_{i=1}^{N} \sum_{j=1}^{M} V_{ij} = 1 \qquad \sum_{i=1}^{N} \sum_{k=1}^{N} A_{ik} = 1$$

Ecological validity. The conditional probabilities v_{ij}, the probability of E_i when C_j occurs, are elements of a $N \times M$ matrix $[v_{ij}]$ where the rows correspond to events and the columns correspond to cues. This matrix, together with the probabilities c_j, define the statistical properties of the ecology. Instead of v_{ij}, the ecological validities of the cues, and the absolute probabilities c_j, the ecology can be represented by the matrix $[V_{ij}]$ where the elements sum to unity (Figure 3.2). The marginal probabilities of this matrix are e_i (rows) and c_j columns). Note that $[V_{ij}] = [v_{ij}]\,[c_{ij}]$, where $[c_{jj}]$ is a diagonal matrix containing the absolute probabilities of the cues.

Utilization. The conditional probabilities u_{jk}, the probability of R_k when C_j occurs, are elements in a $M \times N$ matrix $[u_{jk}]$ in which the rows correspond to cues and the columns to responses (Figure 3.2). This matrix represents the dependence of responses on cues and therefore indicates cue-utilization.

Achievement. The probability of the joint occurrence of E_i and R_k, is represented by an $N \times N$ matrix $[A_{ik}]$ where the rows correspond to events and the columns to responses (Figure 3.2). This matrix shows how responses and events go together and thus represents the validity of the inferential responses (functional validity).

Each element of the main diagonal, A_{ii}, represents the probability of the joint occurrence of R_i and E_i. According to the definition in Equation 3.1, the probability of correct prediction, the achievement, is obtained by summing the elements of the main diagonal. Achievement is thus the trace of $[A_{ik}]$.

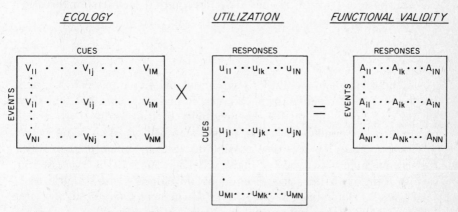

Figure 3.2.   The modified lens model in matrix representation. Notice that the ecological system and the functional validity of the inferences are both represented by absolute probabilities, whereas utilization is represented by conditional probabilities (See Equations 3.4 and 3.5).

It is easily verified that an element A_{ik} of the matrix $[A_{ik}]$ is the sum of products of the ith row of $[V_{ij}]$ and the kth column of $[u_{jk}]$ (See Björkman, 1967).

$$A_{ik} = \sum_{j=1}^{M} V_{ij} u_{jk} \qquad (3.3)$$

Since this is the operation defining matrix multiplication we have

$$[A_{ik}] = [V_{ij}][u_{jk}] \qquad (3.4)$$

The square $N \times N$ matrix $[A_{ik}]$ is the product of the $N \times M$ matrix specifying the ecological system and the $M \times N$ matrix specifying the response system. The matrix $[A_{ik}]$ tells the complete story about the agreement between inferential responses and the events to be inferred. It expresses a fundamental idea in Brunswik's functionalism, namely, that inferential accuracy is a function of the statistical properties of the ecology and the statistical properties of the subject's response system. Although expressed in a different mathematical language (matrix algebra instead of multiple regression statistics) the parallel between the metric and the nonmetric case is obvious.

Equation 3.4 gives precise meaning to Brunswik's suggestion (1956, p. 141) that "cues should be utilized in accordance with their validity." The ecological validity of stimulus C_j is its power as a predictor of an event E_i, which is defined as the conditional probability v_{ij}. A match between ecological validity and utilization means that v_{ij} should equal the conditional probability of response R_i on the occurrence of C_j, which is u_{ji}. Complete matching then means that the utilization matrix $[u_{jk}]$ is the transpose of $[v_{ij}]$. In this case $[A_{ik}]$ becomes a symmetric matrix according to the formula

$$[A_{ii}'] = [v_{ij}][c_{jj}][v_{ji}'] \qquad (3.5)$$

Conclusion. It is the author's intention that Equations 3.3, 3.4, and 3.5 should not be regarded as an exercise in matrix algebra but that they should convey to the reader the possibility of transferring lens model concepts to the nonmetric case (a further step will be taken below when we come to Case II). It is thus possible to write in simple mathematical form what Brunswik advocated many years ago and what is expressed in precise form by the lens model equation developed for the metric case (See Hursch, Hammond, & Hursch, 1964), namely, that the agreement between inferential responses and the events to be inferred is a function of the statistical properties of the ecology and the subject's response system. The properties of these systems set the limits of achievement, which for a given ecology are determined by the characteristics of $[u_{jk}]$, the subject's policy. This may seem rather self-evident, but it (1) stresses the similarities between the metric and the nonmetric situations: and (2) will help in clarifying certain issues in policy formation, for example, how achievement depends on the policy for a given ecology.

Consistency and Congruency

Two additional concepts, referred to as *consistency* and *congruency,* should be added. Since both can be applied to the C-E matrix and the C-R matrix, there are altogether four measures to consider. Each refers to a particular cue or pair of cues. Therefore, consider two cues C_j and C_m. The utilization probabilities (See Figure 3.2) are represented by the two row vectors $[u_{j1}, u_{j2} \ldots u_{jk} \ldots u_{jN}]$ and $[u_{m1}, u_{m2} \ldots u_{mk} \ldots u_{mN}]$, and the conditional ecological probabilities by the two column vectors $\{v_{1j}, v_{2j} \ldots v_{ij} \ldots v_{Nj}\}$ and $\{v_{1m}, v_{2m} \ldots v_{im} \ldots v_{Nm}\}$. As will be seen shortly, simple common principles will be used for defining all four measures, namely, matrix multiplication of vectors. Furthermore, achievement will be defined according to the same principle. All measures to be considered are thus products of vectors in N-dimensional spaces, where the unit vectors are the N responses or the N events.

Response consistency. Response consistency represents the degree to which a person follows a rule (compare the interpretation of R_s^2 in the lens model equation). A subject who always predicts E_1 when C_1 occurs is more consistent than a person who distributes his predictions over several events. High response consistency is necessary for high achievement, whereas the reverse is not true. A subject may very well be consistent in his response system but have a low achievement because he has chosen a less than optimal rule.

A simple and algebraically convenient measure, which expresses the main idea of consistency, is obtained by multiplication of the vector by its transpose. The response consistency h_j^2 of cue C_j is thus

$$h_j^2 = \sum_{K=1}^{N} u_{jk}^2 \tag{3.6}$$

Ecological consistency. This measure is the ecological analogue to response consistency and tells how valid a cue is as a predictor, not of one particular event, but of the set of events associated with the cue (compare R_e^2 in the lens model equation). The ecological consistency g_j^2 of cue C_j is accordingly defined as

$$g_j^2 = \sum_{k=1}^{N} v_{ij}^2 \tag{3.7}$$

Cue-utilization congruency. The intuitive meaning of this measure, which will be used for studying cue-compounds, may be expressed as follows. If two cues are both responded to in a consistent (according to Equation 3.6) but different manner, they can be said to be noncongruent. If, on the other hand, the consistency of both is high and the response patterns very similar the congruency is high. A measure that reflects both similarity of the response patterns and response consistency (although not in a completely independent way) is the following

$$h_{jm} = \sum_{k=1}^{N} u_{jk} u_{mk} \tag{3.8}$$

where h_{jm} will be referred to as the cue-utilization congruency for cues C_j and C_m.

Cue-validity congruency. The ecological parallel to Equation 3.8 is

$$g_{jm} = \sum_{i=1}^{N} v_{ij} v_{im} \tag{3.9}$$

which is related to cue-redundancy in the metric case. If two metric cues are highly correlated, they will of course predict criterion values that are close to each other. When two cues in the nonmetric case are congruent they will predict the same event.

Achievement. Instead of postmultiplying $[V_{ij}]$ by $[u_{jk}]$ as in Equation 3.4, consider the elements of a diagonal matrix $[a_{jj}]$ obtained by multiplying the jth row vector of $[u_{jk}]$ by the jth column vector of $[v_{ij}]$:

$$a_{jj} = \sum_{i=k=1}^{N} u_{jk} v_{ij} \tag{3.10}$$

The element a_{jj} is the probability of a correct prediction when cue C_j occurs. According to Equation 3.2, the sum of these elements, each multiplied by the probability of cue C_j, defines achievement.

Comments. The consistency measures h_j^2 and g_j^2 can vary from $1/N$, which represents complete randomness, to unity, which represents the highest consistency possible; in the latter case all probabilities associated with the stimulus, except one, are 0. Congruency always lies within the range from 0 to 1.

Consistency and congruency of a set of cues can be presented by two matrices obtained in the following way. By postmultiplying $[u_{jk}]$ by its transpose one obtains a matrix where the elements of the main diagonal are the consistency measures of $C_1 \ldots C_m$, and the off-diagonal elements are the congruency measures for all pair-wise combinations of $C_j (j =$

$1 \ldots M)$ and $C_m (m = 1 \ldots M)$. The corresponding matrix for the ecology is obtained by premultiplying $[v_{ij}]$ by its transpose.

In accordance with the above definition of congruency, a_{jj} can be regarded as the congruency between the jth stimulus vector in the R-space and the jth vector of the E-space. A special case of this congruency is matching. This means that the jth vector of $[u_{jk}]$ is identical to the jth column vector of $[v_{ij}]$. It can be immediately seen from Equations 3.6, 3.7, and 3.10 that under this condition

$$a_{jj} = h_j{}^2 = g_j{}^2 \qquad (3.11)$$

showing that the probability of a correct prediction for cue C_j is equal to both the ecological consistency and the response consistency. Here one should note the close correspondence with the metric case, where achievement is $R_e{}^2 = R_s{}^2$, when matching is perfect.

Empirical Studies

The most popular C-E task studied by experimental psychologists is the case of two cues and two events. Although this situation has become a standard experiment among statistical learning theorists, very few attempts have been made to explore it from the Brunswikian approach adopted in this paper. This approach to the two-choice situation has been discussed in some detail in a previous paper (Björkman, 1967). The present discussion is limited to an examination of three issues: (1) maximizing versus matching, (2) the effects of cue-compounds, and (3) the role of feedback. Empirical illustrations will accompany each.

The matching-maximizing issue. Figure 3.3 contains four different utilization matrices, each one representing an inference strategy.

From left to right we have first what may be called simple *matching* (or E-matching); here the person does not pay attention to the connections between cues and events but attends solely to the marginal frequency of the events. According to Equation 3.3 (which is general and can be applied in all the four cases) achievement is

$$A = e_1{}^2 + e_2{}^2 \qquad (3.12)$$

The second case represents simple *maximizing* (or E-maximizing), which provides higher achievement than matching ($e_1 > e_2$)

$$A = e^1; \; e^1 > (e_1{}^2 + e_2{}^2) \qquad (3.13)$$

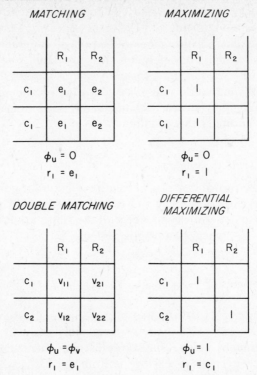

Figure 3.3. Four strategies defined by the conditional probabilities $p(R_k/S_j)$. The ϕ-coefficients refer to the correlation between C and E (ϕ_v) and the correlation between C and R (ϕ_u).

Third comes *differential matching* (named double matching in Björkman's paper). In this case the subject utilizes both the differences in event frequency and the connections between C and E. The cues are "utilized in accordance with their validity" and the achievement is

$$A = c_1 (v_{11}^2 + v_{21}^2) + c_2 (v_{12}^2 + v_{22}^2) \qquad (3.14)$$

Finally we have *differential maximizing* in which case the subject consistently predicts the most frequent event for each stimulus. This strategy gives the highest possible achievement, which can be written as the sum of the diagonal elements of the ecology matrix (since $[V_{ij}]$ is multiplied by an identity matrix):

$$A = V_{11} + V_{12} \qquad (3.15)$$

It is easily verified that differential maximizing results in the highest achievement possible and that matching results in the lowest achievement.

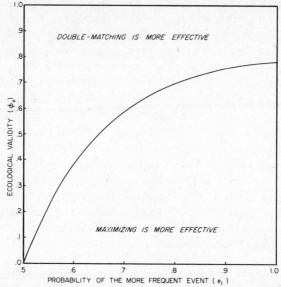

Figure 3.4. The curve separates 2×2 ecologies into those where differential matching leads to higher achievement and those where maximizing is more effective.

But is differential matching or maximizing the more functional performance? As shown previously (Bjorkman, 1967), which of these is the more effective strategy depends on the statistical characteristics of the ecological system. Let the dependency between C and E be measured by the ϕ-coefficient. Differential matching is then always superior if the coefficient exceeds 0.71 (See Figure 3.4). If, for example, $e_1 = 0.60$ ($e_2 = 0.40$) it requires a ϕ-coefficient of 0.41 to make differential matching equally effective as maximizing. So even for rather small differences between e_1 and e_2 maximizing can be the more effective strategy. The issue under consideration is a direct parallel to a well-known problem in clinical prediction: How much can the hit rate be increased when tests and other instruments are used, compared to predictions made solely from information about the base rates. Meehl and Rosen (1955), for example, report several cases where prediction of the most common diagnosis (without any aid of tests) gives more hits than would be the case if the predictions had been made with the use of tests and other clinical instruments.

Experimental findings. As yet there is no theory indicating which strategy a person is likely to follow under given ecological conditions. The situation is even worse because there are only a few empirical studies dealing directly with the question of response strategy. Kroll (1970) used a 4×2 task (four cues and two events). Six groups, each with a different task with respect to the probability of E_1 and E_2, were used. Group 1 served as a control group where no cue was given (simple probability learning) and for Group II all the four probabilities $p(E_1/C_1)$ were set equal to 0.70. In the other four groups the event probability $p(E_1/C_j)$ varied and the overall ecological validity measured by ϕ coefficients was 0.00, 0.54, 0.52, 0.19, and 0.27 for Groups II, III, IV, V, and VI, respectively. The predictability measured by ϕ is thus rather low in all groups and covers a narrow range. There were 16 subjects in each group and they were classified according to which strategy could best describe the behavior during the last two blocks of training. Since the range of overall predictability is rather narrow and since the number of subjects in each group is relatively small compared to the number of possible strategies (five when random performance is included), it is hard to make any definite statements about strategy under various conditions. Of 80 subjects (Group I is disregarded in this connection) the strategies were distributed as follows: matching, 27; maximizing, 12; differential matching, 30; differential maximizing, 6; and random, 5.

The dominating performances are thus the two matching strategies, which altogether account for more than 70 percent of the cases. Inspection of the different groups shows that of the 27 cases of matching, 17 belong to the two groups with the lowest overall predictability (0.00 and 0.19). Note also the low frequency of subjects who utilize the most effective strategy, namely, differential maximizing. This might be due to the relatively low predictability of the task. Although any conclusions concerning the distribution of strategies should be accepted with great care, it seems fair to say that differential matching is the dominant strategy (especially when 10 cases of matching in Group II are either excluded or counted as differential matchers, which is completely correct since the two matching strategies cannot be differentiated in this case).

In a study by Björkman (1969b) of inference behavior in a 2×2 task, 50 subjects were distributed on 5 conditions with respect to ecological validity (measured by the ϕ-coefficient) and base rate. In this experiment the overall validity varied from 0.18 to 0.78. The general findings are similar to those of Kroll. Differential matching accounts for slightly more than 50 percent of the cases, while differential maximizing comes next with the best fit in 11 of the 50 cases. Matching accounts for 6 cases and maximizing occurred only once.

When the strategies were separated on different levels of ecological validity, differential matching was most frequent for intermediate levels of ecological validity. The frequency of differential maximizing increases when the ecological validity increases. Matching, maximizing, and random performance are most apt to occur when the validity is low (See Kroll's study). Due to the small sample of subjects, however, these conclusions should so far be regarded as only suggestive (See Figure 8 in Björkman,

1969b). These findings suggest also that it is not possible to predict with certainty how a person will behave under a certain set of ecological conditions. That is, subjects show considerable variation in their cognitive performance for a given ecology indicating, for example, that the cognitive appraisal of the situation, educational background, and other subject variables are important, but usually uncontrolled, determiners of strategy. In this regard, Kroll (1970) demonstrated that subjects with a knowledge of statistics were more likely to maximize than subjects without such knowledge.

Questions of individual differences in studies of cognitive inference deserve much more attention than has hitherto been the case. The studies by Kroll and Björkman show that even within a rather homogenous sample of subjects one observes a wide variation in inference strategy. The imaginary "average person," who is quite often a differential matcher, has been on the scene long enough and should be substituted, as far as possible, by data on individual subjects. What is needed are models and empirical work that increase our knowledge about individual response strategy. Why do some persons match while others maximize under the same ecological conditions? Related to this issue is also the fact, directly derivable from the lens model, that the same achievement can be attained by different response strategies (See Figure 3.4 for a simple example).

Summers (1968) studied five groups in a 2×2 situation where the event frequencies $p(E_1/C_1)$ were 0.50, 0.60, 0.70, 0.80, and 0.90 and where the values of $p(E_1)$ where $[1 - p(E_1/C_2)]$. The overall predictability, in terms of the ϕ-coefficient, ranged from 0.00 to 0.89. The main finding in this study was that the majority of the subjects deviated somewhat from differential matching towards differential maximizing ("overshooting"). In all conditions the asymptotic performance was above the level corresponding to differential matching. According to Summers this might be due to the contrast between the cue event dependencies and the marginal frequencies.

The three studies just mentioned have one characteristic in common: They describe inference behavior in terms of the four strategies defined in Figure 3.3. There are, however, more experiments dealing with the 2×2 situation (usually under the heading of discrimination learning) originating from statistical learning theory, for example, Popper and Atkinson (1958), Shaffer (1963), and Myers and Cruse (1968). The data reported in these studies do not permit a categorization of subjects according to inference strategy. The author has tried, however, to look into the strategy followed by the average subject. In the studies by Popper and Atkinson and by Shaffer a deviation from differential matching towards undershooting occurs for low levels of ecological validity (measured by the ϕ-coefficient of the C-E matrix), whereas matching or a slight tendency towards overshooting occurs for higher levels of ecological validity. A similar trend, though less obvious, appears also in the data by Myers and Cruse. The deviation from differential matching in these three studies is thus in the opposite direction from the one found by Summers (1968), at least for the lower levels of ecological validity.

Conclusion

Since there is no general theory for inference strategy in non-metric situations (although several "micro-theories" have been suggested) and since an individual's strategy is probably very sensitive to instructions, personal background, education, and so on, I have confined myself to a few main trends in the data referred to. It seems fair to conclude that, in general, differential matching and differential maximizing are the dominant strategies, the latter tending to be more frequent when the task becomes more determinate. Differential matching is most frequent for intermediate levels of ecological validity, whereas matching and maximizing show a relative increase in frequency when the task becomes more uncertain. In other words, the degree of determinism of inferential behavior seems to follow rather closely the determinism of the task. This, of course, is a rough generalization, from which deviations in both directions occur. But lacking a systematic theory that incorporates subject variables and the information of instructions, it seems at present rather fruitless to go into explanations of these deviations.

In this section we have focused on inference behavior in terms of four strategies that are uniquely defined by the C-R matrix with elements u_{jk}. A subject's performance can be categorized as belonging to the one or the other strategy, or to be more precise, one of the four strategies is usually a better description of the person's behavior than the other three.

Though it may be convenient to classify subjects according to certain response strategies, this is an oversimplification; that is, subjects seldom behave exactly in accordance with a certain ideal strategy. As an alternative, it might be useful (and more realistic) to approach inference behavior in the nonmetric situations by methods that do not force subjects into any category. What is aimed for is thus a description of strategy which is "continuous" rather than categorical. Two areas of research now in progress in our laboratory will be chosen as empirical examples. The one concerns inferences to cue-compounds and the other concerns changes of inference behavior when feedback is removed.

Cue-compounds. Consider a situation of the following kind: First, a subject is trained to respond to cues $C_1 \ldots C_m$, which are related to a set of events according to a $M \times N$ matrix with elements v_{ij} denoting the conditional probabilities of E_i when C_j occurs. At the end of training, when the response system has become fairly stable, the inferential behavior as it appears in the C-R matrix can be studied. After this training the cues are combined into compounds, for example, (C_1, C_2), (C_2, C_3, C_7), and so on, and the subject is asked to respond to these compounds according to the same set of categories as before, $E_1, E_2 \ldots E_N$. No feedback is provided during this second phase of the experiment.

Situations where we first learn to interpret single cues and then have to respond to combinations of them are often met outside the laboratory. If one were attempting to predict the likelihood of rain, for example, sometimes the cues would point in the same direction, that is, the humidity is high (C_1) and there are clouds in the sky (C_2). On other occasions the cues are more or less in conflict with each other; that is, the humidity is high (C_1) and the sky is cloudless (C_2). Compound situations are frequently found in several occupations. An X-ray physician, for example, has to make his diagnosis from more or less congruent cues. By the two-stage procedure (first training on single cues and then test on compounds), we can induce experimentally various degrees of conflict between the cues. In this manner we can then study inference behavior under various degrees of cue-utilization congruency (See Equation 3.8). While we have a rather large body of data concerning interpersonal conflicts (See readings on cognitive conflicts), the studies of intrapersonal conflicts by means of the two-stage procedure described above have just begun. The data to be reported here should be regarded as the result of a preliminary attempt to investigate reactions to cue-compounds.

Friedman, Rollins, and Padilla (1968) have suggested a two-stage model, implying (1) that the subject first selects one of the cues in the compound where the probability of selecting a cue is assumed to be proportional to its validity, and (2) once the subject has selected a cue the response probabilities are the same as they were at the end of the training. Friedman et al. found this model valid for a task where the cues had no joint events, that is, E_1 was connected only to C_1, E_2 and E_3 were associated with C_2 only, and so on. This might be an important restriction on their model because the subject can resolve a conflict between two cues in a compound by selecting one of them and then following his previous response pattern. A recent experiment in our laboratory (Lenntoft, 1969) indicates that the two-stage model may not be as relevant for cases where stimuli are associated with the same events as it is in the case of disjoint events.

It will be assumed here that responses to stimulus compounds can be predicted from the C-R matrix for cue-components, without taking the C-E matrix into consideration. It goes without saying that this does not mean that the cue-utilization probabilities would be independent of the ecological validities. Among other things, our discussion in the preceding paragraphs has illustrated how strategies are related to the task characteristics. What the assumption means is simply that the strategy developed during training on component cues determines the strategy when the subject is asked to respond to compounds.

Only compounds of two stimuli have been used in the following experiments. Two types of compounds can be distinguished representing extremes on the continuum of cue-utilization congruency, as defined in Equation 3.8. At the one extreme we have compounds where the two stimuli have been responded to in an identical and highly consistent manner ($h_{jm} = 1$). At the other extreme are those compounds where the response patterns are the opposite of each other ($h_{jm} = 0$), meaning that there is a conflict between the stimuli with respect to the way they were utilized at the end of training. In the first case one can predict with a great deal of confidence that the subject will continue to respond as he did to both components. But what about the other extreme? Will the subject resolve the conflict by arbitrarily restricting his responses to a single response category (high response consistency) or by distributing the responses over the response categories available (low response consistency)? The problem can be seen in a larger context since it concerns our inferences in situations where our previous experience provides us with equivocal information; that is, information that cannot be rationally utilized in the one or other manner.

Experimental findings. What has been done so far is to focus on response consistency for stimulus compounds, h_{jm}^2 as a function of the cue-utilization congruency during the training period, h_{jm}. More detailed descriptions of the experiments have been given elsewhere (Björkman, 1969d).

In the first experiment the task was a 4×2 *C-E* matrix. The cues were Greek letters α, β, γ, and δ and the two events were a red square and a blue square. The subject made his prediction by pushing either of two buttons (red or blue). The conditional probabilities of E_1 for the four cues were 0.80, 0.80, 0.40, and 0.40 for half of the subjects and 0.80, 0.20, 0.40, and 0.60 for the other half. The subjects were given 800 trials of training on the component cues, 600 trials during Day 1 and 200 during Day 2. Immediately after this training they were tested during 320 trials on four compounds, namely (α,γ), (γ,β), (β,δ), and (α,δ), which makes 80 trials per compound. The order in which the compounds were tested was random.

For the two cues in each of the four compounds the cue-utilization congruency was computed for the last 200 trials of component training. This was done for each subject separately. The continuum of congruency was then partitioned into five equal intervals with the following midpoints: 0.10, 0.30, 0.50, 0.70, and 0.90. The number of values within each interval was fairly constant: 33, 26, 49, 29, 35 for the five intervals respectively.

The next step was to compute the average response consistency for cue-compounds for each of the five intervals.

The results are shown in Figure 3.5 (I). As expected, the response consistency for cue-compounds was high when the cue-utilization congruency was high. Also, as expected, when h_{jm} decreased so did the response consistency. An unexpected finding, however, was that after a minimum had been reached the response consistency began to increase as the cue congruency decreased further. The relationship is thus U-shaped. The subjects became more rule bound both when the two cues of the compound had been utilized very congruently during the component training and when they had been utilized in opposite ways.

Quite similar results were obtained in two other experiments. In one of them (II) three groups of 12 subjects were trained on 2×2 C-E matrices with varying ecological validities in the three groups. In this case the compound (C_1, C_2) was interspersed among the component stimuli. During a training period of 400 trials the subjects responded to the compound in 30 percent of the cases, whereas C_1 and C_2 were each presented in 35 percent of the trials. The order of presentation of C_1, C_2, and (C_1, C_2) was randomized. Again the U-shaped tendency appears and, as in Experiment I, the response consistency was somewhat higher at the right extreme of the continuum of cue-utilization congruency. It can also be observed that the response consistency was somewhat higher for the 4×2 situation for the 2×2 case. This finding might be tentatively interpreted in accordance with findings by Erickson (1966) and Kroll (1970) that an increase of the number of cues tends to make the response system more determinate.

The third experiment (III) was designed to test the above mentioned two-stage hypothesis for the case of joint events (See Lenntoft, 1969).

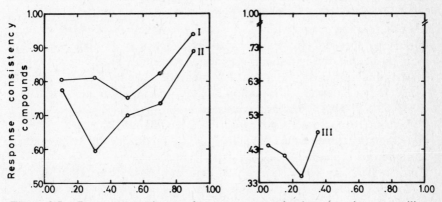

Figure 3.5.   Response consistency for cue-compounds plotted against cue-utilization congruency for the last blocks of training.

Three groups of 10 subjects each received component training on a 2×3 C-E matrices, where $p(E_1/C_1)$ and $p(E_3/C_2)$ both were zero, and $p(E_2/C_1)$, $p(E_3/C_1)$, $p(E_1/C_2)$, and $p(E_2/C_2)$ were nonzero. E_2 is thus the joint event, The ecological validity of C_1 and C_2 was equal but differed from group to group. Since the two cues have only one event in common, the range of cue-utilization congruency becomes narrower than in the other two experiments. However, even within this rather narrow range, the U-shaped function found in the two other experiments remains.

Comments. The results illustrated in Figure 3.5 should by no means be regarded as definite; they represent the first data in a series of experiments. The interesting and unexpected finding is, of course, the high response consistency for low degrees of cue-utilization congruency. Faced with conflicting information subjects prefer to follow a certain policy, a rule, rather than to distribute the responses over the events available. The conflict is resolved by being consistent rather than irregular, or random (as far as people can behave randomly!).

The Role of Feedback in Policy Formation

The experiments to be reported below follow a simple procedure of the following kind. First the subject is trained on C-E material in the usual way. Afterwards, the subject is asked to respond to the same cues but now without receiving feedback. This procedure is similar to the design of retention experiments; that is, after a period of training, there is a test phase where no information about the correct answer is given. There is, however, one important difference. When retention of a previously learned task (e.g., paired-associate material) is tested, there is typically only one test trial for each stimulus. In the following experiments the training is followed by a nonfeedback period comprising a number of trials. Obviously this provides the person with the possibility to develop a response strategy during the nonfeedback trials, a strategy which may or may not be the same as the one during training. Then, does the strategy change and, if so, in what direction does it change? The measure to be used is the response consistency, as defined in Equation 3.6, and the question addressed here is as follows: Does response consistency during the feedback training differ from response consistency during the nonfeedback phase?

The effect of so-called "blank trials" (no feedback) has been studied in numerous probability learning experiments (Anderson & Grant, 1957; Greeno, 1962; La Berge, Greeno, & Peterson, 1962; Reber & Millward, 1968). These studies indicate that blank trials either produce no effect on the response probability or result in a regression toward the initial guessing level. It should be remembered, however, that in these studies, except the one by Reber and Millward (1968), the blank trials were mixed with feedback trials. In the latter study, 500 nonfeedback trials were given after feedback training and the response probability decreased significantly from overshooting to the matching level.

Azuma and Cronbach (1966), using a concept attainment task, found a tendency toward higher response consistency when no framework was given. They interpreted this finding as follows: As long as the subjects receive feedback, various strategies or hypotheses are tested; when the feedback is removed, they are less apt to try different strategies and instead maintain the strategy they found most effective during training.

In the nonmetric *C-E* situations under consideration one can rather safely assume that the subjects try to hit the events at every trial. Those who follow this strategy perfectly will become differential matchers. Others will follow a strategy which is a compromise between trying to hit on every trial and trying to get as many correct predictions as possible. A third, but small category of people, are perfectly rational and predict the most frequent event for each stimulus. In general, therefore, feedback in an uncertain *C-E* task will result in subjects varying their responses, often in accordance with the policy of differential matching, sometimes with a deviation toward undershooting, in other cases with a tendency toward overshooting.

Feedback in probabilistic tasks is thus to be regarded as environmental variation which produces response variation. It is as if subjects attempt to form a cognitive representation that is isomorphic with the environment itself. From these considerations it would follow that removal of feedback is the same as removing the very factor that produces response variation. As a consequence one would expect a reduced response variation (higher response consistency) under nonfeedback trials. This is the hypothesis to be tested by the data reported below.

Experimental findings. Two of the experiments (I and III) are designed in the same way as Experiments I and III on stimulus compounding. Here, however, instead of being tested on compounds the subjects continued as before during Phase 2, but without receiving feedback. Between the feedback phase and the nonfeedback phase, the subjects were instructed that the second task would be the same as the first one, except that no information about the correct answer would be given.

In Experiment I, 800 training trials were followed by 400 trials without feedback. In Experiment III, 400 trials of training were followed by 30 trials without feedback. Experiment II varied the time interval between training and the nonfeedback period. One group of subjects (II-A) completed the nonfeedback trials immediately after training. The other group (II-B) trained for 200 trials with a different C-E task between training and test.

Since these experiments have been reported in more detail elsewhere (Björkman, 1969a), only the major results are presented here. For each subject and cue there are two measures of response consistency, one for the last blocks during training and one for the nonfeedback period.

The difference in response consistency can be analyzed for each stimulus separately, or one can compare each subject's response consistency, averaged over the stimuli, between training and test. Only the latter procedure will be reported here, but the conclusions remain the same regardless of which method is chosen. The results are illustrated in Figure 3.6, where each subject's response consistency during nonfeedback trials has been plotted against the response consistency at the end of training. If no change had occurred the observations would fall around

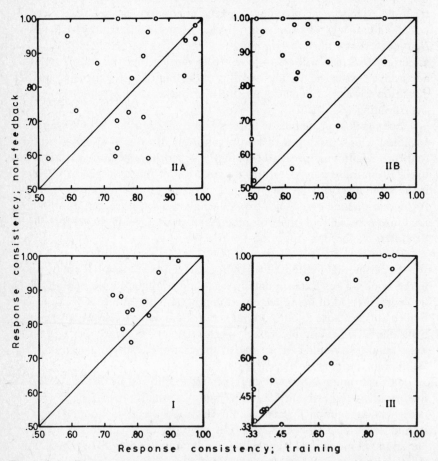

Figure 3.6. Data from three experiments showing the relationship between response consistency during a nonfeedback phase, which follows after training, and the response consistency at the last block of training

the diagonal. In three of the four experiments, however, there is a considerable increase in response consistency when no feedback is provided. The difference is significant at the 1 percent level (*t*-tests for correlated samples) in Experiments I and IIB and significant at the 5 percent level in Experiment III. In IIA the difference is in the predicted direction, but nonsignificant.

Discussion

On the whole, the results are at variance with the findings in probability learning experiments, even those by Reber and Millward (1968) who used the same procedure (first training and then testing without feedback). Although similar in experimental procedure the tasks, however, are different. Reber and Millward (1968) used the traditional (no cue) probability learning two-choice task, whereas ours are (multiple) cue probability learning tasks. The nonmetric *C-E* task used here may be viewed as a set of rules, one for each cue, which are more or less equivocal (e.g., "E_1 goes with C_2, although sometimes there are exceptions so E_2 will occur"). These tasks share this characteristic with the metric multiple and single cue probability learning tasks.

Fortunately, we have some information about the effect of nonfeedback trials for the metric case. Brehmer and Lindberg (1970a, 1970b) conducted experiments using a single cue metric task. The cue-variable was length of lines and the criterion was numbers. For various levels of correlation between the cue and the criterion and for various time intervals between training and nonfeedback test, they have consistently found an increase in response consistency from the training phase to the test phase. (Response consistency in these studies was measured by the correlation between the cue-variable and the subject's response.)

The evidence suggests, therefore, that the effect of nonfeedback depends upon the nature of the inference tasks. When the task consists solely of a distribution of events, without any cues guiding the predictions, response consistency either is reduced or does not change. On the other hand when the task consists of a rule to which some "noise" has been added, the response consistency increases when no feedback is provided. To use Brunswik's (1957) terminology it may be said that "distribution hypotheses" are weakened or unchanged, whereas "correlation hypotheses" are strengthened when feedback is no longer provided.

The author has argued in a previous report (Björkman, 1968) that learning a probabilistic rule as in correlation learning involves two processes: (1) learning the rule, for example, the regression of Y on X; and (2) learning the amount of task error that interferes with the rule, for example, the distribution of values around the regression line. It was also suggested, and supported by experimental data, that a person faced with a task of this kind must learn the rule prior to learning the exceptions from the rule (the "noise").

A further step in this reasoning would be to say that the uncertainty added to the rule to a certain extent induces the subjects to vary their responses. When "noise" is removed, as is done when feedback is no longer provided, the cognitive representation of the task consists primarily of the rule and this will express itself as increased response consistency, whether the task is metric or nonmetric. In the noncue situation, probability learning, there is only a distribution to learn but no rule in the sense described above. In this case, the feedback cannot interfere with any other learning going on concurrently. Thus, when feedback is removed it is not surprising that the response probabilities remain unchanged or decrease somewhat in the direction of the initial response tendencies.

In conclusion, learning theorists, in particular those who tend to equate feedback with reinforcement, may find it somewhat surprising to view outcome feedback as an interfering factor in probabilistic C-E learning. The argument is based on the fact that the subjects are faced both with regularity and irregularity (randomness) and the assumption that the latter interferes with the former. Our reasoning might be viewed as one way of expressing man's preference for deterministic relationships. However, it is not until we remove the interfering influences that the subjects get the full opportunity to express their preference for lawfulness and regularity.

REFERENCES

Anderson, N. H., & Grant, D. A. A test of a statistical learning theory model for two-choice behavior with double stimulus events. *Journal of Experimental Psychology,* 1957, *54,* 305–317.

Atkinson, R. C. A Markov model for discrimination learning. *Psychometrika,* 1958, *23,* 309–322.

Azuma, H., & Cronbach, L. J. Cue-response correlations in the attainment of a scalar concept. *American Journal of Psychology,* 1966, *79,* 38–49.

Björkman, M. Stimulus-event learning and event learning as concurrent processes. *Organizational Behavior and Human Performance,* 1967, *2,* 219–236.

Björkman, M. The effect of training and number of stimuli on the response variance in correlation learning. *Umeå Psychological Reports,* 1968, No. 2.

Björkman, M. The effects of policy formation in a nonmetric task when training is followed by nonfeedback trials. *Umeå Psychological Reports,* 1969, No. 6. (a)

Björkman, M. Individual performances in a single-cue probability learning task. *Scandinavian Journal of Psychology,* 1969, *10,* 113–123. (b)

Björkman, M. On the ecological relevance of psychological research. *Scandinavian Journal of Psychology,* 1969, *10,* 145–157. (c)

Björkman, M. Response consistency as a function of cue congruency in stimulus compounding. *Umeå Psychological Reports,* 1969, No. 5. (d)

Brehmer, B., & Lindberg, L. The relation between cue dependency and cue validity in single-cue probability learning with scaled cue and criterion variables. *Organizational Behavior and Human Performance*, 1970, *5*, 542–544. (a)

Brehmer, B., & Lindberg, L. Retention of probabilistic cue-criterion relations as a function of cue validity and retention interval. *Journal of Experimental Psychology*, 1970, in press. (b)

Brunswik, E. *Perception and the representative design of psychological experiments*. Berkeley: University of California Press, 1956.

Brunswik, E. Scope and aspects of the cognitive problem. In H. Gruber, R. Jessor, & K. Hammond (Eds.), *Cognition: The Colorado symposium*. Cambridge, Mass.: Harvard University Press, 1957.

Burke, C. J., & Estes, W. K. A component model for stimulus variables in discrimination learning. *Psychometrika*, 1957, *22*, 133–145.

Erickson, J. R. On learning several simultaneous probability-learning problems. *Journal of Experimental Psychology*, 1966, *72*, 182–189.

Estes, W. K. The statistical approach to learning theory. In S. Koch (Ed.), *Psychology: A study of a science*. Vol. 2. New York: McGraw Hill, 1969.

Friedman, M. P., Rollins, H., & Padilla, G. The role of cue-validity in a stimulus compounding. *Journal of Mathematical Psychology*, 1968, *5*, 300–310.

Greeno, J. G. Effects of nonreinforced trials in two-choice learning with noncontingent reinforcement, *Journal of Experimental Psychology*, 1962, *64*, 54–61.

Hammond, K. R. New directions in research on conflict resolution. *Journal of Social Issues*, 1965, *21*, 44–66.

Hammond, K. R., Bonaiuto, G., Faucheux, C., Moscovici, S., Frohlich, W. D., Joyce, C. R. B., & Di Majo, G. A. A comparison of cognitive conflict between persons in western Europe and the United States. *International Journal of Psychology*, 1968, *3*, 1–12.

Hammond, K. R., & Brehmer, B. Distrust among nations: A challenge to scientific inquiry. University of Colorado, Institute of Behavioral Science: Program on Cognitive Processes. Report No. 116, 1970.

Hursch, C., Hammond, K. R., & Hursch, J. Some methodological considerations in multiple cue probability studies. *Psychological Review*, 1964, *71*, 42–60.

Kroll, N. E. A. The learning of several simultaneous probability learning problems as a function of overall event probability and prior knowledge. *Journal of Experimental Psychology*, 1970, *83*, 209–215.

La Berge, D., Greeno, J. G., & Peterson, D. F. Nonreinforcement and neutralization of stimuli. *Journal of Experimental Psychology*, 1962, *63*, 207–213.

Lenntoft, K. Joint and disjoint events in a stimulus compounding situation. *Umeå Psychological Reports*, 1969, No. 4.

Marx, M. H. The general nature of theory construction. In M. H. Marx (Ed.), *Theories in contemporary psychology*. New York: Macmillan, 1963.

Meehl, P. E., & Rosen, A. Antecedent probability and the efficiency of psychometric signs, patterns, or cutting scores. *Psychological Bulletin*, 1955, *52*, 194–216.

Myers, J. L., & Cruse, D. Two-choice discrimination learning as a function of stimulus and event probabilities. *Journal of Experimental Psychology*, 1968, *77*, 453–459.

Popper, J., & Atkinson, R. C. Discrimination learning in a verbal conditioning situation. *Journal of Experimental Psychology,* 1958, *56,* 21–25.

Reber, A. S., & Millward, R. B. Event observation in probability learning. *Journal of Experimental Psychology,* 1968, *77,* 317–327.

Shaffer, J. P. Effect of different stimulus frequencies on discrimination learning with probabilistic reinforcement. *Journal of Experimental Psychology,* 1963, *65,* 265–269.

Summers, S. A. Alternative bases for choice in probabilistic discrimination. *Journal of Experimental Psychology,* 1968, *76,* 538–543.

Todd, F. J., & Hammond, K. R. Differential feedback in two multiple-cue probability learning tasks. *Behavioral Science,* 1965, *10,* 429–435.

Tolman, E. C., & Brunswik, E. The organism and the causal texture of the environment. *Psychological Review,* 1935, *42,* 43–77.

Introduction
to Reading 4

It is clear that useful studies of human judgment and learning can be accomplished in more-or-less ordinary circumstances where college sophomores serve as laboratory subjects. But can judgment processes be studied effectively in not-so-ordinary circumstances where hospitalized mental patients serve as subjects? Although the evidence at this point is not sufficient to permit a firm answer, the reading by Gillis and Davis provides an encouraging account of how the lens model was employed to examine disordered thinking.

These authors report on the performances of paranoid and non-paranoid schizophrenics who worked on two different uncertain judgment tasks while under two different drug regimens. In general, theoretical propositions about the nature of schizophrenic thought and the effects of drugs were confirmed. It should be noted that whereas certain features of the study preclude unequivocal generalizations about drug effects, the findings remain important because they demonstrate how the lens model approach to judgment can be utilized to gain new understandings of disordered thought.

4 The Effects of Psychoactive Drugs on Complex Thinking in Paranoid and Nonparanoid Schizophrenics: An Application of the Multiple-Cue Model to the Study of Disordered Thinking[1]

JOHN S. GILLIS
Texas Tech University

KEITH E. DAVIS[2]
Rutgers University

Despite the wide range of cognitive problems that have been investigated within Brunswik's Lens Model paradigm, very little effort has been made to apply this paradigm to problems of disordered thought. The present paper, therefore, is designed to illustrate how the lens model can be useful, both conceptually and methodologically, in this domain. Specifically, this paper shows how the lens model can be used to assess the effects of psychoactive drugs (amphetamine and chlorpromazine) upon schizophrenic thinking.

Cognitive functioning in schizophrenics. A growing body of evidence (e.g., Goldberg, Schooler, & Mattson, 1968; Lang & Buss, 1965; O'Connor, 1957; Raush, 1952; Shakow, 1963; Venables, 1964; Voth, 1947) points to crucial differences between paranoid and nonparanoid schizophrenics with regard to a wide range of cognitive functions. Particularly impressive is Silverman's identification of perceptual differences between these two groups of patients. Based on an extensive review of previous work (1964a) as well as his own investigations (1964b), Silverman has suggested that paranoids and nonparanoids differ with regard to the "scanning controls"

[1] This investigation was supported by Research Grant 12545-01 from the National Institute of Mental Health, United States Public Health Service.
[2] The authors are indebted to the staff of the Veterans Administration Hospital, Ft. Lyon, Colorado, for their cooperation. The authors also wish to thank Richard J. Comtois and Leonard Gerny who assisted in the screening and testing of subjects. Kenneth R. Hammond was a source of stimulation and encouragement for this study.

described by Gardner and his co-workers (Gardner, Holzman, Klein, Linton, & Spence, 1959). Paranoids are hyper-vigilant and exhibit extreme scanning and a wide scope-of-attention. Nonparanoids, on the other hand, demonstrate minimal scanning and a narrow scope-of-attention. Similar notions regarding differential scanning responses, especially the reduced scope of chronic nonparanoids, have been advanced by a number of investigators (Broen, 1966; Lester, 1960; Venables, 1964).

Differential effects on "focus of attention" and vigilance have also been reported for the psychoactive chemicals amphetamine and chlorpromazine (Calloway & Stone, 1960; Evans & Smith, 1964; Loeb, Hawkes, Evans, & Alluisi, 1965; Wikler, Haertzen, Chessick, Hill, & Pescor, 1965). Amphetamine appears to prevent the loss of vigilance in perceptual tasks and to increase "focus of attention," whereas chlorpromazine has directly opposite effects.

It should be noted, however, that the above evidence—with regard to both drug effects and the paranoid-nonparanoid dimension—is derived entirely from perceptual studies. Silverman's (1964b) notions, for example, are based largely on size estimation tasks in which scanning control is inferred from a subject's tendencies to over- or underestimate the size of a stimulus object. Although such studies are useful, none of the data bear directly on what we might call the cognitive consequences of such perceptual response dispositions. It is unknown, for example, whether the paranoid who perceptually scans his environment can effectively integrate this information in a judgmental task. Similarly, there is no information as to whether the diminution of focus of attention through psychoactive chemicals renders one more or less effective in the manner in which he utilizes those cues to which he does attend. The purpose of the present study was to evaluate the "focus of attention" hypotheses generated in perceptual tasks in situations involving complex cognitive behavior.

Judgments in multiple-cue situations. Judgment tasks involving multiple, probabilistic cues, when used in conjunction with Brunswik's Lens Model, appear to be particularly suited for investigating the problems noted above. As a paradigm within which significant aspects of the organism–environment interaction can be studied, the lens model represents the most succinct summary of Brunswik's views. The model has been fully described elsewhere (Brunswik, 1952; Hursch, Hammond, & Hursch, 1964), and it need only be noted here that this approach provides a means of confronting subjects with conditions representative in form of their typical ecologies. Brunswik, among others, stressed that most persons function in situations that are both uncertain and involve a multiplicity of cues. The most frequent judgments that must be made in everyday circumstances are necessarily based on a wide range of indicants, no one of which has a univocal relationship with the "distal variable"—the characteristic or event that must be assessed. If, as Gillis (1969a) has suggested, certain individuals have failed to adapt cognitively to their environment, it is precisely to such multiple-cue, probabilistic situations that they have failed to adapt. And it is within situations representative of such conditions that we are likely to determine to what extent, and in what manner, such failure occurred.

The tasks derived from this multiple-cue model appear especially suited to exploring cognitive over- and underinclusion in that they permit experimenter control over the range of information that must be taken into account for successful performance. It is therefore possible to relate adequacy of performance directly to the task requirements for "narrow or wide scope" of effective cue-utilization.

The primary goal of the investigation was therefore to assess the effect of two diagnostic conditions—paranoid and nonparanoid schizophrenia— and two psychoactive chemicals—chlorpromazine and amphetamine—on performance in probabilistic multiple-cue tasks. It was expected that both the paranoid and amphetamine conditions, because they enhance vigilance and scope-of-attention, would enhance performance on tasks requiring the use of a wide range of cues. Performance on tasks requiring the effective utilization of a limited number of cues, where, in fact, additional cues constituted distractors, would be maximal in the nonparanoid and chlorpromazine conditions.

The multiple-cue tasks employed appeared to tap a kind of functioning similar to what has been traditionally described as "over- and underinclusive" thinking (Cameron, 1936). In order to assess this possibility, a measure of conceptual breadth (Chapman, 1961) representing the more familiar methods of evaluating these concepts was also included in the study. Although there were no firm expectations in this regard, the relationship between multiple-cue performance and overly narrow or broad conceptual responses could thus be evaluated.

Method

Subjects

Subjects were 90 chronic schizophrenic patients hospitalized at the Veteran's Administration Hospital, Fort Lyon, Colorado. All subjects were selected after an initial extensive screening interview. During this interview the patient's diagnosis—paranoid or nonparanoid—was ascertained, ratings on the Venables and O'Connor (1959) scale being a principal determinant of the judgment. Also determined during the screening process was the patient's IQ (Otis alpha), his premorbid adjustment (using Phillips' scale as modified by Farina and Garmezy [Garmezy, 1965]), and his status with regard to a number of demographic indices. A patient was excluded from the study when (1) there was any suggestion of brain damage, or (2) he could not be placed with reasonable certainty into the paranoid or nonparanoid categories. Those subjects selected were then divided into 12 groups having from 5 to 8 members each. 6 of these groups consisted of exclusively paranoid patients and 6 contained only nonparanoids. All 12 groups were matched for age, education, and intelligence. Table 4.1 presents the means and standard deviations for each of the groups of these variables. It was not possible to equate the groups on premorbid status although, as mentioned, the status of most subjects on this variable was determined so that its relationship to performance on the tasks could be evaluated.

Stimulus Materials

Two multiple-cue probability learning (MCPL) tasks were utilized in this study. In each task there were three cues (i.e., three distinctly different aspects of geometric figures), each of which was related in a linear, probabilistic way to the criterion. In the narrow-focus task *(A) only one cue* had any significant predictive validity, the remaining two cues having near-zero correlations with the criterion. In the wide-focus task *(B) each of the three cues* had a significant and roughly equal predictive validity. The correlational structures of the wide- and narrow-focus tasks are depicted in Figure 4.1. In order to perform successfully on Task *A* then, subjects need only learn to take into account a single cue when making their responses. Their performance, in fact, would be impaired to the extent that they utilized the other cues. To perform successfully in the wide-focus task *(B)*, however, subjects must take account of all available information contained in the three cues. In neither task was it possible for a subject to be perfectly correct on every trial; that is, R^2 for both tasks was approximately .85.

Details of the MCPL Tasks

The multiple-cue stimulus materials consisted of a geometric pattern involving a circle, a pointer on its periphery, and a horizontal line within the circle. The relevant cues for the prediction of the criterion variables were: (1) size of circle, (2) position of the horizontal line within the circle, and (3) location of the pointer on the periphery of the circle.

Subjects were informed that the criterion was a number on the back of each stimulus card that ranged from 1–16 and could be predicted with considerable, although not perfect, success if they learned which cues were relevant for this prediction. Subjects were also told at the outset what the three cues were and how each varied. After the subjects were

Table 4.1. Means and Standard Deviation of IQ, Educational Attainment, and Age for Each Cell of the Design

Drug Subject Status Task		Amphetamine				Chlorpromazine				Placebo			
		Paranoid		Nonparanoid		Paranoid		Nonparanoid		Paranoid		Nonparanoid	
		NF*	WF**	NF	WF	NF	WF	NF	WF	NF	WF	NF	WF
IQ	$\overline{X}$	93.4	91.1	91.3	93.0	92.9	94.0	93.6	95.8	91.4	88.8	95.3	97.0
	SD	10.8	13.0	11.3	9.5	10.3	16.2	9.1	10.4	6.9	6.5	14.3	10.0
Education	$\overline{X}$	11.3	10.5	11.3	11.5	11.3	11.1	10.9	11.0	11.4	12.2	10.9	11.0
	SD	7.1	2.5	1.8	4.0	1.5	3.2	1.4	1.9	2.1	2.9	1.7	1.0
Age	$\overline{X}$	33.3	32.1	30.1	36.3	30.8	34.9	33.0	35.9	38.7	32.2	32.0	34.0
	SD	9.5	6.5	7.7	7.8	9.3	8.0	9.9	3.7	7.4	8.2	7.9	7.0
	N	8	8	8	8	8	8	8	8	7	5	7	7

*NF = Narrow-focus task
**WF = Wide-focus task

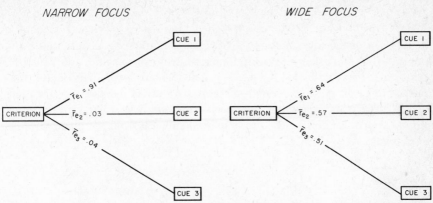

Figure 4.1. Statistical structure of the multiple-cue probability learning tasks. $\bar{r}_{e_1}$ = average correlation between cue 1 and criterion over the entire 75 trials. R_e^2 = overall linear determinacy for all three cues as predictors of the criterion.

given three illustrative practice trials, all subjects completed 75 learning trials. On each trial, subjects were first shown a stimulus array, and then asked to record a prediction on an answer sheet. Following this prediction, subjects were given immediate feedback about the correct answer.

Test of Conceptual Breadth

The measure of conceptual breadth employed was a paper-and-pencil form of a card-sorting task developed by Chapman (1961). Briefly, subjects were presented with a word describing a conceptual category, for example, "fruit." They were then required to circle, from a list of 30 terms, items that belong in this category, and also to designate (by checking the word) items that do not belong in the category. Overinclusive (OI) errors are scored when an item that does not belong in the specified category is circled; overexclusive (OE) errors are scored when items that should be included in the specified category are omitted. Two levels of conceptual breadth were represented by the categories, "fruit" and "birds" being examples of relatively narrow categories while "creatures that fly" and "things to eat" represent the broader levels. In all, subjects were asked to respond to 16 conceptual categories, each having 30 terms that must be appropriately designated as belonging or not belonging in that category.

The primary purpose of employing this task in the study was to evaluate the relationship between MCPL performance and conceptual measures of overinclusion and overexclusion. The test was thus scored for total OI and OE scores without reference to the differential width of the stimulus categories.

Design

The intent of the investigators had been to complete a 2 (Paranoid-Non-paranoid) $\times$ 2 (Tasks) $\times$ 3 (Amphetamine, Chlorpromazine, and Placebo) factorial design with 8 subjects per cell. Because some difficulty was encountered in getting enough subjects who could be clearly classified as paranoid or nonparanoid (while also meeting the other criteria mentioned above), a decision was made to omit subjects from the placebo cells. (See Table 4.1.)

Procedure

Subjects were taken off all medication for three days prior to the administration of the experimental dose. On the day of testing, subjects received (after having taken no food for at least three hours) either (1) 150 mg. chlorpromazine, (2) 15 mg. meth-amphetamine, or (3) a lactose placebo.

One and one-half hours after administration of the experimental drug, testing was begun. Although the initial plan of the study proposed that subjects be tested individually, time pressures rendered this difficult. Subjects were thus tested in pairs.

Each pair of subjects was confronted with the same MCPL task ("narrow or wide focus"), but the composition of each pair was random with regard to diagnosis and drug condition. While interaction between the members of the pair was permitted for a few minutes before and after the testing, they were not allowed to interact while the testing was in progress.

Subjects completed in order (1) Chapman's measure of "conceptual breadth," (2) either the narrow- or wide-focus MCPL task, (3) a 35-item questionnaire designed to assess feelings of internal control over the environment, and (4) a 94-item self-report of current psychological states developed by Davis, Comtois, and Evans (1969). Results of the two questionnaires are not considered in this report.

Results

Performance in the MCPL task was assessed by correlating (over trials) subjects' responses with the correct answers. The resulting coefficients are here referred to as "achievement correlations" (r_a). In order to detect possible improvement over trials, achievement correlations were calculated for three blocks of 25 trials. These coefficients were then transformed into Fisher's Z coefficient for all subsequent statistical analyses.

Based on the structure of the MCPL tasks and the methods of analysis used, it was possible to assess drug and diagnostic influences over all trials or over any single block of 25 trials. It was anticipated that the most valuable comparisons might be made over the second (trials 26–50) and third (trials 51–75) blocks of trials since subjects should, by that time, have developed some stable manner of coping with the tasks.

Two analyses of variance were performed on the achievement *(Z)* scores for the second and third blocks of trials, respectively. These analyses revealed that drug status (chlorpromazine, amphetamine, or placebo) was nearly significant for the second block of trials; F $(df = 1,76) = 2.51$, $p < .07$. This result was almost entirely due to the superiority of the placebo groups over the two drug conditions. Drug status was clearly significant in the third block of trials; F $(df = 1,76) = 4.13$, $p < .05$. Again, this effect was due to the higher achievement correlation obtained for subjects in the placebo condition than in either of the drug conditions. In addition, it was found that the narrow-focus task was less difficult than the wide-focus task; F $(df = 1,76) = 6.44$, $p < .05$. This finding of differential task difficulty for schizophrenics replicates that of Gillis (1969b) who found, however, no such difference with normal subjects.

Paranoid-Nonparanoid Differences on MCPL Performance

It had been expected that nonparanoids would perform better than paranoids in the narrow-focus task, whereas paranoids would be superior in the wide-focus situation. The most direct test of this hypothesis was in the placebo condition. As Table 4.2 indicates, the pathology-task hypothesis was supported in the second block of trials with regard to the narrow-focus task; that is, the nonparanoids demonstrated a significantly higher achievement than did the paranoids. There was, however, no difference between the two groups of patients in the wide-focus task.

Over all drug conditions (chlorpromazine, amphetamine, and placebo), nonparanoids were also noticeably better on the narrow-focus task, although the difference was not significant ($t = 1.53$, $p < .10$). Again over all drug conditions, there was no difference between the two diagnostic groups in the wide-focus task.

Table 4.2.   Comparisons of Achievement Correlations of Paranoid and Nonparanoid Schizophrenics in the Placebo Condition (Trials 26–50)

Task	Group	r_a	t-value	P
Narrow-focus	Paranoid	.36	2.10	.05*
	Nonparanoid	.79		
Wide-focus	Paranoid	.38	0.10	n.s.
	Nonparanoid	.40		

*One-tailed test

Effects of Amphetamine and Chlorpromazine on MCPL Performance

It was expected that amphetamine would facilitate performance on the wide-focus task but impair it in the narrow-focus situation relative to chlorpromazine. Although the predicted difference between the amphetamine and chlorpromazine conditions did occur in the wide-focus task ($t = 1.76$, $p < .05$) during trials 26–50 (Table 4.3), the amphetamine-placebo difference is in the opposite direction and the predicted difference has disappeared by trials 51–75 (Table 4.4). Here one can see that by trials 51–75, both drug groups are performing at a level significantly below the placebo subjects in the wide-focus task.

In the narrow-focus task, results are much the same. Both drugs tend to impair performance relative to placebo in both blocks of trials (See Tables 4.3 and 4.4). In neither block, however, is the drug-induced impairment quite so strong as it was in the wide-focus task. To the degree that consistency of pattern is important, the most striking and unexpected result is that both drugs produced a decrement compared to placebo. These results are in accord with those obtained for normal college students in their first encounter with MCPL tasks (Davis, Evans, & Gillis, 1968).

Relationships among the MCPL, Test of Conceptual Breadth, and Demographic Indices

Comparisons of the mean scores of each of the 12 cells of the design (using Duncan's multiple-range test) yielded no significant differences in terms of either overinclusion (OI) or overexclusion (OE), as determined by the Chapman procedure. Similarly, comparisons of scores on the Chapman test across all drug conditions and both diagnostic states failed to yield any significant differences. There was no relationship between performance on the MCPL task and the conceptual breadth test. Across all 90 subjects, the correlation between the Chapman overinclusion score and MCPL achievement on Block II was .03. The correlation between the overexclusion score and MCPL on Block II performance was −.11.

Performance on Chapman's test was, however, significantly related to IQ. Again across all 90 subjects, IQs obtained on the Otis correlated −.29 ($p < .05$) with the OI score and −.31 ($p < .05$) with the OE score. In short, subjects with higher IQs made fewer errors of either type. Education was also significantly and inversely correlated with overinclusion ($r = -.22$, $p < .05$).

On the other hand, intelligence was *not* associated with performance on the MCPL tasks used here. Thus, the correlation between IQ and achievement for the second block of trials was only .07. An analysis of the

Table 4.3.   Comparisons of Achievement Correlations (r_a) on Two Multiple-Cue Probability Tasks under Three Drug Conditions (Trials 26–50)

Task	Drug Comparison	r_a	t-value	P
Narrow-focus	Amphetamine Chlorpromazine	.32 .35	0.14	n.s.
	Amphetamine Placebo	.32 .62	1.63	n.s.
	Chlorpromazine Placebo	.35 .62	1.57	n.s.
Wide-focus	Amphetamine Chlorpromazine	.33 .18	1.75	.05*
	Amphetamine Placebo	.33 .39	0.64	n.s.
	Chlorpromazine Placebo	.18 .39	1.75	.05*

*One-tailed test

relationship between Block III achievement and IQ yielded an equally low coefficient. Similarly, neither age nor education was significantly related to MCPL performance; that is, all correlations between these variables and Block II and Block III achievement were less than .08.

Finally, premorbid status, as rated according to Phillips' scale (Garmezy, 1965), failed to correlate significantly with either MCPL achievement or the OI and OE indices derived from the conceptual task.

Table 4.4.   Comparisons of Achievement Correlations (r_a) on Two Multiple-Cue Probability Tasks under Three Drug Conditions (Trials 51–75)

Task	Drug Comparison	r_a	t-value	P
Narrow-focus	Amphetamine Chlorpromazine	.45 .52	0.42	n.s.
	Amphetamine Placebo	.45 .68	1.67	n.s.
	Chlorpromazine Placebo	.52 .68	1.24	n.s.
Wide-focus	Amphetamine Chlorpromazine	.27 .25	0.26	n.s.
	Amphetamine Placebo	.27 .53	2.27	.05
	Chlorpromazine Placebo	.25 .53	2.28	.05

Discussion

The results indicate that both the paranoid–nonparanoid dimension of schizophrenia and the drug regimen of a schizophrenic patient are important factors in the performance of rather complex multiple-cue tasks.

That nonparanoids were, as expected, superior on the narrow-focus task adds support to the contentions of several investigators (Broen, 1966; Silverman, 1964a, 1964b; Venables, 1964; Zahn, Rosenthal, & Shakow, 1963) that such patients are hyposcanners who cope with the world by excessively narrowing their stimulus field. More important, however, this finding indicates that such scanning processes have effects on the cognitive functioning of such patients. As shown here, the "narrow" nonparanoid demonstrated superiority on a task having requirements congruent with his characteristic cognitive style. Moreover, the results from the multiple-cue learning task suggest that such patients can utilize, with some effectiveness, those segments of the stimulus situation to which they do attend. This is consistent with findings of a previous MCPL study (Gillis, 1969b) involving a group of schizophrenics composed largely of chronic nonparanoids. In that study, the patient group was able to perform at a level comparable to normal college students *only* when the utilization of limited cues presented in an impersonal context was necessary for predictive accuracy.

The inferiority of paranoids on the narrow-focus task is consistent with the notion that these patients, at least relative to other types of schizophrenics, are "overinclusive" in the sense of being unable to ignore irrelevant aspects of their environment. And, again, the demonstration of this characteristic within the context of an inferential task suggests that the scanning dispositions of such patients are indeed determinants of their judgmental abilities. That such paranoid–nonparanoid differences were not supported with the wide-focus task—that is, that paranoids were not superior in this situation where an "inclusive" response would be successful—is perhaps best explained in terms of the level of difficulty of the task. As Gillis (1969b) noted, the wide-focus situation appears to be a very difficult one for schizophrenics generally, and the limits of achievement for these patients may be such that they preclude any subgroup from performing well. Indeed, it has been shown that learning is slow in these "wide-focus" tasks for nonhospitalized subjects as well (Uhl, 1963).

Clearly the expectations regarding drug influences were not supported in that both drugs impaired performance and their influence was roughly the same in both the narrow- and wide-focus tasks. It should be kept in mind, however, that their similar deteriorative effects may be brought about by quite different processes. Amphetamine, for example, may indeed dispose an individual to take account of diverse cues; but it may also dispose him to use these incorrectly, or to include aspects of the stimulus situation *other* than what the experimenter has designated as "cues." And chlorpromazine may so "narrow" an individual's scope-of-attention or impair his ability to learn that he finds it difficult to cope with *any* task presenting several potential items of information.

To the degree that consistency over learning trials is important, the results with chlorpromazine, amphetamine, and placebo are dramatic in showing a pattern of drug decrement in the MCPL tasks. These data are in fact strikingly similar to those obtained by Davis, Evans, and Gillis (1968) for normal college males, although in that study the drug-induced decrement for these same psychoactive agents was most pronounced in the narrow-focus task.

It is also interesting to note that performance by nonparanoid schizophrenic subjects in the placebo condition was as good as that achieved by college students in the same narrow-focus task used by Davis et al. (1968). Specifically, these investigations found a mean achievement correlation of .71 for normals while the comparable score for nonparanoids in the present study was .80. Although these two studies are not strictly comparable, this finding lends some support to an earlier finding (Gillis, 1969b) that schizophrenics can perform cognitively at a level comparable to that of normals when task content is impersonal and when the task involves the use of limited cues.

The finding that subjects could not learn complex problems when taking chlorpromazine, even at a moderate dose level, is congruent with evidence from a variety of learning situations (Hartlage, 1965), and would appear to be a crucial finding concerning the use of this agent in the treatment of schizophrenics. Regardless of how one conceptualizes the various psychological forms of treatment a patient receives—individual or group sessions, occupational therapy, milieu programs, and the like—most of these certainly involve the goal of a patient's learning some "new" responses to his environment. Although the evidence that chlorpromazine has many beneficial or "antischizophrenic" effects is substantial (Goldberg, Klerman, & Cole, 1965), it may well be that for patients for whom psychological treatment holds some promise, it may be an inappropriate medication. This investigation is in no way definitive in this respect, of course, but it does suggest that the effects of chlorpromazine upon learning complex tasks should receive careful scrutiny.[3]

Perhaps it is not surprising that the MCPL measure and Chapman's conceptual task were found to be unrelated, as there is no necessary over-

[3] It is important to recognize that the findings concerning drug effects must be regarded as only tentative in view of the rather brief drying out time (three days). Although the similarities between these findings and previous findings using normal college students suggest that the drying out time may have been sufficient, the possibility of contamination by prior drug regimen is not eliminated.

lap involved in the functions of responding to a narrow or broad spectrum of cues and the breadth of one's conceptual categories. The significance of this finding is that it does confirm the independence of the cognitive processes sampled, that is, that the multiple-cue task does measure a kind of overinclusive or overexclusive functioning different from that measured by more traditional methods. In addition, the independence of the MCPL performance and intelligence suggests that the cognitive functions involved in these tasks are different from those measured by IQ tests. To the extent that we are confronted in everyday life with the kinds of ecologies represented in form by the multiple-cue model, these tasks provide us with information about cognitive performance which is not only important, but apparently supplementary to information available through other means.

In conclusion, the present study, along with two others (Gillis, 1969b; Davis, Evans, & Gillis, 1968), demonstrates the feasibility and usefulness of Brunswik's paradigm in the investigation of disturbed thinking. In yielding data about the inadequacy of functioning in uncertain situations in which a variety of (sometimes misleading) cues are available, the paradigm represents, apparently somewhat uniquely, vital aspects of the ecology with which some persons have not learned to cope.

REFERENCES

Broen, W. E. Response disorganization and breadth of observation in schizophrenia. *Psychological Review,* 1966, *73,* 579–585.

Brunswik, E. The conceptual framework of psychology. In R. Carnap & C. Morris (Eds.), *International encylclopedia of science.* Chicago: University of Chicago Press, 1952.

Calloway, E., & Stone, G. Reevaluating focus of attention. In L. Uhr & J. G. Miller (Eds.), *Drugs and behavior.* New York: Wiley, 1960.

Cameron, N. Reasoning, regression and communication in schizophrenics. *Psychological Monographs,* 1938, *50,* No. 221, 1–33.

Chapman, L. J. A reinterpretation of some pathological disturbances in conceptual breadth. *Journal of Abnormal and Social Psychology,* 1961, *62,* 514–519.

Davis, D. E., Comtois, R. J., & Evans, W. O. A methodological study of dose and repeated experience effects on the report of current states when under the influence of a sedative-intoxicant (secobarbital). Technical Report No. 3 for U.S. Army Contract Da-49-193-MO-2831, Institute of Behavioral Science, University of Colorado. March 1969.

Davis, K. E., Evans, W. O., & Gillis, J. S. The effects of amphetamine and chlorpromazine on cognitive skills and feelings in normal adult males. In W. O. Evans & N. S. Kline (Eds.), *The psychopharmacology of the normal human.* Springfield, Ill.: Charles C Thomas, 1969.

Evans, W., & Smith, K. Some effects of morphine and amphetamine on intellectual functions and mood. *Psychopharmacologia* (Berl.), 1964, *6*, 49–56.

Gardner, R., Holzman, P. S., Klein, G. S., Linton, H. B., & Spence, D. P. Cognitive control: A study of individual consistencies in cognitive behavior. *Psychological Issues*, 1959, *1*, No. 4.

Garmezy, N. Process and reactive schizophrenia: Some conceptions and issues. In M. Katz, V. Cole, & W. Barton (Eds.), *The role and methodology of classification in psychiatry and psychopathology.* Public Health Service Publication No. 1584. Washington: U. S. Government Printing Office, 1965.

Gillis, J. S. The perceptual-cognitive model: Applications of a multiple-cue paradigm to the study of disordered thinking. In L. L'Abate (Ed.), *The role of models in clinical psychology.* Atlanta: Georgia State College Press, 1969. (a)

Gillis, J. S. Schizophrenic thinking in a probabilistic situation. *Psychological Record*, 1969, *19*, 211–224. (b)

Goldberg, S. G., Klerman, G. L., & Cole, V. O. Changes in schizophrenic psychopathology and ward behaviour as a function of phenothiazine treatment. *British Journal of Psychiatry*, 1965, *111*, 120–133.

Goldberg, S. C., Schooler, N. R., & Mattson, N. Paranoid and withdrawal symptoms in schizophrenia: Differential symptom reduction over time. *The Journal of Nervous and Mental Diseases*, 1968, *145*, 158–162.

Hursch, C., Hammond, K. R., & Hursh, J. Some methodological considerations in multiple-cue probability studies. *Psychological Review*, 1964, *71*, 42–60.

Lang, P., & Buss, A. Psychological deficit in schizophrenia: II. Interference and activation. *Journal of Abnormal Psychology*, 1965, *70*, 77–106.

Lester, J. R. Production of associative sequences in schizophrenia and chronic brain syndrome. *Journal of Abnormal and Social Psychology*, 1960, *60*, 225–233.

Loeb, M., Hawkes, G., Evans, W., & Alluisi, E. The influence of d-amphetamine, benactyzine, and chlorpromazine on performance in an auditory vigilance task. *Psychonomic Sciences*, 1965, *3*, 29–30.

O'Connor, N. Reminiscence and work decrement in catatonic and paranoid schizophrenics. *British Journal of Medical Psychology*, 1957, *30*, 188–193.

Peterson, C. R., Hammond, K. R., & Summers, D. A. Optimal cue-weighting in multiple-cue probability learning. *Journal of Experimental Psychology*, 1965, *70*, 270–276.

Raush, H. L. Perceptual constancy in schizophrenia. *Journal of Personality*, 1952, *21*, 176–187.

Shakow, D. Psychological deficit in schizophrenia. *Behavioral Science*, 1963, *8*, 275–304.

Silverman, J. The problem of attention in research and theory in schizophrenia. *Psychological Review*, 1964, *71*, 352–379. (a)

Silverman, J. Scanning-control mechanism and "cognitive filtering" in paranoid and nonparanoid schizophrenics. *Journal of Consulting Psychology*, 1964, *28*, 385–393. (b)

Uhl, C. N. Learning interval concepts: I. Effects of differences in stimulus weights. *Journal of Experimental Psychology*, 1963, *66*, 264–273.

Venables, P. H. Input dysfunction in schizophrenia. In B. A. Maher (Ed.), *Progress in experimental personality research.* Vol. 1. New York: Academic Press, 1964.

Venables, P. H., & O'Connor, N. A short scale for rating paranoid schizophrenia. *The Journal of Mental Science,* 1959, *105,* 815–818.

Voth, A. C. An experimental study of mental patients through the autokinetic phenomenon. *American Journal of Psychiatry,* 1947, *103,* 793–805.

Wikler, A., Haertzen, C., Chessick, R., Hill, H., & Pescor, F. Reaction time ("mental set") in control and chronic schizophrenic subjects and in post-addicts under placebo, LSD-25, morphine, phenobarbital, and amphetamine. *Psychopharmacologia* (Berl.), 1965, *7,* 423–443.

PART II
The Three-System and *N*-System Cases for Group Judgment

Introduction
to Reading 5

The following ten readings contain contributions relevant to the study of judgment processes in situations involving two or more persons. Each of the contributions should be readily understandable if read separately and in random order. Yet it is nowhere more appropriate than here, to quote the familiar principle that a whole may be greater than the sum of its parts, because the range of specific problems to be covered is so great that it may obscure essential theoretical unities. Indeed, readers should be warned upon beginning this collection of papers that they will be stepping out on a conceptual tightrope stretched over much of the traditional subject matter of social psychology, an area notorious for its theoretical anarchy and diversified empirical scope. One may keep one's balance, however, by moving according to the organizational plan underlying this section of the book.

Hammond's cognitive conflict paper establishes the general framework for all the succeeding material. Slightly revised from an article first published in 1965, it has been included here because it provides an exceptionally challenging and succinct statement emphasizing the critical role of human judgment in social behavior. This shift of emphasis from individual to social behavior leads directly to a new set of research issues with dramatic practical implications.

Central among these issues is the disagreement that occurs when persons with different judgment policies must try to reach consensus in the face of uncertain information. In Reading 5, Hammond discusses the practical and theoretical significance of this phenomenon, distinguishes it from other forms of interpersonal conflict, describes an appropriate paradigm for laboratory research, and offers a prospectus for further research on related problems.

5 The Cognitive Conflict Paradigm[1]

KENNETH R. HAMMOND
University of Colorado

Historical Considerations

The conflicts that occurred in the Western world in the hundred years or so prior to the nuclear turning point were generally motivated by material gain; *A* wanted something, *B* also wanted it, and if power and the threat of violent use of power were not sufficient to settle matters, a violent struggle followed. Both *A* and *B* assumed that they would somehow be better off after the struggle than before. That is the sort of conflict we are familiar with—and in that sort of world the strategist and weaponeer were more useful as consultants than behavioral scientists might have been.

But nuclear weapons made a difference, and awareness of the population explosion made a difference; changes in transportation and communication, the United Nations, and a greatly improved science of medicine and public health made a difference. And the difference is that political and intellectual leaders everywhere are now becoming aware that the major problems on earth are common to all men. Moreover, whether anyone will be better off after a violent struggle is now becoming a vanishing topic for debate.

As a result, there is beginning to be a perceptible change from questions of "who gets what" to questions of "whose solution to our problem is best"? In the future, as I see it, *A* and *B* will still engage in dispute, but it will not be merely power or the spoils of war that cause the dispute. Rather, *A* and *B* will be divided over political solutions to those physical, biological, and social problems that threaten *both*. Control of nuclear energy, control of population, provision of food and medical care, and provision of those social and psychological circumstances that minimize the growth of belligerent, paranoid cognitive and affective systems—all of these problems are now beginning to be seen as threats to world security—threats to the security of all nations, to all cartels, to all labor unions,

[1] This paper is a revised version of the article "New Directions in Research on Conflict Resolution" first published in *The Journal of Social Issues,* 1965, *21* (3), 44–66. Reprinted by permission of the author and the Society for the Psychological Study of Social Issues.

and to all religious groups. The reason for this change may not be so much a matter of soul-searching as it is a growing recognition that systems that are badly imbalanced economically, politically, socially, and psychologically are too dangerous for anyone to create, and once created are too volatile for anyone to ignore.

There is, in brief, a change from a world in which there has been conflict over ends (the "spoils") but agreement as to means (political and economic pressure, including war) to a future in which there will be agreement over ends (world security) but cognitive conflict over means (how to get it).

To forecast such a world is not to forecast utopian bliss; far from it. Conflict over means can be as dangerous as any other kind; it can and does rapidly proliferate into self-contained systems of thought which harden into ideologies, and for reasons we do not understand as well as we should, ideologies become value-laden, as well as affect-laden—and, as we know only too well, enormously resistant to change. We shall call conflict between ideologies *cognitive* since it derives from differences over what men believe to be the efficient, just, and moral ways to solve their problems.

Ideological Differences as Cognitive Conflict

Unhappily, cognitive conflict provides as large a potential for violence and destruction as does traditional conflict over power and gold. The long and bitter religious wars, some of which are still with us, are evidence of this sad fact.

The problem is that cognitive differences not only harden into ideological differences, but such differences increase until they seem capable of resolution only by violent means. The tragedy of the situation lies in the fact that escalation of cognitive conflict occurs despite, indeed through, the efforts of both parties to reduce it. Efforts such as discussion, argumentation, persuasion, and so on, to reduce cognitive conflict are prominent elements of the process of escalation; the traditional treatment more often exacerbates than heals the disease. What bedevils us all—from husband-and-wife arguments to Geneva conferences—is the fact that humans have little or no skill in satisfactorily preventing or resolving cognitive differences, even when we want to.

The research paradigm presented below is not intended to represent, or provide a "scenario" for, diplomatic confrontations or discussions of the sort common to the '60s or even the '70s. In all likelihood, the human race will have to survive these decades without the benefit of findings from psychological research. Rather, the relevance of the paradigm is based on the assumption that we have correctly identified cognitive conflict as a very significant problem of the future.

The purpose of this essay, then, is to stimulate research efforts to uncover information concerning cognitive conflict and its resolution by presenting a new research paradigm for studying both—on the assumption that after the next decade or so it will be cognitive conflict that will provide the greatest potential for precipitating extraordinary warfare.

Requirements of the Research Paradigm

In approaching the problem of developing a research paradigm, the investigator has a choice in his order of priorities. We chose to consider first this question: What phenomena should the paradigm provide (i.e., what should the investigator *see*)? Second, what should the investigator *learn* from the phenomena provided by the paradigm? Third, what scientific *and* nonscientific requirements should the paradigm meet? Each of these questions is discussed in turn below.

What Phenomena Should the Paradigm Provide?

At a minimum, the investigator should see (1) two or more persons with different cognitive systems confronting (2) a problem that is not susceptible to a perfect solution. Each of these aspects of the situation requires separate discussion.

Persons with different cognitive systems. It is not difficult to understand why the investigator should see two persons with different cognitive systems attack a problem—because different cognitive systems give rise to conflicting answers, and conflicting answers lead to conflicting courses of action. The investigator should see two persons offer solutions that follow from their different belief systems; he should see two persons contrast their solutions and observe their efforts to cope with their differences and arrive at a joint decision; he should observe the effect of this experience on their cognitive systems and on their efforts to solve subsequent problems. So much is straightforward; this is the nature of cognitive conflict.

Problems that are not susceptible to perfect solutions. The investigator should see also two persons attempting to cope with (1) a series of problems for which neither can deduce correct answers with infallibility; (2) a set of problems for which their past experience apparently is appropriate, but actually is only partly so; (3) a set of problems for which there is in fact no set of perfect solutions. This much is not straightforward and requires a brief explanation.

1. *Why should neither person be able to deduce a correct answer for each problem?* There is increasing recognition that the world provides problems for which no one can deduce perfect solutions from political and social ideologies on every occasion. Increased dissemination of information has brought increasing suspicion of purely ideological solutions that purport to be infallible. "Working" negotiators show clear recognition of the value of discovering the workable solution, imperfect as it inevitably is, as against the futility of debating the comparative values of purified deductions from competing ideologies. In order to represent this aspect of situations involving cognitive conflict, the research paradigm should require both persons to cope with the fact that their solutions to the problems are less than adequate.

2. *Why should the past experience of each person be only apparently appropriate?* All of us are forced to cope with problems, new or old, by means of whatever cognitive systems we have developed out of our past experiences in dealing with similar, or apparently similar, problems. The greater the apparent similarity the more likely it is that people will rely on familiar concepts and familiar methods. But man faces changing conditions and changing problems; the similarity of present problems to past ones is often more apparent than real. Because the dynamic character of the environment requires cognitive change, the research paradigm should require cognitive change on the part of the subjects. The research paradigm should maintain its representativeness by providing a situation in which each person's past experience seems appropriate but actually is not.

3. *Why should there be no perfect solution to the problem itself?* The paradigm should not allow for a perfect solution to the problem it presents because to the best of our knowledge political problems are not susceptible to such solutions. Indeed, Boulding has said, ". . . we cannot, by reason of the (dynamics) of the social system itself *ever* [italics ours] arrive at a state of knowledge in which we can make exact predictions of social systems. . . . We can make probabilistic predictions . . . [Kenneth Boulding, 1964, p. 71]." This observation by a well-known economist is congruent with the fundamental principle of probabilistic functionalism which argues that the environment is a "semi-erratic medium" to which men must adapt in a probabilistic, "uncertainty-geared" manner (Brunswik, 1952, 1956; Hammond, 1965). Thus, in order to maintain the representativeness of the paradigm, subjects are required to cope with problems that permit only probabilistic solutions.

What Should the Investigator Learn?

At a minimum, the investigator should first learn what "natural" approaches the subjects use to resolve their differences; he should also learn to what extent these efforts are successful. That is, although the investigator may be fairly certain such efforts on the part of the subjects will be unsuccessful, he needs to learn how people cope with cognitive conflict under the circumstances described above.

The investigator should also learn which conditions lead to escalation of cognitive differences, and which conditions retard escalation and reduce such differences. He should learn what conditions abort the discussion and turn the effort away from problem-focus to person-focus, which conditions lead to which forms of conflict resolution, and which forms of discourse prevent conflict resolution as against those that tend to resolve cognitive differences with respect to new problems.

Scientific and Nonscientific Requirements

The paradigm should possess sufficient rigor to allow clear denotation and quantitative specification of both the task variables and cognitive variables; results should meet customary scientific criteria so that research psychologists can use the paradigm in their scientific work on the problem. At the same time, however, the behavior of the subjects must possess sufficient richness and complexity so that the results of the research can be brought to bear on the problems it was intended to cope with. Not only should the paradigm provide appropriate scientific data, but the informed layman should find the research conditions reasonable and the implications of the results should be direct and obvious. Although the results should bear implications for the science of psychology, their principal import should be obvious to the nonprofessional. The research, in short, should be both scientifically meaningful and readily understandable.

Description of the Research Paradigm

The research paradigm produces the following situation: Two persons who (1) attempt to solve problems that concern both of them, (2) have mutual utilities (their gain, or loss, derives from their approximations to the solution of the problem), (3) receive different training in the solution of a problem involving uncertain inference, are then brought together and find themselves dealing with a familiar problem which their experience apparently prepared them for but, (4) find that their answers differ, and that neither answer is as good as it has been, although each answer is logically defensible, (5) and who provide a joint decision as to the correct solution, and, therefore (6) must adapt to one another as well as to the task if they are to solve their problems.

Speaking generally, these features were chosen because they represent the situation in which men of good will find themselves when dealing with a problem for which they have less than adequate solutions because of limitations in their ability imposed by their past training, and for which they have different solutions because of cognitive differences imposed by their past training. The paradigm does not pretend to represent fully or adequately all the important features of such problem situations, if for no other reason than that all relevant or important features are not yet known. But it may reasonably be supposed that no research paradigm will, in the foreseeable future, represent fully or adequately all important features of problems as complex as the one we are addressing. The question the paradigm must face is: Will the use of this paradigm advance our knowledge concerning the resolution of cognitive differences to an *important* degree?

Method

The method is an experimental laboratory method that involves two stages: (1) a *training* stage in which two subjects are trained in such a way that each learns to think differently about a common set of problems, and (2) a *conflict* stage in which the two subjects are brought together and attempt to arrive at joint decisions concerning the problems. The training and conflict phases are discussed in turn. (See Rappoport, 1965, for the first application of this method.)

Training stage. The aim of the training stage is to develop different sets of cue-dependencies in two subjects. For example, in a three-cue probability task Subject 1 will learn to depend heavily on Cue *A*, less heavily on Cue *B*, and least on Cue *C*. Subject 2 will learn the reverse system—to depend most heavily on Cue *C*, less on Cue *B*, and least on Cue *A*. Cognitive differences are thus "built up" in the two subjects in their separate and different training experiences. (See Figure 5.1; note the close relation to Brunswik's Lens Model of behavior.)

Two points about this procedure should be emphasized: (1) the method is *general;* training may be arranged to develop in subjects what-

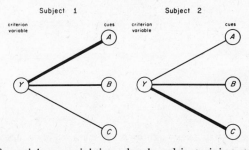

Figure 5.1. Differential cue-weightings developed in training stage

ever degree and kind of cognitive differences the investigator considers appropriate, and (2) the method is quantitative in nature; differences in training may be precisely specified in terms of statistical properties of the multiple-cue task, and differences in cue-dependencies between subjects may be precisely denoted in terms of the statistical properties of the subject's response system. The paradigm, in short, brings cognitive differences between persons under *experimental control.*

Conflict stage. At the completion of training the subjects are told that they have mastered the training task and that their next problem will be to apply what they have learned; furthermore, they will carry out the second part of the task with another subject.

The subjects are then asked to proceed in this way: On each trial they are to observe the data presented on the given trial, form a conclusion as to the correct answer, write down their judgment, and report this judgment to the other person. They are then to discuss whatever differences appear in order to reach a joint decision with the other person. Next they are asked to reconsider their individual decisions in light of the discussion and write down a second private decision which remains private. At this point they are informed of the correct answer.

Conflict task. The nature of the different training task determines the degree and kind of cognitive differences the two persons bring to the conflict situation, and the nature of the conflict task influences the manner in which these differences will be resolved. Thus, for example, in one training task Subject 1's cue-dependencies were Cue $A = .75$, Cue $B = .50$, Cue $C = .25$ and the cue-weightings were reversed for Subject 2; in the accompanying conflict task the cue-weights were set *midway* between

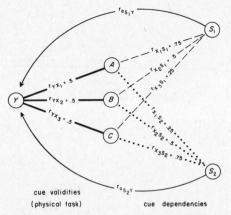

cue validities
(physical task)   cue dependencies

Figure 5.2. Differential cue-weightings of each subject and cue-validities of conflict task

those of each subject, that is, Cue $A = .5$, Cue $B = .5$, Cue $C = .5$ (See Figure 5.2). In this case, resolution of conflict in terms of compromise was therefore enhanced. Because the truth, so to speak, was nearly always somewhere between each person's judgment, a compromise decision was reached more rapidly than would otherwise have been the case.

Note again that the method is *general*. These specific conditions need not always be employed. Just as training may be arranged to develop whatever form of cognitive differences the investigator wishes to study, conflict task properties may be arranged to develop whatever class of phenomena the investigator wishes to study. If, for example, the investigator wished to compare the effect of *social pressure* versus *correctness* in the conflict task, conflict task properties could be arranged to favor the cue-dependencies of the person able to exert least social pressure. One could thus compare the relative weight of social pressure and "cognitive correctness."

Basic data provided by the paradigm. The paradigm makes it possible to ascertain the following basic data:

1. Tr_1: The response Subject 1 would make to the data card if he followed his training exactly.
2. Tr_2: Same for Subject 2.
3. S_1: The response S_1 makes to the data-card and which he announces to S_2 (the *overt* individual judgment).

INTRA - TRIAL EVENTS

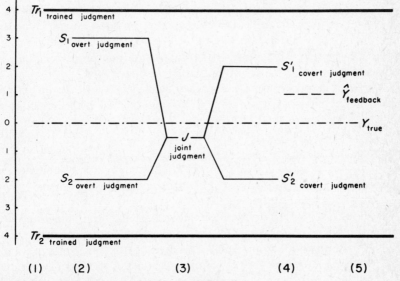

Figure 5.3. Basic data obtained on a single trial

4. S_2: Same for Subject 2.
5. J: The joint decision arrived at by the two subjects.
6. S'_1: The *covert* response Subject 1 makes privately after hearing Subject 2's response, Subject 2's argument, and concurring in a joint decision with him.
7. S'_2: Same for Subject 2.
8. Y: The correct answer, if there were no random error in the problem system.
9. $\hat{Y}$: The answer given to both subjects which includes the error in the problem-system; the random difference between Y and $\hat{Y}$ prevents perfect solution.

The above scores, presented in Figure 5.3 in diagrammatic form, provide the fundamental data of the paradigm. A brief explanation of these follows.

The scores Tr_1 and Tr_2 indicate the degree of underlying cognitive conflict potentially acquired by the subjects. There are major advantages in being able to specify Tr_1 and Tr_2 in a precise, quantitative way. Currently, when psychologists wish to compare reactions of persons supposed to hold different points of view, they must be satisfied with very rough approximations to the cognitive systems of their subjects—such approximations being obtained, for example, via "known group" techniques, or attitude test measures. Because of the approximate nature of such data, group comparisons must be made. In contrast, Tr_1 and Tr_2 specify precisely what the differences between two specific individuals should be.

The joint decision *(J)* which the subjects are required to make provides an essential element of the paradigm; it indicates the objective outcome of the discussion precipitated by the subjects' different individual judgments *(S)*. Subjects are required to make a second covert individual judgment *(S')* so that the effect of the negotiation over the joint decision may be ascertained. The nature of the interaction that produces J may be such that the subjects harden their private positions *(S')*.

The distinction between Y and $\hat{Y}$ is made mainly for technical reasons. Y indicates the "answer" that would be obtained if the set of problems involved a completely determined system. Because of the judgment expressed earlier that the problem set should not be one that allows the subjects to arrive at a correct solution to each problem in the series, $\hat{Y}$ departs randomly from Y. The distinction between Y and $\hat{Y}$ indicates the indeterminacy in the problem set. The investigator may set this indeterminacy to any degree he deems appropriate to a given study.

It should be pointed out that the uncertainty in both the learning task and the conflict task provides an essential psychological component of the paradigm. In the learning stage, the investigator may arrange for his subjects to develop any degree of competence (and confidence) he believes necessary for his study by his choice of amount of uncertainty in the task.

The same is true for the conflict stage. The uncertainty in the task results in the subject being uncertain whether the failure to get every answer right is due to the characteristics of the task, to his own faulty thought processes, or to the incompetence of the other person.

Various measures may readily be derived from the basic data described above. Three examples follow.

Compromise. A comparison of S (individual judgment) and J (joint decision) provides an *overt* measure of compromise $(S - J)$. For example, if J is increasingly found to be midway between S_1 and S_2 over trials, then we find increasing compromise; if J is increasingly found to favor either S_1 or S_2 we find increasing capitulation. A second measure $(S' - J)$ provides an indication of compromise on a *covert* level, for neither subject reports to the other what his final (S') judgment is. *Overt* compromise may, of course, be affected by one set of conditions while *covert* compromise may be affected by another.

Conflict. A comparison of Tr_1 and Tr_2 indicates what the difference between the subject's responses would be if they followed their training exactly. The difference $(S_1 - S_2)$ is a direct measure of the overt conflict that occurs as a result of $(Tr_1 - Tr_2)$. A second measure $(S'_1 - S'_2)$ indicates the *covert* conflict that remains after negotiation has taken place. It is a direct measure of covert conflict which may, of course, be affected by different conditions than is the measure of overt conflict $(S_1 - S_2)$.

Cognitive change: With respect to the conflict task. It will be remembered that the conflict task is different from the task the subjects were trained on. Thus, each subject is required to adapt to the new task by giving up, to a certain extent, his dependency on the cue he has been trained to rely on, and to develop, to a certain extent, a dependency on the cue the other person was trained to depend on. The difference $(S - Y)$ provides a measure of each subject's adaptation to the new task; the difference $(J - Y)$ provides a measure of the extent to which the subjects' joint decision approaches the correct answer in the new task.

Cognitive change: With respect to the other person. Not only does the new task induce each subject to depart from his training, but each subject also induces the other to make a different decision than his training would require. The difference $(Tr - S)$ provides a measure of the extent to which a subject's decision *overtly* departs from what his training would suggest. The difference $(Tr - S')$ provides a measure of the extent to which a subject's decision *covertly* departs from what his training would suggest. And the difference $(S_1 - S'_1)$ indicates the extent to which a subject's *covert* decision approximates (after discussion) his previously announced decision.

Classes of Measures and Dynamics

It should be emphasized that the above measures are merely simple examples of the wide variety of measures that can be derived from the paradigm. At this point, however, it should also be indicated that two classes of measures and two classes of dynamics are inherent parts of the paradigm:

1. *inter*trial measures (e.g., $S_1 - S_2$ over trials);
2. *intra*trial measures (e.g., the relation between $S_1 - J$ and $S_1 - S'_1$ on the same trial).

The two classes of dynamics involve:

1. *external* dynamics (i.e., the effect of such independent variables as differential threat or power on such dependent variables as compromise, conflict, or cognitive change);
2. *intra*trial measures (e.g., the relation between $S_1 - J$ and $S_1 = S'_1$ on the same trial).

Thus, one might hypothesize that one of the internal dynamics of cognitive conflict is the following: The larger $Tr_1 - J$, the less intratrial change will occur (i.e., the smaller $S_1 - S'_1$). Put otherwise, cognitive change $(S_1 - S'_1)$ is a negative function of the discrepancy between training and the joint decision $(Tr - J)$; the more a person is openly forced to depart from his training, the more he clings to it in private.

Any specific investigation may, of course, deal with questions concerning the effect of external dynamics or internal dynamics, or the relation between the two.

Implementation of the Paradigm

Several studies have been conducted using a political decision-making task. Subjects were trained to estimate the "level of democratic institutions" in a given nation on the basis of two cues: (1) the extent to which free elections existed in the nation, and (2) the extent to which state control was a factor in the government.

Each member of a pair of subjects received different training. Subject A was given a task in which the "state control" variable accounted for 98 percent of the variance in the "level of democratic institutions" (criterion) variable; furthermore, the "state control" variable was related to the criterion variable in a nonlinear (one phase of a sine function) manner. Thus, both low and high degrees of state control indicated a "low level of democratic institutions" and a moderate level of state control indicated a "high level of democratic institutions." For Subject *A,* the second predictor variable (free elections) was randomly related to the criterion variable. Subject *A,* then, built up a high degree of dependency on "state control" as an indicator of "level of democratic institutions."

Subject *B* was trained in the opposite way; for him, "free elections" accounted for 98 percent of the variance in the criterion, and it was related to the criterion in a linear way. The "state control" variable, however, was *randomly* related to the criterion. Subject *B,* then, built up a high degree of dependency on "free elections" as an indicator of "level of democratic institutions." (See Hammond & Summers, 1965, and Summers & Hammond, 1966, for theoretical and experimental analyses of the simultaneous learning of linear and nonlinear relationships.)

After each subject had reached criterion performance in training they were brought together in pairs, each member of a pair having received different training as described above. The subjects were told that they had grasped the policy in principle, and now the question was, how well could they apply it to problems involving real nations. Furthermore, "we want to see how well two of you can do the job." As indicated earlier, a data card was presented, each subject recorded an individual judgment *(S₁, S₂)* concerning the "level of democratic institutions," each subject presented his judgment to the other and the subjects discussed their differences (cognitive differences which are bound to occur as a result of differential training) until they reached a joint decision *(J),* then each subject recorded a second private judgment *(S'₁, S'₂)* which was not revealed to the other person; the experimenter then reported the correct answer for that task, the trial was concluded, and another begun. (See Figure 5.4.)

Using this procedure, investigations have been started in the following areas:

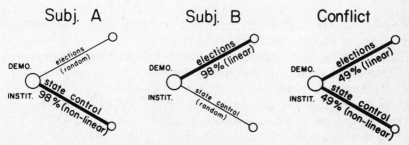

Figure 5.4. Cue-validities in differential training tasks and conflict tasks

Studies Involving External Dynamics

The effect of various types of interchange. Rapoport (1961, 1964) has offered suggestions as to how a discourse between persons with different cognitive systems might be carried on so as to increase the likelihood of resolving those differences. He suggests that, among others, the technique of pointing out to one's antagonist the region of validity of the antagonist's belief system is conducive to conflict reduction. One study (Hammond, Todd, Wilkins, & Mitchell, 1966) examines the results of the use of this technique by one of the two subjects, both of the subjects, and neither of the subjects on compromise, conflict, and cognitive change. The results indicate that Rapoport's suggestion does not lead to effective conflict reduction.

The effect of ambiguous feedback. In the "real world" one does not always discover the "right answer" after making a judgment. It may be that only asymmetrical information can be received; that is, the action following a judgment may preclude receiving information about what the effects of an alternative action would have been, or the feedback may be provided in crude form—one might discover that he was wrong, but not be informed as to how far wrong, and so on.

With this point in mind a study was undertaken to evaluate the effect of ambiguity of feedback on compromise and conflict. Two forms of feedback were employed: (1) one group of subjects was provided with the specific value of the criterion variable after the joint judgment was made; (2) one group of subjects was told only that their joint decision was "right" or "wrong." The results indicate that ambiguous and exact feedback does not differentially affect conflict reduction but does differentially affect compromise (Todd, Hammond, & Wilkins, 1966).

The differential effect of analytical and intuitive thought. As a first step toward analyzing the effect of ideological commitment on the process of conflict resolution, Rappoport (1965) investigated the differential effect of analytical and intuitive modes of thought on compromise. He found that pairs of persons trained to think analytically, that is, to develop a system of thought, a rationale, for their judgments, engaged in more conflict and less compromise than did pairs trained to think intuitively (and equally successfully) about the problem. Although only an initial step, the study suggests the dangers of the application of a predetermined system of thought to a task system not fully understood (and which may have changed, as the task system actually did in the experiment).

Studies Involving Internal Dynamics

The effect of the "critical" trial. In a preliminary study it was found that, on a trial late in the conflict phase of the study, the two persons were faced with a wide divergence in their judgments. In this case, their private judgments closely followed the decision their training would have required. The data suggested that the two "persons" (actually 30 pairs of persons) did not undergo cognitive change as a result of their experience together.

The question these data raised was this: What is the effect of such a "critical" trial involving a large divergence of opinion? Is it more likely to induce cognitive change if it appears early? If this were so, the wide discrepancy between the antagonists would get to the surface early, it could be dealt with, and future problems could be handled by means of the changed belief systems of the antagonists. On the other hand, it might be argued (indeed it has been argued by Roger Fisher, 1964) that it is better to "fractionate conflict," that is, to deal with smaller issues first. Thus, Fisher argues, "It would seem that only by dividing up the issues and considering them separately in small units will we be able . . . to work together in those areas in which we have common goals and common interests and thus obtain the optimal accommodation possible [p. 107]." (Such a division in our situation would mean confronting problems in which differences were small.) But our preliminary results cast some doubt on this hypothesis, for they indicated that the experience with small problems, that is, small divergencies in opinion, did not effect any cognitive change on the part of the subjects—they were as far apart "ideologically" as they ever were (Hammond, Todd, Wilkins, & Mitchell, 1966).

Interpersonal learning. The research paradigm not only makes it possible to study cognitive conflict, but also opens up a new topic for psychology—interpersonal learning. So far as we can discover, psychologists have never studied the process whereby one person learns to predict the behavior of another. To be sure, there have been studies of imitation—where one person's behavior is a cue to a physical state of affairs, and there have been studies of interpersonal perception. But we find no investigations that directly study the situation where a physical state of affairs is used as a cue to another person's behavior, studies where one person *learns* to predict the behavior of another person in a specific situation. The present paradigm permits such studies; indeed, we find that the process of learning to predict another's behavior is an integral part of the conflict situation.

Briefly, we have carried out such studies in the following way. After any given number of trials in the conflict phase, the subjects are shown a data card, and are asked to make a prediction for the criterion value. Then, instead of making a joint decision, each subject is asked to infer what judgment the other person will make in response to a data card; S_1's inference about S_2's judgment about the data card can then be compared with S_2's judgment, which provides a criterion for the accuracy of S_1's inference.

So far we have learned that subjects can learn to predict the behavior of others, and that they exhibit true differential (as well as stereotyped) accuracy, and that "similarity" plays an important role in learning about the "other." More interesting, however, we have found that in an indeterminate situation there are definite limits to the extent that one person can predict the behavior of another. Put otherwise, there are limits to which one person can "know" another—as clear a denotation of the human condition as can be anticipated (Hammond, Wilkins, & Todd, 1966).

Language and communication. As an example of how the paradigm may be brought to bear on language and communication problems, consider the following statement from a political scientist:

> One of the difficulties of Soviet-Russian vocabulary is that the word "compromise" is not of native origin and carries with it no favorable empathy. It is habitually used only in combination with the adjective "putrid." "Compromise for the sake of getting on with the job" is natural to American and British people, but is alien to the Bolshevist way of thinking and to the discipline which the Communist party has striven to inculcate in its members. To give up a demand once presented, even a very minor or formalistic point, makes a Bolshevik-trained negotiator feel that he is losing control of his own will and is becoming subject to an alien will. Therefore any point which has finally to be abandoned must be given up only after a most terrific struggle. The Soviet negotiator must first prove to himself and his superiors that he is up against an immovable force. Only then is he justified in abandoning a point which plainly cannot be gained and in moving on to the next item, which will then be debated in an equally bitter tug of wills [Mosley, quoted in Fedder, 1962].

Such statements are important because they tend to produce in the reader certain beliefs and attitudes toward the possibility of negotiation—beliefs and attitudes that guide behavior. In their own subtle way, such statements appear to be scientific analyses of the possibilities of negotiation between the United States and the Soviet Union. The subtlety lies in the assertion that although "compromise is natural" to the Americans and British, compromise is "alien" to the Bolshevist "way of thinking," the implication being that the assertion is based on a scientific, and therefore impartial, linguistic analysis. In point of fact, we have before us an hypothesis, an important one, to be sure, but one not to be mistaken for a conclusion supported by fact. This hypothesis should be tested before allowing it to guide our behavior.

Evaluation

Having sketched the general methodology of the cognitive conflict paradigm, and indicated with illustrations how it may be employed to investigate certain problems, we turn now to its evaluation.

Can the Investigator See What He Should See?

It should be clear from the foregoing that the paradigm does permit the investigator to see two persons with different cognitive systems confronting a problem which is not susceptible to a perfect solution. He does see two persons offering conflicting answers, observes efforts to cope with differences and arrive at a joint decision, and he does, in fact, observe the effect of this effort on their cognitive systems and on future efforts to solve the problem.

But the reader will want to know whether the paradigm produces "real conflict"; does it produce a genuine interaction worth studying? We are satisfied that it does. We have seen over 100 pairs of subjects in the political decision-making task and have been satisfied that the paradigm produces the kind of interaction we set out to study.

Our examples admittedly involved only the simplest kind of task, inferring the value of a criterion variable from two or three predictor variables, and thus the nature of the discourse was restricted in complexity. It should be noted, however, that such simple cognitive differences as those developed in the study described above are indeed sufficient to provoke a dispute, and indeed, often provoke a dispute that does not get resolved. Although it is too early to draw sound conclusions, current data indicate that even rather simple, quickly induced cognitive differences solidify rapidly. If this proves to be the case, the paradigm will readily permit the observation of conflict between cognitive differences that are highly resistant to change.

Can the Investigator Learn What He Should Learn?

The investigator can learn which conditions lead to escalation of cognitive differences and which conditions reduce such differences by introducing those external conditions he has reason to believe are important, and he can measure the effects of these external conditions on the external dynamics of the conflict situations as well as on such outcomes as conflict, compromise, and cognitive change. Here he is limited only by his imagination. Indeed, we would go so far as to say that we have shown that the paradigm opens up new topics for investigation for psychologists, as well as making it possible for psychologists to test hypotheses that are presented by political scientists and other analysts of conflict, as our examples have indicated.

Of course, we must not claim too much. Although the paradigm does provide a framework for the analysis of general propositions concerning cognitive conflict, we should be able to do more than that. We should, for example, be able to evaluate such propositions by means of a cross-sectional, *ahistorical* study of two given individuals. That is to say, we should be able to study the cognitive systems two specific individuals present to us and predict the kind of cognitive conflict we will observe between them, as well as the conditions that will lead to the best form of resolution of that conflict. And, of course, we should aim to do that with the same sort of precision with which we ascertain the cognitive differences of subjects in our present paradigm in which cognitive differences are developed through historical procedures. It is important to note that the present paradigm makes possible such ahistorical analysis, a form of analysis badly needed if we are to move away from the experimental laboratory.

Does the Paradigm Meet Scientific and Nonscientific Requirements?

Scientific requirements are clearly met by the paradigm: Task conditions are specified, quantified, and controlled by the experimenter; the same is true for response systems and interaction between response systems. Propositions concerning conflict can be put to test. The entire system is congruent with (indeed, is derived from) a general conceptual framework known as probabilistic functionalism, an approach developed by Egon Brunswik. The paradigm can carry meaning for scientific psychology.

But what about nonscientific requirements? The scientific terminology of this paradigm translates readily to the intelligent layman's vocabularly. All of the terms used above such as conflict, compromise, capitulation, and escalation are familiar to laymen and are given concrete meaning in the paradigm. Equally important, the paradigm can be employed to investigate problems formulated by nonpsychologists who have reason to be interested in cognitive conflict.

My view of the future is that the next 20 years will find increasing agreement on ultimate values such as the dignity of man and all that is implied by that phrase, and that conflict between men will be derived from their cognitive differences concerning the means by which physical, biological, and social problems are to be managed so that dignity may be achieved. But cognitive conflict over means is dangerous because of its escalation potential, and because of our notorious lack of scientific information about its control.

If my view of the future is even partly correct, then it follows that research on cognitive conflict is needed; and if it is true that cognitive conflict has a large escalation potential and that our knowledge about it is minimal, then it follows that there is an urgent need to develop theory and method to investigate this phenomenon.

REFERENCES

Boulding, K. Toward a theory of peace. In R. Fisher (Ed.), *International conflict and behavior science.* New York: Basic Books, 1964.

Brunswik, E. *The conceptual framework of psychology.* Chicago: University of Chicago Press, 1952.

Brunswik, E. *Perception and the representative design of experiments.* Berkeley, Calif.: University of California Press, 1956.

Fedder, E. J. Communication and American-Soviet negotiating behavior. *Background,* 1962, *2,* 190–210.

Fisher, R. Fractionating conflict. In R. Fisher (Ed.), *International conflict and behavior science.* New York: Basic Books, 1964.

Hammond, K. R. (Ed.) *The psychology of Egon Brunswik.* New York: Holt, Rinehart & Winston, 1965.

Hammond, K. R., & Summers, D. A. Cognitive dependence on linear and nonlinear cues. *Psychological Review,* 1965, *72,* 215–224.

Hammond, K. R., Todd, F. J., Wilkins, M., & Mitchell, T. O. Cognitive conflict between persons: Application of the "lens model" paradigm. *Journal of Experimental Social Psychology,* 1966, *2,* 343–360.

Hammond, K. R., Wilkins, M., & Todd, F. J. A research paradigm for the study of inter-personal learning. *Psychological Bulletin,* 1966, *65,* 221–232.

Rapoport, A. *Fights, games, and debates.* Ann Arbor, Mich.: University of Michigan Press, 1961.

Rapoport, A. *Strategy and conscience.* New York: Harper & Row, 1964.

Rappoport, L. Interpersonal conflict in noncompetitive and uncertain situations. *Journal of Experimental Social Psychology,* 1965, *1,* 323–333.

Summers, D. A., & Hammond, K. R. Inference behavior in multiple-cue tasks involving both linear and nonlinear relations. *Journal of Experimental Psychology,* 1966, *71,* 751–757.

Todd, F. J., Hammond, K. R., & Wilkins, M. Differential effects of ambiguous and exact feedback on two-person conflict and compromise. *Journal of Conflict Resolution,* 1966, *10,* 88–97.

ASPECTS OF COGNITIVE CONFLICT AND LEARNING

Introduction to Readings 6, 7, and 8

Three of the general problems noted in Reading 5 are examined in the contributions grouped together here. First, Helenius shows that when persons are selected according to similarities and differences between their judgment policies, and must then work together in pairs on a relevant uncertain judgment task, they experience cognitive conflict in much the same way as laboratory subjects who have been trained to hold different judgment policies. Thus, policy differences appear to produce similar effects on social interaction regardless of whether the differences arise from laboratory training or natural experience.

Second, the effects that exact and ambiguous types of outcome information have upon the policies of persons working together are investigated by Bonaiuto. She reports the degree to which they change their policies under such conditions, and discusses some apparent differences in the behaviors of Americans and Europeans.

Third, since language is the medium through which persons in the laboratory and the real world try to resolve their disagreements, Kuhlman, Miller, and Gungor describe research on the role of language in a cognitive conflict situation. Their results indicate that the connotative meanings of words persons use to discuss judgment policies may become an independent source of conflict, apart from original policy differences.

6 Socially Induced Cognitive Conflict: A Study of Disagreement over Childrearing Policies

MAIJA HELENIUS
University of Helsinki

The Problem

Other papers in this volume describe how Brunswik's Lens Model can be adapted to study conflict and decision making in small groups. However, in early work demonstrating the feasibility of this proposition, conflict was generated by first *training* subjects to think differently about a mutual problem. Such "laboratory induced" cognitive conflicts have been studied in a number of important experiments. But the question remained whether people whose social experiences outside the laboratory have led them to think differently about a given problem would behave similarly to people who had been trained to think differently.

   As a research issue, therefore, the problem is to determine if socially induced cognitive differences generate conflict in the same way as laboratory-induced differences. The importance of this problem has been expressed elsewhere as follows:

> If the model is to serve as anything more than an interesting laboratory analogue, it must be shown that socially induced cognitive differences provide the same conflict phenomena as laboratory-induced cognitive differences. Otherwise, we cannot be certain that the conflict we observe is not an artifact of laboratory training [Rappoport, 1969, p. 143].

   The present study examines conflict among women who are given cue information about the backgrounds of children, and then are required to agree on a judgment of the children's social behavior. Instead of training subjects to think differently about the cue material, their "natural" views are assessed. Then they are paired according to a new procedure that allows precise specification of similarities and differences in their cognitive systems.

Earlier Studies

So far, only two cognitive conflict studies have been carried out without using the laboratory training technique. The first was done by Summers (1968). He selected persons who believed that the low status of minority groups could only be changed through increased education, and paired them with persons who believed that both increased education and new government legislation were necessary. When these subject pairs had to reach mutual decisions regarding minority status, their disagreements were described as being caused by socially induced cognitive differences. That is, their previous social experience had led these subjects to think differently about the minority status problem. As Summers, however, was primarily concerned with the effects of rewards and instructions on compromise, socially induced cognitive differences were not manipulated as an independent variable.

Rappoport (1969) assessed cognitive differences among subjects required to judge levels of race friction in hypothetical American communities. His work indicates that subject pairs who are significantly different in the way they interpret certain cue information, have more conflict than those who are similar, show less compromise, and experience more difficulty learning from accuracy feedback information.

Design

Purpose. Socially induced cognitive conflict is investigated here in order to determine whether previously obtained results hold for subjects in a different culture (Finland), working on a different task (childrearing). Furthermore, measures not used in previous socially induced conflict studies are employed to obtain a more elaborate description of relevant behavior.

Task. To construct a meaningful judgment task for females, preliminary research involving questionnaires, interviews, and group discussions centering on childrearing was conducted. This area was selected because it has not been handled in prior conflict studies. In addition, most people have had some contact with it; many have strict opinions about childrearing and many different notions might be considered "right." While talking about childrearing, one can seldom tell which conclusions are correct; thus each person might have different but defensible opinions. Here we have again the basic assumption that cognitive differences may cause serious interpersonal conflict even when people are working together to attain a mutually desired goal. Results showed that the following four characteristics of childhood experience were generally seen as important predictors of later behavior:

1. Demands for obedience.
2. Indulgence of aggressive behavior.
3. Severity of cleanliness training.
4. Nurturance (protective care) of the child.

These four predictors were treated as cue-variables used to construct a set of 20 cases, each of which appeared on a separate card. That is, information ranging over ten steps from minimum to maximum "demands for obedience," "indulgence of aggressive behavior," and so on, was presented on each card. The means and variances of the four cue-variable distributions were kept approximately equal across all 20 cards, and the intercorrelations between the cue-variables were not significantly different from zero. Subjects also received a written description of the meaning of each cue, which served to minimize idiosyncratic differences.

Subjects were told that each card described a different 9- to 10-year-old girl. Their task was to estimate how well each girl would (1) adapt to her teacher in school, (2) adapt to other children, and (3) the degree to which each girl would show initiative or independence. Judgments of the three criteria were made on ten-point scales.

Subjects. Eighty female students majoring in home economics and ethnology served as subjects in the experiment. These fields were selected in order to find students who were not acquainted with psychology. It was also thought that students of various personality types want to study these themes, and thus their attitudes towards the area studied and in general might be different. Freshmen and sophomores were not included in the sample; the age range was 20–30 years, most subjects being 20–22 years of age. The sample included both married students with children and unmarried students because differences between these groups were expected to occur.

Procedure and methods. The experiment was run in two phases, involving a judgment and a conflict stage. During the judgment stage the subjects made their first estimates of the children. This task was administered to all 80 subjects. Like and unlike pairs were then selected from among this group on the basis of their judgments. Although the subjects were not allowed to talk to each other during the judgment stage, they were called to the first experiment phase in pairs, in order to get used to working in two-person groups instead of working alone.

Cognitively similar and dissimilar pairs were selected for the conflict phase according to analysis of their initial judgments. These were first processed using a multiple correlation technique: Only those subjects whose judgments reached R^2 of .70 or greater with the cue-variables were retained. These were apparently people who had been following a mathematically stable policy over the 20 trials.

Then cognitively similar and dissimilar pairs were arranged by analyzing individual policies according to the BC TRY cluster analysis developed by Tryon and Bailey (1966). This analysis allows one to see how a number of variables (subject judgments in this study) group themselves over a standard set of dimensions (cue-variables). Results are plotted in the spheroids shown in Figure 6.1. Note that the relative differences between subjects on the three criterion variables are immediately apparent from the dispersion of the points plotted on the spheroids. It is clear that judgments about initiative (independence) do not lead to much disagreement, so this criterion was dropped from the study.

Subjects are well spread out, however, on the "adaptation to teacher" criterion. Most are located between Cues 1 and 2. Thus both of these cues are considered approximately equally important when estimating a child's adaptation to the teacher. This seems quite natural, as the names of the cues were "demands of obedience" and "allowance of aggressive behav-

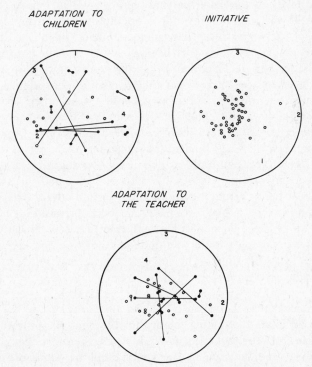

Figure 6.1. Cluster analysis (BC TRY) showing cue-dependencies for subjects in the childrearing judgment task

ior." Cues 3 and 4 tend to be ignored when judgments of adaptation to teachers are being made.

But for the criterion "adaptation to children," subjects are spread all over the plot. This variable has clearly been the most difficult for them to judge, because it seems to be the most inherently complex of the three.

Thus, for purposes of arranging a conflict task, adaptation to children and teacher are the best criteria. Each was used to select a total of 20 pairs for the conflict task. 5 similar and 5 dissimilar pairs were drawn according to responses on the "adaptation to children" scale. And 5 similar and 5 dissimilar pairs were likewise drawn according to responses on the teacher scale.

Conflict task procedure. The general situation here was similar to that used in the judgment phase of the experiment with the exception that subjects were now given accuracy feedback after every trial. Pairs judging the adaptation to children and to teachers criteria were treated in exactly the same way, worked on the same deck of cards, and were given the same mathematically calculated feedback. The only difference was in the label on the criterion variable.

The following general procedure was employed. In order to check the reliability of their previously determined policies, each pair of subjects began by judging 10 new cards having similar statistical properties as the original deck of 20. They then began the conflict task proper, in which they had to reach joint agreements about each of the original 20 cards. For example, on Card 1, the two subjects first noted their own personal judgments of how well the child would adapt to other children, or teachers, as the case might be. These judgments were made on a 20-point scale. (Widening the scale to 20 points made it easier to detect differences of opinion.) The subject pair was next encouraged to discuss their differences and reach a single joint judgment. E recorded this, and turned the card over to show the "correct" value of the criterion. Before receiving this feedback, however, each subject made a second private judgment of the criterion, so it could be determined whether she had honestly changed her mind when agreeing to the joint judgment, or whether she was merely going along with the other. The same procedure was followed on all of the 20 cards.

Accuracy feedback. "Correct" values appearing on the back of each card were calculated by taking the arithmetic mean of the values on the four cue-variables for that card. Each cue was, therefore, given an equal validity. But some uncertainty was maintained by randomly adding 0, $+1$, or -1 to each of the arithmetic means.

Dependent variables. The following measures of subject performance on the conflict task were obtained: (1) absolute conflict $(|S - S|)$, (2) departure from predicted conflict $(|T - T| - |S - S|)$, (3) relative conflict $(|\frac{S - S}{T - T}|)$, (4) relative covert conflict $(|\frac{S' - S'}{T - T}|)$, (5) adaptation to a new task $(|\frac{S - Y}{T - Y}|)$, (6) cognitive change within trials $(|\frac{S - S'}{S - J}|)$, and (7) adaptation of the joint decision to the new task $(|J - Y|)$. All these measures are explained in more detail in the article by Hammond in this volume, pages 195 and 196.

Results

Using trend analysis and multiple regression statistics, all measures were first analyzed separately for the "teacher" group and for the "children" group, to determine whether there were statistically significant differences in response to these two tasks. Had there been significant differences between these two tasks, this would have meant that different results were produced depending upon the content of the task, rather than as a result of experimental conditions (like vs. unlike pairs). Because no significant differences were found, it was concluded that the results are general over the two tasks. Since task content did not affect the results in an important way, the data from the "teacher" study and the "children" study were combined for the analysis reported here.

Absolute conflict $(|S - S|)$**.** Mean conflict scores are plotted in Figure 6.2. Unlike or cognitively different pairs show consistently more conflict than like pairs $(F = 7.2, p < .05)$. But there is no significant trend toward conflict reduction, nor is there any interaction between conflict and trials.

Departure from predicted conflict $(|T - T| - |S - S|)$**.** Figure 6.3 presents mean differences between conflict predicted according to analysis of subject pairs' initial judgments $(T - T)$ and actual conflict $(S - S)$. The data are plotted in two-trial blocks. Trend analysis results show that unlike pairs reduce their conflict across succeeding trials $(F = 6.9, p < .05)$, but like pairs do not. Furthermore, the unlike pairs depart much further from their predicted conflict than do the like pairs.

Relative conflict $(|S - S| / |T - T|)$**.** The results indicate that observed conflict (overt conflict) relative to predicted conflict is not reduced in either group; for unlike pairs it remains at the predicted level of conflict and for like pairs it rises above this level.

Relative covert conflict $(|S' - S'| / |T - T|)$**.** These data indicate

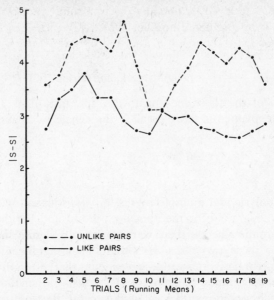

Figure 6.2. Comparison of mean conflict scores obtained for cognitively similar (like) and cognitively different (unlike) pairs

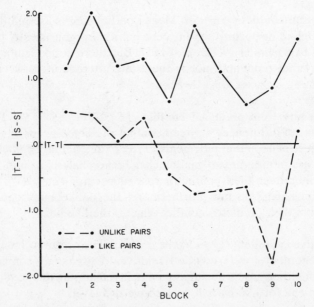

Figure 6.3. Comparison of mean differences between predicted and actual conflict scores for the like and unlike pairs

a gradual drop in covert conflict. However, the linear trend for both groups does not reach conventional levels of statistical significance.

Adaptation to new task ($|S - Y| / |T - Y|$). The data here show no tendency toward increased mutual understanding, nor adaptation toward the new task. In fact, a significant trial blocks effect indicates that subjects are returning to their original policies by the end of the conflict task. Briefly, these results, together with the relative conflict results, suggest that subjects are ending up precisely where they started.

Cognitive change within trials ($|S - S'| / |S - J|$). Comparisons reveal a nonsignificant tendency for like pairs to change their minds on each trial more than unlike pairs.

Joint adaptation to the new task ($|J - Y|$). Both groups of subjects are very similar in the accuracy of their joint judgments, providing a statistically significant U-shaped curve. Errors are fairly large on the first four trials, drop sharply on the next eight, and then rise to about their original level on the remaining eight.

Discussion

Results generally support previous studies showing that socially induced cognitive differences produce conflict in the same fashion as laboratory-induced differences. Since the present findings on overt conflict are approximately similar to those obtained in another culture, using male subjects working on very different substantive problems, it would appear that rough equivalence between natural and artificially induced cognitive conflict is now firmly established.

Results concerning the reduction of cognitive conflict are of special interest in at least two major respects. First, it is clear that no reduction in overt, absolute conflict occurred. This is contrary to earlier findings reported in similar studies done in the United States (e.g., Rappoport, 1969), but it is in principle similar to earlier reports comparing conflict reduction in American and European subjects.

Hammond, Bonaiuto, et al. (1968) report that Americans decrease the differences between them to a much greater extent than Europeans. Thus, working on the same task, Americans reduce the amount of conflict anticipated on the basis of differential training from approximately 70 percent to approximately 40 percent by the end of 20 trials; the European subjects, however, show about as much conflict at the end of 20 trials as at the beginning. The graphs from different European countries are very much alike and none of them indicates reduction of conflict during the

10 last trials which is apparent for the Americans. The graphs of this study show that Finnish students behave similarly to other European subjects.

It is possible, of course, that American society places more value on "cooperation" and "compromise" than does Finnish or European society in general. If such is the case, it is not surprising that laboratory studies seem to suggest that Europeans reduce interpersonal conflict more slowly than do Americans. Another related possibility is that Americans have had, in general, more experience working cooperatively with others than have individuals reared in Finland. In this respect, it is the author's opinion that American schools encourage cooperative working with others more than schools in Finland. If so, individuals educated in American schools may gain considerable experience working with others and listening to their opinions. The situation may be quite different for Finnish students. That is, students in Finnish schools are encouraged to work alone, to make their own decisions, and to accept responsibility for these decisions. Such educational practices could provide the individual with inadequate experience for working cooperatively (and compromising) with another individual in conflict situations such as studied here.

The only result of this study somewhat contrary to the above generalizations concerns the departure from predicted conflict $(|T - T| - |S - S|)$. But here it should be noted that whereas unlike pairs depart significantly further from their predicted conflict than like pairs, the trend changes toward the end of the task. That is, Figure 6.3 shows the unlike pairs rise toward the predicted conflict line on the last block of 2 trials. Which seems, once again, to be more characteristic of European than American subjects.

The second finding of general interest involves the data on relative covert conflict. Scrutiny of these results indicates that discussions between subjects do have an important effect on specific trials, that is, some legitimate shifts in judgments occur. However, the general pattern of subjects' judgments does not seem to be influenced. In other words, the discussion may affect the judgment made on one trail, but on other trials subjects apparently return to their original policies. This suggests that momentary changes in behavior may occur without there being any change in the overall pattern.

During the experiment it was also noted that mothers gave in more easily than unmarried women. Mothers often seemed to be more unsure and were willing to pay more attention to their partner's opinions. It was also more difficult for them to base their estimation on one cue, because they tried to pay equal attention to several factors. Unmarried women seemed to have less complex opinions, their cue-dependencies were more clear-cut, and their judgments seemed to come more quickly and easily.

REFERENCES

Hammond, K. R., Bonaiuto, G. B., Faucheux, C., Moscovici, S., Fröhlich, W. D., Joyce, C. R. B., & Di Majo, G. A comparison of cognitive conflict between persons in Western Europe and the United States. *International Journal of Psychology,* 1968, *3,* 1–12.

Rappoport, L. Cognitive conflict as a function of socially induced cognitive differences. *Journal of Conflict Resolution,* 1969, *13,* 143–148.

Summers, D. A. Conflict, compromise, and belief change in a decision-making task. *Journal of Conflict Resolution,* 1968, *12,* 215–221.

Tryon, R. C., & Bailey, D. E. The BC TRY computer system of cluster and factor analysis. *Multivariate Behavioral Research,* 1966, *1,* 95–111.

7 The Feedback Problem: Cognitive Change in Conditions of Exact and Ambiguous Outcome Information[1]

GABRIELLA BARTOLI BONAIUTO[2]
University of Bologna

Cognitive change is an important psychological feature of all conflict situations involving genuine bargaining or negotiation. It refers to changes in individual decisions that come about as a result of discussion leading to collective decisions. Presumably, this phenomenon can be seen in such situations as collective bargaining or international negotiation, where parties who are initially far apart in their views change to the point of expressing satisfaction with a collective arrangement different from the one they originally proposed.

In the conflict research paradigm described by Hammond (Reading 5), cognitive change is measured by the discrepancy between a person's initial *overt* judgment about an uncertain task and a later *covert* judgment he makes after discussion leading to the adoption of a collective or joint judgment. Accuracy feedback relevant to the joint judgment is only given to subjects after each has made his individual covert judgment. Because this sequential procedure of overt judgment, discussion, joint judgment, covert judgment, and accuracy feedback is followed on each trial in the total experimental series, it is possible to examine cognitive change in the

[1] The research reported here was undertaken in 1966, 1967, and 1968 at the Institute of Psychology, Faculty of Medicine and Surgery of the University of Bologna. It was sponsored by the following organizations: the Italian Ministry of Education, which provided a scholarship and research grant for 1966; the Institute of Psychology of the Faculty of Medicine and Surgery and the Laboratory of Psychology of the Faculty of Pedagogy, University of Bologna, Italy; and the Institute of Behavioral Science, University of Colorado, Boulder, U.S.A., which provided equipment and funds. Statistical calculations were done at the Institute of Behavioral Science, University of Colorado.

[2] The author is indebted to the following people for their assistance: Professor K. R. Hammond, Department of Psychology, University of Colorado; Professor B. Brehmer, Department of Psychology, University of Umeå; Professor L. Rappoport, Kansas State University; Professor P. Bonaiuto, Laboratory of Psychology, Faculty of Pedagogy and Institute of Psychology, Faculty of Medicine and Surgery, University of Bologna.

context of cognitive conflict as a function of increasing information about the task.

The present study investigates cognitive change in relation to two different types of accuracy feedback.

Previous Research

The important role of accuracy feedback in uncertain learning and conflict situations has been recognized for some time. For example, Todd and Hammond (1965) compared the cue learning of subjects given exact feedback—where they can see precisely how far their judgments deviate from correct answers, with similar learning under conditions of ambiguous feedback—where subjects can only see whether their judgments are right or wrong. The former technique makes for much more efficient learning. Analogous findings have also been reported by investigators of concept learning (e.g., Pishkin, 1967; Richard, 1966; Wolfgang & Pishkin, 1966).

In the conflict research area, Todd, Hammond, and Wilkins (1966) have shown that compared with ambiguous feedback, exact feedback enhances the likelihood that subjects who think differently about a mutual problem will resolve their disagreements by adopting compromise judgments. Similar findings suggesting the value of exact feedback have been reported in game theory studies of conflict (e.g., McClintock & McNeel, 1966; Pilisuk, Skolnick, & Overstreet, 1968; Tedeschi, Lesnick, & Gahagan, 1968).

Present Aims

The general purpose of this study is to examine the effects of ambiguous and exact feedback upon cognitive change in subjects performing a cognitive conflict experiment. Prior research showing better learning associated with exact feedback suggests that cognitive change should also be best under this condition. However, in the earlier studies of Hammond and his associates, cognitive change was not emphasized because procedures and measures appropriate for its examination were not available. Moreover, investigators of concept learning and gaming behavior have not been concerned with cognitive change because it is not recognized as an important variable in the theoretical orientations characterizing these problem areas.

In addition to studying the main effects of ambiguous and exact feedback upon cognitive change, this study also involves manipulation of cue-function forms as a second independent variable. That is, since numerous studies (See Slovic & Lichtenstein, this volume) have shown curvilinear cue-criterion relationships to be more difficult to learn than linear cue-criterion relationships, the effects of ambiguous and exact feedback are here studied separately for subjects trained to rely on linear and curvilinear cue-variables.

In sum, the present experiment follows a two-factor design that permits examination of the effects of different types of accuracy feedback and cue-function forms upon cognitive change.

Method and Procedure

Subjects

Twenty pairs of university students were paid to serve as subjects. They were male students from various faculties of the University of Bologna who did not know one another. It should be pointed out that, from a large number of subjects examined, the investigator selected only the 40 subjects who, at the end of training, had best learned the criterion. These were subjects whose judgments correlated $>+.75$ with the correct cue and $<+.25$ with the incorrect cue.

The Experimental Task

Originally used by Todd, Hammond, and Wilkins (1966), and later employed by several other investigators, the "political decision-making" task used here requires subjects to judge the "level of democracy" in various countries. This criterion variable has the form of a 20-point scale ranging from a very low to very high level of democracy. Judgments of the criterion are based on two ten-point cue-variables which show, respectively, the level of "state control" and the frequency of "free elections" in a series of different countries.

The entire task is contained on a deck of cards, with each card representing a specific country. The face of the card gives the values on the two cue-variables for a given country, and the correct criterion value for that country is given on the back of the card (See Hammond & Brehmer, this volume, p. 338, for more details).

Training and Selection

Subjects were first trained individually to rely on either the "state control" or "free election" cue when judging the "level of democracy" criterion. This was accomplished by giving them 60 trials with the task arranged so that the cue to be learned correlated either linearly or curvilinearly $+ .95$ with the criterion, while the other cue was completely uncorrelated with the criterion. It should be noted that while this training version of the task is obviously a simple form of multiple probability learning, it still demands that subjects adapt to a minimal degree of uncertainty.

Subjects were only permitted to go on to the next stage (conflict stage) of the experiment if they were able to learn the high validity cue during training. As mentioned above, the selection criterion here was such that after 60 trials, subject judgments had to correlate at least $+.75$ with the high validity cue, and less than $+.25$ with the low validity cue.

The Conflict Situation

General design. Subjects trained to rely on different cues were paired with one another for the conflict stage of the experiment according to a 2×2 feedback by function form design. Ten pairs received exact feedback on every trial, showing them exactly how far their judgments were from the correct value of the criterion. Within each of these ten pairs, one member had been trained to rely on the curvilinear cue (state control), and one member had been trained to rely on the linear cue (free elections). The same cue function form division existed among the ten pairs given ambiguous feedback; in this condition, however, subjects were only told whether their judgments were right or wrong. All pairs received 20 trials on the conflict task.

Procedure. The subject pairs were tested following the same general procedure in all conditions of the experiment. They were first told that they would work together on a task similar to their prior individual task, however, this time the 20 problems would be more difficult because the countries involved were more complex. They were also told that they might not always agree in their predictions; whenever this occurred, they were to discuss the matter until they could arrive at a decision acceptable to both of them.

In fact, the conflict task was in all ways identical to the training task except that now both cue-variables correlated $+.67$ with the criterion, and there were fewer trials.

It was also explained to subjects that they were to follow a four-point procedural sequence on each of the 20 new trials: (1) record their individual predictions (i.e., overt judgments), (2) arrive at a joint prediction through discussion, (3) record their second individual prediction (i.e., covert judgments), and (4) receive accuracy feedback from E before going on to the next trial.

The Cognitive Change Measure

The amount of cognitive change on each trial of the conflict task was measured using the ratio $\dfrac{S - S'}{S - J}$; where the difference $(S - S')$ represents the discrepancy between the initial overt judgment *(S)* and the later covert judgment *(S')*, and the difference *(S — J)* represents the discrepancy between the overt judgment *(S)* and the agreed upon or joint judgment *(J)*. This measure is essentially a ratio between the individual change of opinion in each subject from the beginning to the end of the conflict trial, and the compromise joint judgment to which he openly agrees. It therefore takes into account the relative character of cognitive change.

The ratio was calculated for each trial, and then the average ratio for each block of two trials was computed. Results can thus be shown as a function of 10 2-trial blocks.

Results

No significant differences were found between the experimental groups with respect to the external dynamics of the conflict task, that is, overt conflict, covert conflict, adaptation to the task, and joint judgments. But significant differences *were* obtained with respect to cognitive change: It is more pronounced in the exact than the ambiguous feedback group. This difference favoring exact feedback shows itself in terms of the average degree of cognitive change across all trials and linear trends across trials.

Average Cognitive Change

The ratio measure of cognitive change averaged across all trials and for all pairs receiving exact feedback is $+.59$, whereas the corresponding mean for those receiving ambiguous feedback is $+.39$. An analysis of variance yielded a significant main effect for groups ($F = 6.88$, $p < .05$, $df = 1,36$) but no other significant main effects or interactions. It therefore appears that when they disagreed in an uncertain judgment situation, ambiguous feedback led our subjects to *stiffen their own viewpoints*. This point is made clear by the trend analysis.

Trends in Cognitive Change

Exact versus ambiguous feedback. Figure 7.1 shows the linear trend of cognitive change for all pairs in the exact and ambiguous feedback groups plotted across the 10 trial blocks. It can be seen here that, in general, the ambiguous feedback subjects return more and more to their original opinions. In other words, with increasing trials these subjects show a tendency toward reduction of cognitive change while the exact feedback subjects show a tendency toward increased cognitive change.

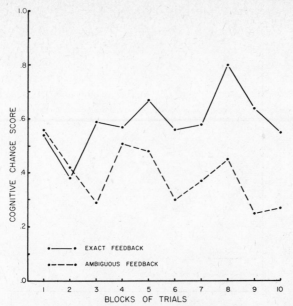

Figure 7.1. Mean cognitive change scores plotted as a function of trial blocks for the exact and ambiguous feedback groups

Analysis of variance of these trends indicates that although neither one is itself significantly different from zero, the difference between them is significant ($F = 4.54$, $p < .05$).

Linear versus curvilinear training. When all subjects given linear and curvilinear training are compared without regard to feedback conditions, no differences in cognitive change can be observed. However, separate trend analyses for these groups reveal that cognitive change in the linearly trained subjects *is* significantly influenced by feedback. That is, whereas curvilinearly trained subjects are not differentially affected by feedback conditions, the linearly trained subjects receiving ambiguous feedback show less cognitive change than those receiving exact feedback.

Figure 7.2 presents a comparison of cognitive change ratios for linearly trained subjects given ambiguous and exact feedback. Trend analyses indicate that the exact feedback group does not differ significantly from a zero trend, but the ambiguous feedback group has a significant negative trend ($F = 5.64$, $p < .05$). Furthermore, the difference between the two trends plotted in Figure 7.2 is also significant ($F = 4.67$, $p < .05$).

These data indicate that linear subjects given exact feedback move toward a new position during the conflict task while those receiving ambiguous feedback gradually return toward their original position.

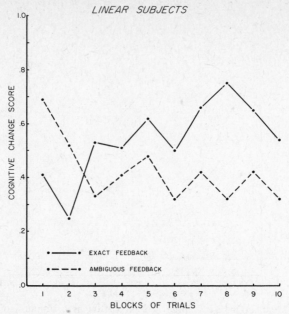

Figure 7.2. Comparison of mean cognitive change ratio scores for linearly trained subjects given ambiguous and exact feedback

Summary of Results

Altogether, the results of this study indicate two generalizations that can be applied to behavior in uncertain judgmental situations. First, in comparison with exact feedback, ambiguous feedback appears to prevent cognitive change. Second, feedback may interact with initial cue learning in such a way that linearly trained subjects are influenced by different types of feedback, while curvilinearly trained subjects are not.

Discussion

The substantive results of this study raise at least two important questions for discussion: (1) Why should exact feedback enhance cognitive change, and (2) why should this effect hold for linearly but not curvilinearly trained subjects? However, a prior issue involving comparison of the present findings with those obtained in an earlier study deserve immediate consideration. Using the same task employed here, Todd, Hammond, and Wilkins reported the following results: ". . . full versus partial information feedback (i.e., exact vs. ambiguous) did not have a marked differential effect on the reduction of conflict, but did have a differential effect on whether conflict would be resolved by compromise or capitulation. Where full information was received as feedback, conflict was resolved by compromise; where partial information was received, it was resolved by capitulation [1966, p. 96]."

The present study also shows no important effect on conflict reduction, but, contrary to the American subjects, for the Italians, the different types of feedback had no significant effect on compromise or capitulation (See comparison Table 7.1). It should be understood that compromise is measured according to the number of trials on which subjects both depart from their initial overt judgment when agreeing on a joint judgment, and capitulation is measured according to trials on which one subject keeps to his original judgment which the other accepts.

The data in Table 7.1 indicate that although the effect of feedback on compromise and capitulation is somewhat similar for American and Italian subjects, it is much stronger (and statistically significant) for the Americans. Given this finding that different types of feedback do not influence the compromise and capitulation behavior of Italians as much as Americans, the following interpretation is suggested.

It seems reasonable to assume that exact and ambiguous feedback influences the two different samples in different ways. In the American subjects, feedback effects show themselves at an *overt* level. Hence the Americans given exact feedback resolve their differences through compromises worked out during discussion. In the Italian sample, it may be that feedback effects manifest themselves at a *covert* level, so that those receiving exact feedback do not change their inclination toward compromise even though their personal judgments are more likely to change. In brief then, comparison suggests that exact feedback has a relatively internal impact on Italian subjects and an external impact on American subjects.

Ideally, this hypothesis could be examined further by comparing cognitive change data in the two samples, but this cannot be accomplished because the variable in question was measured differently in the two studies. Yet to the extent that comparison is possible here, the present interpretation is supported because the Americans seem to evidence less cognitive change than the Italians. It is also noteworthy that an unpub-

Table 7.1. Average Rates of Compromise or Capitulation in American and Italian Experimental Subjects Receiving Exact and Ambiguous Feedback

	Compromise		Capitulation	
	American Subjects	*Italian Subjects*	*American Subjects*	*Italian Subjects*
Exact feedback	.52	.44	.13	.23
Ambiguous feedback	.35	.41	.35	.30

lished study by Fröhlich (1967) done with German subjects produced results showing that exact feedback had no effect on compromise, and that ambiguous feedback led to an increase in overt conflict. Thus, it may well be the case that reactions to different types of feedback information reflect legitimate cultural differences between national groups. This possibility clearly requires further study.

Now, turning to the results of the present study, how is it possible to understand the increased cognitive change brought about by exact feedback? The most plausible interpretation relates to the cognitive and social conditions created in the experiment. Thus, when subjects are required to give their second (covert) judgment, they must be aware of the discrepancy between their first (overt) judgment and the joint decision agreed on with their partners. The immediate decision facing them, therefore, must involve an internal conflict—whether to base their second judgment on the same criteria used for the first, or to use whatever new criteria may have emerged from the subsequent discussion. Our results show that with increasing trials, exact feedback subjects tend to follow the latter course.

A direct explanation for this result was suggested by Todd, Hammond, and Wilkins, who note that exact feedback subjects ". . . discover in the early trials of the conflict situation that the right answers lie approximately midway between their individual predictions even though the amount of discrepancy between the individual judgments varies from trial to trial [1966, p. 96]." With such new learning, subjects begin to emphasize judgmental criteria arising during discussion, and this state of affairs induces cognitive change as the best way of resolving their covert judgment dilemma. In effect, the subjects learn from one another because the exact feedback makes it clear that both of them are at least partially correct.

On the other hand, ambiguous feedback makes it almost impossible for subjects to "learn to learn" from one another. In this case, their original judgment scheme, which was learned and verified during training, is not easily disconfirmed; it retains credibility as the only stable basis for decision making, and cognitive change is therefore hindered.

To recapitulate: The two kinds of information feedback apparently lead subjects to cope with the judgment situation in different ways. In the case of exact feedback, the information provides a basis for them to learn from one another and show cognitive change. It may be said that the cognitive input here modifies the social field dynamics of the judgment situation. In the case of ambiguous feedback, however, there is no important change because cognitive input is not sufficient to produce a reevaluation of prior learning or restructuring of the social field.

Of course, this tentative explanation of feedback effects must be qualified in accord with other findings indicating that cognitive change also varies in different cultures, and among subjects trained on different cue-function forms. Concerning the first point, it has been suggested that sociocultural factors may influence performance in two ways. Subjects may try to resolve tensions by working them out at the level of overt interpersonal relations, thus causing variation in amounts of conflict or in the methods by which it is resolved. Or, they may operate at a more *intra*personal level, and thus show a strengthening or weakening of their prior learning.

Under conditions of ambiguity, Italian subjects seemingly behave according to our proverb which translates approximately as follows: "He who leaves the old way for a new one does not feel well." But our results suggest an additional statement: "He who leaves the old way . . . does not feel well *unless he has exact information about his situation.*"

Finally, it should be noted that under conditions of ambiguous feedback, subjects who have been trained in a linear policy are less likely to change than are subjects who have been trained in nonlinear policies. This finding relates to a larger issue involving the psychological meaning of different types of cue-dependencies.

Briefly, other research in this volume (See Hammond & Brehmer; Moscovici et al.) demonstrates that curvilinear cue-dependency results in a more complex judgment policy than does linear cue-dependency. Linear subjects can base their judgments on a simple rule such as "the higher or lower the cue-value, the higher or lower the criterion." In contrast, subjects trained to use the curvilinear cue have learned to relate middle-range cue-values to extreme values on the criterion. It has been shown, for example, that a curvilinear cue is learned more slowly and is more difficult to verbalize than a corresponding linear cue. The present finding suggests that the less complex a subject's judgment policy, the more attractive it is (and, hence, more resistant to changes) under conditions of ambiguity. That is, in a situation of ambiguity, the clarity and simplicity of a linear response rule would constitute a stable frame of reference; change would therefore be resisted.

In conclusion, it should be clear from the work so far accomplished on the feedback problem that the quality of accuracy information available in an uncertain judgment situation is a very important determinant of behavior. In particular, such major variables as conflict, types of conflict resolution, and cognitive change may all be influenced by the nature of the available information.

REFERENCES

Fröhlich, W. D. Personal communication to Kenneth Hammond, 1967.

McClintock, C. G., & McNeel, S. P. Reward and score feedback as determinants of cooperative and competitive game behavior. *Journal of Personality and Social Psychology,* 1966, *4,* 606–613.

Pilisuk, M., Skolnick, P., & Overstreet, E. Predicting cooperation from the two sexes in a conflict simulation. *Journal of Personality and Social Psychology,* 1968, *10,* 35–43.

Pishkin, V. Availability of feedback-corrected error instances in concept learning. *Journal of Experimental Psychology,* 1967, *73,* 318–319.

Richard, J. F. Generalisation de la couleur avec information constante et information intermittente. *Psychologie Française,* 1966, *11*(2), 117–126.

Tedeschi, J., Lesnick, S., & Gahagan, J. Feedback and "washout" effects in the prisoner's dilemma game. *Journal of Personality and Social Psychology,* 1968, *10,* 31–34.

Todd, F. J., & Hammond, K. R. Differential feedback in two multiple-cue probability learning tasks. *Behavioral Science,* 1965, *10,* 429–435.

Todd, F. J., Hammond, K. R., & Wilkins, M. M. Differential effects of ambiguous and exact feedback on two-person conflict and compromise. *Journal of Conflict Resolution,* 1966, *10,* 88–97.

Wolfgang, A., & Pishkin, V. Effects of age, sex, error correction, social cues and amount and type of memory information in concept learning. *Proceedings of the 74th Annual Convention of the American Psychological Association,* 1966, *1,* 29–30.

8 Interpersonal Conflict Reduction: The Effects of Language and Meaning[1]

CARL E. KUHLMAN,
MONROE J. MILLER,
EROL GUNGOR[2]
University of Colorado

Language is generally acknowledged to have a central role in reducing conflict that arises from differences in ideologies or beliefs. Yet the inadequacies of language for this purpose have been observed not only in laboratory studies of conflict but also in the disputes of everyday life. In addition, the use of different languages adds to the difficulties residing in use of the same language. Indeed, it is with respect to disagreement between persons from different cultures that language and meaning differences present the greatest obstacles to conflict reduction. Despite the ubiquitous role of language, however, the effects upon conflict reduction of differences in meaning existing even in one culture, involving but one language, have not yet been investigated. The purpose of this investigation, therefore, is to examine the role of two specific dimensions of language, connotative and denotative meanings, in the reduction of interpersonal conflict arising from differences in beliefs.

Language and Connotative Meaning

Osgood and his colleagues (Osgood, Suci, & Tannenbaum, 1957; Snider & Osgood, 1968) have focused upon the *connotative* meanings of concepts, that is, the affective responses of persons to particular terms, and have suggested that differences in connotative meanings inhibit the resolution of conflict between persons. Osgood has pointed out that differences in both *denotative* and *connotative* meanings may serve as sources of disagreement and has argued that denotative agreement must be achieved

[1] The research reported here was undertaken in the Program of Research on Cognitive Processes, Institute of Behavioral Science, University of Colorado, and was supported by National Science Foundation Grant GS-1699 and National Institute of Mental Health Grant MH-11928-01.
[2] Now at the University of Istanbul.

before connotative disagreement can be engaged. For example, Osgood (1968) states, "two people must first agree on the referential (or denotative) meaning of a sign before they can agree on their diverse emotive (or connotative) reactions to it [p. 322]." Although connotative meanings have been widely studied, including extensive documentation of cross-cultural differences (See Jakobovits, 1966; Osgood, 1968), as yet there has been no empirical investigation of the relation between differential connotative and denotative meanings and the reduction of interpersonal disagreement.

Denotative Meaning and Interpersonal Conflict

Whereas Osgood's work has focused on connotative meaning, Hammond and his associates have been concerned with the problem of interpersonal conflict arising from differences in denotative meanings. Studies in which subjects are trained to develop different denotative meaning systems have generally shown that even in situations in which subjects have mutual utility for resolving their differences, the reduction of conflict is slow and inefficient. That is, denotative differences between persons are reduced, but rarely to a great extent.

Of particular interest in these studies is the *pattern* of conflict reduction. In virtually every study, conflict is systematically reduced during the first half of the interaction between subjects. During the second half of this interaction, however, the level of conflict is almost never reduced further, and in some cases, conflict actually increases. The generality of this finding is further shown by the results of two cross-national studies (See Brehmer, Azuma, Hammond, Kostron, & Varonos, 1970; Hammond, Bonaiuto, Faucheux, Moscovici, Fröhlich, Joyce, & DiMajo, 1968) in which similar patterns of conflict reduction are shown by subjects from nine different countries.

Osgood's findings of individual differences in connotative meanings suggest that the failure of subjects to reduce conflict further may be due to differences in connotations. That is, subjects may discover differences in connotative meanings as a result of discussion during the first half of their interaction, and this, in turn, may prevent further reduction of conflict as observed in the above studies.

Thus, Osgood has focused upon the *connotative* meanings of terms, whereas Hammond has studied the reduction of conflict due to *denotative* differences; however, no investigation has been made of the relation between connotative *and* denotative differences and the reduction of disagreement. The specific aim of this investigation is to evaluate the effects of *both denotative and connotative* differences on interpersonal conflict and the subsequent reduction of this conflict. It is expected that differences in denotative meanings, which provide the initial conflict between subjects, will be systematically reduced when the words used in discussion evoke similar connotations; however, when these words evoke different connotations, there will be less overall reduction of conflict and the rate of conflict reduction will decrease.

Method

Following the cognitive conflict paradigm developed by Hammond, the present study involves (1) a *training stage* in which pairs of subjects are trained to develop different belief or denotative meaning systems with respect to a decision-making task; and (2) an *interactive stage* in which subjects are required to work in pairs on a series of tasks similar but not identical to the tasks on which they were trained. The training stage allows precise specification of the belief systems of the subjects (i.e., their denotative meaning systems), while the interactive stage provides an opportunity for the subjects to discuss the nature of their differences in attempting to reduce their disagreement.

In addition, the semantic differential technique (Osgood, Suci, & Tannenbaum, 1957; Snider & Osgood, 1968) was used to assess connotative similarities or differences between subjects in each pair.

The experiment utilized a 2×2 factorial design that allowed comparison of the effects on cognitive conflict of differences and similarities in *both* denotative and connotative meanings. Specifically, subjects were assigned to one of four experimental conditions on the basis of their semantic differential ratings *and* the training they received during the first stage of the experiment. The four conditions were: (1) similar denotations and similar connotations, (2) similar denotations but different connotations, (3) different denotations but similar connotations, and (4) different denotations and different connotations.

Procedure

Selection To Establish Connotative Differences and Similarities

Forty-eight male undergraduates were required to rate a series of concepts, including "state control" and "elections"—the two key conceptual elements of the political decisions task to be described below—on a series of ten semantic differential scales which included four evaluative scales: (1) good–bad, (2) nice–awful, (3) sweet–sour, and (4) beautiful–ugly. The subjects were then matched to produce pairs with marked differences or similarities in their semantic differential ratings and assigned to the Different Connotation or Similar Connotation conditions, respectively. To be selected for the Different Connotation condition, subjects in a pair were required to show a mean difference of 3.0 or more in their evaluative ratings of the concepts "state control" and "elections." Inclusion in the Similar Connotation condition required that subject-pairs show a mean difference of no more than .25 in their evaluative ratings of the same two concepts. (The maximum possible mean difference for any pair of subjects was 6.0.) To insure comparability of absolute connotative ratings between the Similar and Different Connotation conditions, subjects with mean absolute ratings between 3.5 and 4.5 were excluded from the Similar Connotation condition.

Training To Establish Denotative Differences and Similarities

All pairs were then instructed that they were to participate in an investigation of "political decision making." They were trained individually to predict the level of democratic institutions in a series of hypothetical nations on the basis of two cues: (1) the extent to which government is determined by free elections, and (2) the amount of state control over the individual present in that nation. The two cues were presented in the form of bar graphs, ranging in value from 1–10, on 5 × 8 inch cards, the level of the bar graph indicating the value of each cue. On the basis of these cues, subjects were to estimate the "level of democratic institutions" for each nation on a 20-point criterion scale. Subjects were shown the "correct answer" after each of the 60 trials. In all cases, the two cues were probabilistically related to the criterion (i.e., $R^2 = .92$), thus making it impossible for subjects to achieve the correct answer on each trial and insuring the indeterminate nature of the task.

Subjects were told the form of the function relating each of the cues to the task criterion, and also told that one of the cues was more important and should be given more weight in their predictions of the criterion than the other cue. Specifically, they were instructed that the elections cue was related to the criterion in a positive linear manner ("The greater the degree of *elections,* the greater the *level of democratic institutions*"), but that the state control cue was related to the criterion in a nonlinear manner ("Neither too little nor too much *state control* means that *the level of democratic institutions is high*").

Different denotations. To establish differences in denotative meanings (or beliefs), one subject in each pair was given a task in which the correlation between the elections cue and the level of democratic institutions was .98, while the state control cue was randomly related to criterion. For the other subject, the elections cue was random, while the state control cue was correlated .98 with level of democratic institutions.

Similar denotations. In order to establish similar denotations between pairs of subjects, both subjects in a pair were trained to depend upon the same cue in making their judgments and to ignore the other. Half of the subject-pairs were trained to depend upon the elections cue and half upon the state control cue.

Subjects were included in the interactive stage of the experiment if they showed a correlation of .90 or greater between their judgments and the cue they were trained to depend upon, and a correlation of less than .20 between their judgments and the cue they were trained to ignore.

Interactive Stage

Upon completion of training, each pair worked together on a decision task similar but not identical to their individual training tasks. They were informed that whereas the decisions they had been making before concerned hypothetical nations, they would now be making judgments about real nations. Consequently, these would be more difficult and might lead to disagreement, in which case they were to discuss their judgments until they reached a mutually acceptable decision. Each subject first recorded his individual judgment of the level of democratic institutions for each nation, then presented his judgment to the other subject, after which they discussed their judgments until they reached a decision acceptable to both. This procedure was repeated until the subjects had made judgments for 20 nations. Four different sequences of the 20 interactive trials were used and matched across the four experimental conditions. The cue-criterion relations for the interactive task were structured so that both cues were equally valid with respect to the criterion.

Amount of conflict. The most direct measure of conflict consists of the absolute difference between subjects' judgments $|S_1 - S_2|$, and is recorded for each pair of subjects on each trial of the interactive sequence. This measure reflects the differences in judgments that are communicated and discussed by the subjects on each trial.

The amount of conflict for subjects in each of the four experimental conditions is shown in Figure 8.1. Pairs of subjects who were denotatively different showed more conflict over trials than pairs of subjects with similar denotations. Analysis of variance indicates that these differences are statistically significant ($F = 23.40$, $df = 1,20$, $p < .01$). Pairs of subjects with different connotations showed a tendency toward greater conflict than pairs of subjects with similar connotations, but these differences are of borderline significance ($F = 3.03$, $df = 1,20$, $p \cong .10$).

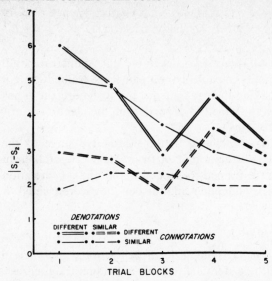

Figure 8.1.   Mean amount of conflict as a function of blocks of 4 trials for subject-pairs in each experimental condition

Denotative differences and conflict reduction. For those subject-pairs who were denotatively different, there was a significant reduction of conflict over the interactive sequence as indicated by a significant Blocks by Denotations interaction $(F = 3.42, df = 4,80, p < .05)$. As expected, subject-pairs with similar denotations did not show a reduction of conflict over trials due to their low initial level of disagreement.

Connotative differences and the pattern of conflict reduction. Figure 8.1 indicates that in the Different Connotation conditions, the amount of conflict observed during the latter portion of the interactive sequence does not decrease and shows some tendency towards increasing. Since previous studies (See Brehmer et al., 1970; Hammond et al., 1968) have shown that conflict reduction during the second half of interaction often differs from that during the first half, an analysis of variance was performed upon conflict scores for the last half of the interactive sequence. This indicates that subject-pairs who are connotatively different show significantly more conflict than subject-pairs who are connotatively similar during this portion of the interactive sequence, independent of the denotative condition $(F = 4.71, df = 1,20, p < .05)$. In addition, subjects who were denotatively different show a tendency toward more conflict than subjects who were denotatively similar during this portion of the interactive sequence, but the difference is relatively small $(F = 3.65, df = 1,20; p \cong .10)$. This finding suggests that differences in connotative meanings contribute to the failure of subjects to reduce their disagreement beyond the levels achieved during the first half of the interactive sequence.[3]

Discussion

The results reported here indicate that both connotative and denotative meanings affect the amount of conflict that persons experience when working together to solve common problems, as well as the rate with which this conflict is reduced. Specifically, the effects of connotative and denotative differences on cognitive conflict may be summarized as follows: (1) differences in denotations are the primary determinants of the amount of conflict during the *initial* stage of the interactive sequence; (2) these differences are reduced during the interactive sequence; and (3) during the *latter* half of the sequence, connotative differences inhibit the further reduction of conflict and may lead to an increase in the amount of conflict experienced. In short, after conflict due to denotative differences undergoes some resolution, differences in connotations persist and become major determinants of the level of cognitive conflict.

The finding that the effects of connotative differences on conflict reduction become apparent *after* denotative differences are reduced is of particular importance. It agrees with Osgood's (1957) suggestion that denotative agreement *precedes* connotative disagreement; that is, before connotative differences can affect attempts to reduce conflict, some agreement about the denotative or referential meaning of the terms used in the discussion must be reached. However, whereas denotative differences are apparently reduced, the results suggest that subjects are not able to reduce their connotative differences.

The results of this investigation also demonstrate the *behavioral consequences* of differential connotative meanings with respect to the reduction of interpersonal conflict. Two ways in which connotations affect the reduction of conflict are suggested. First, connotative similarity *facilitates* conflict reduction. Where substantial cognitive conflict between subjects occurs (i.e., in the Different Denotation conditions), subjects with similar connotations are better able to resolve their conflict than subjects with different connotations. Second, connotative differences *inhibit* conflict reduction. Independent of the extent of their denotative differences, both groups of connotatively different subjects show no further conflict reduction beyond the level achieved during the first half of the interactive sequence. Indeed, the denotatively similar but connotatively different

---

[3] In a subsequent study, which employed female subjects, patterns of conflict reduction different from those in this investigation were obtained. However, it is unclear whether the observed differences in conflict reduction represent basic sex differences or differential effects of connotative differences as a function of sex.

subject-pairs show some tendency toward *increasing* conflict over the latter half of the interactive sequence; in the final block of trials they experience as much conflict as the denotatively different but connotatively similar subjects.

The finding that denotative and connotative differences are both important determinants of interpersonal conflict raises two additional questions: (1) Can information be provided for subjects so that they may reduce connotative differences? (2) Are subjects aware of their differences with respect to *both* denotations and connotations?

The problem of providing subjects with information about denotative differences has been investigated by Hanna and Hammond (1968) who found that quantitative pictorial feedback regarding the nature of denotative differences increases the tendency of subjects to compromise to reduce their differences. Future research must also address the question of whether information about the nature of connotative differences affects the reduction of conflict due to these differences. In addition, the related question, can *subjects learn about* each other's connotative meanings, is also of great importance. Whereas there is some evidence that subjects can learn about the denotative meanings others attach to terms used to discuss cognitive differences (See Bergner & Miller, 1969; Hammond, Wilkins, & Todd, 1966), the problem of learning about the connotative meanings others attach to these terms has never been investigated.

The present findings also have important implications for attempts to reduce conflict between persons who speak different languages and/or have different cultural backgrounds. Specifically, attempts to reduce conflict by facilitating communication must take into account the *denotative* and *connotative* meanings of terms, both of which may differ as a function of language and cultural background. For example, while the *denotative* meaning of the term "compromise" may be readily translated from French into English, it may be far more difficult to convey to the Englishman the *connotative* meaning of "compromise" for the Frenchman. Failure to communicate this, however, may severely retard attempts to reduce disagreement. Osgood and his colleagues (See Jakobovits, 1966; Osgood, 1968) have demonstrated numerous cross-cultural differences in connotative meaning systems, but their findings have yet to be applied to the problem of conflict reduction. This paper constitutes an initial step in that direction.

REFERENCES

Bergner, R., & Miller, M. J. Interpersonal learning: The case of learning about one another. Report No. 115, Boulder, Colo.: Program on Cognitive Processes, Institute of Behavioral Science, Summer 1969.

Brehmer, B., Azuma, H., Hammond, K. R., Kostron, L., & Varonos, D. A cross national comparison of cognitive conflict. *Journal of Cross Cultural Psychology,* 1970, *1,* 5–20.

Brown, L., & Hammond, K. R. A supra-linguistic method for reducing intragroup conflict. Report No. 108, Boulder, Colo.: Program on Cognitive Processes, Institute of Behavioral Science, 1968.

Hammond, K. R., Bonaiuto, G., Faucheux, C., Moscovici, S., Frohlich, D., Joyce, C. R., & Di Majo, G. A comparison of cognitive conflict between persons in Western Europe and the United States. *International Journal of Psychology,* 1968, *3,* 1–12.

Hammond, K. R., Wilkins, M., & Todd, F. J. A research paradigm for the study of interpersonal learning. *Psychological Bulletin,* 1966, *25,* 221–232.

Jakobovits, L. A. Comparative psycholinguistics in the study of cultures. *International Journal of Psychology,* 1966, *1,* 15–37.

Osgood, C. E. Interpersonal verbs and interpersonal behavior. Technical Report No. 64, Urbana, Ill.: University of Illinois, Group Effectiveness Research Laboratory, November 1968.

Osgood, C. E., Suci, G. J., & Tannenbaum, P. H. *The measurement of meaning.* Urbana, Ill.: University of Illinois Press, 1957.

Snider, J. G., & Osgood, C. E. *Semantic differential technique.* Chicago: Aldine, 1968.

INTERPERSONAL LEARNING
FROM *AND* ABOUT *THE OTHER*

Introduction
to Readings 9 and 10

The next two contributions concern yet another important set of questions that arise when judgment is studied in the context of social interaction: What can persons with different policies learn *from* one another concerning the task at hand, and, what can they learn *about* one another? The former question is investigated in a series of experiments reported by Earle, who specifies conditions under which learning from the other facilitates policy changes and judgmental accuracy.

With respect to the latter question, Miller describes both laboratory and field studies that show how interpersonal understanding can be increased when persons learn about each other's judgment policies. This work is also noteworthy because it involves real inimical groups (e.g., police and minority youth) and an ingenious "tape exchange" technique for arranging communication between them.

9 Interpersonal Learning[1]

TIMOTHY C. EARLE[2]
Oregon Research Institute
and
University of Oregon

People learn about the world in two ways: either *individually,* through personal discovery of environmental regularities, or *interpersonally,* through information provided by another person. Although many everyday situations obviously involve mixtures of both individual and interpersonal learning, it will presently be shown how the two processes may be distinguished from one another theoretically and according to their particular areas of application.

In modern experimental psychology, however, the study of human learning has generally been equated with individual learning (e.g., Melton, 1964). Although some social psychology has been concerned with topics relevant to interpersonal learning (e.g., socialization, education; see Lindzey & Aronson, 1968, 1969), direct analytical concern with the process *qua* process is nowhere in evidence. This paper describes some preliminary steps toward a theory of interpersonal learning; it also provides an appropriate research methodology which is illustrated and evaluated in a series of experiments.

Theory

Interpersonal learning involves at least three prime components: the learner, the person being learned from, and the situation being learned

[1] Sponsorship for this study comes from the Personnel and Training Research Programs, Psychological Sciences Division, Office of Naval Research, under Contract No. N00014-68-C-0431, Contract Authority Ident. No. NR 153-311, and from Grants MH-15414 and MH-16437 from the United States Public Health Service.
[2] The author gratefully acknowledges the contributions of Kenneth R. Hammond and his associates at the Institute of Behavioral Science, University of Colorado, Boulder. Paul Slovic and Robyn M. Dawes of the Oregon Research Institute provided invaluable support and assistance. Special thanks are due to Monroe J. Miller for his many contributions. The final form of this paper is due in large part to the editorial skills of Leon Rappoport.

about. In medicine, the area from which illustrative examples are drawn throughout this paper, interpersonal learning may include a student, an expert clinician, and a patient. Any theory of interpersonal learning must discuss these components and the relations among them. More specifically, the theory should embrace (1) the patient's condition (the relations between the surface signs and the basic disorders), (2) what the expert knows about the condition, (3) what the student does not know, and (4) what the student learns from his contact with the expert over time. The theoretical framework that can accomplish this is introduced below.

System Properties

In the conceptual framework of Brunswik (1952) and Hammond (1970) an environmental situation or "system" is said to be composed of *surface elements* and *depth elements:* the surface elements are known to an observer, while the depth elements must be inferred from the surface elements. Such a system may be described in terms of its *laws* and its *consistency*. The laws involve relations between surface and depth elements. The degree of consistency in a system is the degree to which its laws can be inferred from directly observable surface elements.

A patient is, of course, a very complex system. The surface elements here are the primary features of his condition; for example, fever, diarrhea, jaundice, etc. The depth elements are his basic disorders; for example, inflammation of the liver or carcinoma of the lung. The relations between the primary features of the patient's condition and his basic disorders constitute the laws of the system. For example, wheezing and coughing are related in certain ways to lung cancer, while loss of appetite and jaundice are related to inflammation of the liver. Finally, the consistency of a patient-system depends on the relations between his symptoms and underlying disorder. If it were possible for the expert clinician to always predict the basic disorder from surface evidence, then a patient would be a highly consistent system. But many basic disorders cause similar symptoms, and a patient may be host to a number of basic disorders. Patients, therefore, are highly inconsistent systems, demanding the most sensitive and skillful judgment on the part of the clinician.

Intersystem Knowledge: Clinical Judgment

Clinical judgment is the interaction between two systems, clinician and patient; it is the *knowing* of the patient by the clinician. Hammond (1970) has described this interaction in terms of three concepts: matching, consistency, and context of information.

Law matching. Good clinical judgment requires a high degree of intersystem knowledge, which depends in the first instance upon accurate matching between the laws of the patient-system and the laws of the clinician-system. The better the matching, the better the knowledge. Thus, clinical judgment will be good insofar as the clinician can detect and rely upon the significant symptom-disorder relations in the patient-system.

System consistency. Intersystem knowledge also depends on the consistencies of the two systems. A highly consistent patient-system is relatively easily known because its surface elements or symptoms will always be associated with particular depth elements or disorders. But many patients may appear to be highly inconsistent systems, their laws obscured by a confusion of surface elements. In order to achieve knowledge here the clinician must try to make up for lack of consistency in the patient-system by increasing his own. That is, he may impose consistency on the patient-system, and on his own judgment system, by recourse to special diagnostic tests, consultation with expert colleagues, and his fund of prior experience. Indeed, by building up his own consistency in this fashion, he operates in the grand tradition of modern science to make sense out of surface confusion.

Context of information. This refers to the mode and content of communication between systems, factors mediating contacts between the patient and clinician. Unlike matching and consistency, the context of information involves conditions *surrounding* the system which can either facilitate or inhibit intersystem knowledge.

Intersystem Knowledge and Interpersonal Learning

When two persons face an environmental situation, the situation may be thought of as a static, nonknowing system, while each of the persons is a dynamic, knowing system. Interpersonal learning is what one person learns from the other, and this learning depends on the shared knowledge or agreement between the two persons:

$$A_{12} = f(M, C_1 C_2)$$

Agreement between person one and person two is a function of the matching between the laws of their systems and their consistencies. If A_{12} is high, the persons have little to learn from one another; low A_{12} indicates that there is much to be learned. The former case might be illustrated by two expert clinicians who have been practicing together in the same fashion for many years, and the latter by a new intern working with an expert clinician.

Learning in any such situation will depend upon information coming from either the environmental system or the system of the expert other person. Both sources can provide similar information about surface and depth elements in the environmental system, but the expert other can *also* provide information about his ideas—his theoretical conception of how the environmental system functions. In addition to the different quality of information available from these two sources, the context of information may include different forms of communication: oral, written, pictorial, and numerical, in various combinations.

As a general process, then, interpersonal learning can be a very complex matter, depending not only upon the initial agreement between knowing systems as indicated by their match and respective consistencies, but also upon the context of information mediating between them. This complexity makes it all the more important to employ an appropriate research methodology, one which can provide quantitative procedures for the description of changes in the relations among the learner, the person being learned from, and the object or person being learned about.

Methodology

The analytical model for interpersonal learning was described in the general introduction as the "three-system case" for research on human judgment, and later discussed in more detail (See Hammond, Reading 5) as a means of studying conflict. For laboratory investigations of interpersonal learning, however, the model may be summarized as follows. Individual subjects (S_1 and S_2) are trained to rely on different cues in the same two-cue learning task. In their subsequent joint task (common environment), the two cues (X_1 and X_2) are equally relevant to the criterion *(Y)*. The subjects thus begin their joint task with different information; each must now learn from the other, and/or from the task, that the cue he had been trained to ignore is important.

In addition to this cue learning, each person may also have to learn a new rule (function form) relating the cue to the criterion. But regardless of whether cue learning or rule learning is involved (See Summers, 1967, 1969), relevant information can be obtained from both the other person and the task. Consequently, two types of learning—interpersonal learning (from the other person) and individual learning (from the task)—can go on simultaneously. In order to distinguish between them it is necessary to employ analytical techniques based on the lens model equation.

The lens model equation. Originally developed to measure changes occurring between an individual cognitive system and an environmental or task system (Hursch, Hammond, & Hursch, 1964), the lens model equation was elaborated by Tucker (1964) into a form appropriate to the study of interpersonal learning.

$$r_a = GR_eR_s$$

where $G =$ the correlation between the predicted criterion values of the person's system and the predicted criterion values of the task system. Nonlinear cue-criterion relations are transformed to linear relations prior to calculation of G. G therefore is a measure of the *matching* between the laws of the person's system and the laws of the task system.

$R_e =$ the multiple correlation between the task criterion values and the cue-values, a measure of *task consistency*.

$R_s =$ the multiple correlation between the responses of the person and the cue-values, a measure of *person consistency*.

$r_a =$ the correlation between the task criterion values and the person's responses, a measure of *knowledge*.

We thus have the multiplicative function Knowledge $=$ Matching $\times$ Task Consistency $\times$ Person Consistency. In addition to these measures, the person's cue-dependencies, r_{x_is}, are important in determining what information he is using and the source of that information. Very briefly, then, by using the lens model analysis together with appropriate experimental controls, it is possible to show who learned what from whom.

Summary

In general, it should now be clear that the lens model and lens model equation provide both the experimental procedures and analytical techniques needed to investigate interpersonal learning. These methodological tools can be applied very broadly: Any number of persons may be studied, their initial knowledge may be of any kind or quantity, and any degree of agreement may exist between them.

The balance of this paper describes three experiments concerning fundamental conditions of interpersonal learning. Experiment 1 investigates the effects of varying the context of information and rule complexity. The second experiment is entirely devoted to problems involving rule complexity, and the third involves relations between rule complexity and initial agreement among subjects.

Experiment 1: Context of Information and Rule Complexity

Theoretically, it has been suggested that interpersonal learning can either be facilitated or inhibited depending upon the context of information (hereafter abbreviated as *CI*) in which it occurs, and the complexity of the cue-criterion relations to be learned. The present study manipulates *CI* factors to produce five different conditions that should make learning more or less difficult, while, at the same time, the rules to be learned are manipulated through two levels of complexity. The experiment is thus specifically designed to investigate how interpersonal learning varies with changes in *CI* conditions and rule complexity.

Design

CI conditions. In general, the various factors relevant to *CI* conditions include the sources, modes, and contents of communication. Sources may be the task or other person, modes may be verbal or nonverbal, and contents may be information about the surface or depth elements in either the task-system or other-person-system. The following *CI* conditions were arranged to present different types of information in five increments, ranging from a minimum to a maximum of relevant data: (1) data concerning task surface elements; (2) task surface and task depth elements; (3) task surface and depth, plus nonverbal other-subject data; (4) task surface and depth, plus verbal other-subject depth and relational data; (5) task surface and depth, verbal other-subject depth and relational data, plus nonverbal other-subject relational data. The operational meaning of each *CI* condition is described in a later section on method and procedure, but the theoretical importance of the five conditions can be specified immediately.

First, since task surface data alone cannot reveal laws relevant to the criterion, in this condition matching should be low and learning accordingly inhibited. The addition of task depth data in the second condition, however, should allow task laws (i.e., cue-criterion relationships) to be readily inferred, depending upon their consistency and complexity. It is assumed that for a given level of consistency, laws involving simple relationships will be learned more easily. The remaining *CI* conditions involve other-subject data, information over and above that which comes from the task system.

Condition 3 only involves the nonverbal judgmental behavior of the other subject which will probably seem quite variable and confusing to the learner in the absence of verbal explanations. Hence, this sort of added data should increase the learner's inconsistency and thereby impede his progress. In the fourth condition, verbal other-subject data includes explanations of how the other understands cue-criterion relations that are new to the learner. Such information should help the learner match the laws of the task more easily than in any of the previous *CI* conditions, and learning should be facilitated. Finally, the addition of nonverbal other-subject relational data in Condition 5, which will be presented as a straightforward numerical description of the other's judgment policy, should lead to maximum learning efficiency.

In sum, the first three *CI* conditions are all relatively individual or task-oriented because no effective aid can be provided by the other person, while the last two conditions do permit genuine interpersonal learning. By comparing performances in these different *CI* conditions, therefore, it should be possible to specify the contribution of interpersonal learning to overall task adaptation. Conditions 1 and 2 set the baseline for individual performance; Condition 3 is arranged to show how the presence of another may impede learning; and Conditions 4 and 5 should facilitate learning by successively greater degrees.

Rule complexity. Several studies have shown that in judgmental learning tasks, different forms of cue-criterion relationships can be more or less difficult to learn (e.g., Brehmer, 1970; Hammond & Summers, 1965; Summers, 1967). In particular, all of these studies indicate that complex (nonlinear) rules relating cues to a criterion are more difficult to learn than simple (linear) rules.

The task employed in the present study included both a simple positive linear rule and a complex nonlinear (inverted U-shaped) rule. The study is thus generally arranged as a 5 *(CI)* $\times$ 2 (rule complexity) design. Potential interactions between these two independent variables are especially important, because it is assumed that when difficult rules are involved the more favorable interpersonal learning conditions will be required for best performance.

Method and Procedure

Subjects. One hundred male undergraduates were assigned to five experimental conditions, with ten pairs in each condition.

Training task. Subjects appeared in pairs and were instructed that they would participate in an experiment in political decision making. This involved making judgments of the level of democratic institutions according to the amount of state control over the individual, and the extent to which government is determined by free elections. These cues were presented in the form of bar graphs on 5 $\times$ 8 cards, the level of the bar graph indicating the value of each cue. Cue-values varied from 1 to 10. On the back of each card was the criterion, "level of democratic institutions," with values varying from 1 to 20.

Subjects were informed that the relation between *state control* and level of *democratic institutions* was nonlinear ("neither too much nor too little state control will mean that the level of democratic institutions is high"), and that the relation between *free elections* and *democratic insti-*

tutions was linear ("the greater the extent to which government is determined by free elections, the higher the level of democratic institutions"). Subjects also were told that one cue would be more important than the other and should be given more weight in making their decisions; they were not told which one was more important.

One subject in each pair was presented with a deck of 60 training cards in which the correlation between state control and level of democratic institutions was .98. For these subjects, no systematic relation existed between free elections and the criterion. The second subject in each pair was trained on a deck of cards in which the correlation between free elections and level of democratic institutions was .98, while state control and the criterion were unrelated.

Subjects were informed of the correct answer after each trial, and were trained to reach a criterion at which their judgments correlated at least .75 with the cue they were trained to depend on, and not more than .25 with the cue they were trained to ignore. The multiple correlation between the two cues and the criterion in both training decks was .92, making it impossible to achieve the correct answer on every trial.

Interaction task. Subjects were told that the previous session had involved fictitious data, but that the task now facing them concerned real nations. They were shown a new deck of 20 cards similar to those used in training. As before, the free elections cue was related to the criterion in a positive linear manner; the state control cue related to the criterion in a nonlinear manner (inverted U). However, the correlation of each cue with the criterion was now .67. (There was no correlation between the cues.) Subjects were *not* told that the two cues were now equally correlated with the criterion.

CI Conditions

1. *Task surface.* Subjects in this condition were required to make judgments individually with no accuracy feedback and no contact with any other subject.

2. *Task depth.* Identical to Condition 1, except that subjects were informed of the correct answer after each trial.

3. *Nonverbal other-subject depth.* Similar to Condition 2, but after recording his judgment on a particular trial, each subject was then shown a card which provided another judgment about the criterion. The judgment presented on this card was the mean judgment made for that trial by subjects trained on the opposite cue in previous experiments.

4. *Verbal other-subject depth and relational.* Subject pairs were told that because they would be making predictions about real nations, the task was difficult, and they might differ in their predictions. Whenever

disagreement occurred, they were to discuss the matter with one another until they arrived at a decision agreeable to both. They were instructed to first examine the cue-values on a card and record their individual judgments, then inform each other of their decisions, and, if these differed, to arrive at a joint decision. The correct answer was presented after each trial.

5. *Nonverbal other-subject relational.* The same as Condition 4, with one additional feature. After 7 trials each subject was asked to estimate (1) how much weight he placed on each of the cues, and (2) how much weight the other subject was placing on each cue. While the subjects were making these estimates, their judgments on the first 7 interaction trials were entered into a computer and the "weights" (correlation coefficients) each subject actually used were calculated. Subjects were then given this information from the computer to compare with their own estimates. The same procedure was repeated at the end of the fourteenth interaction trial.

Measures of interpersonal learning. Conditions 1, 2, and 3 of the present study included only task information. Conditions 4 and 5 included both task and interpersonal information. Differences in task adaptation between Conditions 1, 2, and 3 and Conditions 4 and 5 indicate the effects of interpersonal learning. Examination of the lens model adaptation parameters, G and R_s, with the R_e constant (from $r_a = GR_eR_s$), together with the cue-dependencies, $r_{x_is_j}$, allows specification of what is learned from the task and what is learned interpersonally from the other subject.

Results and Discussion

The most important results are first, that learning in *CI* Conditions 1 and 3 (task surface and nonverbal other-subject information, respectively) was poorer than in any other conditions, as indicated in Figure 9.1. And second, that whereas nonlinear-trained subjects generally matched the laws of the task better than linear-trained subjects (See Figure 9.2), the latter subjects were more consistent (See Figure 9.3). These results are discussed below.

Since the surface data (cue-values) provided in Condition 1 cannot reveal the laws of the task, it was expected that learning would be very low because, although the subjects might be consistent, they would not be able to match the cue-criterion relations in the task. In Condition 3, however, which included surface, depth, and nonverbal other-subject data, it was assumed that learning would suffer because the added nonverbal information would interfere with consistency. The results mentioned above confirm these expectations. But the poor learning in Conditions

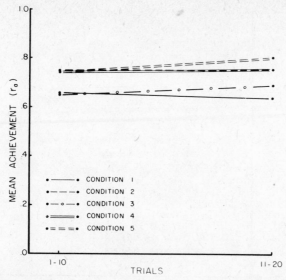

Figure 9.1. Comparison of mean learning scores obtained in different context of information conditions

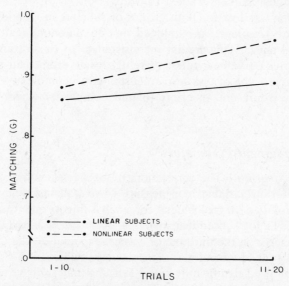

Figure 9.2. Comparison of mean matching scores obtained for linear- and nonlinear-trained subjects

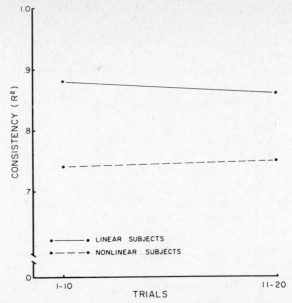

Figure 9.3. Comparison of mean consistency scores obtained for linear- and nonlinear-trained subjects

1 and 3 was due to different patterns of matching and inconsistency among the linear- and nonlinear-trained subjects.

Matching was low for both groups of subjects in Condition 3, while inconsistency was more pronounced among the nonlinear subjects in Conditions 1 and 3. This greater inconsistency for those trained to work with a complex curvilinear rule apparently results from their set to match a more difficult type of task law. Accustomed to complexity, their inconsistency may represent an effort to find complexity where it does not exist.

Specific Judgment Parameters

1. *Task learning.* The correlation, r_a, between a subject's judgments and the criterion variable is a measure of overall task learning; r_a was computed for two 10-trial blocks for each subject, and transformed to Fisher z-scores for subsequent analyses. A $5 \times 2 \times 2$ ANOVA with repeated measures on the third factor was used to analyze the *CI*, rule complexity and trial blocks effects, respectively. Subjects in *CI* Conditions 2, 4, and 5 showed significantly better learning than subjects in Conditions 1 and 3 ($F_{4,90} = 4.01$, $p < .01$). There were no significant main effects for rule complexity or trial blocks, and no significant interactions.

Thus, subjects with *no* task depth information (Condition 1) and subjects with a *confusing* type of information (Condition 3) learned the task less well than those working under more facilitating conditions. These results hold for both types of rule complexity, but since learning is a function of matching and consistency, it is necessary to examine these components in more detail.

2. *Law matching.* The correlation, G, between the predicted criterion values of the subject's system and the predicted criterion values of the task system is a measure of matching between laws of the subject's system and laws of the task system. Nonlinear cue-criterion relations were transformed to linear relations prior to the calculation of G. As with r_a, G was computed for two blocks of 10 trials for each subject, and transformed to Fisher z-scores for subsequent analysis according to the $5 \times 2 \times 2$ design described above.

A significant main effect was obtained for the CI conditions ($F_{4,90} = 7.04$; $p < .01$), with matching lowest in Condition 1, intermediate in Condition 3, and highest in Conditions 2, 4, and 5. Nonlinear subjects achieved greater overall matching than linear subjects ($F_{1,90} = 5.90$, $p < .05$). And finally, while there was a significant linear trend ($F_{1,90} = 12.93$, $p < .01$) indicating increased matching by all subjects over blocks of trials, there was also a rule complexity $\times$ trial blocks interaction ($F_{1,90} = 3.94$, $p < .05$) showing better matching over blocks by nonlinear subjects than by linear subjects.

These task matching results are roughly the same as those obtained for task learning; that is, subjects in Conditions 1 and 3 matched the task less well than subjects in Conditions 2, 4, and 5. This suggests that the differences in learning may have been due to differences in matching. Furthermore, the differences in matching between linear and nonlinear subjects indicate that although both groups learned at about the same level, this was accomplished through different processes. Since nonlinear subjects were better able to match the laws of the task than linear subjects, it follows that the linear subjects must have been more consistent in their judgments than the nonlinear subjects.

3. *Consistency.* The multiple correlation, R_s, between cue-values and subject responses is a measure of subject consistency; that is, the predictability of the subject's responses on the basis of the cue-values. As with the other measures, R_s was first transformed and then analyzed according to the $5 \times 2 \times 2$ design. The only significant main effect was for rule complexity ($F_{1,90} = 24.01$, $p < .01$); and the only significant interaction was between rule complexity and CI conditions ($F_{4,90} = 3.26$, $p < .05$). This interaction is due to the fact that while linear subjects were more consistent than nonlinear subjects within each information condition, their differences in Conditions 1 and 3 were much greater than those in Conditions 2, 4, and 5. Much of the main effect of rule complexity was thus due to Conditions 1 and 3.

These results are in line with the preceding learning and matching results: Failure to find *CI* conditions affecting consistency shows that these conditions only influence the matching component of learning. The interaction between rule complexity and *CI* conditions suggests that there should be differences in law matching *(G)* between linear and nonlinear subjects within *CI* conditions (since there was no effect of rule complexity and no interaction with information conditions). In the analysis of *G*, however, the interaction between rule complexity and information conditions was not significant. Further information on this matter can be gained through analysis of subject cue-dependencies.

4. *Subject cue-dependencies.* The correlation, $r_{x_i s_j}$, between a subject's judgments and cue i is a measure of cue-utilization or dependency. This correlation was computed for both cues in the two trial blocks and then transformed prior to analysis in the standard ANOVA design used above. There were two sets of cue-dependency data, correlations with the cue on which subjects were trained and correlations with the "new" cue. The results are reported separately. *Trained cue correlations:* the *CI* conditions had a significant effect on use of the trained cue ($F_{4,90} = 3.73$, $p < .01$). There were significant interactions between *CI* conditions and rule complexity ($F_{4,90} = 3.28$, $p < .05$) and blocks ($F_{4,90} = 6.20$, $p < .01$). The rule complexity and blocks main effects were also significant ($F_{1,90} = 22.39$, $p < .01$).

Examination of these results shows that with regard to main effects and interactions involving trial blocks and *CI* conditions, subjects in Conditions 2, 4, and 5, reduced their use of the trained cue over trials, while those in Conditions 1 and 3 did not. The main effect for rule complexity occurs because linear subjects maintained use of this cue to a greater degree than nonlinear subjects relied upon their nonlinear cue. However, this finding is complicated by an interaction with *CI* conditions: Linear subjects only reduced their use of the linear cue in Conditions 4 and 5; whereas nonlinear subjects were similar, they showed some departure from use of the nonlinear cue in Conditions 2 and 3.

Very briefly, these findings suggest that linear subjects were *not* able to properly adjust their trained cue correlations until they were given verbal, other-subject depth and relational information (Conditions 4 and 5). But nonlinear subjects *were* able to correctly decrease their trained cue correlations on the basis of both task surface and depth information (Conditions 2, 3, 4, and 5). Consequently, the linear and nonlinear subjects may have differed in matching within information conditions. Since matching involves the use of *both* task cues, however, the new cue correlations must be examined.

New cue correlations. A significant trial blocks effect ($F_{1,90} = 20.56$, $p < .01$) showed that new cue usage improved across trials in all experimental conditions. The *CI* effect was also significant ($F_{4,90} = 6.39$, $p <$ .01): Subjects in Conditions 4 and 5 approached optimum dependence on the new cue, while those in Conditions 2 and 3 only made a moderate shift to the new cue. No significant effect was found for rule complexity, and there were no important interactions.

Despite the failure to find significant effects for rule complexity, however, the data here forms a pattern suggesting that linear- and non-linear-trained subjects differ in their matching ability within different *CI* conditions. Thus, nonlinear subjects show significant dependence on the linear cue in Condition 2, while linear subjects do not begin to use the non-linear cue until Condition 4. This result is in line with the earlier finding that nonlinear subjects begin to reduce their *trained* cue-dependencies sooner than linear subjects. A similar and relevant nonsignificant tendency can also be seen in the matching data, where nonlinear subjects begin to match the task laws in Condition 2, while linear subjects do not show effective matching until Condition 4. It is generally indicated, therefore, that in comparison with nonlinear subjects, the linear-trained require better *CI* conditions before they can begin to depend on a new cue.

Implications for Interpersonal Learning

Taken together, the results of this study support the view that interpersonal learning may function as a very important aid to individual learning. Subject performances on the judgment task were generally best in those *CI* conditions that were designed to be most propitious for interpersonal learning. In this connection it is particularly noteworthy that in a "spurious" interpersonal learning situation (Condition 3), learning can be impeded by the addition of inappropriate information from another person.

With respect to rule complexity, the results suggest that interpersonal learning is of differential importance to linear- and nonlinear-trained subjects: The former benefit more from such learning than the latter. This is not very surprising, since if it is more difficult to shift from dependence on a simple rule to a complex rule than vice versa, those who must make this change will obviously benefit more from whatever aid is available. In the present experiment, the linear subjects required interpersonal learning from the nonlinear subjects in order to learn to use the nonlinear cue.

Finally, going back to the initial example of the student and expert clinician, the findings reported above seem clearly relevant: Complex surface-depth relations that are common in medicine (as well as in other fields) and are extremely difficult to learn to use individually, can readily be taught interpersonally when the "teacher" is able to communicate the proper (relational) information. The present study, however, investigated only two types of surface-depth relations, positive linear and inverted

U-shaped. The generality of the findings reported may therefore be limited by possible differences in the ability of persons to exchange information about varying forms of surface-depth relations. This problem is taken up in the next experiment.

Experiment 2: Variations in Rule Complexity

The previous investigation involved only two types of rule complexity: the relatively simple positive linear function form, and the more complex inverted U-shaped form. In order to study the effects of rule complexity more systematically, however, negative linear and U-shaped function forms must also be considered. Since other research findings (Björkman, 1965; Naylor & Clark, 1968) indicate that negative linear rules are more difficult to learn than positive linear rules, it seems fair to assume that the complexity of a rule depends upon its algebraic sign as well as its linear or nonlinear form.

Moreover, the four types of rules may each entail a different level of learning difficulty. For example, a U-shaped rule may be considered predominantly negative because the relation between the first half of the cue range and the criterion is negative. Similarly, an inverted U-shaped rule, where the first half of the cue range is related positively to the criterion, may be considered predominantly positive. While the U-shaped and inverted U-shaped rules are equally nonlinear, the U-shaped rule is more complex because of its predominant negativity. A negative linear rule is also, of course, more complex than a positive linear rule.

Briefly then, the present study investigates four levels of rule complexity, positive linear, negative linear, inverted U-shaped, and U-shaped (See Figure 9.4), in a constant *CI* Condition which allows significant interpersonal learning to occur.

Procedure

The experimental arrangements involving training and subsequent interaction were generally the same as in the previous study. In this instance, however, the task cues were presented without conceptual labels, simply as numbers. Two hundred male undergraduates served as subjects and were paired in such a way as to fill out the ten experimental conditions shown in Figure 9.5, with ten pairs in each condition. Subject pairs in each condition were tested on a 20-trial interaction task appropriate to their particular training. For example, a negative linear-trained subject and U-shaped trained subject would face a task containing negative linear and U-shaped cues.

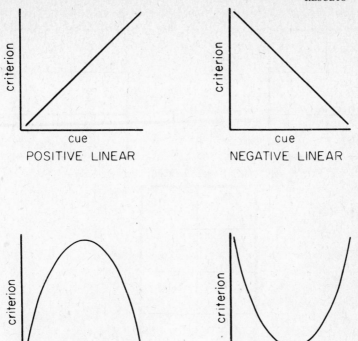

Figure 9.4.   The four levels of rule complexity

Interpersonal learning. Since the *CI* conditions were constant and favorable for interpersonal learning (subjects were given task surface and depth information, plus verbal other-subject depth information, as per Condition 4 in the first experiment), the effects of variations in rule complexity can be determined with respect to both task learning and interpersonal learning.

Results

All of the results described below were tested for significance according to a 4 (subject rule complexity) $\times$ 4 (other's rule complexity) $\times$ 2 (trial blocks) ANOVA design, with repeated measures on the trial blocks factor.

1. *Task learning.* Subject's ability to learn the interaction task was not influenced by the complexity of the rules they had been trained on. The main effect for subject rule complexity was not significant. However, although all subjects learned tasks of varying complexity equally well,

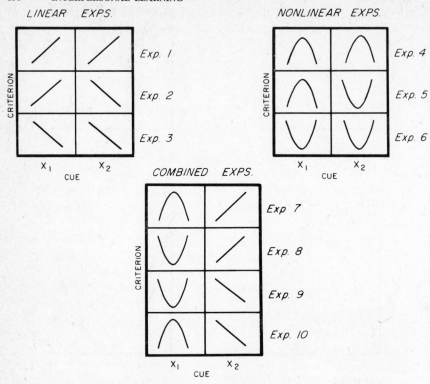

Figure 9.5. Illustration of the ten experimental conditions defining the experiment

their underlying learning processes may have been different. This point is taken up later.

The complexity of the other's rule *did* produce a significant effect upon subject's ability to learn the task ($F_{3,184} = 4.16$, $p < .01$). But this effect was mainly the result of better learning among subjects paired with a positive linear-trained other. In such cases, the interaction task always contained a positive linear cue, and since this type of cue is easiest to learn, even in the absence of interpersonal learning, the significant result must be interpreted as a *task*-learning rather than an *interpersonal*-learning phenomenon.

Finally, a significant trial blocks effect ($F_{1,184} = 4.85$, $p < .05$) showed that all subjects increased their learning across trials. There were no significant interactions.

2. *Matching*. Analysis of the matching component of task learning *(G)*, revealed no significant effect for subject rule complexity, and only a borderline significance ($p < .10$) for other's rule complexity. Briefly then, subject's ability to match cue-criterion relationships in the interac-

tion task is not influenced by the complexity of their prior training, and only slightly influenced by the complexity of their partners. The latter result was again due to pairings with positive linear-trained partners, which insured that the interaction task would contain an easy-to-learn rule. The matching component increased sharply across trials ($F_{1,184} = 11.68$, $p < .01$), and there were no interactions.

3. *Consistency*. Examination of this second component of task learning *(R_s)* yields results quite different from those reported above. Subject rule complexity has a significant effect upon consistency ($F_{3,184} = 5.82$, $p < .01$), while there is no effect for other's rule complexity. Further scrutiny of these data show that positive linear-trained subjects were the most consistent, U-shaped rule trained subjects were least consistent, and those trained on negative linear and inverted U-shaped rules were intermediate. It seems clear, therefore, that the complexity of their rule training influenced the ability of subjects to use rules consistently in the interaction task. But with respect to overall task learning, this difference in consistency apparently has no important effect because it is overridden or swamped by subject's general ability to match task laws regardless of their prior training on more or less complex rules.

As was the case for the other measures reported above, consistency increases significantly across trials ($p < .05$) and there are no significant interactions.

4. *Subject cue-dependencies: (a) Trained cues*. Here for the first time analyses reveal a significant main effect for both subject rule complexity ($F_{3,184} = 2.77$, $p < .05$) and other's rule complexity ($F_{3,184} = 2.18$, $p < .10$). While the latter result is borderline, the two findings taken together indicate interesting complementary processes. The subject rule complexity effect shows that positive linear rules were easiest to maintain, followed respectively by inverted U-shaped, negative linear, and U-shaped rules. The effect for other's rule complexity shows that being paired with a negative linear-trained other best facilitated maintenance of a subject's trained rule, followed, respectively, by pairing with others trained on U-shaped, positive linear, and inverted U-shaped rules.

A significant trial blocks effect ($p < .05$) indicates decreasing use of trained cues across trials. There were no interactions.

(b) New cues. Apart from an obvious trial blocks effect ($p < .01$) showing increased use of the new cue for all subjects, the only significant finding here is for the interaction between subject rule complexity and other's rule complexity ($F_{9,184} = 2.06$, $p < .05$). This interaction was mainly due to heavy use of the new positive linear cue by positive linear-trained subjects, but negative linear-trained subjects also used the negative linear cue to a greater extent than other subjects. Furthermore, both types of nonlinear-trained subjects used the new inverted U-shaped cue more

heavily than linear-trained subjects. The facilitating effect of the trained rule on learning to use a new rule of the same type seems, therefore, to be an inverse function of the complexity of the rule.

Implications for Interpersonal Learning

The most important generalization emerging from this study is that despite training on rules of different complexity, subjects can learn new rules of varying complexity when they are allowed to benefit from relevant interpersonal learning. Thus, in the previous study, it was shown that interpersonal learning could serve as a useful aid to task learning in limited conditions involving a simple and complex rule, and it was further shown that particular forms of interpersonal learning can be more or less beneficial. The present experiment extends these findings by showing that a condition of optimum interpersonal learning can aid task learning across a wide variety of rule complexity conditions.

Results concerning the finer details of task learning, for example, matching, consistency, and cue-dependencies, suggest that while the ways in which subjects benefit from interpersonal learning may vary depending upon their prior experience, the experience of their partner, and the complexity of the material to be learned, the final outcome is always the same—increased task learning. In more practical situations, therefore, it would seem that a student who could not learn a complex relationship working by himself, could do so when provided with interpersonal learning from an expert. And this, of course, is precisely how learning goes on in many professional training programs.

Experiment 3: Interpersonal Learning versus Task Learning

The two previous studies both show how interpersonal learning can aid or enhance task learning, but neither provides an explicit comparison between interpersonal learning and task learning. The purpose of this final experiment is to explore differences between the two types of learning in order to determine whether they yield equivalent benefits for subjects who must learn complex material. More specifically, the question investigated here is: How does the presence of another freely communicating person, who may or may not possess relevant information, influence task learning under different conditions of task complexity?

Information Sources

In an interpersonal learning study such as Experiment 1, the task provides information about its surface and depth while the other subject provides depth information about himself and the task. Experiment 2 included pairs of subjects who were differently trained so that they could provide different, complementary information about the task. Note that if subjects within a pair had been trained identically, they would not have been able to provide useful information to one another; they would have had to rely on information from the task. In other words, instead of being an interpersonal learning situation, it would have been a two-person *task learning* situation, since the subjects are free to communicate but initially have nothing useful to say to one another.

By contrast, in order for interpersonal learning to occur, each person (or one of the two persons) must possess useful information that can be learned by the other person. A typical interpersonal learning situation would be one in which two persons are faced with a common problem about which they have different, partially valid beliefs. Since both persons are initially partially correct for different reasons, the exchange of information through interpersonal learning increases their overall knowledge of the problem. This increase in knowledge about the task is not due solely to interpersonal learning, however—task learning also occurs during the interaction. Assessment of interpersonal learning in an interaction situation is thus dependent on proper control of task learning. The control used in the present study consists of pairs of subjects who could learn from the task, but not from each other. The learning task-knowledge of these control pairs is then compared with that of pairs who could learn from *both* the task and from each other.

Rule Complexity

It has been shown in the previous studies that positive linear rules can readily be inferred on the basis of task surface and depth information but more complex rules require more information in order to be learned. In the present study, two forms of rule complexity are used—positive linear and inverted U-shaped. It is hypothesized that the positive linear rule will be learned in both the task learning and interpersonal learning conditions, while learning of the inverted U-shaped rule will require interpersonal information.

Design and Procedure

Training. For the dyadic task learning conditions, subjects were trained identically on a task composed of either a linear cue and a random cue, or a nonlinear cue and a random cue. Pairs of subjects who think in the same way (use the same cue in the same way, either linearly or nonlinearly) are thus produced to serve as controls.

For the dyadic interpersonal learning condition, subjects are trained entirely differently, that is, on tasks which share no elements. For example, if S_1 is trained on a task composed of a linear cue and a random cue, S_2 would be trained on a task composed of a different random cue and a nonlinear cue. This procedure insures that the subjects will have something to learn from one another in the interaction stage.

Interpersonal interaction. In both task learning and interpersonal learning the interaction task must be composed of elements from both training tasks plus elements unique to the interaction stage. Note that the same task used for task learning is used for task learning combined with interpersonal learning, thus making a direct comparison between the performances of these two groups possible.

Subjects. Forty male University of Oregon students were divided into two groups of ten pairs. One group *(TL)* served in the task learning condition, while the other group *(IPL)* served in the combined interpersonal learning and task learning condition.

Task structure: Training. Four different sets of training materials were used (all numerical), the tasks differing on two factors—cue-criterion correlation and cue-criterion function form or rule. As shown in Figure 9.6 the four tasks were:

1. X_1 linear and strongly correlated with Y, X_2 uncorrelated with Y;
2. X_1 nonlinear and strongly correlated with Y, X_2 uncorrelated with Y;
3. X_1 uncorrelated with Y, X_2 linear and strongly correlated with Y;
4. X_1 uncorrelated with Y, X_2 nonlinear and strongly correlated with Y.

Task structure: Interaction. There were 60 interaction trials on two two-cue tasks. These differed according to which of the cues was related to the criterion by a linear and a nonlinear rule. The two interaction tasks (See Figure 9.6) were:

1. X_1 linear and moderately correlated with Y, X_2 nonlinear and moderately correlated with Y;
2. X_1 nonlinear and moderately correlated with Y, X_2 linear and moderately correlated with Y.

Subject pairs worked on one or the other task depending upon their training and their assignment to a *TL* or *IPL* group.

Linear and nonlinear TL groups. In the linear *TL* group (five pairs), both subjects in a pair were trained on Training Task 1; in the five nonlinear pairs, subjects were trained on Training Task 2. When linear *TL* pairs were brought together for the joint task, they worked on Interaction

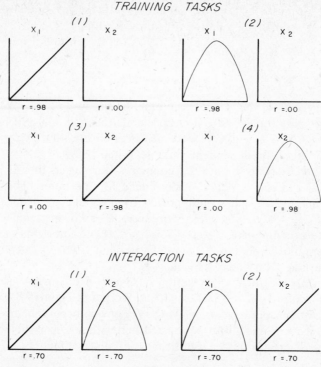

Figure 9.6.   Illustration of the four different training tasks and the two interaction tasks

Task 1; nonlinear pairs worked on Interaction Task 2. Both linear and nonlinear *TL* subjects then worked with partners trained in the same way they were on joint tasks that differed from their training tasks in two ways: (1) the cue they were trained to use had lost validity (.98 → .70); and (2) the cue they have been trained to ignore had gained validity (.00 → .70) and was related to the criterion by a new, unknown rule.

IPL groups. In *IPL* Group *A* (five pairs), one subject was trained on Training Task 3, while the other was trained on Training Task 2; Group *A* pairs worked on Interaction Task 2. In *IPL* Group *B* (five pairs), one subject was trained on Training Task 4, while the other was trained on Training Task 1; Group *B* pairs worked on Interaction Task 1. The only difference, then, between *IPL* Groups *A* and *B* was in the positions of the linear and nonlinear cues. Otherwise, all *IPL* subjects worked with partners trained differently from the way they were trained (different cue, different rule) on joint tasks which differed from their training tasks in the same ways as in the *TL* groups. Subjects in the *IPL* groups (as opposed to the subjects in the *TL* groups) had the opportunity to learn from their differently trained partners the significance of the newly important cue and how to use the rule relating it to the criterion.

Results

In order to analyze the effects of interaction groups (*TL* vs. *IPL*), subject rule complexity (linear vs. nonlinear), and trials (six ten-trial blocks), a $2 \times 2 \times 6$ ANOVA with repeated measures on the third factor was employed for all of the dependent variables listed below.

1. *Task learning.* Figure 9.7 compares learning in the *TL* and *IPL* conditions, and shows better performance for the latter. This superior learning among *IPL* pairs is supported by a significant main effect for groups ($F_{1,36} = 4.39$, $p < .05$). Moreover, a significant main effect for subject rule complexity ($F_{1,36} = 7.48$, $p < .01$) shows that across the two interaction conditions, nonlinear-trained subjects demonstrated better learning than linear subjects.

The only significant interaction obtained was between groups and rule complexity ($F_{1,36} = 15.64$, $p < .01$). Plotted in Figure 9.8, these data reveal that the superior learning of the *IPL* group occurs mainly because linear subjects in this group performed better than linear subjects in the *TL* group. There was also a significant trial blocks effect ($F_{5,180} = 10.32$,

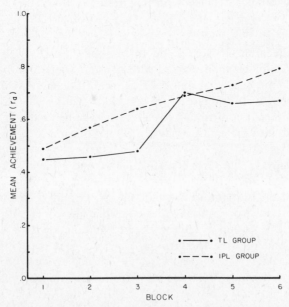

Figure 9.7.   Comparison of mean learning scores obtained in the task learning and interpersonal learning conditions

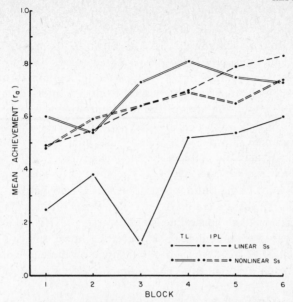

Figure 9.8. Mean learning scores obtained for linear- and nonlinear-trained subjects in the task learning and interpersonal learning conditions

$p < .001$), indicating that all subjects accomplished substantial learning.

Further analysis involving individual comparisons among the various subject groups showed that whereas the learning of linear and nonlinear subjects in the *TL* condition differed significantly, there was no such difference between the linear and nonlinear subjects in the *IPL* condition. It seems clear, therefore, that the overall superiority of learning in the *IPL* condition can be attributed to interpersonal learning; specifically, the interpersonal learning of the linear subjects from the nonlinear subjects.

2. *Matching. (G).* Analysis of this component of task learning yields results similar to those described above: Significant main effects for the interaction groups and rule complexity factors ($F_{1,36} = 7.06$, $p < .05$; $F_{1,36} = 16.33$, $p < .001$, respectively) show that matching was best in the *IPL* condition and among nonlinear-trained subjects. Moreover, a significant trial blocks effect ($F_{5,180} = 6.06$, $p < .01$) and interaction effect between groups and complexity ($F_{1,36} = 22.82$, $p < .001$), completes the parellel with prior results. The interaction here is again due to the poorer performance (lower matching) of the linear subjects in the *TL* group as compared with such subjects in the *IPL* group.

3. *Consistency. (R_s).* The only significant result obtained was for trial blocks ($F_{5,180} = 4.76$, $p < .01$), showing that all subjects increased their consistency during the course of the task. Comparisons of linear and non-

linear subjects in the *TL* and *IPL* conditions were conducted using linear trend analyses, but no significant differences were revealed.

These results indicate that insofar as the variables manipulated in this experiment had important effects on task learning, they were brought about via effects upon the *matching* component of learning. In this connection, linear subjects apparently benefited from *IPL* interaction because it helped them to match the laws of the task, but nonlinear subjects did not benefit because they were able to match effectively on the basis of task information alone. The nature of these matching effects can be better understood by examining subject cue-dependencies.

4. *Trained cue-dependencies (a).* The manner in which subjects used the cue they were trained to depend upon varied only across trials ($F_{5,180} = 3.24$, $p < .01$); there were no other main effects or interactions. Linear trend analyses yielded borderline significant ($p < .10$) effects showing that as compared with nonlinear subjects, the linear subjects in the *TL* condition tended to increase their dependence on the cue learned during training. No such differences were obtained between subjects in the *IPL* conditions.

New cue-dependencies (b). In line with the results reported earlier for task learning, the subject's abilities to learn the new cue in the interaction task were found to be significantly influenced by all three independent variables (groups, complexity, and trials). However, the interaction between groups and complexity ($F_{1,36} = 6.84$, $p < .05$) shows that the main effects were largely due to the fact that linear subjects in the *TL* condition were unable to learn the new nonlinear cue. All other subjects in the experiment more or less correctly adjusted their trained cue-dependencies and learned appropriate new cue-dependencies according to the demands of the interaction task.

Implications for Interpersonal Learning

The general results of this study may be summarized as follows. While the interaction task was learned by both groups, the learning was significantly better in the *IPL* group. This was due to better performance by the linear-trained subjects in the *IPL* group, who were able to acquire relevant information from their nonlinear-trained partners. The nature of this relevant information was such as to increase the linear subject's ability to match the laws of the interaction task. More specifically, this means that the linear subjects in the *IPL* group could shift their cue-dependencies to the nonlinear cue with greater ease than the linear subjects in the *TL* group.

Returning now to the issue raised at the beginning of this experiment; that is, how does interpersonal learning compare with task learning, the results show that the two are quite similar when it comes to the learning of complex task relationships. That is, the mere presence of another person without relevant knowledge to contribute does not facilitate learning. But when the other person does have relevant knowledge, learning is substantially enhanced. From this standpoint, it seems necessary to distinguish *relevant* interpersonal learning from other kinds. It is only when such a distinction is made that one may attribute uniquely important functions to the process of interpersonal learning.

Summary and Conclusion

The work described in this paper is based on a theoretical analysis of interpersonal learning in which the learner, the person being learned from, and the situation being learned about are conceived as interacting systems composed of surface and depth elements. The *laws* of any system were defined as the relations between its surface and its depth elements. The *consistency* of a system was the extent to which the laws could be inferred from directly observable surface elements, and the *knowledge* achieved between two systems was described in terms of the *matching* of the laws of the two systems, their *consistency,* and the *context of information* surrounding the systems.

Three empirical studies were conducted following the lens model research paradigm, and employing components of the lens model equation as measures of different aspects of performance.

The first study focused on the *context of information and rule complexity.* It showed that simple (linear) subjects required interpersonal learning from complex (nonlinear) subjects in order to learn to use a complex (nonlinear) rule; complex subjects did not similarly require interpersonal learning from simple subjects in order to learn to use a simple rule.

The second study concerned *variations in rule complexity.* Results demonstrated that simple (i.e., positive linear) rules could be learned from task information, but that complex (i.e., negative linear, inverted U-shaped, and U-shaped) rules required the exchange of interpersonal information concerning their form before they could be used.

In the third study, it was shown that interpersonal learning is not notably different from individual task learning, except when the other person can convey information relevant to the task. Complex task relationships can then be learned much more easily because persons trained on a simple task rule benefit from contact with those who are familiar with a complex rule.

Altogether, then, this paper provides both a conceptual scheme and demonstrations of research methods appropriate for the study of interpersonal learning, while at the same time offering new substantive knowledge about the parameters governing this process. Finally, it should be emphasized that the problems discussed here are not trivial. The traditional psychology of learning available to education, business, and government systems may serve well enough to convey rote knowledge of various kinds, but as it is increasingly recognized that such systems must impart judgmental skills to many persons, it will obviously be necessary to elaborate new principles of interpersonal learning.

REFERENCES

Björkman, M. Learning of linear functions: Comparison between a positive and a negative slope. Report No. 183, Psychological Laboratories of the University of Stockholm, 1965.

Brehmer, B. Inference behavior in a situation where the cues are not reliably perceived. *Organizational Behavior and Human Performance,* 1970, *5,* 330–347.

Brunswik, E. *The Conceptual Framework of Psychology.* Chicago: University of Chicago Press, 1952.

Hammond, K. R. Inductive knowing. In J. Royce & W. Rozeboom (Eds.), *The Psychology of Knowing.* New York: Gordon & Breach, 1970.

Hammond, K. R., & Summers, D. A. Cognitive dependence on linear and nonlinear cues. *Psychological Review,* 1965, *72,* 215–234.

Hursch, C., Hammond, K. R., & Hursch, J. L. Some methodological considerations in multiple cue probability studies. *Psychological Review,* 1964, *71,* 42–60.

Lindzey, G., & Aronson, E. (Eds.) *Handbook of Social Psychology.* Reading, Mass.: Addison-Wesley, 1969.

Melton, A. W. (Ed.) *Categories of Human Learning.* New York: Academic Press, 1964.

Naylor, J. C., & Clark, R. D. Intuitive inference strategies in interval learning tasks as a function of validity magnitude and sign. *Organizational Behavior and Human Performance,* 1968, *3,* 378–399.

Summers, D. A. Rule vs. cue learning in multiple probability tasks. *Proceedings of the 75th Annual Convention of the American Psychological Association,* 1967, *2,* 43–44.

Summers, D. A. Adaptation to change in multiple probability tasks. *American Journal of Psychology,* 1969, *82,* 235–240.

Tucker, L. R. A suggested alternative formulation in the development by Hursch, Hammond, & Hursch and by Hammond, Hursch, & Todd. *Psychological Review,* 1964, *71,* 528–530.

10 Interpersonal Understanding: Laboratory and Field Investigations[1]

MONROE J. MILLER[2]
University of Pittsburgh

> *You guys come down and see a black dude and bust him just 'cause he's black.*

> *When there's a crime reported, it is our responsibility to question anybody who is suspicious by his presence; it makes no difference whether he is black or white.*

Taken directly from an exchange between police officers and black youth, these remarks indicate an important aspect of interpersonal understanding. The statement of the black youth expresses a common understanding of how policemen think; the policeman's statement reflects an equally common view about the clear-cut responsibilities in law enforcement. Neither shows awareness that they are involved in a difficult mutual problem, nor of the other's view of this problem. In the absence of at least a minimum degree of interpersonal understanding, conflict between these parties appears to defy resolution.

The general purpose of this paper is to demonstrate how the lens model paradigm may be employed to study interpersonal understanding in both laboratory and field settings, and, further, to show how knowledge gained in laboratory experiments may be applied in field settings to increase the level of interpersonal understanding existing in actual or potential conflict situations.

[1] The research reported here was undertaken in the Program of Research on Human Judgment and Social Interaction, Institute of Behavioral Science, University of Colorado and is Publication 136 of the Institute. The research was supported by National Science Foundation Grant G5-1699 and National Institute of Mental Health Grant MH-11928-01.

[2] The author wishes to express his appreciation to Bruce Bartlett, Ray Bergner, Carl Kuhlman, William Wellisch, and Karene Will for their assistance in the experiments reported here, and to Kenneth Hammond for his helpful suggestions and comments throughout.

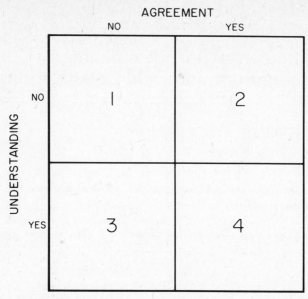

Figure 10.1.   Schematic representation of categories of conflict as a function of levels of agreement and understanding

Interpersonal Understanding

Hammond, Wilkins, and Todd (1966) have defined interpersonal learning as the process whereby two (or more) people learn about one another as a result of their mutual interaction, and have shown how this process may be studied using the lens model paradigm. The practical significance of this work can be seen clearly in the context of relations between inimical parties. For example, two diplomats engaged in negotiation might fail to make progress because of actual disagreement over the desired outcome of the negotiation, or because each fails to understand how the other thinks about the issues before them. What is required to resolve their apparent disagreement would depend upon which of these two instances was involved.

A schematic representation of four possible combinations of agreement and understanding is shown in Figure 10.1. Cell 4 (lower right-hand cell) depicts a situation in which two individuals (or groups) not only agree with one another but also understand how each other thinks and, consequently, the nature of their agreement. Cell 1 depicts the opposite case, in which there is not only disagreement between the parties involved, but the nature of the disagreement is not understood. That is, the parties to the disagreement are unaware of the judgmental policies of one another and therefore cannot identify the basis of their disagreement. Cell 3 shows disagreement between parties who, in fact, understand why they disagree with one another. Cell 2, on the other hand, represents the situation where there is agreement but no understanding of how the other thinks. Consequently, the agreement is not seen and may be perceived as disagreement or conflict.

The importance of interpersonal understanding is most clear when Cells 1 and 2 are considered. In these cases, regardless of whether there is agreement or disagreement, it is effectively impossible to resolve the dispute because of the lack of understanding. Where disagreement exists (Cell 1), it cannot be engaged because there is no starting point of understanding. Even more regrettable, however, is the situation where there is agreement, but lack of understanding about the other party prevents this from being seen. Given the above representation of the role of interpersonal understanding, the treatment of this problem in the traditional social psychology literature will be briefly reviewed and constructed with the potential for investigation of these processes within the lens model paradigm.

Previous Investigations

Most research related to the problem of learning about or understanding another person has been done either in the context of imitative learning or of social perception. Work in the former area has been chiefly concerned with how persons learn to imitate the behavior of a model (See Flanders, 1968, for a general review). However, the utility of such studies for understanding the process of learning about another person is limited for three main reasons: (1) there is usually no substantial interaction between subjects and models; (2) there is no engagement with an environmental problem or task important to both individuals; and (3) the emphasis has been on one person reproducing the responses of the other, rather than learning how the other interacts with the environment. It should be clear, therefore, that the imitative learning model does not lend itself to application in field settings involving conflict.

Consideration of the literature on social perception indicates that with few exceptions, interpersonal learning, as the process whereby one person learns about another with whom he is interacting, has not been studied. Research here has generally concentrated on problems of judgmental accuracy in relation to the characteristics of the perceiver. (See, e.g., Bieri, 1955; Bieri & Blacker, 1956; Mayo & Crockett, 1964.) Consequently, empirical investigations typically involve factors such as the actual or assumed similarity between perceiver and person-object, the cognitive complexity of the perceiver, or his ability to utilize stereotypes appropriate to the judgmental situation.

Little attention has been paid to the *development* of accurate perception and virtually no attention has been given to how specific characteristics of the person-object being judged may gradually reveal themselves to the perceiver. These limitations are even more significant when one considers the problem of studying social perception outside the relatively controlled conditions of the laboratory. For example, in nonlaboratory interactive situations, people often change as the interaction progresses. That is, mutual dynamic change occurs as a function of the interaction itself. Consequently, one is frequently required to learn about another person as that person is changing and as changes occur in oneself with reference to the other person. An adequate research paradigm must not only permit such changes, but must also provide the methodology and measurement techniques for the evaluation of interpersonal understanding under such conditions of mutual change.

Another characteristic of many real social situations is suggested by the remarks of the black youth and the police officer. Both comments have some validity, that is, the variables of race, police responsibility, and crime rate are intercorrelated. Thus, while the reasons for greater frequency of arrests in "black" neighborhoods are viewed separately and differently, they are in fact, interrelated. An adequate research paradigm for interpersonal understanding must also be able to reflect such inter-relationships among variables if evaluation of these processes is to be achieved.

Lens Model Theory and Method

The lens model paradigm. Within the paradigm suggested by Hammond, Wilkins, and Todd (1966), the specific characteristics of environmental and subject systems can be represented in terms of relations between the cues and either (1) the distal variable in the environment, or (2) the subject's responses. The achievement of a subject relative to an interpersonal learning task is indicated by the correlation between one subject's predictions of the responses of the other person and the actual responses made by that person. Specification of the characteristics of subject and environmental systems allows the investigator to evaluate the effects of these characteristics upon interpersonal learning. For example, by training subjects to hold different views about a mutual environmental task, and by controlling the formal structure of this task, it is possible to observe changes in the subjects' cognitive systems as they interact with one another and with the task system. This allows specification of the locus of interpersonal learning, that is, exactly what each subject learns about the other as well as about the environmental task. Moreover, appropriate quantitative measures are available through application of the lens model equation.

The lens model equation. The lens model equation is described in detail in Reading 14 (Hammond & Brehmer). In the present context, however, three parameters derived from the lens model equation are of particular importance: (1) the cue-dependencies of the subject, (2) the linear consistency of the subject and the environmental task (or the other person), and (3) the nonlinear consistency of the subjects and the environment where nonlinearity is present. Each of these parameters provides precise information about the adaptation of a subject to an environmental task *and* to another subject. Thus, in addition to indicating how accurate subjects may be in predicting one another's responses, these components allow precise identification of what each subject must learn about the other in order to maximize their predictive accuracy. In the case of interpersonal learning, the "other person" is considered rather than the environmental task so that the lens model equation describes the characteristics of the judgmental and predictive systems of the persons involved.

Feedback about cognitive systems. Specification of the characteristics of a person's cognitive system makes it possible to present this information to another person who must learn about the first. For example, it is possible to show an individual whether his lack of accuracy is due to predictive inconsistency (low R^2) or inappropriate prediction of the other's use of the cues. Such feedback has been demonstrated to be useful in laboratory studies of probability learning (See Deane, Hammond, & Summers, 1971; Todd & Hammond, 1965) and should also be useful in studies of interpersonal learning. An additional purpose of this paper, therefore, will be to demonstrate the utility of feedback about cognitive systems in the attempt to increase interpersonal understanding.

Application of the paradigm. Aside from the initial demonstration by Hammond, Wilkins, and Todd (1966), there have been few studies of the many factors influencing interpersonal learning (See, e.g., Summers, Taliaferro, & Fletcher, 1970), and only a few preliminary attempts to employ the paradigm in nonlaboratory settings. For example, there has been no study of the effects of the characteristics of subjects' cognitive systems (e.g., weight and form of the relations between proximal cues and subjects' judgments) upon the ability of one person to learn about another. Nor have the effects of such substantive factors as language and motives been evaluated.

The following sections of this paper present findings obtained in two laboratory and two field experiments. The laboratory studies concern first, the problem of how interpersonal learning is affected by different cue-response relationships held by interacting subjects, and second, the effects upon interpersonal learning of differences in the connotative and denotative meanings attached to relevant concepts in a substantive judgmental task. The field studies demonstrate how mutual interpersonal understanding can be increased between parents and delinquent children in one instance, and between minority youth and police officers in another.

Laboratory Investigations

Experiment 1: The Effects of Different Function Forms

This study is concerned with interpersonal learning when individuals facing a mutual problem think differently about the way proximal information is related to a distal variable. Apart from differences in the weighting of proximal cues, there are four major ways in which a cue may be functionally related to a criterion variable (See Figure 10.2): (1) positive linear (as the cue increases in value, so does the criterion variable); (2) negative linear (as the cue increases in value, the criterion variable decreases); (3) U-shaped nonlinear (as the cue increases in value, the criterion variable decreases up to the midpoint; beyond the midpoint the criterion variable increases in value); (4) inverted U-shaped nonlinear (as the cue increases in value the criterion variable also increases up to the midpoint; beyond the midpoint the criterion variable decreases in value).

The most fundamental distinction among these function forms is

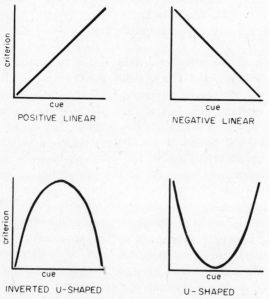

Figure 10.2. Graphic representation of positive linear, negative linear, inverted U-shaped, and U-shaped cue-criterion function forms

that between linear and nonlinear relations. Summers and Hammond (1966) and Sheets and Miller (1971) have shown that nonlinear relations are more difficult to learn than linear relations. Further, nonlinear relations are structurally more complex than linear relations. Consequently, one would expect that a person utilizing a nonlinear function form would be more difficult to learn about than a person utilizing a linear function form.

The second distinction is between linear positive and linear negative relations. Björkman (1965) and Uhl (1966) have shown that positive linear relations are easier to learn than negative linear relations. It would be expected, therefore, that persons utilizing a negative linear function form will be more difficult to learn about than those utilizing positive linear function forms. Since U-shaped nonlinear relations and inverted U-shaped nonlinear relations are of equivalent complexity and familiarity, no differential interpersonal learning would be expected as a consequence of these function forms. Thus, subjects using more complex and/or less familiar function forms should be more difficult to learn about than subjects using less complex and/or more familiar function forms. Finally, it seems likely that certain combined characteristics of the cognitive systems of the learner and person learned about should affect interpersonal understanding. For example, a subject using an inverted U-shaped function form may be more difficult for "positive linear subjects" to learn about than another "inverted U-shaped subject."

Procedure

A two-cue probabilistic task was employed with subjects trained individually to depend on different cues to infer the value of the task criterion. In addition, subjects were trained to utilize one of four different judgmental policies, varying in function form, for relating the cue on which he was trained to the task criterion. Each subject was then paired with another who was trained to rely on a different cue; the other person used either the same or a different function form in relating that cue to the task criterion. The study therefore provides interaction between all possible combinations of the four function forms described in Figure 10.2. Ten experimental conditions were employed, each with 20 subjects (10 pairs) included.

Upon completion of training, pairs of subjects were required to work together to make judgments about a new series of tasks that were similar but not identical to their training tasks. This interaction provided subjects with the opportunity to learn about both the relevant cue for the other member of the pair and the function form of that cue. In all of the ten conditions, the properties of the interaction task were arranged so that the correct answer would be midway between the judgments the subjects would make if they followed their training. Following this interactive sequence, subjects engaged in an interpersonal learning task similar in format to the interactive tasks. This required them to respond to cue information by: (1) recording their own judgment of the criterion value, and (2) predicting the judgment they thought the other person would make. Ten such trials were conducted. (For further detail, see Bergner and Miller, 1969.)

It is important to note three characteristics of the research paradigm with respect to interpersonal learning. It provides:

1. A preparation or training stage in which the investigator makes certain that subjects develop precisely the cognitive systems required for the experiment. In this case, the subjects required to learn about one another unknowingly face the problem of learning that the other person has a different set of cue-dependencies and, in six of the ten experimental conditions, a different function form.
2. An interpersonal interactive stage in which the environmental task properties are specified precisely with respect to the subjects' cognitive systems. In this study, the properties of the environmental tasks were such that both subjects were required to change their cognitive systems if they were to adapt successfully to the new task. Consequently, each subject was required to learn about another person who was changing as the subject himself was changing. This aspect of the procedure is crucial because it introduces realistic complexity which is essential if we are to study important interpersonal processes in the laboratory.
3. An interpersonal learning test stage that contains the same environmental properties as the interactive stage. This allows evaluation of interpersonal learning as a consequence of the interaction between subjects rather than as a consequence of instructions that direct the subject to learn about a stimulus object.

Table 10.1. Mean Predictive Accuracy Correlations (r_a) for Subjects in Each Experimental Condition

Condition	S_1		S_2	
	ff	r	ff	r
1	/	.78	/	.85
2	/	.75	\	.81
3	\	.77	\	.75
4	∧	.68	∧	.65
5	∧	.76	∨	.66
6	∨	.79	∨	.75
7	/	.69	∧	.83
8	/	.72	∨	.82
9	\	.78	∨	.74
10	\	.44	∧	.47

Table 10.2. Mean Predictive Accuracy Correlations According to Function Form of the Learner and the Person Learned About

	Mean Correlation				
	/	\	∧	∨	*Overall Mean*
Learner	.76	.67	.68	.74	.71
Person learned about	.82	.66	.62	.75	

Results

Predictive accuracy. The mean predictive accuracy correlations for each group of subjects in the ten experimental conditions are presented in Table 10.1. The same data, combined according to the function form of the learner and the person learned about, are shown in Table 10.2. These indicate that predictive accuracy is high in almost all cases and that the function form of the learner has no reliable effect on predictive accuracy; however, a one-way analysis of variance indicates that the function form of the person learned about leads to small but reliable differences in predictive accuracy ($F = 6.57$; $p < .01$).

As expected, the subjects with positive linear function forms were most easily learned about ($r = .82$), whereas subjects with negative linear function forms and inverted U-shaped function forms were somewhat more difficult to learn about ($r = .66$ and $.62$, respectively). Contrary to expectations, subjects with U-shaped function forms were second only to posi-

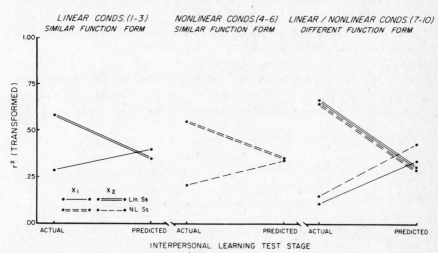

Figure 10.3. Subjects' actual cue-dependencies and predictions of the others' cue-dependencies (transformed r^2) for linear and nonlinear subjects paired with subjects with either similar (Conditions 1–6) or different (Conditions 7–10) function forms

tive linear subjects in ease of learning ($r = .75$). Thus, the function form of the person learned about seems to be the major factor affecting the accuracy of the learner.

Cue-dependencies. Figure 10.3 shows the actual and predicted cue-dependencies for subject pairs with either similar or different function forms. It shows that subject pairs with different function forms did not learn about each other's cue-dependencies as well as subject pairs with similar function forms. This suggests that differences in function form (in addition to differences in cue-dependencies) not only result in greater differences between subjects in their use of the cues, but also makes it more difficult for subjects to learn about each other's cue-dependencies.

Linear and nonlinear components of accuracy.[3] Examination of the linear and nonlinear components of subjects' predictive accuracy indicates that the accuracy shown by pairs of linear subjects is entirely a function of the linear component with no nonlinearity shown. For nonlinear pairs of subjects, of course, it is the nonlinear component which is responsible for accuracy although there is some contribution from the linear component.

Examination of the cases in which linear subjects interacted with nonlinear subjects reveals that nonlinear subjects show greater linearity in their predictions about linear subjects than vice-versa, whereas linear subjects show greater nonlinearity in their predictions about nonlinear subjects than vice-versa (See Bergner & Miller, 1969, for further discussion of these results).

More detailed examination of the linear and nonlinear components of subjects' predictive achievement is required to identify exactly what is learned. The lens model equation parameters, G_{s_i} and C_{s_i} (See Footnote 3), provide the necessary information. Table 10.3 shows the mean values of the parameter G_{s_i} for subjects in the linear cases and the combined linear–nonlinear cases. As expected, in the linear cases the values

[3] The form of the lens model equation used in this analysis is as follows:

$$r_a = G_{s_i} R_{s_i} R_{s_j} + C_{s_i} \sqrt{1 - R_{s_i}^2} \sqrt{1 - R_{s_j}^2}$$

where r_a refers to the predictive accuracy of S_i with respect to S_j
R_{s_i} and R_{s_j} refer to the linear consistency in the predictive system of S_i and the judgmental system of S_j, respectively
G_{s_i} and C_{s_i} refer to the detection by S_i of the linearity and nonlinearity, respectively, in S_j's judgmental system
$\sqrt{1 - R_{s_i}^2}$ and $\sqrt{1 - R_{s_j}^2}$ refer to the nonlinearity in the predictive system of S_i and the judgmental system of S_j

The linear component of predictive accuracy is represented by the parameters $G_{s_i} R_{s_i} R_{s_i}$, and the nonlinear component by the parameters $C_{s_i} \sqrt{1 - R_{s_i}^2} \sqrt{1 - R_{s_j}^2}$.

Table 10.3. Mean Values of the Lens Model Equation Parameters G_{s_i} and C_{s_i} for Subjects in the Linear, Nonlinear, and Combined Linear–Nonlinear Conditions

Parameter		Linear Ss	Nonlinear Ss
	Exp. 1–3	Exp. 7–10	Exp. 7–10
G_{s_i}	.98	.92	.97
	Exp. 4–6	Exp. 7–10	Exp. 7–10
C_{s_i}	.81	.77	.65

are extremely high. In the combined linear–nonlinear cases, the linear subjects do not appreciably differ from the nonlinear subjects with respect to detection of the linearity in the others' judgments (G_{s_i}). Differences in accuracy, therefore, are due primarily to differences in the linear consistency of subjects' judgments and predictions, rather than differences in accuracy of detection of the linearity in the others' judgments. In short, subjects learn about how the other person adapted to the joint task.

Table 10.3 also presents the values of the parameter C_{s_i} (detection of nonlinearity) for subjects in the nonlinear cases and the combined linear–nonlinear cases. In the nonlinear cases, the values of these parameters are essentially high, showing that subjects are able to detect the nonlinearity in the judgmental system of the other person. However, the detection of nonlinearity in these cases is lower than the detection of linearity in the linear cases, as indicated by the comparison of C_{s_i} with G_{s_i}. This is consistent with the finding that nonlinear relations are more difficult to learn than linear relations. In the combined linear–nonlinear cases, linear subjects are able to detect more accurately the nonlinearity in the nonlinear subjects' judgmental systems than vice-versa. Thus, differences in predictive achievement are at least partially due to differences in detection of nonlinearity in the other's judgments.

Discussion

In general, the results described above show that under all experimental conditions, predictive accuracy is quite high. Subjects can learn about each other's cue-dependencies and essentially can detect the linearity and/or nonlinearity in each other's judgment policies. With respect to predictive accuracy, however, analysis demonstrates that the characteristics of the cognitive system of the person *learned about* are a more important determinant of interpersonal learning than the cognitive characteristics of the learner. This finding, that subjects with more complex function forms are the most difficult to understand, independent of the learners' function form, is noteworthy since most previous research in social perception has failed to investigate such attributes in the person being learned about.

The finding that subject pairs with similar function forms are better able to learn about each other's cue-dependencies than those with different function forms is also of considerable interest. Specifically, it is possible to identify sources of differences in interpersonal learning as these relate to cue-dependencies and detection of linearity and/or nonlinearity. Subject pairs who differ in both cue-dependencies and funciton forms are furthest apart in their use of the cues and least accurate in their predictions of the others' cue-dependencies. Yet detection of linearity and/or nonlinearity in the other person's judgmental system is accurate in both cases although it is better when the function forms are the same. This finding emphasizes the need to go beyond response measures and analyze the components of interpersonal learning. The present results also indicate the need for representing a wide range of conditions in experimental studies of interpersonal learning.

The present study illustrates several advantages of the lens model paradigm when compared with traditional investigations of social learning and perception. Two characteristics of the interpersonal learning situation are of primary importance: (1) the properties of the environment and the cognitive systems of the subjects are specified, allowing evaluation of what each individual can and does learn about the other as a result of their interaction; and (2) the fact that each individual is required to change in order to adapt to the interactive task requires subjects to learn about another person who is changing as they are themselves changing. In the present experiment subjects changed in their cue-dependencies and, in four of the conditions, their function forms. Nevertheless, subjects were able to learn about a changing *other* person. The ability to represent and precisely specify these characteristics is a unique capability of the lens model paradigm and lens model equation which permits investigation of interpersonal learning under realistically complex circumstances.

Experiment 2: Connotative Differences and Interpersonal Learning

The previous experiment evaluated the effects of differences in cue-dependencies and function form on interpersonal learning in a *formal* task. This study again focuses on the effects of differential cue-dependencies, but also concerns differences in the affective meanings subjects attach to cue information in a *substantive* task.

Denotative and connotative meanings. In principle, an individual's cue-dependencies (the functional relationship seen between proximal cues and a distal variable) define denotative meanings in a subject's cognitive system. However, when cues are labeled as concepts having various implications regarding substantive issues, then a person's unique past experience with these issues may lead him to attach particular connotative meanings to these concepts. Prior research on cognitive conflict has shown that whereas denotative differences between subjects may be quickly reduced, connotative differences can remain as an important source of conflict (See Kuhlman, Miller, & Gungor, Reading 8).

This study examines the effect of differences in connotative meanings upon the ability of subjects to learn about the judgmental policy of another person with whom they are interacting. It is expected that subject pairs who are connotatively and denotatively similar will show greater ability to learn about the other's judgmental policy than those who are connotatively and denotatively different.

Procedure

The "two-cue political decision-making task" was employed in this investigation (See Appendix A in Hammond & Brehmer), with the procedure used being generally the same as that in Experiment 1. This included a *training stage* in which subjects were trained to develop different denotative meaning systems with respect to the task; an *interactive stage* in which subjects worked in pairs on a task similar to the one on which they were trained; and an *interpersonal learning stage* during which subjects made additional judgments as before, and, in addition, predicted the judgments of the other person in the pair.

The semantic differential technique (Osgood, Suci, & Tannenbaum, 1957; Snider & Osgood, 1968) was used to establish connotative similarities or differences between subjects in each pair. A 2 × 2 factorial design was followed in order to compare the effects on interpersonal learning of differences and similarities in both denotative and connotative meanings. Six subject pairs were assigned to each of four experimental conditions on the basis of their semantic differential ratings *and* their training received during the first stage of the experiment.

The training stage of the experiment insured different denotative meanings, while different connotative meanings were established by requiring a mean difference in semantic differential ratings of 3.0 or more, with respect to the conceptual elements of the task—state control and elections. Connotative similarity was established by holding mean differences in semantic differential ratings to .25 or less. The differential training in denotative meanings was successful as indicated by appropriate cue-response correlations for the subjects, and appropriate connotative differences and similarities were obtained through the semantic differential selection procedure. In addition, it is important to note that half the subjects were trained to depend upon one cue in a nonlinear (inverted U-shaped) manner and half were trained to depend upon the other cue in a positive linear manner.

Results

The mean predictive accuracy correlations for subjects in each experimental condition are presented in Table 10.4. This shows: (1) subject pairs having similar denotative meanings were more accurate in their predictions of one another than those having different denotative meanings, and (2) subject pairs having similar connotative meanings were more accurate in their predictions of one another than those having different connotative meanings. A three-way analysis of variance indicates that both of these differences are statistically reliable. A further finding is that subjects required to learn about a linear person tended to be more accurate in their predictions than those required to learn about a nonlinear person *when* such pairs had different denotative meanings (Note that similarity in denotative meanings in this case also means similarity in function form.). In general, the greatest accuracy in predictions occurred where subject pairs had similar connotative *and* denotative meanings, while those who differed in both these respects showed the poorest accuracy.

Application of the lens model equation for analysis of the components of predictive accuracy reveals that subject pairs having both different denotative and connotative meanings showed a lower degree of consistency (R^2) in their predictions about the other. This was the major contributing factor to their poor performance. Furthermore, the connotatively and denotatively similar subjects were not only more consistent in

Table 10.4. Mean Predictive Accuracy Correlations (r_a) for Subjects in Each Experimental Condition

Connotative Meanings		Denotative Meanings Similar	Different	
Similar	Linear Ss	.83	.74	
	Nonlinear Ss	.85	.80	.81
Different	Linear Ss	.81	.58	
	Nonlinear Ss	.65	.69	.70
		.80	.71	.76

their predictions (higher R^2), but also were somewhat more accurate in reflecting the other's actual cue-dependencies in their predictions.

Discussion

The results presented above confirm the expectation that difficulty in interpersonal learning is caused by connotative differences between subjects, and also demonstrate how analysis by means of lens model equation parameters allows specification of the locus of this difficulty. Moreover, it is also interesting to note that the form of the denotative meaning (linear or nonlinear) affects the ability to learn about another person: It is more difficult to learn about another person who utilizes information in a nonlinear manner than one who utilizes information in a linear manner when subjects in a pair have different function forms.

The implications of these findings for interpersonal interaction in natural settings are important. It is difficult enough to understand another person under favorable circumstances; when these difficulties are compounded by differences in the meanings of the terms used in discussion, the likelihood of achieving mutual understanding is further decreased. One immediate implication of these findings concerns the potential utility of providing feedback about connotative meanings as a means of increasing interpersonal understanding between persons who have such differences. In general, the need to consider differences in meaning in attempts to increase interpersonal understanding between parties inimical to one another in natural settings is further emphasized.

Summary of Laboratory Experiments

The two experiments reported here indicate the generality of the lens model paradigm for the study of interpersonal learning, as well as the analytical power of the lens model equation. They also provide new information about two sets of parameters that influence learning about another person.

The first experiment shows that the function form used by the person learned about, that is, the form of the relation between the subject's responses and the proximal cues, is a primary determinant of the ease with which this person can be understood. Whether subject pairs have similar or different function forms determines how well they will be able to learn about the cue-dependencies of the other person and also affects the consistency of their predictions about the other person.

The second experiment demonstrates that both connotative and denotative differences impede interpersonal learning, particularly when these factors are combined. In addition, the results generally support findings from Experiment 1 showing that subjects utilizing nonlinear (inverted U-shaped) function forms are more difficult to learn about than subjects using positive linear function forms. Again the utility of the lens model equation was demonstrated by data analysis revealing the precise effects of the connotative differences variable.

Finally, when viewed in the larger context of research on cognitive conflict, the two experiments suggest that the lens model approach to interpersonal understanding might fruitfully be applied in more complex field settings. The remainder of this paper describes two different efforts in this direction.

Field Studies

The significance of interpersonal understanding was discussed earlier with respect to conflict situations, particularly those in which the apparent conflict does not necessarily reflect disagreement, but may, in fact, reflect the inability of one party to understand how the other thinks about a significant mutual issue. Figure 10.1 schematized how agreement between individuals may exist but not be perceived due to the lack of understanding between persons. The studies reported in this section of the paper describe two such cases, one involving families containing delinquent adolescents where there is a lack of understanding between parents and child; and a second involving police officers and minority youth in an urban area. While the role of interpersonal understanding may be apparent in the first case, it will be seen that similar problems also exist in the second case.

In more formal terms, it is hypothesized that these situations are represented by Cell 3 in Figure 10.1. That is, it is assumed that a greater level of agreement exists about significant issues than is apparent, but this is masked by the absence of understanding. Conflict may thus be reduced by increasing the level of understanding.

Both of the studies reported below utilize the interpersonal learning paradigm as in the laboratory work, except that certain procedural innovations are employed for reasons of feasibility. Furthermore, attempts to increase interpersonal understanding are made by providing persons with information about the judgmental policies of the other, as suggested by the previous experimental results. In principle, therefore, these investigations represent a preliminary "field test" of the interpersonal learning paradigm.

Experiment 3: Understanding in Families
with Delinquent Children

Problems attending communication between parents and adolescents have been well documented and need not be elaborated upon (See, e.g.,

Miller, 1970; Miller & Bartlett, 1971). However, one of the major consequences of difficulties in communication is a lack of mutual understanding
between parents and adolescents. This can, of course, create difficulties
in all families, but it makes any attempt by members of a troubled family
to work together on specific problems (i.e., the "delinquency" of the
youth) especially difficult. In the present case, therefore, it is important to increase the level of understanding among members of the family because this may allow them to engage their problems more effectively.

Clearly, since the two areas of communication and understanding are
interdependent (e.g., it is virtually impossible to develop understanding
without effective communication), it is first of all necessary to increase
the effectiveness of communication. This is accomplished through use
of the tape exchange procedure.

The tape exchange procedure. One of the main characteristics of
communication in family situations is an imbalance in direction. Parents,
in general, have much more to say to children than vice-versa. When this
is considered in addition to the power and status differential within the
family, it is clear that difficulties that ordinarily attend communication
between persons are compounded by these added burdens. Therefore, a
technique is required that will increase opportunities for effective two-way
communication to occur. The procedure employed here involves tempo-
rary suspension of face-to-face communication and substitution of communication through the exchange of tape recorded messages (See Miller
& Davies, 1971, for a more detailed discussion of the tape procedure).

In practice, one party records a taped message which is played for the
other. The second party then responds by constructing his tape with the
exchange continuing as desired. The major advantage of this technique
is that when "confronted" with a tape recording, people tend to listen
to what it contains. They cannot interrupt the recording, nor influence
what is being said by their presence, authority, or power. Another advantage is that dysfunctional emotional reactions, often common in family
situations, are minimized through the use of tape recordings. This allows
individuals to focus upon the content of what is being communicated
while relatively free of emotional interference.

Procedure

The study included nine volunteer families, each containing a teenage
boy. In six families (experimental), the youth was classified as "delinquent,"
that is, he had been placed in a correctional institution. In the other three
families (control), there was no record of legal difficulties.

All participants were first required to make a series of judgments about "the likelihood of a boy getting into trouble with the law" on the basis of four cues:

1. Discipline in the home.
2. Respect for parents.
3. Time family spends together.
4. Amount of independence allowed.

The cues were presented in the form of bar graphs with values ranging from one to ten. Predictions about the likelihood of a boy getting into trouble with the law were made on a 20-point scale. Preliminary interviews with these and other families had established that the cues listed above were generally seen as important determinants of delinquency.

Twenty-five trials were conducted in each case, with the first five trials serving as practice. As in previous studies, subjects were asked not only to make their own judgments about each case, but also to predict what the "other" would say. Therefore, on every trial, the youth predicted the judgments of each of his parents, and the parents each predicted the judgments of their son.

Following this initial evaluation of the level of understanding, the six experimental families began an exchange of tape recordings, with the

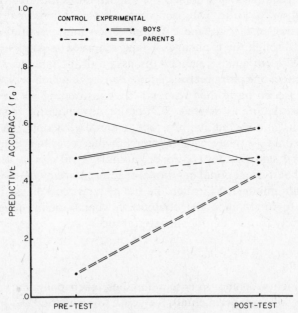

Figure 10.4.   Mean predictive accuracy correlations (r_a) for boys and parents in experimental and control families before and after the exchange of tapes and presentation of feedback

boy constructing a message for his parents and the parents taping a reply. The exchange was continued until each party had constructed and listened to three tape recordings. Then, interpersonal understanding was again evaluated using the same four-cue judgment task employed earlier. The control families did not exchange tapes but received the pre- and post-tests on the judgment task at the same time intervals as the experimental families.

Information feedback. In addition to the exchange of tapes, feedback about judgments and predictions was given to the members of each experimental family halfway through the exchange of tape recordings. Specifically, participants were told about their accuracy in predicting one another's judgments, the consistency of their predictions and the other's judgments (R^2), and their "maximal cue-discrepancies," that is, the cue(s) causing the greatest discrepancies between (1) the judgments predicted for the other person, and (2) his actual judgments. This information was given verbally in the form of further instructions. It should be emphasized that the nature of this feedback derives directly from knowledge gained through laboratory experiments with the aid of the lens model equation. The three control families received no feedback.

Results

The accuracy of predictions made by the experimental and control families before and after the exchange of tapes and presentation of feedback is shown graphically in Figure 10.4. These data indicate that during the pretest, members of the control families were significantly more accurate in predicting about one another than the experimental families, but that the experimental families improved from pre- to posttest to the point that their accuracy was comparable to that of the control families during the posttest. Figure 10.4 further shows that boys in the experimental families were more accurate in predicting the judgments of their parents before *and* after the exchange of tapes than their parents were in predicting the boys' judgments. This distinction did not hold true for the control families.

Application of the lens model equation for analysis of the factors contributing to the levels of accuracy attained indicate that for the control families the level of predictive consistency (R^2) was essentially constant from pre- to posttest. And the extent to which cue-utilization in the judgments of the other was matched by cue-use in predictions also remained relatively constant for these families (See Figure 10.5). However, for the experimental families, Figure 10.5 shows that whereas consistency increased only very slightly from pre- to posttest, there was a marked increase in the accuracy of detection of the cue-utilization of the other person from pre- to posttest. Thus, the increase in accuracy is shown to be

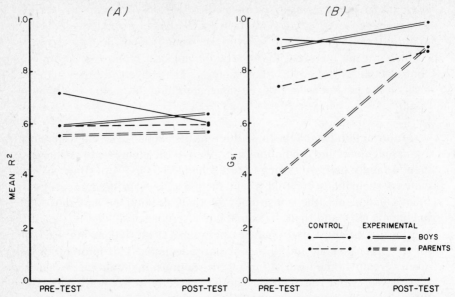

Figure 10.5a. Mean levels of actual and predictive consistency (R^2) for boys and parents in experimental and control families before and after the exchange of tapes and presentation of feedback

Figure 10.5b. Mean levels of accuracy of detection of "others'" cue-utilization (G_{s_i}) for boys and parents in experimental and control families before and after the exchange of tapes and presentation of feedback

a function of more accurate use of the cues in making predictions about the other. It is interesting to note that the level of inconsistency was a greater contributor to predictive inaccuracy during the posttest than during the pretest because of increased accuracy in cue-matching.

Discussion

The major substantive finding of this investigation is the marked increase in accuracy from before to after the exchange of tape recordings and provision of feedback for the experimental families. This demonstrates the effectiveness of the techniques used for increasing understanding, at least with respect to the issue studied here (i,e., getting into trouble with the law).

However, it is not possible to determine the extent to which the increased understanding is a function of the exchange of tape recordings or the presentation of verbal feedback. It is also possible that the tape recordings provided a context which made the feedback information easier to accept. Another interesting result is the greater accuracy of the boys in predicting their parents than vice-versa. This is undoubtedly caused by the differential status and unequal communication in the families. Spontaneous comments from several parents support this interpretation.

Theoretically, the most important finding in this study involves the identification of the *locus* of increased understanding, specifically, the more accurate use of cues in making predictions about the other person during the posttest. Thus, application of the lens model equation reveals the source of the improved accuracy, and indicates the means required to bring this about.

In the context of this particular study, it would appear that information about cue-dependencies offers the more efficient means for increasing understanding. But obviously it is necessary to replicate and extend this research to include many more families and to study long-range consequences before suggesting any general conclusions concerning practical applications.

Experiment 4: Understanding between Police and Minority Youth

Few relationships have led to greater conflict, and even violence, than those between police and minority youth in urban areas. Theoretically, this type of conflict situation appears to belong in Cell 1 of Figure 10.1. That is, not only is there a lack of understanding between the parties involved, but there would also seem to be clear-cut disagreement with respect to mutual concerns. Yet, perhaps nowhere is the need for more effective communication and increased understanding more necessary than between police and minority youth. The quotations at the beginning of this paper were obtained during this investigation and indicate the extreme level of misunderstanding that exists.

While much can be said about the socioeconomic causes of present-day relations between police and minority youth, that is beyond the scope of this paper. The purposes of this investigation are simply to: (1) evaluate cognitive factors that contribute to a lack of understanding, and (2) attempt to increase the level of understanding through the provision of feedback derived from lens model equation parameters.

Procedure

The procedure is essentially the same as that in the previous study, with some modifications appropriate to the circumstances of this investigation. For example, the tape exchange procedure described in the previous investigation is used here, but the recordings were constructed by groups rather than single individuals and played for all the members of the other group.

The subjects were a group of five police officers who patrolled a predominantly black district and a group of five black youths of an average age of 15. All subjects participated on a voluntary basis. The initial level of interpersonal understanding was evaluated through use of a judgment task similar in format to that used previously. Subjects were asked to make judgments about "the likelihood of a boy getting into trouble with the law" on the basis of four cues:

1. Discipline in the home.
2. Respect for parents.
3. Caring about other people.
4. Family income.

As before, cues were presented in the form of bar graphs with values ranging from one to ten, and predictions about the criterion variable were made on a 20-point scale. Twenty-five trials were conducted, with each subject making his own judgment and a prediction of what a member of the other group would say for each trial. After initial evaluation, the youths constructed a tape recording directed at the police officers, who then taped a reply. Three tape recordings were constructed and listened to by each group. Following this exchange, the level of interpersonal understanding was again evaluated using the same judgmental task as before.

Information feedback. The presentation of feedback in this study differed from the previous investigation in the following ways: (1) the data were based upon the average performance of the members of each group rather than individual performance (there was sufficient homogeneity among the members of each group for this purpose); and (2) feedback was presented graphically, that is, subjects were shown graphs of the level of predictive accuracy, the level of predictive and judgmental consistency, and the utilization of the cues in their predictions *and* the actual judgments of members of the other group. Note that as compared with the feedback given in the previous study, the information presented here was much more detailed and concrete.

Results

Figure 10.6 shows the level of predictive accuracy for both groups before and after the exchange of tapes and presentation of feedback. Both groups show a significant increase in the level of their accuracy. (Analysis of variance yields an F ratio for pre-post blocks significant at $p < .01$.)

As in previous investigations, analysis by application of the lens model equation reveals the locus of increases in accuracy of predictions. Figure 10.7 shows the level of predictive and judgmental consistency (R^2) during

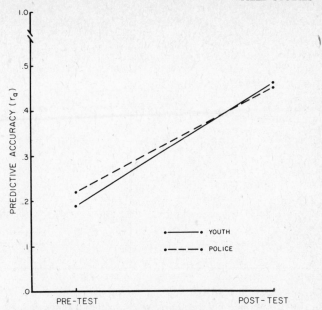

Figure 10.6. Mean predictive accuracy correlations (r_a) for youth and police before and after exchange of tapes and presentation of feedback

pre- and posttests for the members of each group, and the accuracy of detection of the other's cue-utilization (G_{s_i}). These data indicate that consistency remains essentially the same from pre- to posttest, but that the accuracy of detection of cue-utilization increases markedly. Thus, it is the latter change that is responsible for the increased accuracy.

Discussion

The major finding here is that predictive accuracy increases because subjects learn about each other's cue-dependencies as a consequence of the tape-exchange procedure and feedback information. As in the previous investigation, however, the consistency of the subjects' predictions remains basically unchanged.

It would naturally be desirable to provide more precise individual feedback, and to employ control conditions where either only tapes are exchanged or only specific kinds of feedback are provided. But the various constraints imposed by field settings have thus far prevented use of such rigorous designs. The fact remains, however, that understanding was increased, and that the lens model paradigm, therefore, is useful in a complex and demanding situation.

Some of the practical consequences of this study are particularly

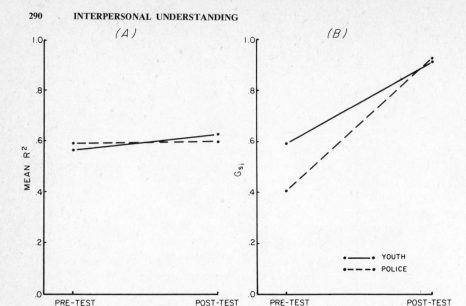

Figure 10.7a. Mean levels of actual and predictive consistency (R^2) for youth and police before and after exchange of tapes and presentation of feedback

Figure 10.7b. Mean levels of accuracy of detection of "others'" cue-utilization (G_{s_i}) for youth and police before and after exchange of tapes and presentation of feedback

interesting because they suggest that "real" changes in understanding and behavior were achieved. After the completion of the posttest, the members of both groups wanted to meet with each other on a face-to-face basis. This was arranged and resulted in a series of discussions that covered an extremely wide range of topics. After participating in several of these joint sessions, several of the police officers remarked that it would not have been possible to meet and have a reasonable discussion with such youths had it not been for the prior use of tapes. The youths, on the other hand, commented (with seeming surprise) that the police officers were human after all. In the case reported here, the police officers and youth desired to set a semipermanent basis for meeting to discuss community issues. This was implemented and continued until the end of the school year during which time other youths and police officers became involved. (In other tape exchanges involving police and minority youths, a number of useful joint projects have evolved. See Miller, 1972, in preparation, for further details.) Note that it was the establishment of communication and the increase in understanding brought about by the experimental intervention that allowed these groups to interact in such a positive fashion.

General Conclusions and Implications

The four studies reported in this paper are quite diverse, varying in rigor, scope, and the types of formal and substantive problems engaged. Taken together, they offer substantial evidence for the generality, adaptibility, and utility of the lens model paradigm for studying interpersonal learning. Yet these investigations merely represent preliminary steps toward better understanding of how persons learn about each other as they interact together. For example, even though function form has been demonstrated in the laboratory to be an important determinant of interpersonal learning, little is known about the effect of other formal parameters in the lens model (e.g., the number of cues used for making judgments, intercorrelations among cues, etc.). Similarly, connotative differences have been demonstrated as an inhibitory factor with respect to interpersonal learning, but it is not known whether feedback about such differences would increase understanding, nor whether other aspects of differences in meaning work against interpersonal understanding.

While the two field studies suggest an important degree of practical utility for the paradigm, they only test the lens model equation parameters in a very limited fashion. For example, feedback was provided in one case through verbal statements, and in the other through more concrete and extensive graphic information. But it was not possible in either case to compensate for the fact that subjects' judgmental policies changed spontaneously during the pre-posttest time interval (which they did slightly). Moreover, in the study with police and minority youth, the feedback had to be presented on the basis of group data even though shortcomings in this technique are obvious. Yet the constraints of field research operated to prevent alternative solutions. Indeed, since feedback has been demonstrated to be so important, techniques must be developed for improving the presentation of feedback in order to increase understanding. One such technique that has enormous implications involves the use of computer graphics.

Hammond and Boyle (1971) have reported the development of "Cognograph," a system for providing graphic feedback information on a visual display unit attached to a large computer. (See also Hammond and Brehmer, Reading 14.)

In a preliminary application of this system with police and probation officers as subjects, the author found that it was possible to teach these individuals to predict the judgments of a youth from a black ghetto with remarkable speed and accuracy. The task here was the same as that used in the police-minority youth study and required judgments of "the likelihood of boys getting into trouble with the law." In this case, after making a series of initial predictions about the youth, subjects were given graphic-pictorial information about the judgmental system of the youth and about their own predictive systems. Specifically, each subject was shown a history of his accuracy on the initial set of trials, a graph of the relative weights placed upon the cues by the youth, and a "lens diagram" indicating the match between the subject's predictive weights and the youth's actual weights. On subsequent trials, the level of accuracy achieved by the subjects was extraordinarily high, with the major limiting factor being the imperfect consistency (R^2) of the youths (See Figure 10.8). Note that the level of accuracy achieved here far exceeds that in the earlier study involving police and youth, indicating the great potential benefits of the cognograph system.

Finally, referring back to the four possible combinations of agreement and understanding schematized in Figure 10.1, it is clear that the present studies merely scratch the surface of many important issues. By showing the theoretical and practical value of the lens model approach to problems of interpersonal understanding, however, these studies provide a strong foundation for future efforts. Further, they have shown that the apparent impasse between conflicting parties indicated by the opening quotations need not be accepted as an inevitable state of interpersonal relations.

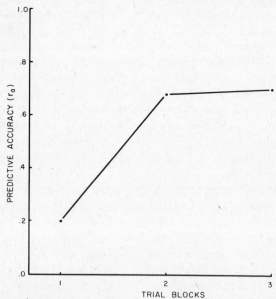

Figure 10.8. Mean predictive accuracy (r_a) for three blocks of trials for police and probation officers instructed about youths through the "cognograph" graphic display system

REFERENCES

Bergner, R., & Miller, M. J. Interpersonal learning: The case of learning about one another. University of Colorado: Program on Cognitive Processes, Report No. 115, Institute of Behavioral Science, 1969.

Bieri, J. Cognitive complexity-simplicity and predictive behavior. *Journal of Abnormal and Social Psychology,* 1955, *51,* 263–268.

Bieri, J., & Blacker, E. External and internal stimulus factors in Rorschach performance. *Journal of Consulting Psychology,* 1956, *20,* 1–7.

Björkman, M. Predictive behavior: Explorations into predictive judgments based on estimation, categorization, and choice. *Scandinavian Journal of Psychology,* 1965, *6,* 129–156.

Deane, D. H., Hammond, K. R., & Summers, D. A. Acquisition and application of knowledge in complex inference tasks. *Journal of Experimental Psychology,* in press.

Flanders, J. P. A review of research on imitative behavior. *Psychological Bulletin,* 1968, *69,* 316–337.

Hammond, K. R. New directions in research in conflict resolution. *Journal of Social Issues,* 1965, *21,* 44–66.

Hammond, K. R., & Boyle, P. J. R. Quasi-rationality, quarrels and new conceptions of feedback. *Bulletin of the British Psychological Society,* 1971, *24,* 103–113.

Hammond, K. R., Wilkins, M., & Todd, F. J. A research paradigm for the study of interpersonal learning. *Psychological Bulletin,* 1966, *25,* 221–232.

Kuhlman, C., Miller, M. J., & Gungor, E. Interpersonal conflict reduction: The effects of language and meaning. See Reading 8, this volume.

Mayo, C. W., & Crockett, W. H. Cognitive complexity and primacy-recency effects in impression formation. *Journal of Abnormal and Social Psychology,* 1964, *68,* 335–338.

Miller, M. J. Communication and understanding in families with delinquent children. Presented at the Rocky Mountain Psychology Association, Salt Lake City, Utah, May 1970.

Miller, M. J. Social consequences of action research: The case of police and minority youth, in preparation, 1972.

Miller, M. J., Bartlett, B., & Wellisch, W. Understanding between delinquents and their parents: The effects of taped communication and feedback, in preparation.

Miller, M. J., Brehmer, B., & Hammond, K. R. Communication and conflict reduction: A cross cultural study. *International Journal of Psychology,* 1970, *5,* 75–87.

Miller, M. J., & Davies, U. Communication and understanding between police and delinquents. University of Colorado: Institute of Behavioral Science, Report No. 138, 1971.

Osgood, C. E., Suci, G. J., & Tannenbaum, P. H. *The Measurement of Meaning.* Urbana, Ill.: University of Illinois Press, 1957.

Sheets, C., & Miller, M. J. The effect of cue-criterion function form on multiple-cue probability learning. *American Journal of Psychology,* in press.

Snider, J. G., & Osgood, C. E. *Semantic Differential Technique.* Chicago: Aldine, 1968.

Summers, D. A., & Hammond, K. R. Inference behavior in multiple-cue tasks involving both linear and nonlinear relations. *Journal of Experimental Psychology,* 1966, *71,* 751–757.

Summers, D. A., Taliaferro, J. D., & Fletcher, D. Judgment policy and interpersonal learning. *Behavioral Science,* 1970, *15,* 514–521.

Todd, F. J., & Hammond, K. R. Differential feedback in two multiple-cue probability learning tasks. *Behavioral Science,* 1965, *10,* 429–435.

Uhl, C. N. Effects of multiple stimulus validity and criterion dispersion on learning of interval concepts. *Journal of Experimental Psychology,* 1966, *72,* 519–527.

THE N-SYSTEMS CASE: SMALL GROUP PHENOMENA

Introduction to Readings 11, 12, and 13

The next three papers relate to situations in which three or more persons engage in an uncertain decision task. When the study of judgment is extended to this point, however, it impinges upon the traditional domain of small group research and inevitably leads to a reconsideration of traditional issues in that area. One such issue that has been very salient in social psychology concerns the influence of the group upon the individual; in particular, group pressures toward conformity. Consequently, this section begins with a brief exploratory study by Kessel suggesting that in three-person decision groups, qualitative characteristics of individual judgment policies are more important determinants of behavior than either prior commitment or group pressure.

The second paper, by Moscovici, Lage, and Naffrechoux, provides a more rigorous set of results consistent with those obtained by Kessel. The paper is particularly impressive because it extends from Moscovici's independent program of research on social influence, and it clearly shows how differences between individual judgment policies can determine patterns of influence in decision-making triads.

Discussion of the n-systems case concludes with a critique of small group research methodology by Cvetkovich. After noting the unrepresentative character of most group tasks, he describes an experiment demonstrating how social interaction and judgment processes may be studied in five-person decision groups functioning through an extended time period.

11 Effects of Group Pressure and Commitment on Conflict, Adaptability, and Cognitive Change

COLIN KESSEL[1]

Department of Psychology
Hebrew University of Jerusalem

Previous work on commitment (Festinger, 1964; Gerard, 1965; Kiesler, 1968) and group pressure (Asch, 1952; Crutchfield, 1959) has indicated that these variables influence attitude change. Group pressure has been found to enhance change, whereas commitment acts to increase resistance to change. The effects of these two variables are examined here in a cognitive conflict situation following the paradigm described by Hammond (Reading 5).

The present research extends the paradigm to a triad situation where two similarly trained individuals form a coalition against a third differently trained individual.

Prior findings about the effects of group pressure and commitment suggest that minority subjects will be more prone to change their views than majority subjects, and that subjects who are committed will be more resistant to change than those who are less committed. Briefly then, if earlier attitude change results are general, noncommitment plus pressure should produce the greatest change, while commitment and no pressure should produce the least amount of change.

In addition to this examination of cognitive change, the effects of commitment and group pressure will also be examined in relation to conflict and adaptability to changes in the experimental task.

[1] This paper is based on a thesis submitted to the Department of Psychology, Hebrew University of Jerusalem, in partial fulfillment of the requirements for an M.A. degree. The author wishes to thank Professor Kenneth R. Hammond for the extensive assistance he gave throughout the study, and Dr. Charles Greenbaum, who acted as supervisor.

Method

Design. The independent variables of commitment (high vs. low) and group pressure (minority and majority) were manipulated according to the 2×2 factorial design presented in Table 11.1.

Subjects. A total of 74 university students participated in the experiment. They were arranged to form either all male or all female three- and four-person groups, as shown in Table 11.1.

Procedure

Training. During their training each subject worked individually, learning to predict the *level of democracy* in a fictitious country from information received about (1) the amount of *free elections,* and (2) the amount of *state control* existing in that country. One group of subjects learned to rely heavily on the amount-of-free-elections variable, which has a linear relationship to the criterion (these subjects are referred to as linear-trained S_1 subjects). The others learned to rely heavily on the state-control variable, which has a nonlinear relationship to the criterion (these subjects are referred to as nonlinear S_2 subjects). For details of training and statistical relationships see Hammond and Brehmer (Reading 14).

Conflict phase. The subjects were placed around a table and seated alternately. They were told that having learned the policy they would now be required to put it into effect while making a series of ten group decisions.

Table 11.1. Experimental Design and Breakdown of Experimental Sessions

| | Commitment | |
	High	*Low*
Pressure[a]	Groups: 7	Groups: 7
	Ss: $N=21$	Ss: $N=21$
No pressure[b]	Groups: 4	Groups: 4
	Ss: $N=16$	Ss: $N=16$

[a] Pressure: This is a triad situation in which two identically trained Ss (majority) participate in the conflict situation with another differently trained S. For purposes of analysis, majority and minority Ss were treated separately.

[b] No Pressure: In this situation two identically trained Ss participate with two other differently trained Ss in the conflict situation. There are four Ss in each group—two trained in one way and two trained in another way.

The procedure then differed for committed and noncommitted groups as follows:

1. Committed Groups: Subjects first recorded their individual answers to each of the ten conflict cards, prior to any interaction with the other subjects. The conflict cards were similar to the learning cards, except that now the two cue-variables were both equally important as predictors of the criterion. The cards were then presented one at a time, and the subjects were requested to announce their answers. They were then required to work together to reach a joint decision. After this joint decision had been reached, subjects were told to record their second, private decision, which was never revealed during the course of the experiment. They were given no feedback concerning the accuracy of their individual or group answers.

2. Noncommitted Groups: The procedure was the same as above with the exception that subjects did *not* record their predictions prior to interaction with the others.

Pressure versus No Pressure. Group pressure was arranged by placing one of the three subjects in the minority. Two subjects learned to rely on the same cue, while the third subject learned to rely on a different cue. These three subjects were then brought together in the conflict phase, one of the three in the minority, and therefore subject to group pressure.

In the nonpressure or balanced four-person groups, two subjects learned one set of cue-dependencies, while another two learned to rely on a second set. In the conflict series, therefore, these groups were equally balanced.

Results

Training

As shown in Table 11.2, training was effective in all groups. It should also be clear, however, that the average high validity cue correlations are significantly *higher* for the linearly trained subjects than for those who received nonlinear training ($F = 45.5$, $p < .001$).

Another noteworthy finding here is that there are no significant differences between the committed and the noncommitted groups. This indicates that any subsequent differences between these two groups cannot be attributed to differentials in their training.

Conflict

Group conflict was measured by calculating the standard deviation of the responses for three sets of pairs in each triad—one pair of like subjects

Table 11.2. Level of Training: Average Correlations for Strong and Weak Cues

	Training	Commitment			Noncommitment		
		High[a]	Low[b]		High[a]	Low[b]	
		$\overline{X}$	$\overline{X}$	n	$\overline{X}$	$\overline{X}$	n
Pressure Three-person groups	Linear S_1	.96	—.15	11	.96	—.10	11
	Nonlinear S_2	.84	—.13	10	.86	.08	10
No pressure Four-person groups	Linear S_1	.96	—.11	8	.98	—.12	8
	Nonlinear S_2	.86	.03	8	.87	—.01	8

[a] High validity cue.
[b] Low validity cue.

(i.e., the two subjects who received identical training) and two pairs of unlike subjects (i.e., one linear subject and one nonlinear subject). These standard deviation scores are averaged out over the ten conflict trials and group scores for conflict within each experimental situation are obtained. One of the advantages of this technique is that it allows for the calculation of a "predicted conflict score." The basic data for this predicted score is provided by the subjects' responses to the training cards; that is, by calculating a regression equation for each subject, responses to the conflict cards can be predicted. These predictions enabled a calculation and a comparison between the four experimental groups for the amount of predicted conflict. Such information is important, since one basic assumption of the experimental design is that there should be no initial differences between the four experimental groups. If such a difference were found, then it might be concluded that any subsequent differences between the four groups could have been a result of the differences in the amount of conflict. It could be argued that the greater the conflict, the greater the resistance to change, or vice-versa. Using a two-way analysis of variance, no significant differences between the four experimental groups were found in terms of their amount of predicted conflict.

Adaptation to Task

The measure $(S - Y)/(T - Y)$ shows the degree to which subject approaches perfect accuracy on each judgment trial while holding constant the differences that would have arisen had the subject continued to make judgments according to his original training. The closer the score approaches zero, the more closely has the subject adapted to the new task.

The committed subjects gave their S responses before interaction and should therefore show much less adaptation than the noncommitted subjects. This expectation was borne out by the results.

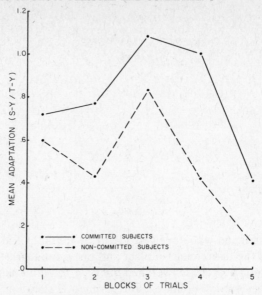

Figure 11.1. Comparison of mean adaptation scores obtained for committed and noncommitted subjects

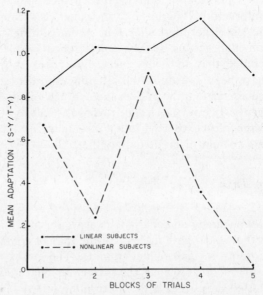

Figure 11.2. Comparison of mean adaptation scores obtained for linear- and nonlinear-trained members of experimental triads

From Figure 11.1 it can be seen that the committed subjects do not adapt to the new task as well as the noncommitted ($F = 9.04$, $p < .001$). Furthermore, Figure 11.2 shows that linearly trained subjects are less adaptable than nonlinearly trained subjects ($F = 30.4$, $p < .001$).

Cognitive Change

The measure $(S - S')/(S - J)$ indicates cognitive change, where S is the individual overt judgment, S' is the individual covert judgment (following the group consensus), and J is the group consensus. Comparisons between committed and noncommitted subjects revealed no significant differences in cognitive change. However, linear subjects were found to change less than the nonlinear subjects ($F = 4.4$, $p < .05$).

With respect to the group pressure variable, there were also no significant main effects or interactions. That is, contrary to the general implications of the literature on group pressure and conformity, cognitive change among minority subjects (whether committed or noncommitted) was not significantly different from such changes in majority subjects.

Summary and Discussion

The main results of this study can be summarized as follows. Among subjects trained to think differently about a given judgment task, comparisons between the committed and uncommitted, working under conditions of group pressure and no group pressure, reveal (1) no significant differences in levels of conflict; (2) significantly better adaptation to the judgment task by noncommitted subjects and those trained to rely on a curvilinear cue-criterion relationship; and (3) no significant effects on cognitive change for either the commitment or group pressure variables, but a significantly greater degree of change in curvilinearly trained subjects.

It therefore appears that in a laboratory situation of cognitive conflict, hypotheses based on traditional attitude change experiments concerning the effects of commitment and group pressure are not confirmed. The one exception to this conclusion is the result showing that the committed do not adapt themselves as readily to changes in the judgment task as do the noncommitted. This result is clearly in line with much prior research demonstrating that various forms of induced commitment to an attitude tend to harden that attitude against change. Yet, even here, it was found that a cognitive factor (linear or curvilinear training) serves as a more significant determinant of adaptability than commitment, since the F-ratio obtained for the former effect was more than three times larger than that obtained for the latter.

Furthermore, because adaptation to change obviously requires flexibility in the sense that subjects must depart from their training, it is not surprising to see that the only significant effect on cognitive change is also related to training. Curvilinear training may "set" subjects in such a way that they are more likely to change in a functionally adaptive direction. Or, since linear training was apparently more effective than curvilinear training (See Table 11.2), it may be that a negative transfer effect interfered with the subsequent adaptation of linearly trained subjects.

While the results thus plainly indicate that cognitive processes can be of equal or greater importance than commitment and/or group pressure, the question now arises whether or not these social variables have been properly manipulated. It should be acknowledged immediately that this is a reasonable criticism. Although the operational procedures employed here to generate commitment and group pressure seemed to be adequate, there is no doubt that much more powerful techniques might have been used.

For example, commitment in this study was arranged simply by having subjects record their individual responses in advance, prior to any communication with other group members. They did not make public statements of their views, as has been done in many attitude change experiments. Similarly, the group pressure in this study only involved a majority-minority ratio of 2:1; considerably less of a majority than has been present in the traditional pressure experiments originated by Asch.

But if the present findings must be qualified as indicated above, it should at the same time be emphasized that the influence of cognitive factors was probably inhibited by the absence of accuracy feedback during the group trials. Thus, if subjects had been told about the correctness of their responses on every trial (as in most prior research on the conflict paradigm), then even very strong manipulations of commitment and group pressure might have been negated by new learning.

Further research will be necessary in order to clarify this problem. In general, however, the results obtained here suggest that when the conflict paradigm is applied to situations involving three (or more) persons, the way in which they have been trained to think about their judgment task may be more important than their previous commitment or the pressure exerted by a majority of others.

REFERENCES

Asch, S. E. Studies of independence and conformity. *Psychological Monographs,* 1956, *70,* No. 90, 1–70.

Crutchfield, R. S. Personal and situational factors in conformity to group pressure. *Acta Psychologica,* 1959, *15,* 386–388.

Festinger, L. *Conflict, decision and dissonance.* Stanford, Calif.: Stanford University Press, 1964.

Gerard, H. B. Deviation, conformity and commitment. In I. D. Fishbein (Ed.), *Current Studies in Social Psychology.* New York: Holt, Rinehart & Winston, 1965.

Kiesler, C. A. Commitment. In R. Abelson et al. (Eds.), *Theories of Cognitive Consistency.* Skokie, Ill.: Rand McNally, 1968.

12 Conflict in Three-Person Groups: The Relationship between Social Influence and Cognitive Style

SERGE MOSCOVICI[1]
ELISABETH LAGE
MARTINE NAFFRECHOUX[2]
Laboratory of Social Psychology
Ecole Pratique des Hautes Etudes
Paris

Experimental research on interpersonal conflict has generally been limited to the conflicts of interest provided by game theory, and has concentrated upon the search for "rational" mathematical solutions while minimizing the role of social psychological variables. However, in prior studies (Abric et al., 1967; Faucheux & Moscovici, 1968) we have shown that such variables produce important effects upon the strategies of players. Following the very same general perspective, which emphasizes the importance of social interaction in conflict, we now consider conflicts of meaning or cognitive conflict. The present study specifically concerns social influence processes affecting the resolution of cognitive conflict.

One might think that during such a conflict convergence or polarization of viewpoints would simply depend upon the information individuals exchange about the task before them. Yet, since the evidence favoring one individual or the other is never entirely perfect, its acceptance cannot become imperative on purely intellectual grounds. Hence, if the individuals are to arrive at a consensus, it is necessary for one to persuade the other to change his opinion, or for agreement to be arrived at through reciprocal influence leading to mutual change. Influence processes may also help individuals to reduce their own uncertainty; that is, the *intra-*

[1] Fellow (1968–1969) at the Center for Advanced Study in the Behavioral Sciences. I also wish to acknowledge the assistance extended to me by the Aquinas Foundation.
[2] The main statistical computation and analysis of data have been done by Professor K. R. Hammond and colleagues. Continuous collaboration with him has been very fruitful and most rewarding. It is a pleasure to acknowledge the help of Claude Faucheux and J. C. Abric.

personal conflict indicated by variability in their responses. Thus, as real life teaches us, negotiation in a conflict setting usually involves at least a subtle exchange of influence as well as information.

As a theoretical issue, the role of influence in situations of "conflict and conformity" has been reviewed by Cohen (1963). He suggests that the decisive factor in opinion change is the dependence of the individual upon a majority of others who serve as a source of authority. But this formulation is questionable in the light of our recent findings (summarized in Moscovici & Faucheux, 1972). Based on a reinterpretation of Asch's earlier studies in this area, and our own new results, we propose that the real effect of influence in changing opinions or judgments depends upon the *behavior style*—the organization of responses—of the persons concerned. In other words, we believe that in situations involving cognitive conflict the role of personal influence is determined by behavior styles reflected in response consistencies, and not by the fact of being in a majority or minority.

With respect to this proposal, the paradigm developed by Hammond and his co-workers is of exceptional interest because it allows experimental confrontations between persons who have acquired different cognitive styles—linear or nonlinear—that vary in the consistency of their structure (See Hammond & Summers, 1965).

Prior research has established that, in general, a linear person arrives at his decisions by following a simple principle according to which cue information may be directly related to the judgment required. For him, correlations between elements in the task are very definite and maintain coherent relations with each other. By contrast, a nonlinear person arrives at his decisions using a more complex principle that involves a curvilinear relationship between cue information and the required judgment. His response pattern corresponds to a vague style based on general indications; he typically cannot say exactly what aspect of the given information is important to him, nor can he express a simple principle explaining the relationship between the cue material and his judgments. Consequently, his response system is frequently characterized by a greater degree of variability and inconsistency (See Hammond & Brehmer, Reading 14).

It follows that when persons with these two different cognitive styles must work together on a judgment task, the situation created is well suited to the study of influence in relation to consistency.

In order to investigate this supposition empirically, we arranged an experiment to manipulate the network of potential influence in conflict groups according to both consistency and the presence of a numerical majority. This was accomplished by varying the number of persons (two or three) making up the groups, and within these groups, the proportion of linears versus nonlinears (one or two).

Presumably, when two consistent (linear) persons are matched with a third person who is less consistent (nonlinear), a strong majority is created that opposes a relatively weak minority. The situation is different when a consistent (linear) person is confronted by two who are less consistent (nonlinear): The pressure exerted by the majority here should be weaker, because the person in the minority may hold firmly to his position, while the two in the majority may only form a pressure group rather than a solidly constituted block. Thus, it is assumed that influence will always flow from the more consistent to the less consistent and not from the majority to the minority.

Two-person groups involving one who is more consistent than the other were also arranged to serve as a control providing a basis for comparison in the absence of the majority-minority condition.

The three-person group situations outlined above all deal with the same cognitive conflict generated by the divergence between linear and nonlinear judgment processes. Only the dynamics of influence should vary — simple in the dyads, in triads it can either take the direction indicated in Asch's work, which emphasizes the impact of a unanimous majority upon an isolated minority, or it may follow the pattern we have suggested where consistency of behavior style is the important casual factor.

In many respects, the experiment described below is imperfect and limited. The manipulation of variables is not as pure as one might have wished, and the ratio of majority to minority (2:1) is relatively small. However, our analysis of cognitive factors is more detailed than in earlier studies of conformity and influence. Taken together with other relevant findings, the results appear very encouraging and are of indisputable interest.

Design

Subjects

Eighty male subjects participated as subjects. They were all medical and public works students, recruited through their corporative association for a remunerated experiment.

Procedure

The experiment was conducted using the two-cue political decision-making task described by Hammond and Brehmer in Reading 14.

All subjects were trained individually to rely upon a cue that was related in either a linear or nonlinear manner to the judgment criterion.

A total of 60 trials was allowed for this purpose. To verify that a suitably high level of training had been accomplished with each subject, his last ten trials were checked to make sure they contained no more than a total of five one-point errors of judgment made on a 20-point scale. In cases where this limit was exceeded, subjects repeated blocks of 20 trials until their errors reached the appropriate level.

Triads were formed containing two linearly trained subjects and one nonlinear subject, referred to hereafter as the *linear* triads ($N = 10$). *Non*linear triads ($N = 10$) included two nonlinear subjects and one linear subject. The dyads ($N = 10$) were all formed of one linear and one non-linear subject.

In the interaction phase of the experiment, subjects in all the three- and two-person groups had to agree on a common judgment for each of 30 trials arranged so that both the linear and nonlinear cues were equally relevant to the criterion. It is here that we witnessed the development of conflict. Once this phase of the experiment was completed, the aims of the experiment and the manipulations involved were revealed to subjects during a discussion period.

The effectiveness of the experimental manipulation concerning group structure is examined below; major findings are presented in the section headed "consistency and influence."

Results

Analyses included individual responses given before the group consensus was reached on each trial. We have constructed indices of these basic data in order to test certain predictions. It was also important to examine cognitive conflict and its resolution immediately, because these phenomena constitute the essential substance of Hammond's paradigm. We then turned to the process of influence between the most consistent (linear) and the least consistent (nonlinear) subjects. It was at this point that we combined different group situations, comparing the power of persuasion of a consistent or inconsistent minority to that of a consistent or inconsistent majority. At the end of this analysis, we were in a position to answer our essential question: Is disagreement reduced as a consequence of pressure exerted by a greater number of persons or does behavior style play the decisive role?

The Evolution of Cognitive Conflict

Confrontation between persons with different cognitive styles involves a divergence in judgments about the same stimulus objects. In this instance, the conflict is due to the disparity between the importance assigned

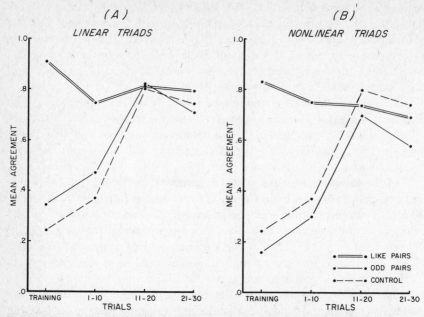

Figure 12.1a. Comparison of agreement scores obtained for control dyads and linear-trained members of the experimental triads

Figure 12.1b. Comparison of agreement scores obtained for control dyads and nonlinear-trained members of experimental triads

by the linear and nonlinear subjects to the corresponding cue material. This conflict can be seen in Figures 12.1 and 12.2.

Figure 12.1 shows the evolution of agreement as measured by the correlation[3] between subjects in the dyads and the linear (Figure 12.1a)

[3]
$$r_A = \frac{R^2_{S_1} + R^2_{S_2}}{2} - \frac{\Sigma d}{2}$$

This expresses:

Agreement = Policy Consistency − Policy Differences

where r_A is the correlation between responses S_1 and S_2

$R^2_{S_1}$ and $R^2_{S_2}$ are the multiple correlations between manifest responses of each subject and the two cues

Σd is an index of systematic differences between the policies of two subjects considering the importance they give to the two cues

Perfect Agreement:

$$r_A = 1.00; \quad \Sigma d = .00; \quad R^2_{S_1} = R^2_{S_2} = 1.00$$

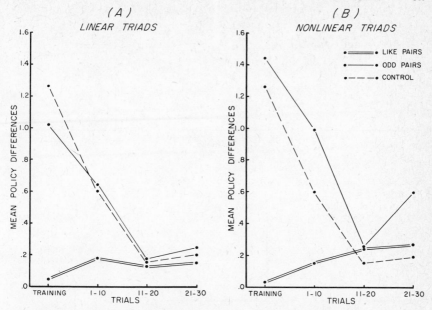

Figure 12.2a. Comparison of differences in cue-weightings (policy differences) among control dyads and linear-trained members of the experimental triads

Figure 12.2b. Comparison of differences in cue-weightings (policy differences) among control dyads and nonlinear-trained members of the experimental triads

and nonlinear (Figure 12.1b) triads. Similarly, Figures 12.2a and 12.2b show the difference in cue-weightings (Σd), which partially account for the agreement scores indicated in Figure 12.1. By inspection, it is easy to see an agreement between subjects with the same cognitive style—the "like pairs," both linear and nonlinear—at the beginning of the interaction trials. At the same time, however, there is substantial disagreement between subjects with different cognitive styles ("odd pairs") in both the dyads and triads.

Figures 12.1 and 12.2 indicate two additional points worth noting: (1) whereas there is high agreement between subjects of the same cognitive style, it is nevertheless not complete (the maximum 1.00 is nowhere attained; the highest agreement score is .81); and (2) the effect of being in the minority or majority is different in the linear and nonlinear triads. Consequently, the number of partners present does have a certain importance (See, for example, studies by Bixenstine & Levitt, 1966; Wilson et al., 1965), but its importance depends on cognitive style.

General reduction of disagreement between odd pairs occurs during the second block of interaction trials. Indeed, odd pairs reach the same

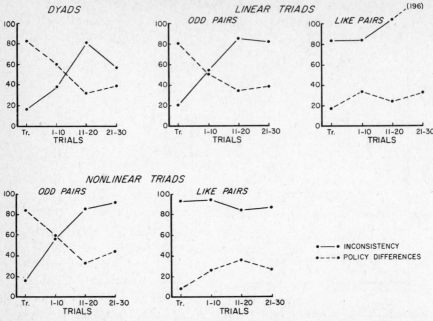

Figure 12.3. Comparison of the inconsistency and policy difference components of disagreement for the control dyads and various pairs from the experimental triads

level of agreement as like pairs who do *not* increase their agreement over trials. This convergence of all groups toward a given level of agreement has been observed in other studies (See Hammond & Brehmer, Reading 14) and its occurrence in triads as well as dyads is significant. It indicates that the interaction trials apparently have the effect of reshaping important aspects of the subject's situation.

Further analyses tracing changes in the components of disagreement (response consistency and policy differences)[4] support this view. Figure

$$1 - r_A = 1 - \frac{R_{S_1}^2 + R_{S_2}^2}{2} + \frac{\Sigma d}{2}$$

Disagreement = Policy Inconsistency + Policy Differences

The indices used in Figure 12.3 are the following:

Inconsistency: $\dfrac{1 - \dfrac{R_{S_1}^2 + R_{S_2}^2}{2}}{1 - r_A} \times 100$

Policy Differences: $\dfrac{\dfrac{\Sigma d}{2}}{1 - r_A} \times 100$

12.3 shows that for all odd pairs, responses diverge at the beginning of the interaction because of policy differences, that is, differences in how they consider the realities represented by the cue material. But toward the end of the interaction trials, disagreement derives from variations in the line of behavior followed by each partner—their inconsistency. Such inconsistency is apparently due to difficulty in stabilizing responses, that is, coordinating one's behavior with that of the other's and thereby introducing a new coherence into one's behavior. Continual changes in the positions subjects adopt are therefore responsible for the persistence of their overt disagreements, regardless of their initial cognitive style.

The conflict thus moves from the level of relationships with stimulus material, to relationships between responses; from that of weighting elements of the "real," to that of controlling exchanges with others. For subjects, the original problem of making correct judgments is now transformed into a search for a socially acceptable interpersonal consensus. In the psychological space created by the changed cue-criterion relationships and the change in the nature of conflict, influence can now act more freely.

Consistency and Influence

Subjects showing higher response variability or inconsistency are likely to be the most susceptible to influence from others. Examining the relationship between the cues subjects were trained on and their later responses, it was found that nonlinear subjects fluctuated significantly ($p < .001$) more than linear subjects, an indication that the former should yield to pressure exerted by the latter.

A relatively direct way of seeing how much someone modified his behavior and was influenced during the interaction is provided by measures of the degree to which subjects deviate from their training.[5] Table 12.1 shows that whether we compare the linear subjects to the nonlinear subjects in the same triad (regardless of which type was in the majority), or in different triads where the majority or minority position in the group is held constant, the analyses of variance always yield a significant F-ratio.

The nonlinear subjects deviate more from their training, taking the

[5] Formulae for computing the measure of departure from training:

$$\frac{T_1 - S_1}{T_1 - T_2} \qquad \frac{T_2 - S_2}{T_2 - T_1}$$

where T is the response the subject would give if he were going entirely according to his training

S is the subject's manifest response

Table 12.1 Departure from Training—Analysis of Variance

	Conditions	F	df	P	Trend
Triads	Linear 2L versus 1NL	4.41	1/18	<.05	cubic
	Nonlinear 2NL versus 1L	3.61	1/18	<.10	cubic
Majority	2L versus 2NL	12.58	1/18	<.01	cubic
Minority	1L versus 1NL	3.94	1/18	<.10	quadratic

linear cue into account, while the linear subjects continue to favor their initial cue the whole time. And this occurs even in the case of a single linear subject facing two nonlinear subjects. Everything happens as if, in the implicit negotiation of the group members, one party tends to up-hold its viewpoint, while the other is ready to go back on its viewpoint and make concessions. Moreover, linear and nonlinear majorities and minorities are not only different in terms of their resoluteness, but also in terms of their cohesion. This is indicated in Figures 12.1 and 12.2 which show that overall agreement (r_a) and similarity in cue-weighting (Σd) is stronger in triads with a linear majority.

Unquestionably, the finding reported above indicates that the linear subjects—whether in the majority or minority—were more rigid and more influential than nonlinear subjects. It should be noted that their impact was not due to judgmental accuracy; analysis of variance of these scores ("adaptation to reality")[6] shows that linear subjects remain closer to their training and are thus *less* accurate than the nonlinear subjects ($F = 4.80$, $p < .05$).

It is evident from the above results that, in this experiment, cognitive style has a more decisive effect than majority pressure. When they are in the majority, linear subjects have a strong influence on the minority nonlinear subject. (One might even say that their exchange with the non-linear subject anchors them more deeply in their cognitive structure.) Moreover, an analysis of adaptation to reality scores (judgmental accuracy) shows that the linear majority responds in closer accord with its training

---

[6] Index of adaptation to reality:

$$\frac{S - Y}{T - Y}$$

where T is the response the subject would give if he were going entirely according to his training

S is the subject's manifest response

Y is the correct value of the variable being judged

as compared with isolated linear subjects who tend to be more correct in their answers ($F = 9.65$, $p < .01$). These minority linear subjects depart further from their initial viewpoint, as do all minority subjects. Linear subjects, therefore, appear less rigid when they are isolated than when they are together. However, even when isolated, they are sufficiently consistent to influence the nonlinear majority.

Conclusions

One might have thought that disagreements arising from different viewpoints concerning a mutual problem would be resolved entirely within a cognitive framework. Our results show that change is not only due to a cognitive disequilibrium, but also to the influence that subjects exert upon each other. It appears that cognitive structures determine the response style of the partners, and this style, in turn, influences the acceptance or rejection of information proposed by the other.

It might also have been expected that a decisive factor in resolving judgmental differences would be the dependency of the minority upon the majority. The majority-minority distinction certainly does play a part, but perhaps only in the situation where a subject is already inclined to accept the others' point of view. It seems instead that cognitive parameters are more important in determining the manner in which subgroups are constituted in triads; that is, in which conflict is resolved. It is the cognitive style imposed by training that determines the respective positions of partners in the process of influence; the majority or minority social position only accentuates this fact.

The results of this experiment confirm all other findings we have obtained concerning the role of behavior style in the process of influence. Furthermore, the present study allows us to point out an additional consideration of general importance. Most research in this problem area is conducted at the level of overt responses. For example, subjects may begin with different responses, and with time, one expects them to move toward each other. Does it suffice to observe such a movement on the overt level without ascertaining whether changes are also occurring at a covert level, and what those changes may be?

Hammond's paradigm offers the possibility of studying influence processes in situations where high-level cognitive functioning is required, and where behavioral responses are only a consequence of such functioning. Situations having this fundamental character, which we have previously discussed on the perceptual level (Moscovici et al., 1969), have not to our knowledge received the attention they deserve. Perhaps predominant theoretical formulations have prevented this, or perhaps the lack of adequate experimental techniques has been an obstacle. But if we wish to understand one of the major phenomena of social psychology, we should approach the study of relationships between cognitive organization, perception, and social behavior, and we now have this possibility.

REFERENCES

Abric, J. C., Faucheux, C., Moscovici, S., & Plon, M. Rôle de l' image du partenaire sur la coopération en situation de jeu. *Psychologie Française,* 1967, *12,* 267–275.

Bixenstine, V. E., & Levitt, C. Collaboration among six persons in a prisoner's dilemma game. *Journal of Conflict Resolution,* 1966, *10,* 488–496.

Cohen, B. P. *Conflict and conformity.* Cambridge, Mass.: M.I.T. Press, 1963.

Faucheux, C., & Moscovici, S. Self-esteem and exploitative behavior in a game against chance and nature. *Journal of Personality and Social Psychology,* 1968, *8,* 83–88.

Hammond, K. R., & Summers, D. A. Cognitive dependence on linear and nonlinear cues. *Psychological Review,* 1965, *72,* 215–224.

Moscovici, S., & Faucheux, C. Social influence, conformity bias and the study of active minorities. In L. Berkowitz (Ed.), *Advances in experimental social psychology.* Vol. 5. New York: Academic Press, 1972.

Moscovici, S., Lage, E., & Naffrechoux, M. Influence of a consistent minority on the responses of a majority in a color perception task. *Sociometry,* 1969, *32,* 365–380.

Wilson, W., Chun, N., & Kayatani, M. Projection, attraction, and strategy choices in intergroup competition. *Journal of Personality and Social Psychology,* 1965, *2,* 432–435.

13 Small Group Dynamics in Extended Judgment Situations[1]

GEORGE CVETKOVICH[2]

Western Washington State College

Nearly 30 years ago, Brunswik (1943; also 1952, 1956) raised some important questions regarding experimental methods in psychology. He was particularly concerned with the extent to which commonly used laboratory settings are representative of the conditions people face in real life, and he argued that the representative sampling commonly applied to the selection of experimental subjects must likewise be applied to the selection of laboratory conditions. To accomplish this end Brunswik advocated the development of a research methodology intrinsic to psychology, a methodology that would incorporate elements representative of the causal texture of the environment encountered by individuals in natural settings.

There is little indication that experimental psychology has to any large extent adopted the particular type of methodological approach advocated by Brunswik; that is, a methodology founded on his theory of probabilistic functionalism. However, some recent efforts in social psychology have been directed towards assessing the "match" between commonly used laboratory settings and the real-world ecology. Efforts in this direction have either been motivated by concerns about generalizations based on laboratory findings (as recognized by Brunswik) or because of discrepancies between the results of laboratory and nonlaboratory research.

Numerous attempts illustrative of this latter concern can be found in the literature. To cite but two examples, Hovland (1959) and Bauer (1964) have attempted to reconcile discrepancies in the results of laboratory and nonlaboratory investigations of attitude change by specifying the differences between the two settings, but analyses of this type can only be performed after a large body of research evidence has accumulated in a particular content area. Additionally, once differences in the characteristics of laboratory and nonlaboratory settings are pointed out,

[1] The investigation was supported by National Science Foundation Grant G-1912 whose principle investigator is Leon Rappoport.

[2] Thanks are due to Benson Penick, Terry Applegate, and Sandra Foster for skilled assistance in collection and analysis of data and especially to Leon Rappoport for valuable suggestions.

attempts are rarely made to bring the laboratory setting in line with the natural setting. Often the research model that has served as the basic means of laboratory investigation for a particular content area remains unchanged. Thus, concern with differences between the laboratory situation and the real world seems to terminate once these differences are identified.

More recently, other investigators have taken a more systematic approach to identifying the general situational and motivational characteristics that distinguish laboratory behavior from behavior outside the laboratory. The work of Orne (1962) and Rosenthal (1966) are both illustrative of this general approach.

Orne has proposed that the behavior of any experimental subject may be influenced, not only by traditionally defined characteristics of the experimental situation, but also by the demand characteristics of the experiment. Briefly, demand characteristics are defined as "the totality of cues which may convey an experimental hypothesis to the subject [1962, p. 121]." These may include among other things explicit and implicit communications by the experimenter, rumors about the research, and the experimental procedure itself. The extent to which behavior during the study is related to demand characteristics determines both the probability that the study can be replicated with minor modifications and the degree to which experimental results can be applied in nonlaboratory settings.

In a similar vein, Rosenthal has cautioned experimenters about the dangers of unintentionally influencing subject behavior in line with experimental hypotheses through the use of subtle unconscious cues. Rosenthal and others have demonstrated this experimenter bias effect in a number of animal and human studies and have identified some of the cues inadvertently used by experimenters.

The general thrust of the work noted above has been to make explicit the long recognized fact that human subjects, unlike the inanimate objects studied by the physical sciences, think, perceive, and react to experimental conditions in ways that may be beyond the control of the experimenter. It has yielded a number of suggestions as to how one may insure that subjects are responding to experimental conditions and not to extraexperimental factors. But whereas these suggestions can reduce one threat to ecological validity by eliminating experimenter bias vis-à-vis subjects, they have little to do with the experimenter bias that often leads to the arrangement of unrepresentative laboratory tasks and conditions.

It is the thesis of the present report that selection of experimental tasks has commonly been arbitrary; often a matter of expediency, sometimes a matter of theoretical convenience, but rarely a matter of careful selection according to criteria of representativeness. The present discussion is limited to one aspect of the total problem. Specifically, we are concerned with tasks and conditions commonly used in the study of small decision-making groups. In addition to the above considerations this particular topic was selected because group decision making is an intrinsically important problem.

Although most decisions are made by individuals, individuals often join with others to make decisions. Within the group, varied resources and knowledge can be pooled, often leading to more accurate decisions. Even when the group does not directly provide solutions to problems, affective ties and relationships between group members can act as a supportive matrix for the individual. Thus, the group provides protection, encouragement, and in general acts as an effective mediator and means of adaptation to an often hostile physical and social environment.

The present discussion is organized into three parts: (1) a brief review of the experimental tasks commonly used in small group research with special attention given to the representative characteristics of these situations, (2) results of a preliminary study developed on the basis of representative considerations, and (3) a discussion of the substantive and methodological issues suggested by the study.

Representative Characteristics of Group Tasks

Small group research has, in the past, focused mainly on structural and organizational variables influencing the achievement of group goals. It has been shown, for instance, that group problem-solving ability is affected by group size (e.g., Gibb, 1951), communication network available to the group (e.g., Bavelas, 1950; Shaw, 1954, 1964), group leadership (e.g., Lippitt & White, 1947, 1958; Maier, 1950), and heterogeneity of group membership (e.g., Hoffman, 1959; Hoffman & Maier, 1961). Likewise, interpersonal relationships among group members are affected by clarity of group goals (Raven & Rietsma, 1957), relative status of group members (Maas, 1957), and individual deviations from group norms (Schacter, 1951).

Briefly, past studies of this type have been attempts to *manipulate* aspects of group organization that influence decision making. Scant empirical attention has been given to those factors that *determine* group organization.

The nature of the task facing the group is particularly important in this respect. The experimental study of the effects of the task, however, has been hindered since prior studies have not employed tasks representative of those facing real-life groups. This is true in at least three major ways.

First, tasks most often used are fully determined and mechanistic (e.g., arithmetic problems, motor cooperation problems, simple reasoning problems), and therefore do not possess the characteristics of uncertainty. The environment faced by nonlaboratory groups, however, is often quite uncertain, equivocal, or probabilistic. Fully determined tasks can be performed by an individual or even a computer—uncertain tasks often require the collective wisdom of a group.

The functional importance of the group in reducing uncertainty for the individual has of course been recognized for some time. Early social psychological research on the development of norms, for instance, demonstrated that groups replace absent definitions of objective reality with subjective "social" definitions (e.g., Sherif, 1935, 1936). However, no systematic attempt has been made to understand the processes whereby groups adapt to uncertain environments, particularly when these environments demand repeated group decisions.

Second, most tasks used in prior research do not permit learning. Either all knowledge necessary for successful completion is known before the task is begun (e.g., arithmetic problems) or there is simply no correct solution available. In either case, when relevant feedback is not provided, laboratory groups cannot improve the accuracy of their performance by learning.

The absence of studies on group learning is somewhat surprising given the historical and contemporary importance of the concept of learning to individual psychology. Among the behavioral sciences, anthropology has been most concerned with investigating group learning as a process of adaptation to the external environment (i.e., culture). Social-psychological research, particularly laboratory investigation, has been restricted primarily to comparisons of individual and group performance, with most of this work being concerned with productivity.

Finally, the amount of time members of laboratory groups spend together, as a group, is less than that of groups in real life. Typically, laboratory groups meet once (for an hour or less) and work for a limited time on a number of problems (e.g., Anderson, 1961; Emerson, 1954). In contrast, real-life groups, particularly if working on problems of any consequence, are very likely to have an extended history and may not be limited in the length of time spent on any one problem.

Several considerations suggest that the behavior of well-established groups differs from that of short-termed groups. One important factor is that groups need time to develop organization and structure. Newly formed groups are severely handicapped because of their lack of organization (Anderson, 1961; Fox & Lorge, 1962; Lorge, Tuckerman, Aikman, & Moss, 1955) and may demonstrate high variability of performance (Perlmutter & deMontmollin, 1952). As a result, their achievement is often found to bear a closer relationship to that of the least proficient members than to more proficient members (Faucheux & Moscovici, 1958). As far back as 1935, however, Daschiell noted that long-term groups are highly stable in performance and will at times perform at a level above that of their *most* proficient member.

Persistence of the group through time is also important to the interpersonal relationship between group members. A number of recent studies indicate differences in the behavior of participants in long-term versus short-term interactions. Particularly relevant here are findings showing that individuals who believe that they will spend extended time with others are more likely to attempt to resolve disagreements with them (Darley & Berscheid, 1967; Kiesler & Kiesler, 1967).

In sum, the tasks used in most prior small group experiments are not representative of real-life conditions where groups typically (1) recognize that their task is certain or uncertain, (2) try to improve their judgments by observing the outcomes and consequences of their decisions, and (3) have an extended history.

Mixed motives. A fourth representative characteristic of group tasks is their reward structure. Two types of reward are commonly considered to be most important: (1) rewards determined by the individual's own efforts, and (2) rewards determined by the combined efforts of the group. Past research has recognized that in real life these two cases rarely occur in their pure form (Kelley & Thibaut, 1969). Therefore, considerable effort has been directed towards the investigation of mixed cases in which the individual may be motivated toward *both* his own gain and the common group gain.

One current approach to decision making in mixed motive situations is research based on game theory formulations. The essential rationale of this research is that game situations provide the answer to the "long felt need in social psychology for a well controlled interaction situation" and that "decisions made by subjects in the game are very similar to decisions that are made in real-life bargaining and conflict situations [Gallo & McClintock, 1965, p. 70]."

Close analysis of the experimental situation, however, reveals that while game situations may meet the mixed motives criterion of representativeness, they do not meet any other. The commonly used Prisoner's Dilemma (PD) game is a prime example.

In its most general form the PD game consists of two opponents who are faced with the selection of one of two alternative moves. Payoff to each opponent is dependent upon both one's own and other's selection. If both players select the noncooperative move, they lose a fixed amount. If one player selects the noncooperative move and the other player selects the cooperative move, the noncooperative player wins while the cooperative player (the sucker in PD parlance) loses.

While runs of the PD game can go on for hundreds or even thousands of trials, subjects can learn nothing more about the task than the information given by the payoff matrix at the outset. Uncertainty exists within the game situation, but it is irreducible uncertainty concerning the strategies one's opponent will use. Learning can only occur if one detects trends in his opponents moves, but this is not learning about the task structure.

More important, however, many gaming studies eliminate the major means of conflict reduction utilized in real life—verbal discussion of the conflict problem. If communication between opponents is permitted at all, it usually consists of experimenter contrived messages, cryptic in content and devoid of task relevant information. Considering the content of most game situations, of course, the possibility for substantive communication is small. A player can only try to persuade his opponent to cooperate by messages that convey threat, shame, or emotional pleas of interdependence or by messages about own intentions and expectations.

Because of the minimal social characteristics of devised games, empirical findings encourage pessimistic interpretations of interpersonal conflict. Prisoner's Dilemma studies have consistently shown that conflict (i.e., noncooperation) generally increases over trials. This is true even when very large payoffs are used (e.g., Gumpert, Deutsch, & Epstein, 1969).

Cognitive conflict. An alternative to the game approach has been proposed by Hammond. Although his model represents a complex interaction situation, it allows the precise specification of both subject and task variables. Additionally, the experimental situation has two important characteristics: (1) it requires decisions in the face of uncertainty while (2) providing for the improvement of judgments through the presentation of judgment accuracy feedback. Equally important, the restraints of the experimental situation are minimal, thereby allowing the full richness and complexity of subject behavior to be displayed, including free discussion of task-relevant material.

Despite the advantages noted above, this paradigm has in the past provided little, if any, opportunity to examine the reward structure considerations discussed earlier. It has recently been shown, however, that the cognitive conflict model can be modified so as to generate a mixed motive situation, thus adding to the representativeness of this approach (See Rappoport & Cvetkovich, 1970). The present study, therefore, is designed to illustrate the usefulness of this approach for investigating small group behavior. Specifically, this study concerns the effects of several mixed motive conditions upon the behavior of five-person groups committed to long-term interaction involving a series of uncertain decisions.

Summary

Prior research on group decision making does not represent the conditions under which most real-life decision groups meet. Uncertain situations that provide feedback relevant to performance accuracy and invoce extended periods of interaction have received little empirical attention. Game theory research, while being representative with respect to mixed motives, neglects other representative factors.

The innovation of the present work is that it studies laboratory groups working on a task that captures characteristics of *non*laboratory tasks. The work is designed to investigate activities leading to the achievement of the two major goals of any successful decision-making group: making a valid decision and maintaining group harmony. By studying these activities in a representative situation the present work includes within a single analytic framework both cognitive and emotional functioning of the group.

Design

According to the cognitive conflict model three situational factors are definitive of cognitive conflict. These are: (1) mutual aims or goals, that is, shared fate; (2) equivocal information, that is, uncertainty; and (3) discrepant cognitive processes, that is, individual differences in thinking (Rappoport, 1965). These characteristics were incorporated in the following task.

Task. The task required judgments of a criterion variable based on information provided by three cues probabilistically related to the criterion. Specifically, subjects were asked to decide how soon survivors of a nuclear blast could safely leave a shelter given information about (1) the "dirtiness" of the blast, that is, strontium yield; (2) intensity of blast, that is, megaton rating; and (3) distance from ground zero.

The content of the task was selected because subjects have had no specific experience in making such judgments and, therefore, all learning about the task occurs within the experimental setting. At the same time, however, general exposure to task materials (through mass media, etc.) is sufficient to persuade subjects that the task is plausible and valid. Additionally, selection of particular cues is based on Civil Defense literature. Therefore, the task has some degree of scientific validity as well as considerable face validity for the typical subject.

Judgments of the criterion variable were made on a 20-point response scale ranging from a minimum of "10 to 14 days" to a maximum of "105 to 109 days" in five-day increments. Information on each of the cues was presented in the form of a ten-step bar graph. In the instructions to subjects, detailed explanations were provided for each category of each cue.

The mathematical structure of the task was such that "dirtiness of blast" correlates $+.80$ with the correct answer, while the other cues are only slightly related to the criterion. Additionally, none of the three cues are highly related to each other. The multiple correlation between all three cues and the criterion is .84. In general, therefore, judgmental accuracy requires heavy reliance on the "dirtiness" cue; but the nature of the relationship of all cues to the criterion, that is, the multiple R, makes perfect accuracy impossible. A schematic representation of the task structure is presented in Figure 13.1.

Subjects. Twenty male college students were divided randomly into four groups of five persons each. Analysis of individual judgments on the first day indicated that all subjects were highly similar in the way they initially thought about the task (mean intercorrelation between any two subjects $= +.70$; $p < .01$). Therefore, the level of judgment similarity among members of each group did not differ significantly from that of the other groups (Chi square $= 0.12$).

Procedure. Groups met on each of eight successive days. Preliminary work indicated that this period was optimal for the purposes of the study: It is long enough for subjects to learn about each other and the task, yet short enough so as not to exhaust their interest in the task. On each day 10 trials of the total 80-trial task were presented. Relationships among cue-values and between cues and criterion for the trials presented on any one day did not differ significantly from those of the total task.

The following steps were followed on each trial: (1) subjects were shown a cue card presenting information on dirtiness of blast, intensity of blast, and survivors' distance from ground zero; (2) they made individual judgments of the earliest date survivors of such a blast might safely leave

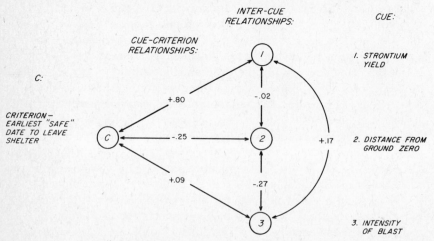

Figure 13.1. Graphic description of the mathematical structure of the judgment task (all cues have linear function form)

the shelter; (3) they discussed the cue information and arrived at a single joint judgment about length of stay in the shelter; (4) each subject made a second individual judgment of the criterion; (5) the correct answer was shown; (6) payoff for that trial for each subject was computed (See "Payoff conditions" below); and (7) the next cue card was exposed.

Furthermore, prior to Trials 1, 6, and 10 on each day, subjects were asked to rate how much they liked each of the other persons in their group, and to predict the judgment each of the other group members would make on the next trial given the cue information for that trial.

Payoff conditions. All subjects were paid a daily wage for participation in the study. Additional pay was dependent upon the pay structure used for the group to which the subjects were assigned. The four pay conditions are listed below.

1. *No pay.* Group members received only a set wage for participation in the study.

In the remaining three conditions each subject received the same daily wage as "No pay" subjects, but also received an additional amount on each trial determined by two factors: (1) accuracy of joint judgment (group-determined pay), and (2) closeness of group judgment to first individual judgment (individual-determined pay). Accuracy of joint judgment was determined by the discrepancy between the joint judgment and the correct answer. If the joint judgment was within a specified range of accuracy, each member of the group received an equal amount of pay.

Closeness of joint judgment to individual judgment was taken as a measure of individual domination of the group judgment. It is assumed that the closer subject's individual judgment is to the joint judgment, the more influence he has exerted upon the group "to see things his way." According to this criterion, only that subject whose initial individual judgment was nearest the joint judgment received pay for domination. If two or more subjects were equally close to the joint judgment, pay for domination was divided between them.

2. *Equal individual- and group-determined pay (Equal).* Approximately equal amounts of pay were given for joint accuracy and for domination of group.

3. *High group and low individual pay (High Accuracy).* Proportionately more pay was given to subjects for accuracy of the joint judgment than for domination of the group.

4. *High individual and low group pay (High Dominance).* Conceptually the reverse of the High Accuracy pay condition; proportionately more pay was given for domination of the group than for joint accuracy. Actual amounts of pay given in each of the four conditions are presented in Tables 13.1 and 13.2.

Table 13.1.   Amount of Money Given to Each Subject in Each Group for Accuracy of Joint Judgment (Group-Determined Pay).

If Joint Judgment Is:	Exactly Correct	Off by 2 or Fewer Units	Off by 3 or More Units
No pay group	$0.00	$0.00	$0.00
High dominance group	$0.10	$0.05	$0.00
Equal pay group	$0.30	$0.20	$0.00
High accuracy group	$0.50	$0.40	$0.00

Measures

Group conflict. Two measures of cognitive conflict between group members were taken: (1) overt conflict was measured by discrepancies in the initial individual judgments of group members; (2) covert conflict was measured by discrepancies in the second, post-discussion judgments of group members. In each case the standard deviation of the individual judgments on each trial was taken as the operational measure of conflict.

Learning. Three indices of learning were derived: (1) group learning about the task was measured by the difference between the joint judgment and the correct answer on each trial, (2) individual learning about the task was measured by the difference between initial individual judgments and the correct answer on each trial, and (3) learning about the judgment policies of others in the group was measured by the difference between the judgments predicted for subjects and their actual initial individual judgments.

Conflict reduction. Two measures related to conflict reduction were utilized: (1) duration of conflict was measured by the amount of time intervening between subjects' statements of their first individual judgments and their mutual agreement upon a joint judgment, and (2) compromise was scored if on any trial the joint judgment fell within ± 1 unit (on the 20-point response scale) of the average of the initial individual judgments. The ratio of such trials to total trials indicates the percentage of compromise trials for each group.

Table 13.2.   Amount of Money Given Only to That Subject Having Initial Individual Judgment Closest to Joint Judgment (Individual-Determined Pay).

No pay group	$0.00
High dominance group	$0.40
Equal pay group	$0.20
High accuracy group	$0.05

Cognitive change. If the group discussion causes group members to reappraise their initial thinking about the task, their second individual judgments should differ from their first. Thus, cognitive change is measured by the discrepancy between first and second individual judgments.

Group cohesion. Subject's liking for each other member of the group was assessed at the conclusion of every session. Each subject's "liking" scores were then averaged so as to yield a measure of group attraction for that subject. In addition, these mean individual ratings were averaged across group members, thus yielding a measure of the cohesiveness of the total group.

Results

Conflict

Overt conflict. As seen in Figure 13.2, groups working under different pay conditions differed in overt conflict ($F = 18.18$, $p < .01$). Individual comparisons showed that the No Pay group was significantly higher in conflict ($\overline{X} = 2.9$) than the other three groups ($F = 7.22$, $p < .001$). The Equal Pay group ($\overline{X} = 1.9$) was significantly lower than the other groups ($F = 7.32$, $p < .05$). Levels of conflict in the High Accuracy and High Dominance groups were intermediate to the No Pay and Equal Pay levels and were not significantly different from each other ($F = 1.67$, $p < .10$).

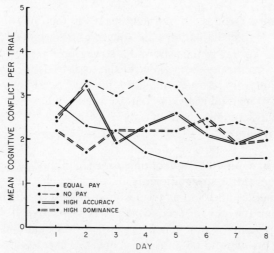

Figure 13.2.   Average overt conflict per trial for each group plotted as a function of days

Comparison of average level of overt conflict between the first four days and the last four days showed that the High Accuracy, Equal Pay, and No Pay groups decreased conflict significantly as days progress ($F = 4.98$, $p < .01$). However, the High Dominance group remained at the same level of conflict from first to last day block ($F < 1$).

Covert conflict. Group differences on covert conflict are similar to those for overt conflict: The No Pay group was highest in covert conflict ($\overline{X} = 1.9$; $F = 19.37$, $p < .001$); the Equal Pay group was lowest ($\overline{X} = 0.4$; $F = 27.12$, $p < .001$); and the High Accuracy and High Dominance groups fell between these extremes. In addition, however, the High Dominance group was significantly higher in covert conflict than was the High Accuracy group ($\overline{X} = 1.5$ and 0.9, respectively; $F = 15.38$, $p < .01$).

Learning

No single group was significantly superior in overall ability to make accurate joint judgments ($F < 1$), nor in accuracy of individual judgments ($F = 2.02$, $p > .10$). Moreover, members of all groups were similar in their ability to predict accurately the judgments of others in their own group ($F = 1.15$, $p > .10$). On all measures of learning, groups increased in accuracy as days progressed ($F = 3.02$, 15.05, and 3.77; $p < .05$ for group judgment, individual judgment, and prediction of others' judgment, respectively).

Conflict Resolution

Compromise. Groups differed significantly in their use of compromise as a tactic of conflict reduction (Chi square $= 64.4$, $p < .001$). Both the Equal Pay and No Pay groups showed a strong preference for the use of compromise. Specifically, 80 percent of the total trials for the Equal Pay group were compromise trials. Similarly, the No Pay group compromised on 68 percent of its total trials. In contrast, the High Dominance and High Accuracy groups compromised on only 34 percent and 25 percent of the trials, respectively.

Duration of conflict. Length of time to reach mutual agreement among group members differed significantly between groups ($F = 15.37$, $p < .05$). High Accuracy and No Pay groups took longest to reach joint agreement (averaging 166 and 152 seconds per trial, respectively). On the other hand, joint agreement was reached rapidly in the Equal and High Dominance groups ($\overline{X}$ time $= 66$ and 40 seconds). There was no significant difference between the discussion times of the High Accuracy and No Pay groups, nor between the times of the High Dominance and Equal Pay groups. All groups required significantly less time to reach agreement during final days than they did during initial days ($F = 7.67$, $p < .001$).

Cognitive Change

As shown in Figure 13.3, the groups differed significantly in the extent of cognitive change following discussion ($F = 7.13$, $p < .01$). In general, extent of change varied inversely with the proportion of pay given for individual domination. Thus, members of the High Accuracy group changed individual judgments to a greater extent than did members of the other groups ($F = 10.83$, $p < .001$). Likewise, members of the High Dominance group changed least ($F = 25.22$, $p < .001$), while the Equal Pay members (intermediate in dominance pay) were intermediate in amount of change. The No Pay and Equal Pay groups did not differ significantly in terms of cognitive change.

A comparison of average change during first four days with average change during last four days indicated that in all four groups *less* change is likely to occur on later days ($F = 4.31$, $p < .01$).

Group Cohesion

Increases in cohesion from initial level for each group are plotted as a function of days in Figure 13.4. As shown here, groups differed significantly

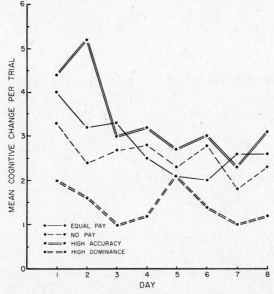

Figure 13.3. Average cognitive change per trial for each group plotted as a function of days

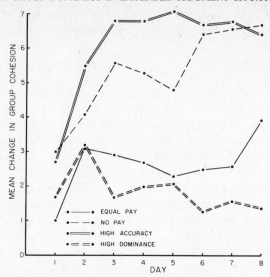

Figure 13.4.   Average increase in cohesion from initial level for each group plotted as a function of days

in extent of relative increase ($F = 75.33$, $p < .001$). Both High Accuracy and No Pay groups increased significantly more than did the High Dominance and Equal Pay groups ($F = 74.52$, $p < .001$). Additionally, High Accuracy, No Pay, and Equal Pay groups all showed continuing increases from first to last four days ($F = 6.17$, $p < .05$), while the High Dominance group did not change significantly ($F = 1.11$, $p > .10$).

Discussion and Conclusion

Substantive Findings

The findings reported here indicate that different payoff conditions can influence: (1) amount of cognitive conflict, (2) frequency of compromise and duration of conflict, (3) willingness of group members to change thinking about the group problem, and (4) group cohesion. Variations in payoffs, however, did not effect learning about task nor learning about judgment policies of other group members. Each of these findings is discussed in turn.

The conflict results are only partially consistent with prior findings (e.g., Deutsch, 1949a, 1949b; Julian & Perry, 1965; Miller & Hamlin, 1963; Mintz, 1951; Smith, 1959) showing that interpersonal conflict is induced by allocation of larger proportions of pay for individual domination of the group. Although present results do show that the High Dominance group is higher in covert conflict than the High Accuracy group, the Equal Pay and No Pay groups are lowest and highest, respectively, in both overall overt and covert conflict. Furthermore, no difference is found between High Accuracy and High Dominance groups in level of overt conflict. Thus, present findings indicate a complex relationship between conflict and competitiveness of pay condition, whereas previous work has reported a simple linear relationship.

The discrepancy may be explained by two important differences between this and previous work. First, the term interpersonal conflict as used by prior studies refers exclusively to competitive conflict as measured by competitive behavior. The present study is more directly concerned with noncompetitive aspects of individual and group behavior primarily measured by disagreements in judgment.

Second, the reward structure used here is truly "mixed": An individual in the High Dominance condition can gain by accepting the judgments of others, although not as much as he could make by persuading others to accept his judgments. The present work also examines an intermediate condition allocating approximately equal amounts for both individual- and group-determined pay, plus a no-pay "control" condition. Prior work has typically compared the extreme conditions involving only group-determined or individual-determined pay.

The frequency of compromise is also found to be related to reward structure in a complex manner. Briefly, both high *and* low proportion of pay for individual domination of group is associated with infrequent compromise. On the other hand, frequent compromise is found in groups where pay is approximately equal for domination and group accuracy, and where no pay besides a standard daily wage is received. It is important to note that use of compromise does not vary with degree of conflict in the group. Groups high and low in conflict (Equal Pay and No Pay) use compromise with the same frequency. Thus, frequency of compromise, as measured here, is not an artifact of initial level of disagreement.

Cognitive change results indicate that the degree to which individuals are willing to change their judgments decreases as the proportion of pay given for individual domination of the group increases. *It would seem that unwillingness to change personal beliefs represents a functional strategy in conditions where gain is geared to individual domination.* Greatest gain can be achieved for domination of group by (1) making a judgment discrepant from the collective consensus, and (2) persuading others in the group to accept that judgment as the joint judgment. Therefore, if an individual continually changes his individual judgment (and implicitly accepts the joint judgment policy), he loses his opportunity to profit by domination. But where the larger proportion of pay is given for joint accuracy the situation is quite different. Individuals working in this condition can accept new information arising during the group discussion and change their individual judgments accordingly, with little fear or suspicion that other group members will attempt to profit from their "open-mindedness."

Group cohesion was also found to vary according to differences in payoff structure. A plausible explanation of this finding is suggested by the previous discussion concerning cognitive change. Because of the large proportion of pay received for individual domination, the High Dominance group is probably characterized by suspicion and mistrust—conditions unlikely to foster long-term group cohesion.

The rather low level of cohesion in the Equal Pay group can be interpreted in a similar manner. This group also receives fairly high pay for domination (approximately 50 percent), which evidently contributes to mistrust among group members.

In addition to being lower in cohesion than the other two groups, High Dominance and Equal Pay groups required less time to agree on a joint judgment. One possible explanation for this finding is that individuals in these groups dislike their group partners to the extent of curtailing their interaction time. Such an interpretation is in agreement with findings of studies by Exline (1962, 1963), who showed that persons reduce interaction with those who disagree with them through a variety of avoidance mechanisms (e.g., reduced eye contact, discussions having a high incidence of personal reference).

Finally, the findings that all groups were similar in their collective and individual accuracy and in their ability to predict the judgments of others are generally in line with prior work that shows that learning of either fully determined (Deutsch, 1949a) or uncertain (Rappoport & Cvetkovich, 1970) tasks is not affected by payoff structure.

However, it must be emphasized that the task used here is very simple. Over the total eight-day period, average error of judgment of all groups differed only .27 units from the standard error of estimate using a least squares linear regression statistic based on all three cues. It follows from this that future research more directly concerned with group differences in learning an uncertain task might profitably use a more difficult task.

In sum, the present results suggest that in an uncertain situation requiring group members to work together toward a common goal, competitiveness induced by payoffs: (1) does not affect learning, (2) has a complex effect upon cognitive conflict and the means utilized to reduce this conflict, and (3) decreases both cognitive change and group cohesion.

As in many exploratory studies, the substantive results obtained here appear to raise more questions than they answer. Additionally, since only one group was run under each of the different conditions, it should be clear that pending further research, the present results are primarily useful for their heuristic value.

Methodological Considerations

Setting other matters aside, however, the main value of the work is that it serves as a demonstration of how the cognitive conflict model can profitably be applied to small group research. For example, just as the model has been used here to study group cohesion, it should also lend itself well to the study of group pressure, commitment, and group structure. While each of these variables has received extensive prior investigation, rarely has this been done with proper attention to maintaining representative experimental task conditions. In this connection, a few final comments are in order.

Four task conditions were included in the present study: uncertainty of problem, feedback concerning adequacy of judgment, length of group discussion, and mixed motive payoffs. Selection of these particular characteristics was partially dependent upon an informal comparison of commonly used laboratory tasks and tasks seemingly typical of those confronting real-life groups. The extent to which these and other conditions are common to most tasks confronting small decision-making groups should be seen as an empirical question. It suggests the necessity for empirical nonlaboratory investigations leading to an objective taxonomy of group tasks. This suggestion was of course anticipated by Brunswik, who believed that ecological sampling of this nature was propaedeutic to the development of the science of psychology.

Other investigators have also argued for the development of a taxonomy of tasks confronting small groups (e.g., Hoffman, 1965, 1961). Most previously proposed classification systems have, however, considered only the supposed thinking processes involved in the solution of the task (e.g., simple versus complex cognitive tasks). The implicit model for classifications of this type has been the *individual*. Rarely have task classifications considered both individual thinking processes as well as task characteristics that might be important in influencing group structure and development.

It is also necessary to recognize that although future investigations in natural settings aimed at the development of a task taxonomy is suggested, this is not the only direction consistent with representative design. Hammond (1966) has specified two different approaches to representative research in psychology. On the one hand, *substantive situational* sampling attempts to capture through empirical investigation the characteristics of the environment confronting individuals in everyday life. An example of this approach would be Brunswik's own work (1956) related to the study of depth perception. On the other hand, *formal situation* sampling is concerned with the relationships between environmental variables. Within the present context, it is important that the investigator have a theory about the environment confronting small decision groups and that an attempt be made to represent this environment in the laboratory.

The "theory" of the environment utilized here is extremely simple. Briefly, we have assumed that a major reason people seek to solve problems in groups is because many problems are too difficult to solve individually; that is, they may be highly complex and uncertain. Other "representative" characteristics follow directly from this assumption. If a task is difficult or uncertain, a group will attempt to improve its judgments by taking into account the consequences of its decisions (feedback) and, if given the opportunity, will work on the problem until the group members are satisfied with the accuracy of the group's decisions (longitudinal considerations). Additionally, most groups in such situations seem to operate under a mixed motive payoff scheme as we have defined it here, such that especially dominant or accurate persons stand to make greater gains.

In addition to advantages related to ecological validity, it is clear that the adoption of a representative approach to laboratory investigations would also result in some general changes in experimental social psychology. Ring (1967) has described what he refers to as the "fun and game" approach to social psychology. According to Ring, a hallmark of such research is the use of "contrived, flamboyant, and mirth-producing experiments," designed more to impress fellow investigators than to collect meaningful data. He argues for changing the "frivolous" values underlying such research and offers several suggestions directed towards such a change. We would add to Ring's list of suggestions the acceptance of a "representative" approach to the development of laboratory settings.

REFERENCES

Anderson, N. H. Group performance in an anagram task. *Journal of Social Psychology,* 1961, *55,* 67–75.

Bauer, R. A. The obstinant audience: The influence process from the point of view of social communication. *American Psychologist,* 1964, *19,* 319–328.

Bavelas, A. Communication patterns in task-oriented groups. *Journal of the Acoustical Society of America,* 1950, *22,* 725–730.

Brown, LaRue, & Hammond, K. R. A supra-linguistic method for reducing intragroup conflict. Mimeographed Report. Institute of Behavioral Science, University of Colorado, 1968.

Brunswik, E. Organismic achievement and environmental probability. *Psychological Review,* 1943, *50,* 255–272.

Brunswik, E. *The conceptual framework of psychology.* Chicago: University of Chicago Press, 1952.

Brunswik, E. *Perception and the representative design of experiments.* Berkeley, Calif.: University of California Press, 1956.

Darley, J. M., & Berscheid, E. Increased liking as a result of the anticipation of personal contact. *Human Relations,* 1967, *20,* 29–40.

Daschiell, J. F. Experimental studies of the influence of social situations on the behavior of human adults. In C. Murchison (Ed.), *Handbook of Social Psychology.* Worcester, Mass.: Clark University Press, 1935.

Deutsch, M. A. An experimental study of the effects of cooperation and competition upon group processes. *Human Relations,* 1949, *2,* 199–231. (a)

Deutsch, M. A. A theory of cooperation and competition. *Human Relations,* 1949, *2,* 129–215. (b)

Emerson, R. M. Deviation and rejection: An experimental replication. *American Sociological Review,* 1954, *19,* 688–693.

Exline, R. V. Need affiliation and initial communication behavior in problem-solving groups characterized by low interpersonal visibility. *Psychological Reports,* 1962, *10,* 79–89.

Exline, R. V. Explorations in the process of person perception: Visual interaction in relation to competition, sex, and need for affiliation. *Journal of Personality,* 1963, *31,* 1–20.

Faucheux, C., & Moscovici, S. Etudes sur la creativité des groupes: I. Tache, situation individuelle, et groupe. *Bulletine Psychologie,* 1958, *11,* 863–874.

Fox, D. J., & Lorge, I. The relative quality of decisions written by individuals and by groups as the available time for problem solving is increased. *Journal of Social Psychology,* 1962, *57,* 227–242.

Gallo, P. S., & McClintock, C. G. Cooperative and competitive behavior in mixed-motive games. *Journal of Conflict Resolution,* 1965, *9,* 68–78.

Gibb, J. R. The effects of threat reduction upon creativity in problem-solving situations. *American Psychologist,* 1951, *6,* 324.

Gumpert, P., Deutsch, M., & Epstein, T. Effect of incentive magnitude on cooperation in the Prisoner's Dilemma game. *Journal of Personality and Social Psychology,* 1969, *11,* 66–69.

Gurnee, H. Group learning. *Psychological Monographs,* 1962, *76* (13, Whole No. 532).

Hammond, K. R. New directions in research in conflict. *Journal of Social Issues,* 1965, *21,* 44–66.

Hammond, K. R. Probabilistic functionalism: Egon Brunswik's integration of the history, theory, and method of psychology. In K. R. Hammond (Ed.), *The Psychology of Egon Brunswik.* New York: Holt, Rinehart and Winston, 1966.

Hammond, K. R. Inductive knowing. Paper presented at Conference on the Psychology of Knowing, Institute for Advanced Study in Theoretical Psychology, University of Alberta, May 1969.

Hammond, K. R., Todd, F. J., Wilkins, M., & Mitchell, T. Cognitive conflict between persons: Application of the "lens model" paradigm. *Journal of Experimental Social Psychology,* 1966, *2,* 343–360.

Hoffman, L. R. Homogeneity of group members personality and its effect on group problem solving. *Journal of Abnormal and Social Psychology,* 1959, *58,* 27–32.

Hoffman, L. R. Conditions for creative problem solving. *Journal of Psychology,* 1961, *52,* 429–444.

Hoffman, L. R. Group problem solving. In L. Berkowitz (Ed.), *Advances in Experimental Social Psychology*. Vol. 2. New York: Academic Press, 1965.

Hoffman, L. R., & Maier, N. R. F. Quality and acceptance of problem solution by members of homogeneous and heterogeneous groups. *Journal of Abnormal and Social Psychology*, 1961, *62*, 401–407.

Hovland, C. I. Reconciling conflicting results derived from experimental and survey studies of attitude change. *American Psychologist*, 1959, *14*, 8–17.

Julian, J. W., & Perry, F. A. Cooperation contrasted with intra-group and intergroup competition. Paper presented at the Midwestern Psychological Association, Chicago, 1965.

Kelley, H. H., & Thibaut, J. Group problem solving. In G. Lindsey and E. Aronson (Eds.), *Handbook of Social Psychology* (2nd ed.), Vol. 4. Reading, Mass.: Addison-Wesley, 1969.

Kiesler, C. A., Kiesler, S. B., & Pallak, M. C. The effect of commitment to future interaction on reactions to norm violations. *Journal of Personality*, 1967, *35*, 585–599.

Lippitt, R. O., & White, R. K. The "social climate" in children's groups. In R. G. Barker, J. Kounin, & H. Wright (Eds.), *Child Behavior and Development*. New York: McGraw-Hill, 1957.

Lippitt, R. O., & White, R. K. An experimental study of leadership and group life. In E. Maccoby, T. M. Newcomb, & E. L. Hartley (Eds.), *Readings in Social Psychology* (3rd ed.) New York: Holt, Rinehart and Winston, 1958.

Lorge, I., Tuckerman, J., Aikman, L., Spiegel, J., & Moss, G. Problem solving by teams and by individuals in a field setting. *Journal of Educational Psychology*, 1955, *46*, 160–166.

Maas, H. S. Personal and group factors in leader's perception. *Journal of Abnormal and Social Psychology*, 1950, *45*, 54–63.

Maier, N. R. F. The quality of group discussion as influenced by the group leader. *Human Relations*, 1950, *3*, 155–174.

Miller, L. K., & Hamlin, H. L. Interdependence, differential rewarding, and productivity. *American Sociological Review*, 1963, *28*, 768–778.

Mintz, A. Non-adaptive group behavior. *Journal of Abnormal and Social Psychology*, 1951, *46*, 150–159.

Orne, M. T. On the social psychology of the psychological experiment: With particular reference to demand characteristics and their implications. *American Psychologist*, 1962, *17*, 776–783.

Perlmutter, H. V., & deMontmollin, G. Group learning of nonsense syllables. *Journal of Social Psychology*, 1952, *47*, 762–769.

Rappoport, L. H. Interpersonal conflict in cooperative and uncertain situations. *Journal of Experimental Social Psychology*, 1965, *1*, 323–333.

Rappoport, L. H., & Cvetkovich, G. Effects of reward structure and cognitive differences in a mixed-motive two-person conflict situation. *American Journal of Psychology*, 1970, *83* (1), 119–125.

Raven, B. H., & Rietsma, J. The effects of varied clarity of group goal and group path upon the individual and his relationship to his group. *Human Relations*, 1957, *10*, 29–45.

Ring, K. Experimental social psychology: Some sober questions about some frivolous values. *Journal of Experimental Social Psychology*, 1967, *3*, 113–123.

Rosenthal, R. *Experimenter effects in behavioral research.* New York: Appleton, 1966.

Schacter, S. Deviation, rejection, and communication. *Journal of Abnormal and Social Psychology,* 1951, *46,* 190–207.

Shaw, M. E. Some effects of problem-solving complexity upon problem solution efficiency in different communication sets. *Journal of Experimental Psychology,* 1954, *48,* 211–217.

Shaw, M. E. Communication networks. In L. Berkowitz (Ed.), *Advances in Experimental Social Psychology.* Vol. 1. New York: Academic Press, 1964.

Sherif, M. A study of some social factors in perception. *Archives of Psychology,* 1935, No. 187.

Sherif, M. *The psychology of social norms.* New York: Harper & Row, 1936.

Smith, E. E. Individual versus group conflict. *Journal of Abnormal and Social Psychology,* 1959, *58,* 134–137.

Thibaut, J. W., & Kelley, H. H. *The social psychology of groups.* New York: Wiley, 1959.

Introduction
to Reading 14

In this final reading, Hammond and Brehmer provide a comprehensive overview summarizing the theoretical and practical implications of research on human judgment and social interaction. They begin by defining international conflict as a crucial problem area characterized by distrust rooted in the quasi-rational nature of policy formation. They then review findings from many relevant prior studies of cognitive conflict and conclude that persons cannot resolve such conflicts unless they receive technical help to clarify their thinking. This is particularly important because experiments show that, when left to their own cognitive devices, persons are not able to act upon their judgment policies in a consistent fashion.

Hammond and Brehmer go on to suggest appropriate aids to cognition in the remainder of Reading 14. Based upon the visual display of components in judgment policies that have been analyzed by computer, these aids allow persons to literally see their own policies and those of others, and also to see the consequences of policy changes. Inconsistency may thus be reduced while the possibility for rational agreement is correspondingly increased.

14 Quasi-Rationality and Distrust: Implications for International Conflict [1]

KENNETH R. HAMMOND
University of Colorado

BERNDT BREHMER [2]
University of Umeå, Sweden

Introduction

Distrust is one of the major principles controlling international relations. Distrust contributes heavily to the arms race and to the anxiety about clandestine nuclear testing; it creates spies, spy-ships and spy-satellites; it is responsible for policies of containment-encirclement, and for failures at Geneva and the United Nations. Distrust is a prime enemy of civilization, and its burden is a constant threat to life itself because men everywhere assume distrust to be inevitable in the present system of world diplomacy.

Rather than accepting distrust and its consequences as somehow inevitable, however, if it is viewed as a product of the form and materials of international relations, then it can be argued that the form and materials of international relations should be analyzed, understood, and *changed*. The task will be difficult, and success may seem implausible. But if ever a problem cried out for creative intellect and energetic endeavor, for the reasoned pursuit of the implausible, it is this one.

The approach taken here is threefold. First, we show that policy-formation is a product of quasi-rational thinking, an uncertain and ambiguous process that must rely almost entirely upon language—also an uncertain and ambiguous process—for its communication, and that the

[1] The research discussed here was supported in part by National Science Foundation Grant GS-1699 and National Institute of Mental Health Grant MH-16437-01.

[2] The authors wish to express their appreciation to the following persons without whose contributions the present paper could not have been prepared. Hiroshi Azuma, Mats Björkman, Gabriella Bartoli Bonaiuto, P. Bonaiuto, Peter Boyle, LaRue Brown, Werner Fröhlich, Maja Helenius, John Gillis, C. R. B. Joyce, Colin Kessel, Lubomir Kostron, Monroe Miller, Serge Moscovici, Leon Rappoport, Dirk Schaeffer, Charles Sheets, David Summers, Denis Varonos, and John Wilson. Special thanks are due to E. Rex Krueger, Director of the Computing Center of the University of Colorado, for providing the special facilities required for the research reported here.

uncertainty and ambiguity of these processes lead directly to mistrust and conflict.

Second, we translate the process of policy-formation, and the problem of quarrels arising from policy differences, from conventional terms into psychological terms and show the results of our research on this problem.

Finally, we describe the kind of technology necessary to cope with quarrels arising from policy differences, and indicate how such technology can be used in the immediate future.

It must appear strange indeed to consider man's greatest evolutionary achievements, the ability to think and to use language, as possible sources of his greatest weakness, the willingness to slaughter his fellowman. Yet the assumption that man's cognitive powers are capable of solving the complexities of the interconnectedness of contemporary life, including international affairs, if only the urge for differential gain could be restrained, seems to us to be gratuitous. Perhaps man's cognitive resources are *not* good enough.

In fact, we are not willing to accept uncritically the assumption that the unaided cognitive processes of men of good will are sufficient to overcome the difficulties of *all* cognitive tasks. Furthermore, it seems plausible that if man's visual abilities can be extended by technological means (e.g., the telescope, television), if his auditory abilities can be extended by technological means (e.g., the telephone, radio), then technological methods might be invented to extend the limits of his cognitive abilities even beyond those new frontiers established by conventional computer science. Were this to be achieved, we should expect man's *aided* efforts to cope with cognitive tasks, including those of international affairs, to be more successful than his *unaided* efforts. We begin, then, by focusing on the cognitive elements in international policy-formation, with no prior commitments to the superlative powers of unaided cognition.

I. Policy-formation

The term "policy" is used here to mean "a guide for action," or "a general rule for making decisions in specific cases." Policies are based on *given* data, data that are more or less palpable, more or less concrete, data that are used as the basis of inferences about some condition or state of affairs *not given*. The specific cognitive organization of the data given defines a specific policy for inferring the nature of the state of affairs not given.

Statesmen (and others) who manage international affairs derive their policies from experience and folklore; policies are not *deduced* from scientific laws or empirical regularities; they are *inductive* in character.

Moreover, inductive inferences concerning world affairs are based on *uncertain* data. The relations between the data given and the circumstances to be inferred are not reliable; they are merely probabilistic. Inductive inference based on uncertain data is a key cognitive process in international affairs.

The critical feature of this cognitive process is its ambiguous character: It is partly implicit, partly explicit, partly rule-bound, partly creative, and partly analytical, as well as partly intuitive. It is the role of these elusive characteristics of inductive cognitive processes in policy-formation that we wish to consider first.

Quasi-rationality of Inductive Policies

When analyzing policies, persons tend to describe them as "rational" or "irrational," or "sane" or "insane." Such concepts are *normative* rather than *descriptive.* That is, they express an *evaluation* of the policy. Evaluative analyses, however, are not likely to increase our understanding of the cognitive processes that produce policies; instead, what is needed are descriptive, psychological methods of analysis.

In this connection, we suggest that the cognitive processes that underlie policy-formation be considered in terms of the analytical and intuitive dimension of thinking. These two forms of thinking are not different in kind; rather, they are the endpoints of a continuum. Most instances of thinking, we assume, fall somewhere on this continuum, rather than at any one of its endpoints. Thus, most instances of thinking will have *both* intuitive and analytical components. We will refer to this composite as *quasi-rational thought.*

The analytical end of the continuum is characterized by a form of thinking that is *explicit, sequential,* and *recoverable.* That is, it consists of a series of steps that transform information according to certain rules. These rules, whatever they are, can be reported by the thinker. Thus, it is possible to reproduce the analytical process.

Intuitive thinking, on the other hand, is *implicit, nonsequential,* and *nonrecoverable.* Usually, the thinker can report no more than the outcome of his thinking. While analytical thinking is characterized by explicit transformations of information, intuitive thinking is more of an associative process, controlled by one's past experience of what leads to what. Most thinking, however, is neither purely analytical, nor purely intuitive; rather it combines analytical and intuitive components. Information is transformed according to explicit rules, but the conclusions reached through these transformations are checked, revised, and even distorted by past experience; indeed, past experience may even substitute for some of the steps in the thinking process. It is this process we refer to as *quasi-rational.*

International Problems Evoke
Quasi-rational Thought

Having indicated that the inductive cognitive processes providing the bases of policy-formation are quasi-rational, we now wish to argue that international problems also evoke quasi-rational cognitive processes. Policy-formation concerning international affairs will not be purely intuitive because it will be driven toward explicitness and coherence by analysis and criticism. During the course of the defense of the policy, its premises will become exposed, its logic sharpened, and its organization improved. Argument will drive out intuition—to a point.

But only to a point, for policy-formation will not be perfectly analytical either. There are no established scientific rules by which information can be organized and integrated. That process must be a matter of judgment. Lacking an appeal to a set of scientific laws, or even to empirical regularities, statesmen have no alternative other than to rest their case with "it is my judgment that . . . ." Again and again those associated with policy-formation have emphasized the judgmental character of the process of organizing and integrating the facts brought to them. In doing so they make explicit their awareness of the fact that, however much effort is made to reason carefully and logically, every organization of the facts is in large part intuitive and creative and, therefore, not recoverable for analysis and point-for-point criticism.

It is for these reasons we refer to the process of policy-formation as quasi-rational. It is not a capricious, whimsical process, but neither is it explicitly logical—nor can it be otherwise in the present state of affairs.

Policy-formation from the Expert's
Point of View

Those who have participated directly in policy-formation are frank in admitting that it is not a rigorous, analytical process. A former Director of Intelligence and Research of the Department of State put it this way:

> We in the State Department . . . know how fruitless it is to try to run Communist intentions through the computer, or to try to quantify what is going on in Buddhist pagodas or to extrapolate the psyche of Fidel Castro. We are paid to make educated guesses, but that is something different. It is not very systematic. . . [Hughes, 1967].

And the quasi-rational character of inductive inference involved in policy developments makes a striking appearance in the reflections of a former Presidential Assistant, Richard Goodwin (1966).

During several years I spent in Washington—at the State Department and as an assistant to Presidents Kennedy and Johnson—few intellectual tasks were more frustrating than the occasional effort to answer the great, the ultimate questions of foreign policy: Why should we try to contain China? Why should we help the underdeveloped nations? What is the urgency of preventing nuclear spread? Such questions, in fact, are ordinarily raised in arguments with critics but rarely in the councils of decisions. *It is precisely because there is no sure and resistless logic by which such questions can be answered* that discussion often dissolves into empty generalities and false scholarship. . . . All that any leader can do is to call upon wisdom, judgment, and national principle, a sense of history and knowledge of present reality, and act on the speculative and intuitive guess that results (italics ours).

Soviet diplomacy is also aware of the quasi-rational character of policy-formation. For example, the *Diplomatic Dictionary* (Vol. 1, 1960) makes the distinction between scientific thought and policy-formation very clear.

. . . the application of conclusions arrived at on the basis of analyzing international relations or the domestic affairs of individual countries to the practical actions of a diplomat cannot be compared *with the application of a scientific theorem to earlier established data*. The methods of diplomatic activity are based on the attainment of definite objectives, connected with a change of reality, and are used in a constantly changing situation. By no means do the methods add up to any set of standard rules, because the attainment of assigned diplomatic foreign policy objectives with the aid of these methods depends to a considerable degree on the particular operating procedures of the persons applying the methods (italics ours).

In brief, the reports of those experienced in international affairs support our contention: Policy-formation *must* be quasi-rational because of the form and materials of the task. Because verification remains as cloudy as inspiration in the international system, the development of foreign policy cannot reach the criteria of scientific thinking.

A Double Standard

While many statesmen readily emphasize the intuitive, creative aspects of their own efforts to develop policy, they do not easily acknowledge the same process in their opposite numbers. The *other* side, it appears, is far more logical and precise in its (cold) analytical plans; in short, a double standard prevails. For although statesmen are quick to assert the complex nature of integrating the vast amount of data they must consider, and quick to deny any machinelike quality in their thinking (the hint is that they can never be replaced by a computer), they frequently attribute machinelike rigidity of thought to those on the other side. This double standard is not a fault; the bureaucracy responsible for foreign affairs makes it a necessity. For to consider one's opponent as less than perfectly rational is to argue that he is not understandable—an argument traditionally unacceptable to those who must make decisions.

Should the above remarks seem to overestimate the assignment of coherence and single-mindedness to the adversary, and the danger that results from such projection, we refer to remarks by George Kennan (1967):

> Plainly, the government has moved into an area where there is a reluctance to recognize the finer distinctions of the psychology of our adversaries, for the reason that movement in this sphere of speculation is all too undependable, too relative, and too subtle to be comfortable or tolerable to people who feel themselves confronted with the grim responsibility of recommending decisions which may mean war or peace. In such times, it is safer and easier to cease the attempt to analyze the probabilities involved in your enemy's mental processes or to calculate his weaknesses. It seems safer to give him the benefit of every doubt in matters of strength and to credit him indiscriminately with *all* aggressive designs, *even when some of them are mutually contradictory* (italics ours).

Kennan's remarks show how policymakers are driven to quasi-rational thought by bureaucratic necessity. And the process goes on. As this essay is being written, the principal argument for an ABM system is based squarely on the premise that the USSR should be given ". . . the benefit of every doubt in matters of strength and . . . credited . . . indiscriminately with all aggressive designs. . . ." And inside the Kremlin the same system is used, of course.

The Danger of the Double Standard

The danger is that the formulation of the opponent's policy is usually wrong. As we shall show below, a quasi-rational system can be approximated but it cannot be understood on every occasion, even by the application of analytical processes. Thus, the opponent will behave in unexpected ways. Unexpected behavior creates suspicion and fear which can then trigger a new cycle of distrust.

As a consequence of its quasi-rational nature, policy-formation cannot be perfectly understood by anyone—as the meager research on this topic shows; yet statesmen are forced to believe that such policies *can* be perfectly understood. This asymmetry produces unavoidable errors of judgment. Both the obscurity and semi-erratic nature of the opponent's process of policy-formation, and the errors produced by the assumption that it is perfectly coherent, produce lack of understanding and thus distrust. In short, ambiguity of intent and the resulting distrust are direct and inevitable products of the quasi-rational form of policy controlling international relations.

The fact that the conduct of international affairs must be based on quasi-rational thinking is a matter to be pondered long and hard. Does the very survival of man depend on such fallible cognitive processes? One need only consider the enormous destructive power controlled by man in order to answer that question. Furthermore, it must be recognized that quasi-rational thought processes have only recently begun to be investigated in a serious, systematic way; we have hardly any information about this form of thought. It is this gap in our scientific knowledge toward which our efforts are directed. Because it is our belief that man's survival does indeed depend to some unknown, but certainly large, degree upon quasi-rational cognition, we want to call attention to its role in the international system. Without wishing to appear dramatic, it seems to us there is no more important problem on earth.

Quasi-rationality cannot be avoided, at least in the immediate future. But it doesn't have to be avoided if scientific research can make it understandable. And if technical means can be developed to analyze, clarify, and explicate it—it *can* be understood. We shall presently indicate how this may be accomplished. First, however, we need to consider the manner in which language, the basic material of international relations, also leads to mistrust.

The Fallibility of Words and Deeds as Devices for Communicating Policy

In view of the long history of dissatisfaction with the ambiguities of language and its failures as a means of conveying ideas, no detailed discussion is required here. And, of course, the same ambiguity surrounds deeds. Obviously, *some* words ("we declare war") and *some* deeds (Pearl Harbor) are completely clear. But during the course of the ordinary practice of international relations, words and deeds fall so far short of clarity that they provide political analysts and historians the materials on which they subsist for generations; agreement may never be reached as to the intent behind a given statement or deed. And because propaganda is an accepted part of international technique, the difficulty is further increased, for the line between propaganda and residual truth is not sharp.

Furthermore, there are the obvious difficulties created by the necessity for translation from one language to another. Not so obvious are the differential *affective* connotations of words that are translated perfectly. Comparative psycholinguistics, a discipline in its infancy, makes it apparent that the different emotive values of the same word in different societies gives rise to problems that are little understood, barely touched by research, and unknown to most diplomats. It probably is fair to conclude that frequently they hardly know what they are saying to one another.

One need only refer to President Kennedy's comments in a televised speech after meeting with Chairman Krushchev in 1961, for a striking example.

> The facts of the matter are that the Soviets and ourselves give wholly different meanings to the same words—war, peace, democracy and popular will.
>
> We have wholly different views of right and wrong, of what is an internal affair and what is aggression, and, above all, we have wholly different concepts of where the world is and where it is going.

But no one knew what to do about the problem Kennedy put before the world. No one suggested the creation of a *new* method of discourse that would prevent the Soviets and the Americans from attaching "wholly different meanings to the same words," or that would make it unnecessary for a President to go to a summit conference in order to discover this fact. No one suggested *change*.

New Directions: Scientific and Technological Research

When the technology that can be brought to bear on the solution of a practical problem concerning things is compared with the technology that can be brought to bear on a practical problem concerning the behavior of humans, the asymmetry in achievement is shocking.

The disparity between thing-technology and human-technology is particularly obvious in the field of international relations. Here the gap between the precision and reliability of engineering techniques possessed by nuclear warriors and nuclear statesmen is not only obvious but frightening. Control of nuclear technology remains at the mercy of the same quasi-rational psychological processes that controlled bows and arrows, and communication concerning nuclear policy remains tied to the fallibilities of language— precisely the same form and materials employed over the centuries with such consistently dismal results.

In the following pages we shall show that a scientific approach to the reduction of international tensions is possible. Feeble as our effort may be when compared with the achievement of, say, the space scientists, we shall try to show the reader that all the essential ingredients of a scientific research effort— theory, model, analytical technique, empirical results— are present in what follows. Most important, both theory and research point directly to the kind of technology required to cope with the problem and indicate how such technology can be used. We now turn to research dealing with the problem of conflict brought about by differences in quasi-rational belief systems.

II. Studies of Conflict

Conflict between persons has generally been studied by psychologists within the framework of game theory (Rapoport & Chammah, 1965) or negotiation processes (e.g., Deutsch & Krauss, 1960). Interpersonal conflict that arises entirely from cognitive differences (as opposed to differential gain), however, has never been investigated in a systematic manner, except by means of the research paradigm described in detail earlier in this volume.

To summarize, conflict is studied in a situation where two persons: (1) attempt to solve problems that concern both of them; (2) have mutual utilities (their gain [or loss] derives from their approximations to the solution of the problem); (3) receive different training in the solution of a problem involving uncertain inference, are then brought together and find themselves dealing with a familiar problem that their experience apparently prepared them for; but (4) find their answers differ, and that neither answer is as good as it has been, although each answer is logically defensible; (5) must provide a joint decision to the correct solution; and (6) must adapt to one another as well as to the task if they are to solve their problems.

Results from International Studies

Since the paradigm was first introduced in 1965, results obtained in the following countries—England, Canada, Sweden, France, Germany, Italy, Czechoslovakia, Greece, Israel, Japan, as well as the USA—have turned out to be *remarkably similar* (See Figure 14.1). They show that conflict is not reduced even under the intentionally benign conditions of these experiments. The subjects in these experiments failed to resolve their differences; indeed, there is a tendency for disagreement to *increase* toward the end of a 20-trial set.

The widespread generality of the results is striking, particularly so in view of the fact that the experiments were conducted by researchers who were not in communication with one another, who were unaware of the results from other studies, and who did not receive special training in the conduct of the studies. Replications have occurred, but no contradictory results have been obtained.

In addition to finding the results of these studies to be general across widely varying subject populations, other studies (five in number) have found similar results across both sexes and different task content and structure. In addition, similar results have been obtained regardless of whether the participants in the studies were *trained* to bring different policies to the interactive situation or whether persons with precise differences in policy were *selected* to participate in the study. In brief, these

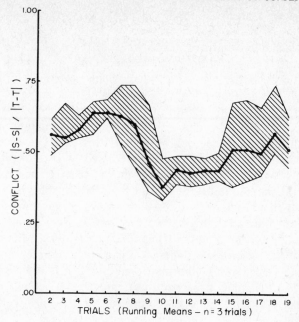

Figure 14.1.   Results from 11 experiments, using the lens model cognitive conflict paradigm, carried out in 11 countries: Canada, Czechoslovakia, England, France, Germany, Greece, Israel, Italy, Japan, Sweden, and the United States. The figure displays the median amount of conflict as well as the 25th and 75th percentile for the 11 experiments for each trial. The technical basis for measuring conflict is described in Appendix 14.A.

studies consistently show that policy differences are not reduced under conditions highly conducive to the reduction of such differences.

These results carry considerable significance for the social psychology of human interaction; they bear out our original contention that cognitive factors in themselves can be responsible for prolonged disagreement. They indicate that it is unnecessary to appeal to differential gain, or to affective distortion of cognitive processes, in order to explain why men fail to change their belief systems, their policies, as a result of discussion. Not only is it evident that rational men of good will do not reduce their differences, these results suggest—although they do not prove—that rational men of good will *cannot* achieve agreement even when they want to, and even when conditions highly favor reduction of differences. If this conclusion is correct, it is a far-reaching one; the dismal history of man and his quarrels becomes more understandable.

What is called for at this point, however, is a more detailed analysis of the psychological process underlying these empirical results. For that we must first turn to a brief description of the analytical technique.

Analytical Method

Although space does not permit us to devote more than a few sentences to our general theory of quasi-rational thought, it is appropriate to indicate here that our analytical techniques have been developed in accord with the following four theoretical assumptions: (1) ecological "real-world" relations between palpable, proximal data and impalpable, distal states-to-be-inferred are probabilistic ones; (2) the corresponding inference process is also a probabilistic one; (3) proximal-distal relations are one-many, that is, a distal state-to-be-inferred is mediated by several proximal variables; and (4) higher organisms integrate the several uncertain proximal data given in order to infer some distal state, or variable, not immediately apparent to them. These basic assumptions are represented by a modified form of Brunswik's Lens Model. (Further remarks concerning the general theory may be found in Hammond, 1964, 1965, 1966, 1969.)

Earlier, we described a policy as a judgment, an inference, based on a set of uncertain data. In the metric case (which is the case under discussion here) the relation between cues and decisions can be described by means of a multiple regression equation.

$$J = B_0 + B_1X_1 + B_2X_2 + \ldots\ldots + B_nX_n \tag{14.1}$$

where J is the decision

B_{1-n} are the weights given to the X_{1-n} different cues

B_0 is the intercept

From these general multiple regression statistics, Hursch, Hammond, and Hursch (1964) developed the Lens Model Equation, which permits the mathematical description of the relation of two probabilistic systems. This equation (indicated below) provides the primary basis for the analysis of the inductive process.[3]

$$r_a = \frac{R_e^{\,2} + R_s^{\,2} - \Sigma d}{2} + C(1 - R_e^{\,2})(1 - R_s^{\,2}) \tag{14.2}$$

[3] Although our remarks are confined here to those circumstances where metric analyses are appropriate, Björkman (this volume) discusses analytical techniques for the nonmetric case. See also Tucker (1964) for an alternative form of this equation.

In addition, it should be noted that our use of correlation statistics as an analytical tool is not arbitrary; it follows directly from our psychological theory. According to this theory, human cognitive systems have irreducible error when studied at a molar level, as for instance, in the form of relations between cues and inferences. This postulate makes it necessary to use an analytical method that makes it possible to estimate the size of this error, rather than a method that conceals the error. Correlation statistics make it possible to obtain such estimates and are, therefore, appropriate for our purposes.

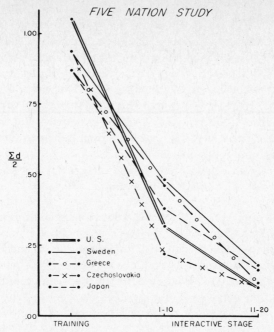

Figure 14.2. Policy differences ($\Sigma d/2$) as a function of blocks of trials for the five-nation study

where r_a = the correlation between subject's judgments and the variable estimated

$\quad R_e$ = the multiple correlation between the cues and the variable estimated

$\quad R_s$ = the multiple correlation between the cues and the subject's judgments

$\quad \Sigma d$ = the sum of the products $(r_{e_i} = r_{s_i})$ $(B_{e_i} - B_{s_i})$ where r_{e_i} = the correlation between cue_i and the variable estimated, r_{s_i} = the correlation between cue_i and the subject's judgment, B_{e_i} = the beta weight for the correlation between cue_i and the variable estimated, and B_{s_i} — the beta weight for the correlation between cue_i and the subject's response

$\quad C$ = the correlation between the variance unaccounted for by the multiple correlation in the task and the variance unaccounted for by the multiple correlation in the subject's response system

Application of the Lens Model Equation to the Analysis of Policy Conflict

Consider the situation in which two persons make decisions from the same information for a series of cases. These two persons may or may not make the same decisions. Whether they will make the same decisions or not is, of course, dependent on the similarity between their policies. That is, it depends on how similarly they *weight* the information available to them and how *consistent* their policies are. It will also depend on the similarity of the *form* in which they use the data. The contribution of the first two factors to the similarity of the subjects' decisions, or their agreement, may be seen in Equation 14.3. This equation is a modification of the Lens Model Equation; it has been adapted to our problem so that we may evaluate the relative effects of these two components before considering the effect of the third. Thus,

$$r_A = \frac{R_{s_1}^2 + R_{s_2}^2}{2} - \Sigma d \tag{14.3}$$

where r_A is the correlation between the decisions made by person s_1 and those made by person s_2

R_{s_1} is the multiple correlation between the n cues and the decisions made by person s_1

R_{s_2} is the multiple correlation between the n cues and the decisions made by person s_2

Σd is the sum, over the n cues, of the products $(r_{x_{i_{s_1}}} - r_{x_{i_{s_2}}})$ $(B_{x_{i_{s_1}}} - B_{x_{i_{s_2}}})$

where $r_{x_{i_{s_1}}}$ is the correlation between cue n and the decisions made by person s_1

$r_{x_{i_{s_2}}}$ is the correlation between cue n and the decisions made by person s_2

$B_{x_{i_{s_1}}}$ and $B_{x_{i_{s_2}}}$ are the beta weights determined by fitting a multiple regression equation to the relations between the cues and the decisions made by the persons

But agreement is also a function of the *form* (linear or nonlinear) of the subjects' integration of the data. In order to simplify our discussion at this point, however, Equation 14.3 will presuppose that the relations between the judgments made by the subjects and the cues are linear. When the equation is applied to nonlinear cases (as it will be below), appropriate transformations of the data will be employed.

In Equation 14.3, r_A is a measure of the agreement between the two persons. The multiple correlations between the cues and the decisions made by the persons, R_{s_1}, R_{s_2}, are indices of the *consistency* of the policies of the persons. If the persons have perfectly consistent policies, that is, if there is no error in the policies, these multiple correlations will be 1.00. If, on the other hand, the policies are inconsistent, these multiple correlations will depart from unity. As can be seen from Equation 14.3, agree-

CANADIAN   STUDY
(MALES / FEMALES)

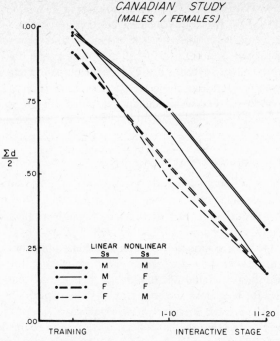

Figure 14.3.   Policy differences ($\Sigma d/2$) as a function of blocks of trials for the Canadian study comparing male and female subjects

ment, r_A, cannot reach unity if the policies are inconsistent, that is, if Rs_1 and/or Rs_2 are less than 1.00.

As indicated in Equation 14.3, Σd is an index of the *differences in how the persons weight the cues* available to them for their decisions (See also Equation 14.2). If the persons use the information in different ways, Σd will depart from 0.00 and agreement can never be perfect. Ignoring for the moment the matter of integration form, it is apparent that agreement is a function of the two parameters indicated above; if Equation 14.3 were written in conventional language it would appear roughly as follows: Agreement = Policy Consistency minus Policy Differences.

Note that these two factors, consistency (R_s^2) and policy differences (Σd), can substitute for each other. Consequently, a given level of agreement (r_A) can be reached through a wide range of combinations of R_{s_1}, R_{s_2}, and Σd. Therefore, even if there are no differences in how the persons weight the information ($\Sigma d = .00$), when the policies of the subjects are less than perfectly consistent (R_{s_1} and/or $R_{s_2} < 1.00$) then disagreement will occur simply as a function of inconsistency in the policies. In short, disagreement in overt judgment does not necessarily imply fundamental policy differences.

On the other hand, it is also possible for two persons to agree from time to time, even though their policies are different, if their policies are not perfectly consistent. Consequently, inconsistency in policies may produce agreement in principle, but disagreement in fact; as well as disagreement in principle, but agreement in fact. Inconsistency, in short, serves to hide from the policymakers the real sources of their agreement or disagreement.

We turn now to the experimental analysis of these components of agreement, with the aim of discovering their empirical significance.

Analysis of the Components of Agreement

Analysis of the components of agreement shows a highly consistent set of results providing a clear indication of the reason for the failure of the subjects in our cross-national study to reduce their differences. What we have found is this: *Subjects do, in fact, reduce the differences in their policies*— the differences in their cue-weighting systems approach zero. At the same time, however, they *decrease their consistency;* they become more erratic, and their judgments, the overt product of their policies, continue to differ. Both overtly and in terms of their experience, the persons in these studies are as far apart at the end of a set of trials (after approximately one to two hours' discussion) as they are at the beginning and they are unaware of the fact that their policies have become highly similar. In short, we have found that under the most benign circumstances, rational men of good will continue to disagree on an overt level despite convergence of their policies on a covert level because of the inconsistency in their policies.

This broad interpretation of our results naturally raises questions concerning their generality. Therefore, we now describe five studies, all of which pursue the generality of these results. The first study shows that the results are general over a widely differing *subject* population; the second shows that the results are general over both *sexes;* the third shows that the results are general over *task content* (as well as over subjects); the fourth shows that the results are general over *task structure;* and the fifth study shows that the results hold for subjects whose policy differences are *socially induced* as well as for subjects who were trained to develop different policies. In summary, the results are highly general.

Results from the Five Studies

Results will be presented with respect to policy differences first, then with respect to consistency. Finally, the relative contributions of each of these factors to the overt disagreement between the subjects will be compared.

Policy Differences

Subject generality. A cross-national comparison was made in connection with results obtained in five different countries: Czechoslovakia (Kostron), Greece (Varonos), Japan (Azuma), Sweden (Brehmer), and the United States (Hammond). Data from these countries were chosen because they constitute new information that confirms previously published cross-national data which indicated that differences between overt judgments are not reduced (See Hammond, Bonaiuto, Faucheux, Moscovici, Fröhlich, Joyce, & Di Majo, 1968).

The subjects in this study were trained to make predictions about the future level of democracy in a (fictitious) country from two variables: (1) the current level of *state control* over the individual, and (2) the extent to which the government is, at present, determined by *free elections*. The elections variable was related to the criterion variable in a positive linear way, the state control variable in a nonlinear way (an inverse U-function). One subject in each pair was trained to depend on the elections variable, the other to depend on the state control variable. The subjects were then brought together to work on a new task. In the new task, the two predictor variables had equal validity, although the subjects were not told this, nor were they told that they had been differently trained. (Details concerning these studies are presented in Appendix 14.A.)

Figure 14.2 presents the results with respect to the change in policy for the five-nation study. As can be seen from this figure, policy differences (Σd) are sharply reduced in all five countries, and at about the same rate in all five countries. This impression is confirmed by the analysis of variance performed on these data, which revealed no differences among the five countries; the main effect of country, as well as the country by blocks interaction, was nonsignificant. As may be expected from observation of the graph, the blocks effect was highly significant (F 2/90 = 281.67, $p < .01$). Thus, there appear to be no cross-national differences with respect to the ability to reduce differences in policy. For the subjects in all five nations, the differences in policy account for a very small part of the disagreement at the end of the 20-trial sequence.

Generality over sexes. The *second* study (carried out by Schaeffer) compares males and females (Canadian subjects), using the same task as in the five-nation study. This included four groups: (1) male pairs, (2) female pairs, (3) female linear, male nonlinear, and (4) female nonlinear, male linear. Clearly, the results of the five-nation study are replicated over sex differences (See Figure 14.3).

There are no differences among the four groups, the only effect to reach significance was the blocks effect (F 2/12 = 149.90, $p < .01$).

Task content. A *third* study was concerned with the effects of the content of the task on the course of conflict. Two experiments were carried out in three different countries: Italy (Bonaiuto), Sweden (Brehmer), and the United States (Sheets). In the first experiment, the political decisions task used in the two studies described above was employed. The second

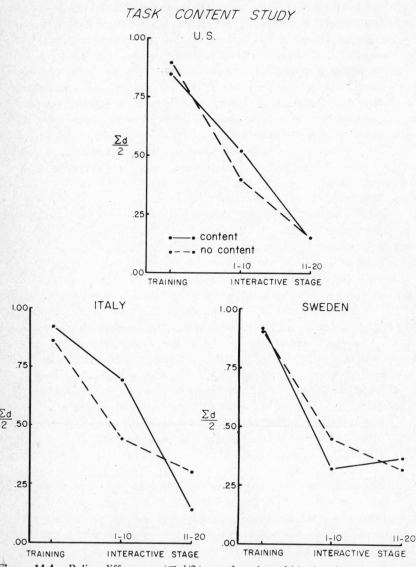

Figure 14.4. Policy differences ($\Sigma d/2$) as a function of blocks of trials for political decisions task and contentless task for United States, Italian, and Swedish subjects in the Task Content study

experiment used a "contentless" task, where the subjects were required to infer the state of a criterion variable, simply marked *C,* from the state of two cue-variables, indicated only as *A* and *B.* Except for the lack of content, the *structure* of this task was identical to that of the political decisions task. (It should be noted that American and Swedish samples used in this study are not the same as those used in the five-nation study.)

Figure 14.4 presents the results comparing the reduction of policy differences ($\Sigma d/2$) in the contentless task and the political decisions tasks for the three nations.

Analysis of variance revealed cross-national differences in the form of a country by blocks interaction ($F\ 4/100 = 3.92$, $p < .01$). This interaction accounted for only a minor proportion (2 percent) of the variance, however. Thus, although the effect is statistically significant, its psychological significance is doubtful, especially in the light of the total set of cross-national data.

THE TEN EXPERIMENTAL CONDITIONS

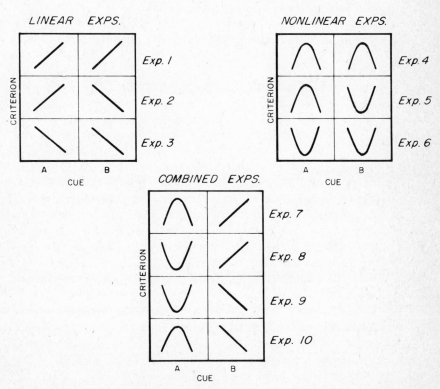

Figure 14.5. The ten different combinations of cue criterion function forms used in the Task Structure study

No other effect involving country was significant, nor was any effect involving task content ($p > .01$). The blocks effect was, as in the studies above, highly significant ($F\ 2/100 = 165.05,\ p < .01$).

Task structure. In the above three studies the tasks used had the same statistical structure with respect to function form; one cue was related to the criterion variable in a positive linear way, and the other by an inverse U-function. This specific task structure was employed because of our theoretical argument that the *form* in which the data are utilized may also contribute to policy conflict. The study of task structure examines the question of the extent to which differences in function form affects the reduction of $\Sigma d/2$.

Ten different task structure combinations were used to vary cognitive function form. These combinations were derived from all possible combinations of two of the following four cue-criterion relations: positive linear, negative linear, U-shaped, and inversely U-shaped. The ten combinations are shown in Figure 14.5.

Figure 14.6 displays the results for the linear, nonlinear, and combined linear-nonlinear experiments separately. As may be seen from the graphs, the results are highly similar in all ten conditions. There were no significant differences between them ($p > .01$); only the blocks effect was significant ($F\ 2/194 = 328.71,\ p < .01$).

Socially induced versus laboratory-induced conflict. The four studies described thus far used subjects that were *trained* to depend on various cues in different ways. Training subjects has the enormous advantage of making certain that subjects are making inferences according to the precise conditions required by the experiment; it has the disadvantage of creating the suspicion that the results might somehow be an artifact of the training conditions. Therefore, the fifth study (carried out by Rappoport, 1969) *selected* subjects according to their *preexisting* cognitive systems instead of training them. In the selection stage of the experiment, the subjects were required to predict the future level of racial strife in a community from three cue-variables: (1) level of integration in education, (2) level of integration in job opportunities, and (3) level of integration in housing. The subjects were selected to have negative correlations between their judgments, and the mean correlation was —.57.

The procedure in the conflict stage was identical to that in the experiment described above. The feedback given to the subjects in the conflict stage was such that the correlation between the "level of integration in housing" and the criterion variable "future racial strife" was —.93. The other two cues were unrelated to the criterion variable. Thus, task structure and task content were varied as well as the procedure for developing interpersonal conflict.

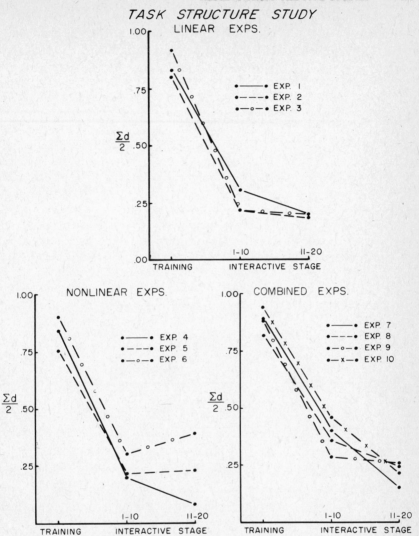

Figure 14.6. Policy differences ($\Sigma d/2$) as a function of blocks of trials for the linear, nonlinear, and combined linear-nonlinear experiments in the Task Structure study

The data regarding Σd from Rappoport's study show the same results as from previous studies (See Figure 14.7). The negative trend in Σd is highly significant ($F\ 1/8 = 12.06,\ p < .01$).

It is worth reiterating the fact that the course of conflict reduction as measured by differences in overt judgments between *untrained* subjects is virtually identical to that observed in the case of *trained* subjects. Rappoport's results concerning conflict reduction with untrained subjects have

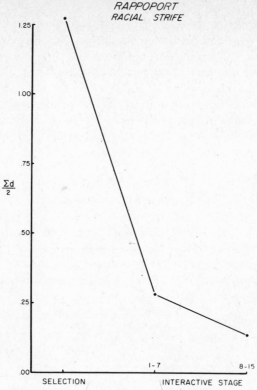

Figure 14.7. Policy differences ($\Sigma d/2$) as a function of blocks of trials for the study using selected, rather than trained subjects

been confirmed by Brown and Hammond, 1968; Helenius, Reading 6; and Summers, 1968.

The data all point to the same conclusion: Policy differences are rapidly reduced on a *covert* level when subjects interact with each other. Thus, the original observation of the failure to reduce overt conflict (as evidenced by the data in Figure 14.1) is not due to any inability to reduce the differences in how the subjects utilize the cues upon which they base their decisions.

Consistency

We turn now to the evaluation of the generality of the second principal result—consistency (as measured by R_s^2) decreases over trials.

Subject generality. The contribution to agreement from consistency is given by $\dfrac{R_{s_1}^2 + R_{s_2}^2}{2}$ (See Equation 14.3).

Figure 14.8 displays the results with respect to this measure for the five-nation study. As can be seen from this figure, the interaction reduced the consistency of the policies of the subjects. The analysis of variance indicated the blocks effect to be significant ($F\ 2/90 = 44.00$, $p < .01$), but there were no differences among the countries ($p > .01$).

Sex differences. Figure 14.9 illustrates the results concerning consistency from the study comparing males and females. There are no differences among the four groups. The blocks effect was, however, significant ($F\ 2/72 = 36.20$, $p < .01$).

Task content. The consistency results from the study comparing the political decisions material with the contentless material are shown in Figure 14.10. In addition to a significant blocks effect ($F\ 2/100 = 24.42$, $p < .01$), there was a main effect due to task content ($F\ 1/50 = 14.37$, $p < .01$) and a country by content interaction ($F\ 2/50 = 6.41$, $p < .01$). These effects account for minor proportions of the variance (7 percent and 6 percent respectively), however, and do not change the general pattern: Consistency is reduced in the interaction of the subjects. This is true for both types of content, as well as for all three countries, as shown by the absence of a content by blocks interaction, and a country by blocks interaction.

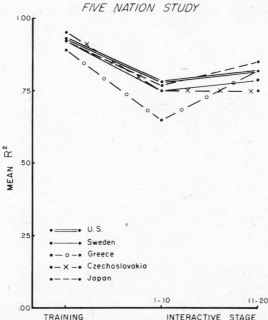

Figure 14.8. Mean policy consistency $[(R^2_{s_1} + R^2_{s_2})]$ as a function of blocks of trials for the five-nation study

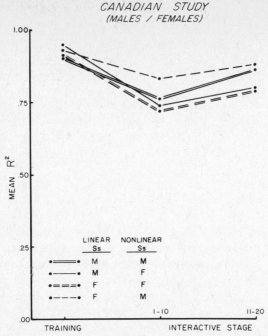

Figure 14.9. Mean policy consistency $[(R_{s_1}^2 + R_{s_2}^2)/2]$ as a function of blocks of trials for the study comparing male and female subjects

Task structure. Figure 14.11 shows the results from the ten experiments which varied task structure. The analysis of variance revealed no differences among the experiments within each of the groups. It is of interest to note, however, that the subjects in the nonlinear groups were less consistent than those in the combined linear-nonlinear groups (F 2/97 = 9.02, $p < .01$). There were no differences between the linear experiments and the combined linear-nonlinear experiments ($p > .01$). The blocks effect was significant for all three groups of experiments (linear experiments: F 2/54 = 12.66, $p < .01$; nonlinear experiments: F 2/54 = 17.42, $p < .01$; and combined experiments: F 2/72 = 30.60, $p < .01$).

Socially induced versus laboratory-induced differences. Finally, Figure 14.12 shows that the same decrease in consistency is obtained with selected subjects as with trained subjects. The trend analysis performed on the data in Figure 14.12 showed, however, that the decrease in consistency was not significant ($p > .01$). This is mainly due to the small number of pairs (five).

It should be noted that in no case is consistency so greatly reduced that the participants can be said to be approaching randomness in their judgments; the mean R is always greater than .7.

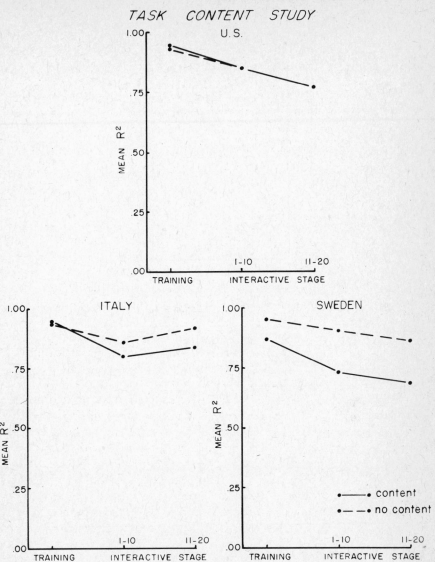

Figure 14.10. Mean policy consistency $[(R^2_{s_1} + R^2_{s_2})/2]$ as a function of blocks of trials for the political decisions and contentless tasks for United States, Italian, and Swedish experiments for the Task Content study

    The results, therefore, all indicate that the consistency of the policies of the subjects decrease as they interact with each other. This result is general over various conditions; in no study do we find that consistency is not decreased. The decrease in consistency increases the disagreement between subjects, and thereby counteracts the effects of the decrease in

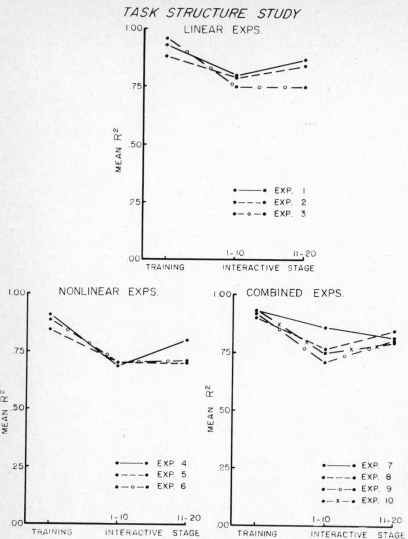

Figure 14.11. Mean policy consistency $[(R^2_{s_1} + R^2_{s_2}]$ as a function of blocks of trials for the linear, nonlinear, and combined linear-nonlinear experiments in the Task Structure study

policy differences, which would otherwise increase the agreement between subjects. Thus, the structure of the conflict changes as the interaction between the subjects in the conflict stage proceeds: The effects of policy differences and inconsistency change as the interaction proceeds. We now turn to a comparison of the relative contribution of these two factors to the disagreement between the subjects at various stages of conflict.

RAPPOPORT
RACIAL STRIFE

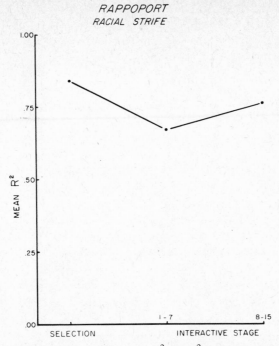

Figure 14.12. Mean policy consistency $[(R^2_{s_1} + R^2_{s_2})/2]$ as a function of blocks of trials for the study using selected, rather than trained subjects

The relative contribution from policy differences and inconsistency to disagreement. Disagreement may be defined as $(1 - r_A)$. As can be seen from Equation 14.3, disagreement is a function of inconsistency and policy differences. The relation between disagreement, inconsistency, and policy differences is given in Equation 14.4.

$$1 - r_A = [1 - \frac{1}{2(R^2_{s_1} + R^2_{s_2})}] = [1/2(\Sigma d)] \qquad (14.4)$$

To make possible an easy comparison of the contributions from policy differences $(\Sigma d/2)$ and inconsistency $[1 - (R^2_{s_1} + R^2_{s_2})/2]$, their relative contributions were computed as $[1/(1 - r_A)]\Sigma d/2(100)$ for policy differences and $[1/(1 - r_A)] [1 - (R^2_{s_1} + R^2_{s_2})/2](100)$ for inconsistency.

Figure 14.13 shows the relative contributions from inconsistency and policy differences to disagreement as a function of blocks for the five countries in the cross-cultural comparison. As can be seen from this figure, the contribution from policy differences steadily *decreases* over blocks while the contribution from inconsistency steadily *increases*, so that in the last block, most of the conflict is caused by inconsistency, rather than policy differences.

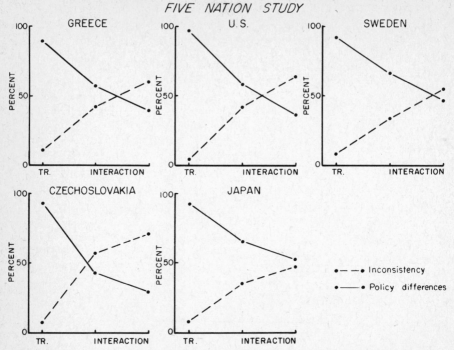

Figure 14.13. The relative contributions (percent) of policy differences ($\Sigma d/2$) and inconsistency $[1 - (R^2_{s_1} + R^2_{s_2})/2]$ to disagreement as a function of blocks of trials for the five-nation study

Figure 14.14 displays the relative contributions of inconsistency and policy differences for the experiment comparing males and females. As can be seen from the figure, the results are the same as in the five-nation study: The differences in policy account for less and less of the disagreement, while inconsistency accounts for more and more. The same picture emerges from the comparison of the political decisions task with the contentless task (See Figure 14.15), although the results are somewhat less clear than those of the two studies above.

The results from the study comparing the ten different combinations of function form are, on the other hand, perfectly unambiguous; in all ten experiments inconsistency accounts for the major part of the disagreement at the end of the interaction between the subjects (See Figure 14.16a–c). Similar results are obtained in the experiment with selected untrained subjects (See Figure 14.17).

The results of these five studies show that the structure of the disagreement between the subjects changes when they interact. Furthermore, recent findings obtained with three-person groups (See Moscovici, Lage,

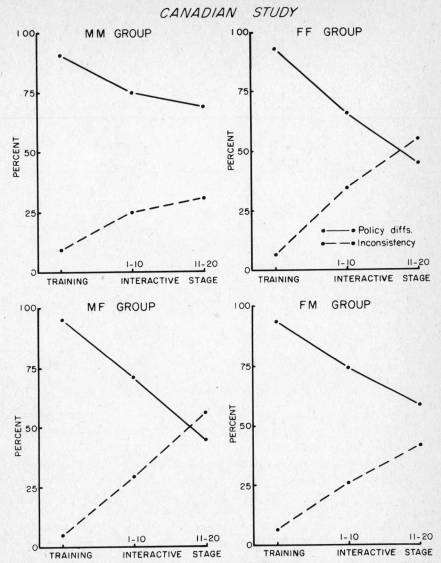

Figure 14.14. The relative contributions (percent) of policy differences $(\Sigma d/2)$ and inconsistency $[1 - (R_{s_1}^2 + R_{s_2}^2)/2]$ to disagreement as a function of blocks of trials for the study comparing male and female subjects

& Naffrechoux, Reading 12) are also in line with this conclusion. In the beginning of the interaction, most of the disagreement is caused by the policies that the subjects hold; at the end, most of the disagreement is caused by the policies that the subjects do *not* hold.

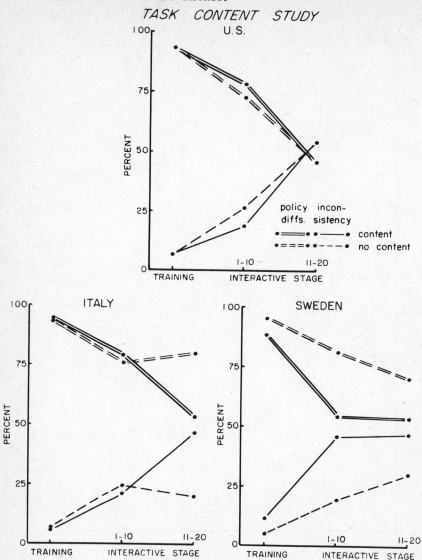

Figure 14.15. The relative contributions (percent) of policy differences $(\Sigma d/2)$ and inconsistency $[1 - (R_{s1}^2 + R_{s2}^2)/2]$ to disagreement for the political decisions task and the contentless task for United States, Italian, and Swedish subjects

Behavioral consequences. One might well wonder what the behavioral consequences of the covert reduction of policy differences and increased inconsistency are. A study by Brown and Hammond (1968) shows one effect of covert convergence.

In this study, groups of four persons were made up of two pairs. Both

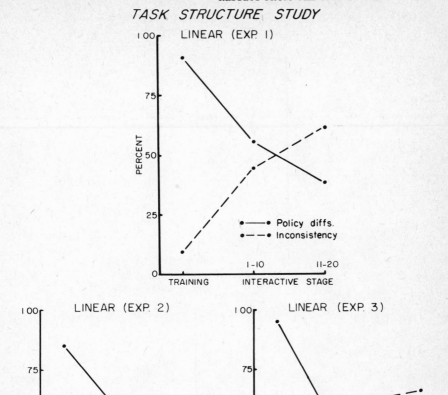

Figure 14.16a. The relative contributions (percent) of policy differences ($\Sigma d/2$) and inconsistency $[1 - (R^2_{s_1} + R^2_{s_2})/2]$ to disagreement for the linear experiments in the Task Structure study

pairs were selected on the basis of the *similarity* of their policies; however, they were also selected so that the two pairs held *opposite* policies. (See Figure 14.18 for a description of the policies involved.) Thus, groups of four persons were made up so that there was agreement *within* pairs and disagreement *between* pairs.

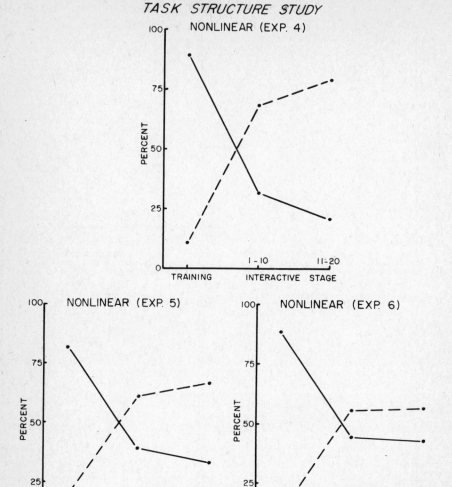

Figure 14.16b. The relative contributions (percent) of policy differences $(\Sigma d/2)$ and inconsistency $[1 - (R_{s_1}^2 + R_{s_2}^2)/2]$ to disagreement for the nonlinear experiments in the Task Structure study

The results of the interaction with respect to four groups of four subjects each are shown in Figure 14.19. It is clear that the wide discrepancies in Σd are sharply reduced—the dissimilar pairs converge to the same degree of similarity as the similar pairs. Moreover, consistency (See Figure 14.20) has decreased for all subjects, which, of course, should add

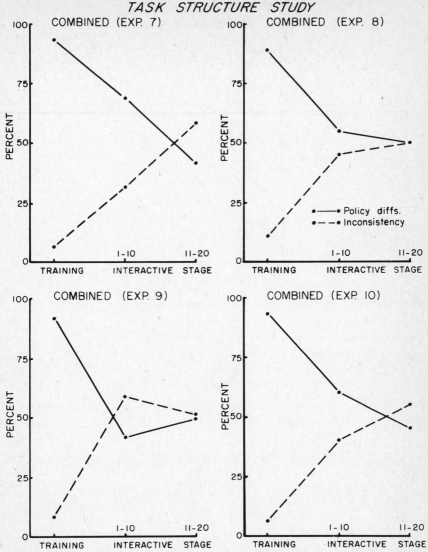

Figure 14.16c. The relative contributions (percent) of policy differences $(\Sigma d/2)$ and inconsistency $[1 - R_{s_1}^2 + R_{s_2}^2)/2]$ for the combined linear–nonlinear experiments in the Task Structure study

to the confusion as to who is in fundamental agreement (or disagreement) with whom. Figure 14.21 shows the relative contribution of policy differences and consistency to conflict in similar and different pairs.

In order to test the hypothesis that covert convergence and increased inconsistency would lead to such confusion, after each of two 2-hour discussion sessions, the participants were asked to identify those persons

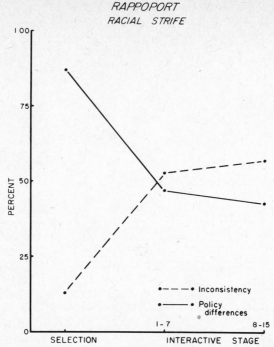

Figure 14.17. The relative contributions (percent) of policy differences ($\Sigma d/2$) and inconsistency $[1 - (R^2_{s_1} + R^2_{s_2})/2]$ to disagreement for the study using selected, rather than trained subjects

who held beliefs *similar* to their own and those who held *different* beliefs. The results were clear: Accuracy of choice was not better than chance, a result that indicates that the mathematical-statistical analysis showing convergence and increased inconsistency has empirical, behavioral significance.

In short, although overt conflict persisted (as it does in all studies of cognitive conflict), the subjects in this study could not discriminate between those persons whose initial belief systems were similar to theirs and those whose belief systems were different (See also Blake & Mouton, 1961, for a similar finding)—a result that gives us confidence that our analytical technique is not a mere mathematical exercise.

All of the above results point to the same explanation for the failure of policy conflict to be reduced—increasing inconsistency makes conflict reduction impossible, even though the participant's policies are in fact becoming increasingly similar. Unaware of the fact that they have less and less to quarrel about, the conflict between participants continues. These results, then, lend support to our analysis of the causes of interpersonal conflict, and demonstrate in a striking way the importance of cognitive factors in conflict.

BROWN / HAMMOND   STUDY

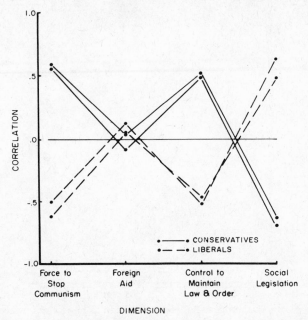

Figure 14.18.   The two types of policies (liberal vs. conservative) used in the Brown-Hammond study

Research Conclusions

Taken at face value, the results obtained are not inconsequential by any standard. Not only do the results speak to an important problem, but also replications of this order are not ordinarily found in social-psychological research. In general, the results indicate:

1. Overt differences in judgment arising from different cognitive systems are not reduced under conditions highly conducive to their reduction.
2. Although the policymakers experience a continuation of divergence in judgment, their policies are becoming increasingly similar in principle.
3. Inconsistency in judgment is the prime factor that prevents convergence in overt judgment.

A Choice in Research Strategy

At this point we are faced with a choice in research strategy. On the one hand we could choose to continue to pursue the validity of the above conclusions; we could question the procedure at every point, carry out new experiments to test alternative hypotheses, and try to develop a new and

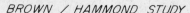

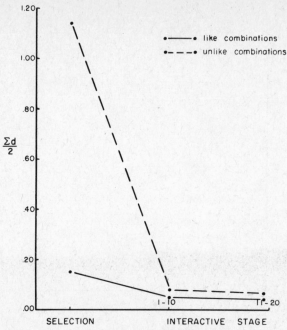

Figure 14.19. Policy differences *(Σd/2)* as a function of blocks of trials for similar and different combinations of subjects

competing theory, new methods, and new techniques to investigate the entire question from a totally different point of view. And, of course, all of that should be done.

On the other hand, what if these results are in fact true? What if they describe man's cognitive limitations as they really are? If these results are substantially correct, we are faced with quite a different challenge, namely, what can be done to *reduce* interpersonal cognitive conflict? If the results tell us something that is substantially correct, then what should the next steps be? Should we continue to verify the facts or to attempt to meet the challenge that arises on the assumption that facts are correct?

We chose the latter course for several reasons: First, the results have already been replicated under a wide set of circumstances; second, if the conclusions are correct it would be regrettable to fail to meet the challenge of developing means to cope with the problem; finally, we believe the results to be substantially correct and, therefore, chose to discover what could be done about reducing conflict that arises from differences in quasi-rational belief systems.

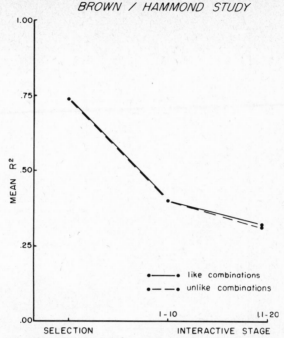

Figure 14.20. Policy consistency $[(R^2_{s_1} + R^2_{s_2})/2]$ for pairs of subjects with similar and different policies as a function of blocks of trials

III. Scientific and Technological Aids to Conflict Reduction

What we have observed in the above studies are the efforts of two people to resolve their differences. But those efforts are without *aids*. By *aids* we mean, of course, scientific and technological aids, as a telescope is an aid to vision, or a computer is an aid to calculation. And what we must now consider is this question: If man's cognitive resources are insufficient to enable him to reduce his differences without aids, what scientific and technological aids need to be invented so that he *can* reduce his differences? Our theory of quasi-rational thought, combined with the empirical results reported above, indicates what needs to be done.

First, since policies converge covertly while judgments remain overtly disparate, it is clear that we need to *bring the fact of convergence to the surface* where the participants can become aware of it and make use of it. And when their policies do not converge, the participants should know in which respects they do not; that is, they should become aware of the *correct differences* in their policies at any given point in time.

BROWN / HAMMOND STUDY

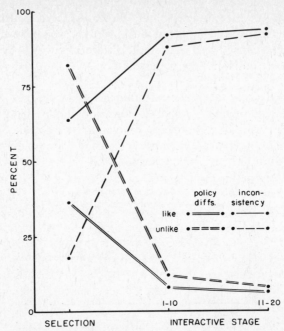

Figure 14.21.   The relative contributions of policy differences *(Σd/2)* and inconsistency $[1 - (R^2_{s_1} + R^2_{s_2})/2]$ to the disagreement between subjects with similar and different policies as a function of blocks of trials

Second, since it is inconsistency in the application of policy that prevents convergence in overt judgments, the participants should be aided in the effort to *remove inconsistency.*

Third, since the participants *need to change* so as to increase convergence without increasing their inconsistency, the participants should be aided in their efforts to change toward stable policies.

Making the Components of Policy Differences Explicit

Scientists shun words in favor of mathematics because of the weaknesses of language as a device for relating symbols to concepts. Precisely rational policies such as scientific laws are represented by mathematical symbols rather than words, and pictorial devices such as graphs serve the same purpose. But it is just the quasi-rational character of policies (international policies included) that has prevented their representation by a mathematical and pictorial symbol system. The question is, can we invent procedures to represent the components of differences in quasi-rational policies in quantitative-pictorial terms? And if we can, what could be gained by it? Precisely this: The problem would become explicit. It would be there for all to see in a "language" all could understand. Differences in policy components would be clear, because they would be displayed in terms that were clear. Most important, differences would be subject to change in a form that could be understood.

Quantitative-pictorial display of policy. During the past three years, we have developed techniques that demonstrate clearly that it is possible to represent quasi-rational policies in quantitative-pictorial form. We proceed as follows: First, the *quantitative* part of the requirement can be met by calculation of the components of agreement indicated above; second, the *pictorial* requirement can be met by computer-produced graphic display procedures. (We will forego the description of the computer equipment other than to say that we use what is known as a "visual interactive display unit." (See Figures 14.22a and 14.22b.)

An example of a quantitative-pictorial display (See Figures 14.23a and 14.23b) shows how the discrepancy in cue-weights can be presented in quantitative-pictorial form. In this display the thickness of the line indicates the "weight" each policymaker places on each policy dimension

Figure 14.22a.   The console

Figure 14.22b. The cue-weighting display

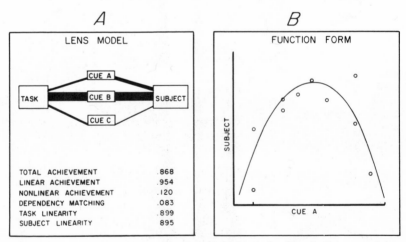

Figure 14.23a. A weighting comparison; width of the line indicates weight attached to each cue

Figure 14.23b. A function form

(weights being calculated in terms of the lens model equation). Thus, simply by pushing a button on the keyboard, the policymakers may see in *pictorial* terms precisely where and how much they differ *quantitatively* in the various aspects of their policy. (It is, of course, possible to display the weighting in other forms, e.g., see Figures 14.22a, 14.22b; we chose to illustrate policy differences in the lens model form because it will serve to remind the reader that our technological procedures follow directly from our psychological theory.)

In addition, Figure 14.23b indicates how two policymakers may discover the *form* in which they are using the data to arrive at a policy judgment. Policymaker *A,* for example, may be relating the data from a given cue to his judgment in a *linear* form, whereas Policymaker *B* may be relating the same data in his judgment in a *curvilinear* form. Again, by simply pressing a button, the policymakers may see the quantitatively determined forms that are producing differences in policy judgments. It should be noted that these precisely determined ("least-squares best-fit") curves would be virtually impossible for one policymaker to describe in words to another policymaker—even if he knew precisely *what* to try to convey to the other.

The above will serve as examples of the kind of information that can be presented instantaneously in quantitative-pictorial form following a series of policy judgments. Several other such procedures have been developed and tested (e.g., the *history* of policy judgments, a history that can indicate which set of circumstances led to a wide discrepancy between policymakers and which circumstances led to agreement). The specific set of policy characteristics presented will depend on the circumstances of conflict (as well as future research). The prime advantage to the policymaker of the quantitative-pictorial procedure just described is that it makes explicit where agreement and disagreement lie, or, in other words, what is *causing* disagreement.

What the *analyst* needs to know can also be presented to him in both quantitative and pictorial fashion. The analyst will need to know, among other things, all of the components of agreement (including consistency). In general, the analyst will want to see a much more detailed and technical explication of the components of agreement than will the participants. The prime advantage for the analyst is his ability to *see,* in quite a literal sense, two cognitive systems and the product of their interaction.

Before proceeding to our second and third requirement, let us pause to consider the significance of this effort to explicate the components of disagreement in terms of our initial discussion of international policies. In what sense are the above described visual display procedures related to that discussion?

The point of view of the other. Beneath all the self-conscious talk of diplomats and men of affairs lies one principal hypothesis concerning the barriers on the road to peace. This hypothesis was expressed quite simply by Albert Einstein in a note to Soviet scientists during the cold war period of the 1950s. He asked them to "see the world through the eyes of the other." More recently, McGeorge Bundy, a former White House advisor with considerable claim to being a practical man, echoed this maxim by saying "Where the danger comes is . . . in the human tendency to suppose that one's own reality is the only reality, so that the observation by the other man is highly misleading."

In brief, it is very frequently argued that what is needed is to make the (quasi-rational) policies of the quarreling parties explicit to them. But this is precisely the message that language fails to convey; one cannot explain what one does not see clearly or understand fully oneself. And until the above procedures were invented, it was, in fact, simply not possible to "see the world through the eyes of the other"; there were no technical means by which this could be accomplished. Moreover, one did not know *what* to see. It is now technically possible, however, to present to quarreling parties the *appropriate* elements of disagreement in quantitative-pictorial terms so that they can, in fact, "see the world through the eyes of the other."

But what are the appropriate elements? Two experiments, performed to investigate this problem, give some information pertaining to this question. Both experiments used the lens model paradigm described above. One subject in each pair was trained to have a nonlinear policy, the other to have a linear policy. In the first of the experiments (which used the above described political decisions material) the subjects in the experimental group were asked to estimate the weights they gave to the cues (elections and state control) when making their decisions, as well as the weights given to these cues by their opponents. While the subjects were making these estimates the actual weights they employed were calculated. These were given to the subjects when they had finished their estimation task. Thus, the subjects could compare their estimated weights with the actual weights for their own judgments, as well as for the judgments of their opponents. The subjects made these estimates after Trials 7 and 14, and the weights calculated were always based on the preceding 7 trials. The control group was not given any special information but went through the 20-trial conflict sequence without any interference from the experimenter.

As can be seen from Figure 14.24, the information about the cue-weights had no effect whatsoever on the reduction of the policy differences. Nor did the information influence the consistency of the subjects' policies. Both groups reduced their policy differences rapidly. This result is parallel to those obtained in the experiments described earlier in this paper. Thus, the subjects seemed to be able to reduce their differences in

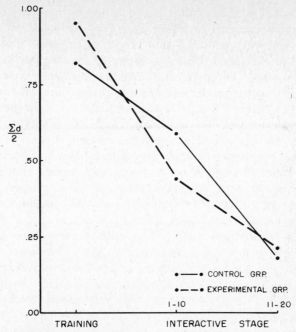

Figure 14.24. Policy differences *(Σd/2)* as a function of blocks of trials for experimental and control groups in the experiment investigating the effects of information about cue-weightings

cue-dependencies regardless of whether special information about their actual cue-weights was given or not. In fact, the reduction is so rapid that there is hardly room for any additional reduction of these differences. Consequently, additional information about cue-weights can hardly be expected to influence the reduction of the differences in policies. Information about differential cue-weightings is not conflict reducing.

However, it has consistently been shown (See Hammond et al., 1968) that in experiments where one subject in each pair has a linear policy and the other a nonlinear policy, the linear subjects change their policy at a much slower rate than the nonlinear subjects. This result suggests that the fundamental problem in this situation is not the differences in cue-weights but the differences in function form, that is, the differences in the forms of the functions relating the judgments made by the subjects to the cue-values. And this conclusion suggests in turn that if the subjects were given information about this aspect of their policies, they might be able to reduce their differences more rapidly. A second experiment was performed to test this hypothesis.

The procedure in the second experiment was identical to that in the first experiment, with the exception that the subjects in the experimental group were asked to *draw* on graph paper the functions relating their judgments, as well as the judgments of the other person. When the subjects had completed these figures, their actual judgments for the preceding seven trials were plotted as a function of cue-values in the same diagrams so that the subjects could compare their actual function forms with what they believed these function forms to be— for both their own judgments and for the judgments of the other person. This information was given after Trials 7 and 14 in the 20-trial conflict sequence, and was found to lead to a more rapid reduction of the differences between their policies (See Figure 14.25). The difference between the experimental group and the control group was significant at the .05 level ($F\ 1/13 = 6.00$).

As expected, the information about the function form influenced only the rate of change in the policies of the *linear subjects.* The nonlinear subjects changed their policies at the same rate in both the experimental and control groups.

Thus, "seeing the world through the eyes of the other" does have some effect on the reduction of differences in policy, however, it is important that the parties are able to see the *appropriate* aspects of the world through the eyes of the other. In this situation, the appropriate aspects appear to be the forms of the functions relating the judgments to the cues. In other, more complex situations, this might not be enough.

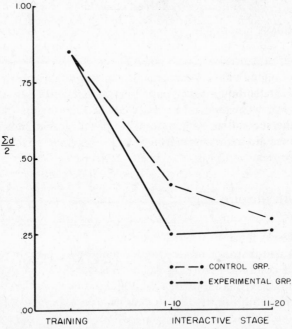

Figure 14.25. Policy differences *($\Sigma d/2$)* as a function of blocks of trials for the experimental group and the control group in the experiment investigating the effects of information about the policy function form

For instance, if the policies use a great number of different cues, reduction of the differences in policy might be possible only if the subjects are given both cue-weights and function forms.

It is interesting to note that the subjects in these experiments were not able to give very accurate descriptions of their own policies. Nor were they able to give very accurate descriptions of the policies of their opponents. This was true in the cue-weight experiment as well as in the function form experiment. Most important, no subject seemed to be aware of the fact that his policy was inconsistent. This result gives support to our hypothesis that language is an inadequate means for communication of policies.

The results of these two experiments, then, indicate that "seeing the world through the eyes of the other" does help to reduce conflict provided that the appropriate aspects are seen. They also indicate that this cannot be accomplished by means of ordinary verbal communication. In fact, it cannot be accomplished when the subjects use graphical means of communication either, for the simple reason that the subjects cannot describe their policies in an accurate way. Thus, these results show the necessity of using other forms of communication, where the policies of the persons are made explicit by means other than those the subjects themselves have at their disposal. In short, reduction of policy conflicts must rely on technological aids.

The technological aids we have developed for making policy characteristics explicit are intended to clear away operational and linguistic confusion by eliminating false differences and pinpointing real differences. This, of course, is precisely what scientists gain when they translate verbal theories into mathematical equations. And it is what differing policymakers would gain. And although that gain is clearly a step forward, certainly more is needed. For what the above procedure cannot do is cope with *inconsistency*—the second requirement indicated above. Nor can it provide a supralinguistic aid for *change*. The next section indicates how these two goals can be achieved.

Coping with Inconsistency and the Necessity for Change

These problems must be discussed together, for changes in policy must be brought about in a manner that eliminates inconsistency, otherwise conflict will continue. Our first step is to identify and explicate a new policy acceptable to both parties.

In the research studies described above, we required the participants to reach a joint decision acceptable to both in each case (i.e., on each trial). Because they had to come to an *agreement* on a joint decision, the participants are unwittingly producing (over time) a new policy on which, in fact, they are agreeing. Now our computer unit is not only capable of storing the joint decisions, it is capable of *reproducing* the joint policy and *displaying* its components in quantitative-pictorial form on the display unit.

In addition, the difference between the original policy of each policy-maker and the Emergent Joint Policy is displayed in quantitative-pictorial form, thus making it clear to both participants precisely how much, and in what form, each will have to change his original policy in order to make it conform with the policy on which agreement has emerged. However, although we are able to identify and explicate a new policy potentially acceptable to the quarreling parties, we need to know whether emergent joint policies are *stable,* whether they are sufficiently consistent to avoid producing conflict.

The results from our experiments indicate that the emergent joint policies are indeed stable and consistent; furthermore, results from different experiments are highly similar. Figures 14.26 and 14.27 illustrate some of our results. The data are taken from the five-nation study, de-

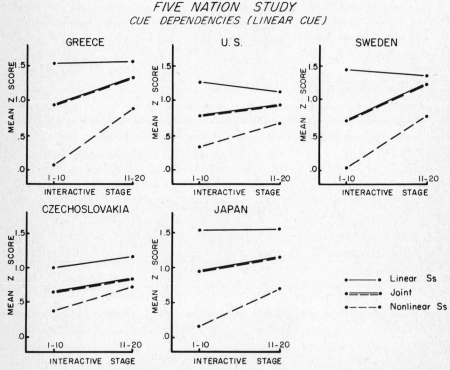

Figure 14.26. The dependency on the linear cue by linear and nonlinear subjects for their decisions and their dependency on this cue for their joint decision as a function of blocks of trials

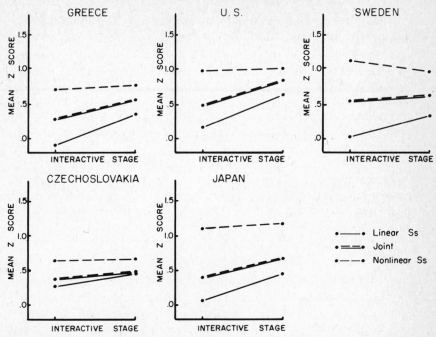

Figure 14.27. The dependency on the nonlinear cue by linear and nonlinear subjects for their decisions and their dependency on this cue for their joint decisions as a function of blocks of trials

scribed above. For each pair in this study, the weight given to each of the two cues by each subject was computed, as well as the weights given to the cues in arriving at the joint decision. Figure 14.26 shows the mean weights for the linear and nonlinear subjects for the elections cue as well as the weight given to this cue in the joint decisions for each of the five countries for the first and last ten trials in the conflict stage. Figure 14.27 shows the corresponding results for the state control cue.

As can be seen from these figures, the results for the five countries are nearly identical. In fact, there are no significant differences ($p > .01$) among the countries with respect to either of the subjects' joint policies. For all five experiments, the dependency for the joint decision is approximately midway between the cue-dependencies for the two subjects. Thus, the subjects achieve an almost perfect compromise. Furthermore, the relations between the cues and the joint decisions are highly stable. The mean squared multiple correlation between the cues and the joint decisions over countries and blocks of trials is .80; there were no significant ($p >$

.01) differences among the countries or between the two blocks. Thus, the emergent joint policy is at least as stable and consistent as the individual policies, and, in general, somewhat more so.

The emergent joint policy is unknown to the subjects; it is uncovered by our analytical procedures. The subjects do not discuss a joint policy, they discuss specific cases. In any one case, a perfect compromise is usually hard, or impossible, to achieve. Therefore, it is not apparent to the subjects that they have, in fact, achieved the compromise policy illustrated in the figures above. In fact, it is almost impossible for the subjects to discover this. From the decisions that they have made on a specific trial, they cannot infer the relation between the cues and the joint decision. This can be done only by means of our technological procedures or others similar to those described here. In short, technological aids can be used to overcome the limitations of quasi-rational thought; they can uncover hidden compromise as well as covert convergence.

Expediting Change

We now turn to the problem of enabling the policymakers to execute the changes they wish to make in order to produce a policy on which they can agree. For even though we have identified a stable emergent joint policy—one which has emerged from the interactive history of the policymakers—they may well wish to modify their original policies in the direction of the emergent joint policy but not accept it fully. In brief, what needs to be done is to invent a technique for aiding the participants to change their policies.

Of course, the technique should be compatible with the quantitative-pictorial form of communication. That is, since we now have policy components displayed in quantitative-pictorial form in order to avoid the ambiguities of language, it is inappropriate to ask the negotiators to retreat to linguistic efforts that we know to be ineffective and dangerous. The new procedure must allow the policymakers to operate directly on the quantitative-pictorial display immediately.

In an effort to reach this goal we have employed a device known as a "light pen" in connection with the Visual Interactive Display Unit. The policymaker is provided with a display indicating the components of his policy and those of the emergent joint policy. If one person wishes to indicate that he does not find all features of the emergent joint policy acceptable, he indicates with the light pen the change he is willing to make in his policy. He does this simply by moving the light pen over the surface of the display screen so as to modify his old policy to make it fit the new one. As he does so, he is, in fact, *writing a new program* which is stored in the computer memory system and which can be recalled to the display unit immediately. That is, he is now *making* policy in quantitative-pictorial terms.

More specifically, if a policymaker wishes to indicate that he is prepared to decrease the *weight* to be placed on a specific cue, he does so simply by indicating, with the light pen, how large a change he wishes to make. Or, if he wishes to change the *form* of the relation between a cue and his judgment he does so simply by using the pen to create the relation between a cue and his judgment. Most important, however, is the fact that he can see the *consequences* of the change he makes.

For instance, it is possible to generate a series of probable future states of the world. The new policy that has been worked out on the screen can be applied to these cases with perfect consistency by the computer. Also, the old policy held by the policymaker (or any other policy) can be applied to these cases, and he can see how much of a difference his new policy makes. If he considers the outcome of the new policy unacceptable, he can go back to the initial display of the policy components and make a revision of his policy.

It is, of course, also possible to work the other way: The policymaker can indicate, for each of the cases given to him by the computer, what decision he would like to make. The computer can then give him back the policy that will enable him to make these decisions. Thus, the policy can be modified in two ways—either by operating directly on the components of the policy or by making a series of decisions. In the first case, the policymaker can observe immediately the consequences of his new policy in terms of actual decisions implied by the policy, and the differences between these decisions and those that would result from another policy. In the second case the policymaker can get back the components of a policy which will generate the desired decisions. In both cases the policy will be perfectly explicit.

It must be emphasized that these procedures enable a policymaker to obtain a policy that has perfect consistency ($R^2 = 1$), a feat that unaided policymakers seldom achieve; and it should be remembered that inconsistency is the prime factor in producing disagreement between persons with quasi-rational policies.

To summarize, we began this section on scientific and technological aids to conflict reduction by indicating that such aids would be required to accomplish the following objectives:

1. make participants aware of the similarities and differences of their policies
2. reduce inconsistency
3. make change possible

Moreover, we indicated that these objectives must be accomplished by quantitative-pictorial methods in order to avoid the hazards of the ambiguities of language. We took steps to meet these objectives by employing a Visual Interactive Display Unit (a computer-related device), which made it possible to display the appropriate policy characteristics and which, when combined with the light pen, made it possible to execute change in policy while avoiding inconsistency.

IV. Summary

This essay consists of three main parts. In Part I we indicated why we believe that a major research effort should be made to understand conflict which arises from cognitive differences. At the risk of being considered incautious we placed the need for that effort in the context of international affairs, because the fate of the international system now encompasses the fate of man.

We endeavored to show that quasi-rational thought forms the base of the inductive policies that control our destiny and that, although this cognitive process has hardly been brought under research scrutiny, it is essential to increase our understanding of it.

Part II presented briefly, and in very general terms, our theory of quasi-rational thought and the analytical technique derived from theory and model. In addition, we presented the results of some 25 experiments based on the above conceptual framework and carried out in a dozen different nations. The results of these studies all lead to the same conclusion: Overt differences in judgment, the visible product of policies, do not converge. Policy differences, however, do converge covertly—a fact of which the participants are unaware. The prime reason for the joint occurrence of these two phenomena lies in the inconsistency of quasi-rational thought. For although covert policy differences decrease markedly, inconsistency occurs in an amount sufficient to keep the overt judgments of the participants apart, and they continue to experience conflict.

Because of the large number of replications of these results, we chose to assume that they are substantially correct and that these studies point to the need for technological aids for conflict resolution. Acting on those assumptions, in Part III we described the techniques we have developed for displaying the components of interacting cognitive systems so that both analyst and participant can see what it is that is causing the policymakers to agree or disagree. In addition, we described the techniques we developed that will enable participants to change their policies, so as to achieve agreement while avoiding the risks of inconsistency.

Whether the techniques presented here will "work" remains to be seen. However, just as the research results we have reported required nearly ten years of effort, the full testing of the wide variety of special techniques available within this framework will undoubtedly require another five to ten years of investigation. Our main reason for describing our technological effort is to make it possible for other scientists (and engineers) to join in the search for new techniques—a matter to which we turn briefly.

Epilogue

The above analysis of distrust unavoidably recapitulates a part of what has been said many times about the failure of man to prevent war. What is new is the argument that scientific research combined with the appropriate technology can now enable us to *change*.

Heretofore, it has been customary to attribute the generally dismal state of international relations to ineradicable defects in the character of man—his malicious greed, his thirst for power, all clearly found in the character of the Other and equally clearly disavowed by the Self. This view, which has led to one disaster after another, can be replaced by a more scientific one. Instead of the denigration of one man by another, or the endless pleading and wringing of hands, it is now possible for science to develop a technology that can remove the ambiguities of traditional discourse and clarify cognition in ways never before open to us.

Our immediate aim should be to establish research programs concerned with the analysis of quasi-rational policymaking and the development of a technology to increase our ability to clarify it, to understand it, to communicate it unequivocally, and to *change* it. There is the challenge to those scientists and engineers who wish to direct their talents toward the search for peace.

APPENDIX 14A

The general research paradigm employed for studying cognitive conflict is described in detail by Hammond (1965). The method involves two stages: a *training* stage in which two subjects are trained in such a way that each learns to think differently about a set of problems, and a *conflict* stage in which the two subjects are brought together and attempt to arrive at a joint decision concerning the problem. The training stage is employed in order to allow the experimenter to arrange the cognitive differences between the subjects to fit the requirements of the study. For example, the larger the differences in training, the greater the subsequent cognitive conflict.

Since a certain "political decision-making" task has been used very extensively for research with the paradigm, this task is described in detail below.

Preconflict Training

The subjects appeared two at a time and were asked to participate in an experiment on political decision making. They were separately trained to predict the future "level of democracy" in various countries on the basis of present "level of state control exerted over an individual" and the present "extent to which elections determine the government."

The level of state control and the prevalence of elections were presented on scales printed on the face of each of a series of 60 cards. The criterion, level of democracy, was indicated on a scale on the back of each card. Both subjects were informed that the scale of state control was related in a curvilinear fashion to the criterion, "neither too little state control nor too much is good," while the scale of elections was related linearly to the criterion, "the more the electorate determines the government the better."

Differential Training

For one subject the variable state control had a correlation of approximately .95 with level of democratic institutions, while the correlation between the election variable and the level of democratic institutions was zero. For the other subject the reverse was true. As a result, the subjects were trained in opposite ways, although they were not made aware of this. For both subjects the relation between the two information scales and the criterion was less than perfect. The multiple regression coefficient (R) between the two scales and criterion was .95, thus, it was impossible for the subjects to get the correct answer on every trial. The two prediction scales were statistically independent of one another. The subjects were trained to a criterion of 10 successive trials in which their judgments correlated at least .75 with the variable they were trained to depend on and not more than .25 with the variable they were trained to ignore.

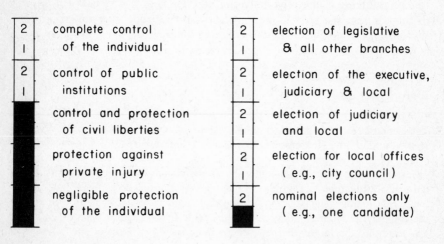

STATE CONTROL   ELECTIONS

Figure 14.A₁. An example of a card used in the training and conflict tasks

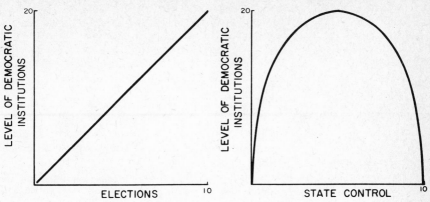

Figure 14.A₂.   Relations between each variable and the criterion

Conflict Situation

After training, the subjects were brought together and informed that they were to
make the same kind of predictions they had made before. They were not told that
they had received different training. They were told that whereas the training
session had involved fictitious data, the new instances for which they were to make
predictions were taken from the "real world of nations" and therefore the task
would be a little more difficult. Because of this greater complexity they might not
always agree in their predictions, and whenever this occurred they were to discuss
the matter with one another until they could arrive at a decision acceptable to both.
The subjects were not informed that the conflict task was in fact different from the
one they were trained in; that in the conflict situation the two information scales
were *equally* correlated with the criterion scale ($r = .67$) (See Figure 14.A₃). After
observing a card and before communicating with one another, the subjects were
told to record their individual predictions on the answer sheet provided; they were
then to inform each other of their predictions, and then to arrive at a joint prediction. Following the joint decision, they were to indicate secretly what they now
thought the correct judgment was. They were then told the "correct" answer. The
subjects made predictions for 20 "nations" in the conflict situation. All subjects

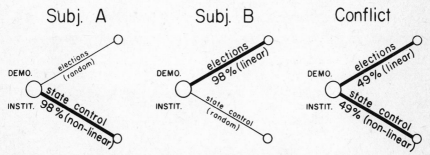

Figure 14.A₃.   Differences in differential training tasks and conflict tasks

in all countries received similar printed instructions, translated into their own language from the original American version. The British version was identical to the latter.

REFERENCES

Björkman, M. Stimulus-event learning and event learning as concurrent processes. *Organizational Behavior and Human Performance,* 1967, *2,* 219–236.

Blake, R., & Mouton, J. S. Comprehension of own and outgroup positions under intergroup competition. *Journal of Conflict Resolution,* 1961, *5,* 304–309.

Brown, LaRue, & Hammond, K. R. A supra-linguistic method for reducing intragroup conflict. University of Colorado: Program on Cognitive Processes Report No. 108, Institute of Behavioral Science, September 1968.

Brunswik, E. *The conceptual framework of psychology.* Chicago: University of Chicago Press, 1952.

Brunswik, E. *Perception and the representative design of experiments.* Berkeley, Calif.: University of California Press, 1956.

Deutsch, M., & Krauss, R. M. The effect of threat on interpersonal bargaining. *Journal of Abnormal and Social Psychology,* 1960, *61,* 181–189.

Goodwin, R. Reflections on Vietnam. *The New Yorker,* April 16, 1966.

Hammond, K. R. Toward a recovery of rational man. *Colorado Quarterly,* 1964, Fall, 101–120.

Hammond, K. R. New directions in research in conflict resolution. *Journal of Social Issues,* 1965, *21,* 44–66.

Hammond, K. R. Probabilistic functionalism: Egon Brunswik's integration of the history, theory and method of psychology. In K. R. Hammond (Ed.), *The psychology of Egon Brunswik.* New York: Holt, Rinehart and Winston, 1966.

Hammond, K. R., Bonaiuto, G. B., Faucheux, C., Moscovici, S., Fröhlich, D., Joyce, C. R., & Di Majo, G. A comparison of cognitive conflict between persons in Western Europe and the United States. *International Journal of Psychology,* 1968, *3,* 1–12.

Hammond, K. R. Inductive knowing. University of Colorado: Program on Cognitive Processes Report No. 113, Institute of Behavioral Science, 1969.

Helenius, M. Socially induced cognitive conflict: A study of disagreement over childrearing policies. See Reading 6, this volume.

Hughes, Thomas L. Policy-making in a world turned upside down. *Foreign Affairs,* 1967, *45,* 202–214.

Hursch, C., Hammond, K. R., & Hursch, J. Some methodological considerations in multiple-cue probability studies. *Psychological Review,* 1964, *71,* 42–60.

Kennan, G. Memoirs: *1925–1950.* New York: Atlantic, Little & Brown, 1967.

Lall, A. *Modern international negotiation.* New York: Columbia University Press, 1966.

Rapoport, A., & Chammah, A. *Prisoner's dilemma.* Ann Arbor: University of Michigan Press, 1965.

Rappoport, L. Cognitive conflict as a function of socially-induced cognitive differences. *Journal of Conflict Resolution,* 1969, *13,* 143–148.

Summers, D. A. Conflict, compromise, and belief change in a decision-making task. *Journal of Conflict Resolution,* 1968, *12,* 215–221.

Tucker, L. R. A suggested alternative formulation in the developments by Hursch, Hammond, and Hursch and by Hammond, Hursch, and Todd. *Psychological Review,* 1964, *71,* 528–530.

Name Index

Subject Index